Robert Dale Owen.

ROBERT DALE OWEN

A BIOGRAPHY

BY

RICHARD WILLIAM LEOPOLD

1969

OCTAGON BOOKS

New York

To

ARTHUR MEIER SCHLESINGER

PREFACE

STUDENTS of American life have long been impressed by the remarkable breadth of interests shown by many leading public men a century ago. Just because they dispersed their efforts so widely, however, some of these have gradually and rather undeservedly faded from the pages of history. In such a group belongs Robert Dale Owen, one of the most versatile figures in an age of versatility. As editor, educator, and labor leader, as politician, diplomat, and man of letters, as legislator, feminist, and champion of a new religious faith, as advocate at one time or another of all sorts of reforms ranging from birth control to Negro emancipation, and as author of all sorts of books from theological discussions to treatises on architecture and plank roads, Owen was one of the best known and most publicized men of his generation. Surprisingly enough, he has been also one of the most neglected. To be sure, his name is familiar to specialists in social history and to those seeking to keep alive Indiana's past; but the absence of a critical, full length biography, based on more materials than Owen's writings alone and portraying in detail the vicissitudes of his thought and activity, has led scholars into frequent errors concerning his career and has obscured from the general reader a man whose life tells us much about the America of a hundred years ago. It is to repair such a deficiency that this work has been undertaken.

In attempting to recover Owen from unwarranted obscurity, I have guarded against exaggerating the importance of a man who performed ably in many fields but achieved greatness in none. Possessed of a mind more facile than consistent, more receptive than original, Owen frequently changed his opinions, even on such fundamental issues as capitalism, religion, educational methods, and the rights of the Negro. He was not always a reformer; he was not always an "incorrigible idealist." His biography cannot be fitted into one mold; his place in history cannot be summarized in a phrase.

Fundamental to any comprehension of Owen's career is the fact that he lived not one life but three. Responding to his various environments, he was in turn a radical reformer, intent on eliminating all irrationalities and injustices in the world; an able politician, eager to promote the interests of an expanding, self-assertive West; and finally a cosmopolitan intellectual, dabbling as a free lance in the problems of the Civil War, relying upon his pen for a livelihood, but concerned primarily with the propagation of spiritualism. Between these three periods of Owen's life there was only a tenuous connection. The actors, as well as the setting, constantly changed. During the New York years Owen promised to become the country's outstanding social critic and freethinker, but in the forties he turned his back on the many humanitarian crusades of the day and within another decade abandoned his militant agnosticism for a creedless Christianity. During the Indiana years Owen stood high in the ranks of the Western Democracy, but in the sixties he broke with his old party and demanded suffrage for the Negro he had helped to exclude from the Hoosier state. During his last years Owen was, perhaps, America's ablest advocate of spiritualism; but by combatting radicals within the fold and exposing mediums of doubtful moral character, he gained the enmity of those who came to control the movement and has thus been conveniently relegated to oblivion by later spiritualists. Hence there is no group, no cause, no party, outside of Indiana, which seeks today to perpetuate his fame.

Yet on many occasions Owen came near to achieving lasting renown. A brilliant career in radical journalism was prevented only by his return in 1833 to the Indiana backwoods. If the influence of *Moral Physiology* could be accurately determined, he might be known as a leading pioneer writer on sociological problems. His name might have been enshrined in the annals of the Smithsonian Institution if he had not, apparently, disagreed with its first Secretary. His reputation as an educator might have been made secure if in 1852, after helping devise the Hoosier public school system, he had consented to run for the office of State Superintendent and thus perfect the organization. Had he not lived his most fruitful years in southern Indiana, he might today be remembered among feminists with Susan B. Anthony and Elizabeth C. Stanton and among abolitionists with William Lloyd Garrison and Theodore Dwight Weld. But these are all might-have-beens. The fact remains that Owen is largely forgotten, and the fault is partly his.

Although no large collection of Owen's papers has survived, the sources for this study are abundant. The biographer's problem has been to condense and to select, without omitting or neglecting any of his subject's multifarious interests, those interests that make him so significant. In order to depict Owen as he was seen by foe as well as by friend, it has been necessary to go beyond his own writings, printed and unprinted, and seek information in manuscripts, scattered from Portland, Oregon, to Manchester, England, as well as in broken files of newspapers, buried away in local Indiana libraries. This research was assisted by two fellowship grants, one from the Social Science Research Council in 1935–1936 and one from Harvard University in 1936–1937.

It is a pleasure to acknowledge some of the kindnesses that facilitated the writing of this biography. I am under deep obligation to several members of the Owen family, to Mrs. Grace Zaring Stone and Mrs. Aline Owen Neal for permission to use manuscripts in their possession, and to Miss Caroline Dale Snedeker and the late Rosamond Dale Templeton for information and advice. Other manuscripts, still in private hands, were made available by Mrs. Donald R. Macdonald, the Misses Mary Fretageot and Louise Embree, and the Reverend Thomas C. Pears, Jr. Transcripts of Owen letters in the Lane and Brownson Papers have been courteously supplied by Miss Nellie B. Pipes and Arthur M. Schlesinger, Jr. The Honorable William L. Bryan furnished me with extracts from the minutes of the Board of Trustees of Indiana University.

I am indebted to the New Harmony Memorial Commission for being allowed to reproduce the Wilson portrait of Owen now hanging in the Old Fauntleroy Home. Of the many librarians who have been indefatigable in their efforts I can single out for special thanks only Miss Esther U. McNitt and Dr. Christopher B. Coleman, of the Indiana State Library, and Miss Louise M. Husband and the late Nora C. Fretageot, of the Workingmen's Institute, New Harmony.

I wish to acknowledge, finally, the assistance rendered by my colleagues at Harvard University. The manuscript was read in its various stages by Professors Frederick Merk and Paul H. Buck. Their comments, growing out of their wide knowledge of the field covered, as well as their cheerfully given advice, were extremely helpful. But my greatest debt of gratitude is to Professor Arthur M. Schlesinger, who first suggested the subject to me and who, over a period of several years, has given me unsparingly of his time. Without his genial humor, constant encouragement, and stimulating criticism this work would not have been possible.

R. W. L.

CAMBRIDGE, MASSACHUSETTS
July, 1940.

CONTENTS

PART ONE

THE REFORMER

PART TWO

THE WESTERN DEMOCRAT

PART THREE

THE INTELLECTUAL

APPENDICES

ILLUSTRATIONS

PART ONE
THE REFORMER

CHAPTER I

BACKGROUNDS

AMONG the most versatile figures in American social history is Robert Dale Owen. Born before the day of the specialist, possessed of a facile pen, an extraordinary adaptability, and a strong faith in human progress, he engaged in a myriad of activities, wrote on a wide variety of subjects, and performed useful services in many fields. Though largely forgotten today, he was in the half century after 1825 one of the best known and most publicized men of his time. His biographer is faced with the problem of portraying not one life but several; for, yielding to his changing environments, Owen was in turn a radical reformer, a Western Democrat, and a cosmopolitan intellectual.

Robert Dale Owen was born in Charlotte Street, Glasgow, on November 7, 1801. He entered a world seething with strife and unrest. Not until his fourteenth birthday did Great Britain finally emerge from the shadow of Napoleon. Peace abroad did not bring peace at home. The post-war collapse in prices caused widespread depression and unemployment; the distressed workers not unnaturally attributed their plight to the introduction of the new labor-saving machinery.

The Industrial Revolution in England was in 1801 still in its infancy. Steam power was not widely used; transportation of bulk awaited Macadam and the canals; the large scale production of iron and steel lay in the distant future. Only in a few branches of manufacture, notably the textile, had the adoption of mechanical devices brought into being the modern factory system. With the birth pangs of that system Owen's family was intimately connected. His maternal grandfather, one time partner of Richard Arkwright, had in 1786 opened the first Scottish owned cotton spinning factory. His father

was, a generation later, widely known as one of the most successful industrialists in the United Kingdom. Owen himself
passed his boyhood in close proximity to his father's mills and,
like many others who came of age in the days of Peterloo, was
keenly aware of the human misery that followed in the wake of
the inventions of Kay, Hargreaves, and Crompton.

In his autobiography Owen traced his ancestry to a great-
great-great-grandfather, the first Earl of Breadalbane.[1] That
claim to noble blood had a curious ring coming from one who
in his earlier years had endorsed communism, championed the
cause of labor, and lived for two decades under the democratic
influence of the American West. There had been a time when
Owen, like Webster, would have rejoiced to have been born in
a log cabin. American log cabins, however, were a far cry from
the palatial Charlotte Street home in which Owen first saw the
light of day and in which lived his maternal grandparents,
David and Ann Campbell Dale. Of the latter, who bequeathed
to Owen her noble lineage but not her extraordinary beauty,
little is known except that she died some years before her grandson's birth. David Dale, on the other hand, was one of Glasgow's leading citizens. By sheer ability he had risen from
humble origins to become a magistrate of the city, an officer
of the Royal Bank, and a wealthy manufacturer. Although
he belonged to the first generation of mill owners, Dale set a
splendid example in providing decent working conditions for
his employees. He died in 1805; but his strong social conscience, his practical philanthropy, and his ardent Calvinism
were a continuing influence upon the environment in which his
grandson grew to manhood.[2]

Dale's deep religious fervor was inherited by his eldest
daughter, Ann Caroline. That Owen's mother fed her children
the Presbyterian creed in generous doses is not to be doubted,

---

[1] Robert Dale Owen, *Threading My Way. Twenty-Seven Years of Autobiography* (N. Y., 1874), 23.

[2] *Threading My Way*, 22–40; *The Life of Robert Owen, Written by Himself*
(London, 1857), I, *passim*; George Stewart, *Curiosities of Glasgow Citizenship*
(Glasgow, 1881), 45–64.

but that fact is given undue emphasis in her son's autobiography.[3] As a young lady she was cheerful, gregarious, and self-reliant, not afraid to give her hand to an utter agnostic. As a parent she was loving and tender, and the devotion that she inspired is evident in the few surviving letters that young Owen wrote before her death.[4] Ann Caroline never interfered with the public career of her husband, though in the last years it led to virtual separation. Nor did she hinder her four sons from seeking their happiness in the New World across the sea.

It is unlikely that there was any noble blood in the Owen strain. The boy's paternal grandmother came from a family of fairly prosperous farmers of Newtown, Montgomeryshire. Her husband, Robert Owen the elder, was born of poor parents at Welsh Pool in the same county. Settling in Newtown after his marriage, he earned a livelihood as a saddler, ironmonger, and local postmaster. That Robert Dale Owen ever saw his paternal grandparents is doubtful; that they exercised no influence upon his life is certain.[5]

If most of Owen's forebears have sunk into obscurity, the fame of his father has increased with the passing of the years. Robert Owen, factory reformer, educational theorist, and Utopian socialist, was born in Newtown in 1771. As the sixth child he received only a meager schooling and before his tenth year set out for London to make his fortune. After spending some time as an apprentice, he moved to Manchester, a city then caught in the first flush of prosperity and opportunity created by the Industrial Revolution. Yielding to the spirit of the times, he set up on borrowed capital as an independent producer of cotton thread. Success followed success; and in 1799 he not

[3] *Threading My Way*, 58, 75–77.
[4] *Life of Robert Owen*, I, 45–55. R. D. Owen to Mrs. Robt. Owen, Jan. 4, Aug. 12, 1830, Robert Owen Papers, nos. 176, 291.
[5] *Life of Robert Owen*, I, 1. On the gravestones in the Newtown cemetery is inscribed the information that Anne Owen died July 13, 1803, aged sixty-eight, and that her husband's decease occurred the following March in his sixty-fifth year.

only purchased, as representative of the Chorlton Twist Company, David Dale's mills at New Lanark but also married the Scot's daughter. On the first day of the new year he assumed personal supervision of the largest cotton factory in Scotland.[6]

Robert Dale was the appropriate name given by the new manager to his eldest son. Young Robert was followed in rapid succession by William, Ann, Jane Dale, David Dale, Richard, and Mary. The first two chapters of *Threading My Way* describe the author's early years amid this large family at Braxfield, an estate situated on the Clyde near his father's mills. The curious will find the pages delightful reading, but they tell more of Owen the septuagenarian than of Owen the child. The biographer must look elsewhere if he is to analyze the forces that really shaped the character of his subject.

As a youth Owen was influenced by the refined, aristocratic, and semi-isolated life on a country estate. Mention of other children is conspicuously absent from his memoirs; elsewhere he admitted that he seldom associated with them. Depending on private tutors for his rudimentary education, he grew to adolescence a shy, retiring lad, sorely wanting in self-confidence.[7] The presence of three sisters, as well as four young maiden aunts, may well have developed his taste for feminine company. But it was his high station, financially and socially, that was most important. David Dale had amassed a large fortune, and his son-in-law followed in his steps. Although the family did not belong to the old landed gentry, it was fast establishing its claim to membership in the new mercantile aristocracy. In his early humanitarian crusades the elder Owen had no direct contact with the working class but sought to convince the factory lords that reform from above would accrue to their advantage. For all their altruism, Dale and his successor were little more than benevolent despots in manufacturing. The younger Owen

---

[6] *Ibid.*, I; Frank Podmore, *Robert Owen, a Biography* (2 v., London, 1910); G. D. H. Cole, *Robert Owen* (Boston, 1925).

[7] Owen to Nicholas P. Trist, Aug. 13, 1829, Trist Papers, VI.

thus came to think in terms of philanthropy rather than of equality, and the large tract of land to which he fell heir in the
American West confirmed that habit. Therein lies an explanation for the cleavage in his thought from that of a Paul Brown,
a Thomas Skidmore, or a George Henry Evans.

Another force in his early life was the strong religious tone
that pervaded Owen's home. In the Scriptures he read his
first stories. When he became ill, he received both spiritual and
temporal medicine. Daily Bible lessons, evening prayers, and
attendance at church twice each Sunday were the custom. No
youthful reading or play disturbed the first day of the week.
Owen later recalled that he had occasionally broken the Sabbath, that he had been terribly addicted to yawning in his pew,
and that he had sometimes fallen asleep during prayer. But
those failings had only confirmed his feelings of innate depravity. He accepted without question the teachings of Calvin as expounded by John Knox. Heaven and hell were vivid realities.[8]

In the last analysis, Robert Owen exercised the greatest influence upon the boy's formative years. He transmitted a philosophical optimism, an undying faith in the perfectibility of
man, that the son never outgrew. Robert Dale Owen was none
the less a child of the eighteenth century for having been born
in the first year of the succeeding one. Similarly, he embraced
the life of a reformer in direct imitation of his father. To be
sure, the elder Owen, before 1813, was known chiefly as a
successful manufacturer who had given the world conclusive
proof that large profits under the new industrial order comported
with a decent regard for the health and happiness of the wage-
earner. After 1813 his interests widened. He soon became
famous for his activities in providing better education for poor
children, for his agitation for improved conditions of work in
the nation's factories, for his attacks on religious intolerance,
and for his plans to abolish poverty and unemployment. The
suppression of intemperance was another favorite reform; it

---

[8] *Threading My Way*, 75–88. An earlier account is R. D. Owen, *Prossimo's
Experience* (*Popular Tracts*, no. 4, N. Y., 1830).

was not until his twelfth year that the younger Owen saw a man drunk.[9]

One illustration of the father's influence was the son's renunciation of Christianity. Although an agnostic, Robert Owen did not interfere with the sectarian instruction given his children by his devout wife.[10] In fact, it was not until 1817 that he publicly scored all religions as false in character and injurious in effect. Some five years earlier precocious Robert had sought to convert his unbelieving sire. The result was unexpected. For the first time the youthful Calvinist heard of the Mahometans with their rival Bible and Savior and learned that the multifarious Protestant sects constituted but a twelfth of the world's religious bodies. Not unnaturally the puzzled lad was impressed by his father's inquiry, "Are you *quite* sure that the one is right and the eleven wrong?" For a year longer the proselytist struggled to retain his own faith; but in the end, unable to understand why an omnipotent and benevolent deity should create evil if men were to receive eternal damnation for committing it, he sorrowfully abandoned his mother's creed. Henceforth, until well into middle age, the younger Owen did not believe in God.[11]

Before his twenty-fifth year Owen came to share many other views with his father. He considered education to be moral as well as mental instruction. Its principal purpose was to build character, for he believed that character was determined largely by one's early environment. The son also held that capitalism had failed and that only the establishment of small, self-sufficient villages with all property owned in common could cure the depression of the worker under the new industrial economy. Like his father, he regarded labor-saving machinery as a good in itself but as a curse in a society founded on private ownership of property. Both Owens rejected the dismal science of

[9] Podmore, *op. cit.*, 161–172, 184–241; *Life of Robert Owen*, I, 103–156; *Threading My Way*, 93–94.

[10] *Threading My Way*, 76; John Griscom, *A Year in Europe* (2d edn., N. Y., 1824), II, 254.

[11] *Threading My Way*, 82–88.

Malthus. Both considered marriage ceremonies illogical and indissoluble unions dangerous.

After 1826 Owen became intellectually independent of his father. Gradually the thought of the two men diverged until the day arrived when they held widely different views on social reform. In his autobiography the son did not hesitate to criticize certain theories of his sire. But *Threading My Way* did not express the sentiments of young Robert Dale Owen who, in dedicating an earlier book to his father, had written,

I trace the formation of a great part of my own character, and the origin of a great part of my own feelings and sentiments to yourself. In teaching me to think, you led me to examine principles, intimately connected with the best interests of mankind. . . . I have seen these principles partially applied to practice, and have witnessed the many beneficial effects which were produced.

With the optimism that ever characterized the two men, the son referred in conclusion to a new experiment of Robert Owen, saying, "But its success will scarcely create in my own mind a stronger conviction than I already entertain, of the certainty and facility, with which poverty and vice and misery may be gradually removed from the world." [12]

[12] Robert Dale Owen, *An Outline of the System of Education at New Lanark* (Glasgow, 1824), 3–4.

CHAPTER II

GROWTH OF A REFORMER

THE ordered regularity of the years in which young Owen grew to manhood was broken by several incidents of more than passing interest. In his twelfth year a serious illness, during which his life was despaired of, transformed a sturdy, athletic boy into a physical and nervous weakling. Fifteen months elapsed before his recovery was assured, and even then further relief from the usual schoolboy's routine was deemed necessary.[1] Thus it happened that a thirteen-year-old lad accompanied Robert Owen on the tour of the British industrial centers to collect evidence that led to the Factory Act of 1819. The impressions left by that experience were significant in the growth of the reformer.

In his father's model factories at New Lanark Owen had seen the Industrial Revolution in its most favorable light. On his survey of the textile mills of England and Scotland he discovered the reverse of the medal. He encountered child labor in its most appalling form. He witnessed boys and girls five years his junior toiling from fourteen to sixteen hours a day, kept at the machines only through fear of the lash. In antiquated, ill-lighted, and poorly ventilated buildings he found working conditions intolerable. He felt for himself the hot air that registered seventy-five degrees and breathed the damp atmosphere laden with fiber and dust. From the lips of surgeons he learned that more than a fifth of these children were crippled by excessive toil or brutal punishment. Small wonder that such horrors disturbed the dreams of the sensitive youth.[2] The father had condemned the system as worse than American slavery, and the son was soon to agree.[3]

[1] *Threading My Way,* 122–125; Podmore, *Robert Owen,* I, 94–95.
[2] *Threading My Way,* 125–126.
[3] *Life of Robert Owen,* I, 112–113; *New Harmony Gazette,* May 28, 1828.

The next step in the growth of the reformer came with Owen's departure for collegiate training at Hofwyl. The schools of Philip Emanuel von Fellenberg, located six miles from Berne, Switzerland, were at that time among the most important institutions of learning in Europe. Their founder, a member of the Swiss patrician class and a friend of Pestalozzi, combined with sound practice the best pedagogical theories of the French Revolution. Assuming that extremes of wealth would always exist, Fellenberg tried to teach rich and poor according to their respective needs but in close proximity to each other. An essential was that both groups receive instruction in agriculture and mechanics. Through this dual yet separate system Fellenberg hoped that the poor would learn to respect the rich and the latter, to appreciate the dignity of manual labor. The increase of trade schools throughout the world was a goal to which he aspired.[4]

In the years after Waterloo Hofwyl attracted the notice of reformers in England. The disgraceful state of British schools made any new system significant, but it was Fellenberg's use of industrial and agricultural instruction that aroused greatest interest. Here was a practical alternative to the inexpensive Lancasterian method which depended upon advanced students acting as monitors for the beginners. If the poor could pay the cost of their training while obtaining it, a new era of education might dawn in England. In 1816 Dr. Andrew Bell and Henry Brougham inspected Hofwyl; a year later at New Lanark Charles Pictet, an ardent supporter of the system, persuaded Robert Owen to visit Fellenberg on his forthcoming Continental tour.[5] In December 1818 *The Edinburgh Review* declared that "sending two or three young persons to the academy would

[4] Charles A. Bennett, *History of Manual and Industrial Education up to 1870* (Peoria, 1926), 128–156; [Henry Brougham], "Mr. Fellenberg's Institutions at Hofwyl," *Edinburgh Review*, XXXI, 150–165 (Dec. 1818); Griscom, *A Year in Europe*, I, 265–277; *Threading My Way*, 159–160.

[5] Robert Southey, *The Life of the Rev. Andrew Bell* (London, 1844), III, 95–98; "Report of the Committees: Education of the Lower Orders," *Parliamentary Papers, 1818*, IV, 194–197; *Threading My Way*, 146–147; *Life of Robert Owen*, I, 179.

probably be the best means of importing a knowledge of all
of Mr. Fellenberg's improvements into this country." A few
months previous Robert Dale Owen and his brother William
had left Braxfield to become the first English students at
Hofwyl.[6]

Attendance at this progressive institution proved a splendid
experience for the youthful reformer. Already trained by his
father to esteem education as the most effective means of uplift-
ing the underprivileged, he received ample confirmation of his
ideas from what he saw in Switzerland. There he witnessed an
enlightened attempt to meet the challenge of the Industrial
Revolution. There he studied pedagogical theory in practice
and was converted to Pestalozzian methods. There he came to
value a broad curriculum that embraced history, science, modern languages, art and music, as well as mathematics and the
classics. There he felt the benefit of regular gymnastics and
learned the rudiments of agriculture and mechanics. But Hofwyl did more than make the young Scot an educational reformer.
It taught him the virtues of tolerance and democracy. Religious
instruction at Fellenberg's never became doctrinal discussion,
and every opinion was allowed free expression. There were no
artificial stimulants to study, no fag masters, no disciplinarians.
The students governed themselves under a written constitution
and maintained order through their own elected officers.[7]
Throughout his life Owen recalled with pleasure his Hofwyl
training. In 1873 he suggested that its form of student government be adopted by the newly created Purdue University. At
the same time he paid high tribute to Fellenberg's college when
he declared that it had given him "a belief which existing abuses

----

[6] [Brougham], "Mr. Fellenberg's Institutions at Hofwyl," *loc. cit.*, XXXI,
164; *Life of Robert Owen*, I, 179. Although the younger Owen's statements
are not clear, it seems he spent three years at Hofwyl beginning in the autumn
of 1818. If his manuscript notebook entitled *Aufsatze* contains exercises done
at Hofwyl, it indicates Owen had arrived by Dec. 1818 and remained until at
least Apr. 1821.

[7] Bennett, *op. cit.*, 128–156; *Threading My Way*, 149–159, 163, 166–168;
Griscom, *op. cit.*, I, 275 n.; Brougham in *Parliamentary Papers, 1818*, IV, 194–
197.

cannot shake nor worldly scepticism destroy, an abiding faith
in human virtue and in social progress." [8]

The democratic character of Owen's college life can easily be
exaggerated. Although cosmopolitan Hofwyl gave the hitherto
sheltered boy his first contact with the outside world, it did
not cause him to mingle with social inferiors. The particular
institution that he attended drew solely from the wealthy
classes. Many of its students were of noble, even of royal
birth. One of Owen's roommates was the grandson of a Russian
general; a boon companion was a German count. [9] The manual
training which attracted the attention of contemporary observers did not constitute so vital a part of the curriculum as it did
in the "poor school." The latter was the really novel contribution of Fellenberg's educational scheme, yet so little contact
was there between it and the academy that eight years after
leaving Switzerland Owen was unable to describe its plan of
mechanical and agricultural training. [10] Certainly Fellenberg
never carried out the type of education that Owen was to advocate in 1829, the mingling of the children of the rich and poor
in one boarding school without distinction as to food, clothing,
or instruction.

Owen's Continental schooling was brought to a close in 1821
with a memorable trip down the Rhine. During the previous
summers he had crossed into Italy; and now, fresh from his
study of German literature, he viewed the river upon which
he had come to look with the pride of a native. After bidding
a fond farewell to Hofwyl, he and William drove in an open
calèche to Basel whence they began the descent of the valley.
At Mannheim they placed their carriage on a small boat and
floated through picturesque, rocky gorges to Coblentz. Thence
they proceeded to Cologne, with its magnificent cathedral, and

[8] *Threading My Way*, 175; R. D. Owen to Richard Owen, Apr. 26, 1873,
Purdue Collection. Owen's three accounts of Hofwyl life appeared in *The Free
Enquirer*, July 29, 1829; *Atlantic Monthly*, XV, 550–560; XXXI, 585–597
(May 1865, May 1873). The last became the fifth chapter of his autobiography.
[9] *Threading My Way*, 163.
[10] *Free Enquirer*, July 29, 1829; *Threading My Way*, 161.

on to Düsseldorf. Leaving the river, the brothers traveled over sandy Hanoverian roads to Hamburg. Sailing from that port after being windbound for three weeks, they reached Braxfield late in the year.[11]

Upon his return to Scotland Owen found his future activity clearly marked out.[12] With his father becoming more and more absorbed in the work of reform, the son quite naturally served as his lieutenant both in the field of business and humanitarianism. Public affairs now frequently drew Robert Owen from New Lanark; and the management of the mills with their fifteen hundred laborers would devolve at such periods upon the younger man. Only fragmentary glimpses of his industrial experience survive. In 1822 he prepared a detailed report on the effect of shorter hours upon wages and production. Two years later he and William were each given a $50,000 share and made partners in the firm.[13] Thus from first hand knowledge the younger Owen learned that competition tended to debase quality; and nothing that he saw in these years shook the belief, already obtained from his sire, that under a system of private property mechanical improvements were a curse to mankind.[14]

More important in the growth of the reformer was Owen's connection with the New Lanark schools. Education of the workers' children according to *A New View of Society*, rather than the less spectacular efficiency of factory management, was the magnet which drew 25,000 visitors to the banks of the Clyde in the decade before 1825. As a teacher and sometimes superintendent of these progressive institutions, Owen had the opportunity to meet such outstanding British and foreign educators as Henry Brougham, William Allen, John Griscom, and William Maclure. On several occasions he publicly defended the schools from the intolerance of the local presbytery;

---

[11] *Threading My Way*, 171–191.

[12] *Life of Robert Owen*, I, 146.

[13] Robert Owen Papers, no. 129; Robt. Owen to Jeremy Bentham, Dec. 31, 1823, Bentham Papers; *Threading My Way*, 33, 294.

[14] *Threading My Way*, 274–275.

and such a controversy in 1823 was responsible, in part, for the writing of his first book.[15]

An Outline of the System of Education at New Lanark was a thin, paper-covered volume of a hundred pages, describing in simple terms the physical basis, curriculum, and pedagogical principles of the schools. Where the father in his *New View of Society* had sought to persuade the world that his ideas would cure its ills, the son was content to portray those ideas in practice. Thus the application of Robert Owen's dictum that man's character is formed for him, not by him, required the elimination of all punishments and rewards and a provision for clean, cheerful, stimulating surroundings. At New Lanark learning proceeded from the known to the unknown, and pupils studied first those natural objects that they saw in daily life. Owenite teaching depended on lectures rather than texts, employed maps, charts, and scientific specimens, and emphasized practical rather than literary subjects. Singing and dancing, however, were taught for their pleasure and health-giving qualities.[16]

In an expository work of this sort the young author's opinions appear only occasionally. In explaining that religious instruction was given solely to placate public opinion, Owen criticized the doctrine of original depravity as an obstacle to reform. He revealed a rational standard of morality when he declared, *"Whatever, in its ultimate consequences, increases the happiness of the community, is right; and whatever, on the other hand, tends to diminish that happiness, is wrong."* Nor did he hesitate to suggest amendments to his father's system. He especially desired better teachers, a more rigid exclusion of child labor from the mills, and the transformation of day schools into boarding schools. Owen rejected the widely held theory that to educate the poor was to invite revolution. The world, he

[15] *Threading My Way,* 139, 200; R. D. Owen to the editor of the *Edinburgh Star,* June 10, 1823, R. D. Owen to the editor of the *Glasgow Chronicle,* Sept. 20, 1823, clippings mounted in the scrapbook of Jane Dale Owen.

[16] *Outline of the System of Education at New Lanark,* 9–16, 34–52, 69–71.

believed, had progressed too far for any one to deny that *"true knowledge uniformly conduces to happiness."* [17]

As a first effort, Owen's performance was highly creditable. The book was characterized by good organization, clarity of style, and a moderation in statement that was seldom found in the writings of the father. The general accuracy of the picture was corroborated by other observers. Even in a digression on religion, the one serious fault, the author refrained from a gratuitous expression of his agnosticism.[18] All in all, the work constituted a significant contribution to the literature of education. It proved to be the only complete description of the New Lanark schools at their fullest development.

Shortly after the publication of this first book, Owen became better acquainted with English reforms and reformers. Early in March 1824 he accompanied his father on one of the latter's periodic trips to London. Some eight years before, as a convalescent youth, Owen had first visited the capital, meeting such notables as Thomas Clarkson, William Allen, and the elder Peel.[19] Now, however, he went as an ardent liberal, intent on telling what he knew of Hofwyl and obtaining any knowledge that might be used in a future social experiment. Much of his time he spent inspecting educational institutions, — the London infant schools, Andrew Bell's academy, and Rowland Hill's self-governing college at Hazelwood. He collected all sorts of information ranging from child labor to steam engines, from textile manufacture to a machine for paring potatoes.[20]

Nor were great personalities ignored. At a public dinner

---

[17] *Outline of the System of Education at New Lanark*, 6–8, 12, 66, 74–77.

[18] In his public letter of Sept. 20, 1823, to the editor of the *Glasgow Chronicle*, Owen had declared, "I have heard many arguments advanced for and against the authenticity of the Scriptures, and I do acknowledge myself as yet unable to decide between them. Indeed I consider it presumptuous in a person of my age to decide dogmatically on a subject upon which the greatest minds . . . are at issue."

[19] *Threading My Way*, 127–137.

[20] "Journal, Begun 6th March 1824, Concluded 22d April 1824" (MS.), Mar. 17, 22, Apr. 8, 17–22; *Threading My Way*, 280–281. "Journal," Mar. 10, 11; "[Notes on Mechanical Contrivances]" (MS.), *passim*, especially no. 5.

Owen heard Wellington and Canning and recorded in his diary that "the nothing of their speeches was well expressed." In the Caledonian Chapel he listened with delight to Edward Irving's frank discussion of matrimony. He won the friendship of two Americans, the painter Chester Harding, then at work on a portrait of Robert Owen, and the novelist John Neal, who was writing for *Blackwood's*.[21] But it was a dinner at Jeremy Bentham's that marked the high spot of the London visit. The great utilitarian had been impressed by Owen's little book and invited him to an evening symposium. On those occasions the guests sat at a table on a raised platform and were encircled by a sort of trench three feet wide. In this trench, with his head at the level of those seated, the seventy-eight-year-old philosopher exercised for a half hour after the meal, while pouring forth the wittiest and most eloquent invective against kings and priests that Owen had ever heard. When the group broke up at midnight, Bentham clasped the young man's hand, saying in farewell, "God bless you, — if there be such a being; and at all events, my young friend, take care of yourself." [22]

Despite its many interesting incidents, Owen's London journey exercised no significant influence upon his thought. It was helpful rather than essential to his growth as a reformer. In 1824 his father still sought social change through the enlightened self-interest of the nobility, not through the triumph of the workers. A chasm still separated the New Lanark manufacturer and the radical political economists. There is no mention of Francis Place, the Mills, or Richard Carlile in Owen's journal. This silence is the more important because the British birth control propaganda had already begun.[23] Owen may

[21] "Journal," Mar. 17, Apr. 11; *Threading My Way*, 206; R. D. Owen to John Neal, July 26, 1824, Irving T. Richards, "The Life and Letters of John Neal," III, 1824–1825, an unpublished doctoral dissertation in the Harvard College Library.

[22] *Threading My Way*, 203–205. See also a similar, earlier account in *The Free Enquirer*, Sept. 1, 1832.

[23] Norman E. Himes, *Medical History of Contraception* (Baltimore, 1936), 212–220.

have been aware of or influenced by Place's writings on that
subject, as he was later to be; but neither his diary nor any
other record bears evidence of the fact. At best that diary
portrays the setting in which Owen might have lived his life
if it had not been for the American adventure, made possible
by the events of the following summer.

While the younger Owen had been growing to manhood, his
father had gradually sketched the outlines of a new economic
order. The genesis of his socialism may be traced to 1813
when he discussed the reformatory effects of proper environmental conditions on the collective character of a group. In
1817 he proposed to abolish unemployment by settling from
500 to 1,500 of the idle in "Villages of Unity and Coöperation"
where material needs would be cared for through common labor
and debased lives remolded. These self-supporting units for
character building were to be established and directed by some
benevolent agency, whether it be an individual, a county, or
the national government. In 1820 he again advanced this
scheme, not as a temporary panacea but as a specific alternative
to the existing social order. Capitalism, Robert Owen declared,
had failed to provide "employment at wages sufficient to support the family of a working man beneficially for the community" and must be replaced by another system based *"on
the principle of united labour . . . property, and equal privileges."* [24] Thus did the squire of Braxfield pronounce the doom
of free competition.

After 1820 the elder Owen took steps to give his theory of
socialism a practical trial. By 1822 his plan was endorsed by
several philanthropic societies, and $250,000 were subscribed
to begin an experiment. In the next year he carried the gospel
into poverty-stricken Ireland without material effect, while at
Westminster a committee of the House of Commons reported
unfavorably on the scheme. Nowise discouraged, the Welsh-

[24] Robert Owen, "A New View of Society," "Report to the Committee of the
Association for the Relief of the Manufacturing and Laboring Poor," "Report
to the County of Lanark, of a Plan for Relieving Public Distress," *Life of
Robert Owen*, I, 253–332; IA, 53–64, 263–310.

man continued his agitation, and a principal reason for the visit to London in March 1824 was to raise a loan for a socialistic enterprise, presumably at Motherwell, near Glasgow.[25] Some preliminary arrangements had already been made by the following summer when the arrival of Richard Flower at Braxfield turned the manufacturer's attention to the New World.

Across the Atlantic several religious communities employing common labor were already in operation.[26] The most successful was that of the Rappites, a sectarian society located at Harmony, Indiana, on the east bank of the Wabash some fifty miles above its mouth. Composed of sturdy Württemberg peasants who, fleeing to America early in the century to escape a tyrannical orthodoxy at home, had adopted celibacy and common ownership of property, this group had twice hewn thriving settlements out of the wilderness. Several factors explained their prosperity in Indiana. The linen, woolen, cotton, and leather goods fashioned in their workshops, together with the whiskey from their distilleries, found a ready sale in a region far removed from Eastern markets. Some produce was supplied to new settlers, but the greater part was conveniently and profitably sent by flatboat to New Orleans. Perfect social relations prevailed among people possessed of a common religious tie. Strong leadership was provided by the society's founder, George Rapp; and business ability was contributed by his adopted son, Frederick.[27] Why the Rappites left Indiana to begin a third home in Pennsylvania has never been satisfactorily explained. It is possible that too much success, which threatened primitive communal life and labor, rather than too little was the cause.[28] However that may be, the decision to move

[25] Podmore, op. cit., I, 275–282, II, 349, 355; R. D. Owen, "Journal, Begun 6th March 1824, Concluded 22d April 1824," Mar. 8, 12, 14, 16, Apr. 2, 3, 5, 13, 16; R. D. Owen to Neal, July 28, 1824, Richards, op. cit., III, 1824–1825.

[26] Morris Hillquit, History of Socialism in the United States (5th edn., N. Y., 1910), 13–37.

[27] John A. Bole, The Harmony Society, a Chapter in German American Culture History (Phila., 1904).

[28] "Diary of William Owen from November 10, 1824 to April 20, 1825," Indiana Historical Society, Publications, IV (Indps., 1906), 53; Threading My

was made by June 1824; and Richard Flower, one of the English settlers at Albion twenty-five miles away, was commissioned to offer the Harmony estate for sale in Europe.[29]

Flower did not visit New Lanark on blind chance. Robert Owen had already shown interest in the American coöperative communities and had once sought from Rapp information upon the effect of the change from private to common ownership of property.[30] Flower found his host a good listener and, according to Chester Harding who was present, took advantage of his ignorance of conditions in the pioneer West. The artist advised his patron to try the experiment in an Eastern state where both population and intellect were greater. His words, however, were not heeded; and in August Robert Owen agreed to cross the ocean to inspect the land at Harmony with a view to establishing there a communistic settlement.[31]

Credulity alone does not explain the manufacturer's willingness to locate his project in America. Aside from the advantages of free political and religious institutions, the Wabash estate was a genuine bargain. In 1817 the philanthropist had estimated the cost of starting a coöperative village in England at $480,000; Rapp's property, real and personal, would not cost a third of that amount. Harmony was already a complete and tested economic unit. It was surrounded by cheap land, if more were needed. During the previous winter Robert Owen had spoken favorably of the United States to Harding, and undoubtedly the cordial reception that he was soon to receive there influenced his final decision.[32]

Robert Dale Owen enthusiastically seconded his father's plan. There is every reason to believe that he regarded social-

Way, 240. See also George B. Lockwood, *The New Harmony Movement* (N. Y., 1905), 31–32.

[29] Philadelphia *National Gazette*, June 16, 1824 (advt.).

[30] Podmore, *op. cit.*, I, 232–233; Robt. Owen to George Rapp, Aug. 4, 1820, George Flower, *History of the English Settlement in Edwards County, Illinois* (E. B. Washburne, ed., *Chicago Historical Society's Collection*, I, Chi., 1882), 372–373.

[31] Margaret E. White, ed., *A Sketch of Chester Harding, Artist* (Boston, 1890), 122–123.

[32] *Sketch of Chester Harding*, 87–88; *Threading My Way*, 240–241.

ism or communism — the words were often used interchange-
ably — as the best remedy for industrial ills. To his diary he
had confided that the present was the most important era in
world history and that "the signs of the times are astonishing
& encouraging." He was eager to engage in communal life and
to do so on the American frontier added a touch of romance.[33]
It was not yet evident to the well-born Scot that participation
in the experiment would lead to a permanent residence in
America. Yet even if he could have foreseen the future, it is
doubtful whether the younger Owen would have hesitated. The
barrage of criticism then leveled against the young republic
by British magazines did not prejudice his mind, for the same
reviewers who gloated over Ashe and Faux were bitterly hostile
to his father's reforms. On the contrary, friendship with Neal
and Harding, as well as his innate liberalism, probably disposed
him favorably toward that astonishing nation beyond the sea.

Despite young Owen's eagerness to embark upon the American adventure, more than a year elapsed before he saw the
promised land. When the father sailed for the United States
in October 1824, he decided to leave his eldest son in charge
of the mills and to take William as an amanuensis.[34] Disappointed by this arrangement, Robert suggested almost at
once that it be changed. It was of the utmost importance, he
wrote, that some community should be begun in the spring.
If it proved to be impossible, however, he hoped his father
would let him cross the ocean at that time to study American
agriculture and inspect the Pestalozzian school at Philadelphia.
In forwarding this letter, William said of his brother, "He seems
in great spirits and very enthusiastic . . . and he thinks that
he is himself spoilt for every life but that of a community." [35]

[33] "Journal," Mar. 16, 1824; Owen to Neal, July 28, 1824, Richards, *op.
cit.*, III, 1824–1825; R. D. Owen to Robt. Owen, Oct. 18, 1824, as summarized
in Wm. Owen to Robt. Owen, Feb. 7, 1825, Robert Owen Papers, no. 58;
Threading My Way, 240–241.
[34] "Diary of Donald Macdonald" (MS.), Oct. 2, 1824; *Threading My Way*,
241.
[35] R. D. Owen to Robt. Owen, Oct. 18, 1824, as summarized in Wm. Owen
to Robt. Owen, Feb. 7, 1825, Robert Owen Papers, no. 58.

Nothing came of this proposal, and Owen had to wait impatiently at New Lanark. The strain was slightly relieved, happily, by a business trip to Holland, at which time he studied the Dutch attempt at Fredericksoord to end pauperism through coöperative labor colonies.[36]

Early in August 1825 Robert Owen returned to Braxfield, bringing a glowing account of his work in America. He had achieved far more than he had expected.[37] He had been cordially received by President-elect Adams, Calhoun, and De Witt Clinton. The people at large seemed favorably disposed. In January he had agreed to purchase Rapp's property. The next month distinguished audiences crowded the House of Representatives at Washington to hear him lecture. He had then announced that his experiment would begin in April and that the village, renamed New Harmony, would be the half-way house in which his followers might prepare themselves for life in the communistic colonies that would be formed on its outlying lands.[38] Final negotiations were soon completed, and with the departure of the last of the Rappites the undertaking was formally commenced on April 27. By June more than eight hundred persons had flocked to the Wabash, although the founder had estimated that three years would be required to gather so many. Faced with such encouraging prospects, even William Owen, theretofore scornful of the backwoods where the poor were content to live on hog and hominy and where the rich did nothing but drink, speculate, and talk politics, was cheered. A letter written by him in August breathed a spirit of optimism.[39]

[36] R. D. Owen, "The Dutch and Their Country," *New Harmony Gazette*, Nov. 15, 22, 29, Dec. 6, 1826, Jan. 17, 24, 1827; *Free Enquirer*, Jan. 15, Nov. 12, 1831. See also "Home Colonies," *Quarterly Review*, XLI, 522–550 (Nov. 1829).

[37] "Diary of Donald Macdonald," Aug. 7; *Threading My Way*, 260. Cf. Robt. Owen to Wm. Allen, Apr. 21, 1825, Robert Owen Papers, no. 56.

[38] "Diary of William Owen," *loc. cit.*, IV, 30, 41–42, 93, 96; Robert Owen, *Two Discourses on a New System of Society* (London, 1825), 24–25.

[39] *New Harmony Gazette*, Oct. 1, 1825; *Niles' Weekly Register*, July 23, 1827; *Co-operative Magazine*, I, 15–16 (Jan. 1826). Cf. Wm. Owen to Robt. Owen, Feb. 7, 1825, Robert Owen Papers, no. 58.

Such news only increased young Owen's eagerness to be off. Yet another two months had to pass while Robert Owen settled his business affairs. Finally the appointed day arrived. Late in September father and son left Braxfield for Liverpool where on October 1 they sailed upon the packet-ship *New York*, Captain Bennett commanding. The great adventure had begun.[40]

[40] "Diary of Donald Macdonald," Oct. 1, 1825.

CHAPTER III

NEW HARMONY

THE modern traveler, whose luxurious floating palace breasts the turbulent Atlantic in four days, can scarcely appreciate the monotony, inconvenience, and perils encountered by his great-great-grandfather on the best packets of an earlier day. Life on shipboard seemed to many tourists of that period like being in prison with the chance of being drowned. A later passenger of the *New York*, crossing at the same season as Owen, complained:

At *best*, a sea voyage is a confinement at once irksome and odious, in which the unfortunate prisoner is compelled for weeks or months, to breathe the tainted atmosphere of a close and crowded cabin, and to sleep at night in a sort of a box, about the size of a coffin. . . . At *worst*, it involves a complication of the most nauseous evils that can afflict humanity, — an utter prostration of power, both bodily and mental, a revulsion of the whole corporeal machinery, accompanied by a host of detestable diagnostics, which at once convert a well-dressed and well-favoured gentleman, into an object of contempt to himself, and disgust to those around him.[1]

Owen's enthusiasm was not dampened by the annoyances of an ocean voyage. His shipmates were a jovial lot; and the presence on board of the operatic troupe of the elder Garcia, then on its way to win the plaudits of New York, afforded many evenings of delightful music. The spirit of adventure that gripped the Owens and their two prospective communal companions, Donald Macdonald and Stedman Whitwell, was vividly expressed in an ode written by the latter and set to music by Señor Garcia himself.

> Land of the West! we come to thee
> Far o'er the desert of the sea:
> Under thy white-wing'd canopy,
> Ebor Nova.

[1] [Thomas Hamilton], *Men and Manners in America* (Phila., 1833), 9–10.

Land of the West! we fly to thee,
Sick of the old world's sophistry;
Haste then along the dark blue sea,
Ebor Nova.

Land of the West! we rush to thee
Home of the brave, soil of the free!
Huzza! she rises o'er the sea —
Ebor Nova.[2]

With the words of this stirring tune still ringing in their ears, the travelers saw the long voyage come to an end. Over the bay, gleaming in the bright sunshine of a clear autumnal morning, rose the white sails of a busy port and, behind, the hundred spires of a growing city. It lacked a day of the twenty-fourth anniversary of Owen's birth. In later life, recalling the feeling of youth, he wrote, "I had reached the Canaan of my hopes, and its first glimpse was beautiful even beyond my dreams."[3]

Owen landed in a New York seething with excitement. Two days before, midst pomp and ceremony, Governor Clinton had solemnized the "marriage of the waters," completing the Erie Canal and initiating the greatest celebration in the history of the city. To this fanfare the annual November elections added their political turmoil. Yet, despite these competing events, the arrival of the Owens attracted much attention. The newspapers gave the father's address, written at sea, good publicity and withheld hostile comment.[4] Prominent citizens from all walks of life flocked to the Howard House where the party was staying. So charmed was the son by the first Yankees he met that he went at once to a notary and declared his intention of becoming an American citizen.[5] A few days later Robert Owen spoke before a distinguished group of literary

[2] *New Harmony Gazette*, Mar. 15, 1826; "Diary of Donald Macdonald," Oct. 1–Nov. 5, 1825; *Threading My Way*, 260–263.

[3] "Diary of Donald Macdonald," Nov. 6; *Threading My Way*, 264.

[4] *N. Y. American*, Nov. 8, 1825; *Mercantile Advertiser*, Nov. 8, 1825; *National Advocate*, Nov. 9, 1825.

[5] *N. Y. National Advocate*, Nov. 18, 1825; *Niles' Weekly Register*, Nov. 26, 1825; *Threading My Way*, 264.

and scientific men in City Hall and drew applause by condemn-
ing the practice of buying cheap and selling dear. Only after
that speech did the New York press begin to voice criticism.[6]

Such criticism was to be expected. Widespread industrial
distress in the young nation was absent. At the very time that
Robert Owen was launching communism on the Indiana frontier, improved methods of transportation and the reduced price
of homesteads on the public domain were making it easier and
cheaper for the discontented of the East to begin life anew as
individual landowners in the West. The New Harmony experiment, moreover, was undertaken in a transitional period of
American social history. In the first half century of independence a national identity had become manifest in nearly
all aspects of life, especially in religion, literature, orthography,
music, and the drama. After 1825 changed economic conditions
and the influence of foreign ideas created a new age, featured
by the rise of the common man. In the extension of political
equality, the increased material comforts of everyday existence,
and the manifold crusades to ameliorate the lot of the unfortunate, this new humanitarianism was notable. But when Robert
Dale Owen arrived on the American scene, few signs of this
reform spirit were in evidence. Universal manhood suffrage
had not yet been established in New York, and the beginning
of the modern labor movement was still two years distant.
The advent of Unitarianism and Universalism indicated a growing liberalism within the confines of organized religion, but
the freedom to think and act beyond the bounds of all faiths
had yet to be won. In 1825 Susan B. Anthony was only five
years old, Garrison had not yet established *The Liberator*, and
Dorothea Dix was to teach school in Boston for another decade.
Fifteen years remained before Fourierism, as expounded by
Albert Brisbane, was to start America on its most important
quest for a communal Utopia. The brief and insignificant influence in the United States of Robert Owen's "social system" sug-

[6] "Diary of Donald Macdonald," Nov. 18; *National Advocate*, Nov. 19,
1825. Cf. *ibid.*, Nov. 21, 22, 23, 1825.

gests that the New Harmony enterprise was of foreign inspiration, directed largely by men of foreign birth, in an attempt to
solve a problem that did not yet exist upon American soil.

Hostility to Owenism did not stem solely from economic
theory or nativism. The outspoken agnosticism of the leader
and the prevalence of similar views among his followers shocked
the orthodox. The Welshman failed to heed the conservatism
of American religion, and even his friends regretted that he
refused to keep his opinions to himself.[7] As a result, the public
journals eagerly pounced upon a dismal report, given by a supposed itinerant Baptist minister, of the confusion and decay
in the old Rappite village. The Owenites, it was said, had
abolished all sermons, converted the town church into a dance
hall, and were teaching the doctrines of Tom Paine in their
schools.[8] In Philadelphia, whither the socialists traveled on
their way west, this story was repeated; and the press generally
proved much less friendly than in New York. The enmity of
the Quaker City papers, whose items on New Harmony were
copied even in Indiana, continued during the life of the community and went far to mold adverse sentiment throughout the
nation.[9]

This unfortunate publicity was partially counteracted by the
decision of William Maclure to associate himself with the social
experiment. Born in Scotland sixty-two years before but an
American citizen for over twenty, Maclure was well-known as
a geologist, a patron of science, and an advocate of agricultural education. Although a liberal in religion and political
economy, Maclure's interest in New Harmony arose chiefly
from the opportunity to establish there the manual labor school

---

[7] *N. Y. National Advocate*, Dec. 2, 1825.

[8] St. Louis *Missouri Republican*, Sept. 19, 1825, reprinted in Philadelphia
Democratic Press, Nov. 8, 1825; *N. Y. Daily Advertiser*, Nov. 21, 1825. See also
"Diary of Donald Macdonald," Nov. 11, 1825; W. Pelham to W. C. Pelham,
Sept. 7, Nov. 27, 1825, Caroline C. Pelham, ed., "Letters of William Pelham
Written in 1825 and 1826," *Indiana As Seen by Early Travelers* (Harlow Lind-
ley, ed., *Indiana Historical Collections*, Indps., 1916), 370, 394.

[9] *Poulson's American Daily Advertiser*, Dec. 1, 2, 1825. Cf. Lawrenceburg
Indiana Palladium, Aug. 26, 1825; *Niles' Weekly Register*, Jan. 18, 1827.

that he had attempted to found in Spain. Curiously enough he had been in New Lanark in September 1824, just prior to Robert Owen's first departure for America; but apparently his mind was not made up until a year later, during which time he was urged to join the enterprise by his close friend, Madame Marie Fretageot, by philanthropic Philadelphians, and perhaps by Owen himself.[10] Maclure, however, refused to invest in the project a sum equal to Owen's, declined to be responsible for any money already expended, and limited his liability to $10,000. He donated books and instruments to the experiment and later bought land for himself; but his chief contribution was to gather on the Indiana frontier a group of scientists and educators whose presence gave New Harmony, both during the experiment and after, much of its intellectual significance.[11]

Foremost among this talented group was Thomas Say, already famous as the leading descriptive entomologist in the United States. Gerard Troost and Charles A. Lesueur, like Maclure, were foreign born and, like Say, were distinguished members of the Philadelphia Academy of Natural Sciences. Troost ranged over geology, mineralogy, chemistry, and other subjects; Lesueur, in addition to his skill as a painter and draftsman, had collected fossils and shells for the first study of the fish of the Great Lakes. With these scientists Maclure brought two Pestalozzian teachers, Marie D. Fretageot and William Phiquepal D'Arusmont, both born abroad and both accompanied by pupils from the schools that they were then conducting in Philadelphia under Maclure's auspices. Also in the party were John Speakman, an original member of the Academy of Natural Sciences, and Cornelius Tiebout, a talented engraver.[12]

[10] Maclure to Benjamin Silliman, *American Journal of Science*, IX, X, *passim*, especially Sept. 10, 1824, *ibid.*, IX, 160; Marie D. Fretageot to Robt. Owen, Feb. 17, 26, 1825, Robert Owen Papers, nos. 60, 64.

[11] *New Harmony Gazette*, Aug. 8, 1827; Maclure to Fretageot, June 9, Aug. 21, 1826, Fretageot Papers; "Diary and Recollections of Victor Colin Duclos," *Indiana As Seen by Early Travelers*, 537; memorandum by R. D. Owen in the Stone Papers.

[12] *Dictionary of American Biography*, XI, 190–191; XVI, 401; XVIII, 530–

With such companions and a few English recruits, Robert
Dale Owen resumed his westward journey. Crossing the mountains by carriage, he reached Pittsburgh where New Harmony
was the chief topic of conversation. Near by, the final arrangements with Rapp were made.[13] Finding the season too advanced for regular steamboat service, the party hired the
keelboat *Philanthropist*; and on December 8 the long drift
down the Ohio began. For a month, however, ice interrupted
near Beaver the progress of this so-called "Boatload of Knowledge." As the temperature rose the vessel moved again, floating slowly past the famous river towns, then in their infancy,
Steubenville, Wheeling, Marietta, Cincinnati, and Louisville.
In spite of his intellectual and sociable fellow travelers Owen
chafed at the numerous delays. His father had gone ahead by
stage, arriving at his settlement on January 12. Not until
eleven days later did the *Philanthropist* reach Mt. Vernon, the
Ohio port for New Harmony. Even then some proposed to
continue to their destination by water, a matter of another
ten days. With the promised land only fifteen miles away,
Owen refused to listen to such a plan. That very evening he
borrowed a horse and hastened through the darkness to obtain
his first taste of community life.[14]

New Harmony, the scene of Owen's youthful dreams and
the home of his middle years, stood on rich bottom land close

---

531, 647–648; *American Journal of Science*, VIII, 188; X, 151; W. S. H. Ruschen-
berger, *A Notice of the Origin, Progress, and Present Condition of the Academy
of Natural Sciences of Philadelphia* (2d edn., Phila., 1860), 64–65.

[13] Paul Brown, *Twelve Months in New Harmony* (Cincinnati, 1827), 9. On
Jan. 3, 1825 Robert Owen agreed to give $120,000 on time for all of the real
and some of the personal Rappite property. Other personal effects were to be
paid for after appraisal. On Apr. 21, 1825 Owen decided instead to deliver
$95,000 in cash at once and thus get a better bargain. A receipt for $125,000,
however, was made by Rapp on Dec. 10, 1825 and some payments were still
due in May 1827 and 1828. Robert Owen probably invested from $120,000 to
$150,000 in the experiment, but poor management led to greater losses. Data
from documents loaned by Mr. & Mrs. J. S. Duss to the Workingmen's Institute;
Robt. Owen to Wm. Allen, Apr. 21, 1825; penal bond dated May 21, 1825,
Robert Owen Papers, nos. 56, 66; Maclure to Fretageot, June 20, 1826, Fretageot Papers; *Threading My Way*, 292–293.

[14] "Diary of Donald Macdonald," Jan. 8, 10, 23, 1826; *New Harmony
Gazette*, Jan. 18, 1826; *Threading My Way*, 268–269.

to the Wabash. The traveler approaching from Mt. Vernon received his first glimpse of its setting from the brow of a semi-circular range of hills that rose some sixty feet above the valley, a half mile south of the village. To the east stretched a large tract of recently cleared meadow land, encompassed in part by undulating hills and in part by the silent forest. To the north, beyond another clearing, likewise sown with corn, wheat, and small grain, flowed the river, behind which rose in unbroken array the luxuriant and lofty woodlands of the Illinois bank. To the west and south of the village the plain was lined with orchards, while the slopes of the surrounding hills contained fifteen acres of carefully cultivated vineyards.

As the traveler descended from his coign of vantage and followed the road along the plain, signs of industry met his eye. A brickyard, a tanyard, and a ropewalk paralleled his path. To the right appeared a cotton factory and a steam mill. To the left, screened by the trees that lined the banks of a branch of the Wabash, stood a three-story flour mill. The unpaved streets of the village, delightfully shaded by locusts and maples, met at right angles. The junction of the Mt. Vernon road running north and south with the Princeton road running east and west marked the center of the town and there, in the north-west quarter, stood the most impressive building, the residence raised in the wilderness by the faithful for Father Rapp. Across the street to the south was a steepled frame church, and a scant ten feet from its door was a brick cruciform struc-ture, already rechristened New Harmony Hall and dedicated to the discussions and amusements of the new social system. Scattered about without fixed design were six large brick build-ings, many frame dwellings, numerous log cabins, and such economic necessities as granaries, warehouses, machine shops, a brewery, a dye house, and manufactories for soap, shoes, and candles. Such was the physical setting for the communal life of Robert Dale Owen.[15]

[15] William Hebert, *A Visit to the Colony of Harmony, in Indiana, in the United States of America* (London, 1825); "Diary of William Owen," Indiana

On Owen's arrival the Preliminary Society of New Harmony numbered slightly less than one thousand members, the great majority of whom had joined the previous spring. This group, representing every state in the Union but two and almost all nations of northern Europe, was extremely heterogeneous. In its ranks were native born and foreign born, Western farmer and Eastern mechanic, intellectual theorist and unlettered backwoodsman, pious Christian and scoffing atheist. Except for the leaders, probably more than half came from west of the mountains; for the experiment attracted both poor agricultural workers in search of free land and respectable citizens of Albion, Mt. Vernon, Princeton, and Evansville. No standard of professional skill or utility to the community had guided the selection of these people. Membership was open to all who signed the constitution and stated their reasons for joining.[16]

Owen found the economic status of the community anything but encouraging. Broken machinery, want of efficient workmen, and the absence of capable superintendents had brought the profitable Rappite manufactures to a standstill. Only those trades dependent on individual initiative flourished. In the agricultural department the alleged neglect of the departing Harmony Society, insufficient sowing, and a general lack of coöperation led to a food shortage as early as September. Vegetables were then being purchased, and it was predicted that potatoes, flour, and other provisions would be needed by winter. In December the general store was threatened with depletion and could no longer supply many of the necessities of life.[17] By this material failure the Preliminary Society cre-

Historical Society, *Publications*, IV, 71–77; "Pelham Letters," *loc. cit.*, 378; "View of New Harmony," *New Harmony Gazette*, Oct. 1, 8, 15, 22, 1825; Bernhard, Duke of Saxe-Weimar Eisenach, *Travels through North America during the Years 1825 and 1826* (Phila., 1828), II, 107–123; *Threading My Way*, 241–243; Nora C. Fretageot, *Historic New Harmony, a Guide* (3d edn., n.p., 1934).

[16] *New Harmony Gazette*, Oct. 1, 29, 1825; *Evansville Gazette*, July 16, 1825; "Diary of William Owen," *loc. cit.*, IV, 89–90, 97–99; Flower, *History of the English Settlement in Edwards County*, 282–283.

[17] T. C. Pears, Jr., ed., "New Harmony, an Adventure in Happiness. The Papers of Thomas and Sarah Pears," Indiana Historical Society, *Publications*,

ated a large debt, the settlement of which plagued the later community and led to strained relations between Robert Owen and William Maclure.

The social and intellectual progress of the group showed a better record. Certain evenings were set apart for concerts, dances, and meetings to legislate on communal affairs. An exposition of Robert Owen's thought was given in the Hall on Sunday mornings, but at other hours adequate facilities were given to visiting preachers. A day school had been begun in June, followed somewhat later by a boarding school designed to relieve parents of all care of their children.[18] On October 1 had appeared *The New Harmony Gazette*, the first paper in Posey County. Complete mental freedom and varied activities, however, were offset by individual inequalities, personal hardships of pioneer life, and the lack of economic progress. These shortcomings caused the members to regard with childlike faith the return of Robert Owen as the solution of all their difficulties. "Expectation hangs on him," wrote a follower, "and should he be delayed until Spring, the spirit of Harmony will be severely tried in many." [19]

The sincere joy manifested in New Harmony at the new arrivals delighted both father and son. After the reports they had received in the East, they were prepared for anything, even complete dissolution. Perhaps the mere fact that the experiment held together encouraged Robert Owen to take a bold and unexpected step, though there is some evidence that he was considering it before he reached Indiana.[20] Within a fortnight the founder decided to scrap the Preliminary Society, which

---

XI (Indps., 1933), 24–26, 52; "Pelham Letters," *loc. cit.*, 381–382, 401; Wm. Owen to Robt. Owen, Dec. 16, 1825, Robert Owen Papers, no. 54; *New Harmony Gazette*, Oct. 22, 1825; *Co-operative Magazine*, I, 48 (Feb. 1826).

[18] *New Harmony Gazette*, Oct. 29, Dec. 21, 1825; "Pelham Letters," *loc. cit.*, 365, 387; "Pears Papers," *loc. cit.*, XI, 18, 26; *N. Y. National Advocate*, Nov. 22, 1825.

[19] "Pears Papers," *loc. cit.*, XI, 24. Cf. *ibid.*, 26, 82; "Pelham Letters," *loc. cit.*, 398, 403; Wm. Owen to Robt. Owen, Dec. 16, 1825, Robert Owen Papers, no. 54.

[20] *Threading My Way*, 285; "Pears Papers," *loc. cit.*, XI, 46.

had been intended to last for three years, and form at once a community of complete equality. In the half-way house hitherto in operation no member had been compelled to place all his property in a common fund, and great differences in labor and living facilities had been tolerated in order to attract scientists and educators. During this training period title to the New Harmony estate remained with its purchaser. But on January 26, 1826, by approving the Society's appointment of a committee to draft a new constitution, Robert Owen abandoned his original plan, located the experiment in the village instead of on its adjoining lands, and left unsettled both the debt previously incurred and the title to the estate for which he had paid more than $100,000.[21]

As a member of the constituent committee the younger Owen had his first oportunity to influence the course of the social experiment. At once he drafted his own blueprint for Utopia, but the frame of government ultimately adopted ignored his suggestions on the vital points. His wise proposals for an easy amendatory process and a six-month probationary period for new members were rejected, and his opposition to a strong executive board was overruled. On the other hand, the right of all members to enjoy equal rank, food, clothing, and housing, passed over by Owen in silence, was specifically asserted in the final draft.[22] Unfortunately both Owen and his colleagues placed too much trust in paper constitutions. Firm leadership, a consistent policy, and sociable feelings among the participants were necessary for the success of the enterprise. Thus, although the new constitution was immediately adopted on February 6 and membership in the new community was opened to those in the old, obstacles arose at once. Despite the election of a capable executive committee, of which young Owen was not

[21] "Constitution of the Preliminary Society, May 1, 1825," *New Harmony Gazette*, Oct. 1, 1825.

[22] "Constitution of the New Harmony Community of Equality," *New Harmony Gazette*, Feb. 15, 1826. Owen's proposed draft is entered in the "Minutes of the Constitutional Convention" (MS.) for Feb. 3. These unprinted "Minutes" are the best source for the events from Jan. 25–Feb. 6, 1826. See also "Pears Papers," *loc. cit.*, XI, 56–63; "Pelham Letters," *loc. cit.*, 406–409.

a member, it was found expedient within a fortnight to appeal to Robert Owen who had wished to remain aloof from the governing body. In another two weeks the complex instrument was suspended for twelve months, and the founder was forced to take hold.[23] Thus did the precipitate abandonment of the modified individualism of the Preliminary Society for a theoretical equality initiate a period of constant changes that continued until the experiment came to an end more than a year later.

Even before the new constitution had time to prove its inadequacy, the first of the many secessions that were to disturb the progress of the socialists occurred. Some time prior to February 15 several native Methodist backwoodsmen, disliking the irreligion of many of their fellow communists, leased from Robert Owen twelve hundred acres of land two miles east of New Harmony. There they founded Macluria, an independent coöperative settlement, the profits of which were to be reserved for canceling the debt to the New Lanark manufacturer. A steady increase in numbers during the spring and summer gave hopes of success that were never realized.[24] About March 1, however, their example was followed by some English farmers, formerly of Birkbeck's colony at Wanborough, who, hoping for better results in a smaller, less cosmopolitan group, formed a third community one mile east of the village. Like Macluria, this Feiba-Peveli adopted its own constitution and was similarly indebted to the elder Owen for its property and ready money. Thanks to a wise restriction of its membership, this society enjoyed comparative prosperity for two years.[25]

Two days after the withdrawal of the English farmers, practically the entire "Boatland of Knowledge," led by Robert Dale Owen, his brother William, and Robert L. Jennings, a British

[23] *New Harmony Gazette*, Feb. 22, 1826; "Pears Papers," *loc. cit.*, XI, 76.

[24] *New Harmony Gazette*, Feb. 15, 22, Mar. 29, 1826; "Pears Papers," *loc. cit.*, XI, 67; "Diary of Donald Macdonald," (n. d.) ; Bernhard, *op. cit.*, II, 115; *Co-operative Magazine*, I, 193–194, II, 46 (June 1826, Jan. 1827).

[25] *New Harmony Gazette*, Mar. 8, Apr. 12, 1826, Sept. 26, Nov. 7, 1827, Mar. 19, 1828; "Pears Papers," *loc. cit.*, XI, 67, 78; "Diary of Donald Macdonald," (n. d.) ; Bernhard, *op. cit.*, II, 115; *Co-operative Magazine*, II, 46 (Jan. 1827).

born, ex-Universalist minister, resigned to form still another small community. Like its predecessors, self-interest was the motive; but where the first split had been along religious lines and the second along national, this third seems to have resulted from intellectual and social differences. The widespread dissatisfaction, however, caused by the loss of the distinguished scientists and educators, as well as the unwillingness of the younger Owen and his associates to settle on uncleared land outside of the village, spelled defeat for the movement. Midst harsh words and bitter feelings, the learned ones took up again their positions in the parent society.[26]

The return of the seceders led to neither peace nor progress. Other defections were attempted, and it became evident that the motley group could never be fitted into one congenial community.[27] Further ill-feeling was created by Robert Owen's repeated attempts to secure compensation for the money he had paid Rapp. Whatever his enthusiastic followers may have thought, the squire of Braxfield had no idea of donating his New Harmony estate to any coöperative enterprise. At various times he had talked of renting it, selling it, or accepting as payment the profits of the Preliminary Society. That organization, however, had expired while insolvent; and the constitution of its successor merely provided that the founder's property should be held in perpetual trust for the community.[28] Although obviously dissatisfied, Robert Owen was unable to obtain a better arrangement, and the matter was left for the time in that state. Meanwhile his disciples, disappointed by his lack of leadership, began to desert. Several of the original members left in April,

[26] "Pears Papers," *loc. cit.*, XI, 67, 71–72, 75, 78; "Diary of Donald Macdonald," undated entry preceding March 4.

[27] Maclure to Silliman, Mar. 16, 1826, *American Journal of Science*, XI, 189–190; *New Harmony Gazette*, Apr. 12, 1826.

[28] "Pears Papers," *loc. cit.*, XI, 76–77; Brown, *op. cit.*, 14–16, 23, 106–116. Previous proposals to settle the question of the property may be found in *The New Harmony Gazette*, Oct. 1, 1825, Feb. 15, 1826; "Diary of William Owen," *loc. cit.*, IV, 90; "Pelham Letters," *loc. cit.*, 393, 416–417; "Notice to Farmers, Traders and Others," Robert Owen Papers, no. 57; R. Owen, *Two Discourses on a New System of Society*, 25.

never to return; and during that month the Duke of Saxe-Weimar predicted the speedy dissolution of the experiment. Although optimistic reports continued to appear in the *Gazette*, there was in the spring of 1826 little harmony along the banks of the Wabash.

The formation of an independent community of intellectuals, attempted in March and April, finally took place in June. William Maclure had watched with increasing disgust the extravagance and mishaps of the experiment in which he had chosen to develop his pedagogical theories. Soon convinced that only a small coöperative unit could be self-supporting, he was ready by summer to terminate entirely his association with Robert Owen. But although he refused to waste any more of his fortune on the heterogeneous population of the village, he was willing to purchase land and buildings with which a select few could conduct under mutual labor and ownership an agricultural and trade school. After much discussion and threats the New Lanark manufacturer reversed his earlier stand and agreed to subdivide his enterprise further into four more small communities.[29]

Under this new arrangement Robert Dale Owen joined most of the "Boatload of Knowledge" in an Education Society with Maclure as patron. Besides Say, Troost, Lesueur, D'Arusmont, and Madame Fretageot, it included Joseph Neef, pioneer Pestalozzian teacher in the United States, and Joseph Applegath, a former instructor in the New Lanark schools. It was hoped that this society would become self-supporting by intelligent coöperative farming, by the labor of its pupils in the mechanical arts, and by such tuition as it received for teaching the children of the other New Harmony communities.[30]

In spite of its talented membership, its possession of the

[29] Maclure to Silliman, Mar. 16, 1826, *American Journal of Science*, XI, 190; Maclure to Fretageot, June 9, 20, July 9, 1826, Fretageot Papers; *New Harmony Gazette*, June 7, 1826; Brown, *op. cit.*, 18–19.

[30] *Co-operative Magazine*, I, 374, II, 47 (Dec. 1826, Jan. 1827); Brown, *op. cit.*, 34; Fretageot to Maclure, July [?] 11, 1826, and a mutilated indenture in the Maclure Papers; Maclure to Fretageot, June 9, 24, July 31, Aug. 11, 21, [21?], 29, Sept. 19, 1826, Jan. 3, 1827, Fretageot Papers.

choicest real and personal property in the village, and the gradual extinguishment of its debt through the munificence of
Maclure, the Education Society made little progress toward a
self-sustaining coöperative community. As superintendent and
occasional instructor, Owen had a good opportunity to discover its faults. Jealousy was rife. D'Arusmont was disliked
on all sides, and a long smoldering quarrel between Neef and
Madame Fretageot finally culminated in an open break. Applegath left the scene, while Troost and Lesueur occupied themselves exclusively with research.[31] The chief difficulty, however,
was to secure enough students to make the experiment financially sound. Maclure's dreams of a tripartite boarding school,
with Madame Fretageot, Neef, and D'Arusmont presiding over
their respective disciplines, never materialized. At no time
was the eight hundred quota anticipated by the patron even
half filled; and the great majority of the children enrolled at the
society's most prosperous period came from the other New
Harmony settlements. When the younger Owen and his associates decided that these scholars too must pay the regular
tuition fee, there was loud protest in the village. The demand
was refused, the children withdrawn, and attendance in the
society's schools fell to eighty.[32]

The Education Society's troubled course was further aggra-
vated by forces beyond its control. On July 4, 1826, Robert
Owen issued a Declaration of Mental Independence in which
he denounced religion, private property, and the marriage system as the trinity of the world's evils. Although such sentiments
were not uncommon at New Harmony, this dramatic and much
publicized speech alarmed people in the East who might otherwise have sent their children to Maclure's institutions.[33] In

---

[31] Brown, *op. cit.*, 82, 116–117; Maclure to Fretageot, July 9, Aug. 11, 29,
Sept. 19, 25, 1826, Fretageot Papers; Fretageot to Maclure, July [?] 11, 1826,
Mar. 2, 1827, Maclure Papers.

[32] Maclure to the editor, July 4, 1826, *Révue Encyclopédique*, XXXI, 801–
802 (Sept. 1826); Brown, *op. cit.*, 34; Fretageot to Maclure, July [?] 11, 1826,
Maclure Papers.

[33] *New Harmony Gazette*, July 12, 1826; Maclure to Fretageot, Aug. 2, 1826,

August the elder Owen proposed a scheme of free, mutual instruction for those not attending the schools of the Education
Society, a proposal regarded by some as an attack on the latter
and an answer to his son's demand for tuition fees.[34] In September the manufacturer again changed his mind and tried to undo
the work he had done in June. Moved by the agitation of certain self-styled republicans who resented the exclusiveness of
the intellectuals and by the realization that he had unwisely
parted with his most valuable buildings, he proposed to reunite
his followers in one large community. This step threatened
the existence of the Education Society and initiated a new
period in the communal life of Robert Dale Owen.[35]

The progress of events had made the younger Owen's position
increasingly difficult. In the outbreak between Neef and
Madame Fretageot, he had had the unenviable distinction of
being the latter's sole supporter. He had been as responsible as
any for the separate community of intellectuals, the protests
against which his father finally felt compelled to assuage. The
widening breach between Maclure and the elder Owen made it
impossible to combine loyalty to both parent and patron.[36]
As a solution he agreed to fill the editorial vacancy in *The New
Harmony Gazette*. Whether he resigned from the Education
Society does not appear. But after mid-October he no longer
participated actively in the government of any of the communities, all of which were approaching final dissolution.

Owen filled with marked ability the post in which he so suddenly found himself. Gifted with a strong, if not highly original
mind and possessed of a facile pen, he improved at once the
standard of Posey County's only paper, then floundering for
want of a capable pilot. To be sure his journal differed greatly

---

Fretageot Papers; John B. McMaster, *A History of the People of the United
States*, V (N. Y., 1900), 95–96.

   [34] *New Harmony Gazette*, Aug. 9, 16, 23, 30, Sept. 6, 1826; Maclure to
Fretageot, Aug. 29, Sept. 19, 25, 1826, Fretageot Papers.

   [35] *New Harmony Gazette*, Aug. 9, 30, Sept. 9, 1826; Brown, *op. cit.*, 41–57,
60–68.

   [36] Maclure to Fretageot, July 21, Aug. 11, 21, [21?], Sept. 19, 1826, Jan. 3,
1827, Fretageot Papers.

from its contemporaries. It avoided the politics, personalities, and sentimental tales so common in the press of the day. News was a secondary matter; for, as a former editor had written, the first object was "to disseminate a correct knowledge of the principles, practice, and local affairs of this Society." [37] Thus it was highly appropriate that this paper should carry the strongest endorsement Owen ever made of the necessity for coöperative communities as an alternative to a decadent capitalism, six essays entitled "Wealth and Misery." [38]

Under the younger Owen the *Gazette* went beyond a discussion of the new "social system." It became the critic of every irrationality in society. Where the prospectus had stated that the paper would not combat the errors and follies of mankind, the new editor considered it his "duty to exhibit . . . every prejudice however popular which we see producing misery to the world, or which we discover retarding the progress of science or general improvement." [39] Under that mandate Owen urged reforms in English grammar, medicine, and female costume. He criticized a Hoosier governor for advocating internal improvements instead of public schools. He openly questioned the wisdom of Christianity and condemned both strict Sabbatarianism and indissoluble marriage.[40] Already Robert Dale Owen the freethinker was emerging, the man who asserted his right to discuss openly all matters pertaining to human happiness, religion, morals, and sexual relationships not excepted. Like his father, however, he had not yet learned the wisdom of keeping such matters separate from the experiment in common property and mutual labor.

The most difficult task falling to Owen as editor was to report on the progress of the community. His predecessors had never told their readers the complete story of the continual dissension and change, and he experienced a similar embarrassment as affairs at the end of 1826 approached a crisis. Nor was

[37] "Pelham Letters," *loc. cit.*, 396.
[38] *New Harmony Gazette*, Nov. 8, 15, 22, 29, Dec. 6, 13, 1826.
[39] *New Harmony Gazette*, Jan. 10, 1827. Cf. *ibid.*, Oct. 1, 1825.
[40] *New Harmony Gazette*, Dec. 6, 20, 1826; Jan. 10, Apr. 4, May 2, 1827.

his load lightened by his father, who not only exercised the right of censorship but also contributed misleading articles on the bright prospects of the society.[41] By sticking to the truth, the son won the praise of his sire's most bitter critic. Yet, as a result, the tone of his editorials grew less and less hopeful. The cessation of the weekly social gatherings was ruefully admitted in January.[42] During the next month the official organ lapsed into complete silence on community matters.

While the *Gazette* pursued its circumspect policy, signs of the experiment's ultimate failure multiplied. The new organization adopted in October proved unpopular. As a bait for its formation, Robert Owen had declared he would place his New Harmony estate in a common fund and that members would not be permitted to retain any private property except that necessary to pay debts or support families elsewhere. When neither of these prerequisites was fulfilled, the poorer element in the village raised its voice in complaint. In January the manufacturer further infuriated his followers by leasing a large amount of valuable property, formerly used by the whole community, to a group of newcomers who agreed to start a colony south of the village. During this same period his constant quarrels with the Education Society made a break with Maclure inevitable.[43]

Then on February 1, 1827, or "doomsday" as it came to be called, the founder took a step that virtually recognized the failure of his enterprise. Once again he dissolved his main community. The best of its members he settled in small groups outside of the town, while all others were given notice that they must support themselves or leave New Harmony. The growing unrest that had theretofore pervaded the scene in the form of fires and depredations was now climaxed by an attempt of

[41] Brown, *op. cit.*, 70, 72–74, 79–81; *New Harmony Gazette*, Oct. 11, Nov. 8, 15, 29, 1826.

[42] Brown, *op. cit.*, 72; *New Harmony Gazette*, Dec. 6, 1826, Jan. 3, 31, 1827.

[43] Brown, *op. cit.*, 60–84; "Lease to W. G. Taylor and Associates, Jan. 13, 1827" (LWI copy); "Pelham Letters," *loc. cit.*, 414; Maclure to Fretageot, Nov. 28, 1826, Jan. 3, 1827, Fretageot Papers.

the discontented to celebrate the funeral of the "social system."
With the collapse of the experiment being reported in the Eastern press, the official organ could not remain silent.[44] At the end
of March, with an optimism his subsequent action belied,
Robert Dale Owen published a carefully prepared statement
of the situation on the banks of the Wabash.

The social experiment, he declared, had not failed. On the
contrary, its success was demonstrated by the many small, independent coöperative communities then clustered about New
Harmony. The first community of complete equality, formed
in February 1826, had almost been wrecked, he admitted, by
the unexpected permission given all members of the Preliminary
Society to join. To save the day the founder had in June
proposed a subdivision, and some of the groups then brought
into being had since become well established. Others had
failed, and for their benefit Robert Owen had agreed in October
to make a second test on a large scale. The innate, anti-social
habits of his heterogeneous followers had, however, proved too
great an obstacle; and in February 1827 the manufacturer returned to his first plan, that of small, voluntary communities
outside of the village. Thus, the son concluded, "It is not in
the town itself, but on the lands of Harmony that the Community System is in progressive operation." [45]

This editorial, repeated in substance by the father in two
later speeches, became the official explanation of the New Harmony experiment.[46] Young Owen, however, left much that was
significant unsaid. He did not call the premature termination
of the Preliminary Society a blunder; and in blaming free membership for most of the difficulties of its successor, he failed to
note that neither his father nor he, after his own draft constitution had been rejected, had made any visible protest at the

---

[44] Brown, *op. cit.*, 75, 85–86; "Pelham Letters," *loc. cit.*, 415; Fretageot to
Maclure, Mar. 2, 1827, Maclure Papers; *Co-operative Magazine*, II, 243;
Threading My Way, 289. *Democratic Press*, Mar. 23, 1827; *N. Y. Evening
Post*, Mar. 26, 1827; *N. Y. Enquirer*, Mar. 30, 1827.

[45] *New Harmony Gazette*, Mar. 28, 1827.

[46] *Ibid.*, May 9, 30, 1827.

time against allowing all upon the scene to join the permanent community. The son felt "too inexperienced" to judge the wisdom of his sire's executive ability. He praised the squire of Braxfield for persevering in the face of great pecuniary loss but made no mention of the ill-will created by his many attempts to compensate himself at the expense of his followers for the money paid Rapp. The growing hostility between William Maclure and his associate was passed over in discreet silence. Nor was any explanation given why the same economic unit that had brought prosperity to the Harmony Society should fail to provide the bare necessities of life for the Owen community.

Criticism of this official interpretation was not slow in appearing. Headed by Joseph Neef and Paul Brown, the self-styled republicans wrote an open letter, bluntly calling the experiment a failure and assigning as the cause the incompetent direction of Robert Owen. No democratic coöperative community could exist, they argued, where one man owned all the property. The Welshman was excoriated for his persistent refusal to share his land with his disciples or even sell it to them cheaply. The critics denied that the social system was then in operation on the New Harmony estate. The outlying groups were shown to be so insignificant and so burdened with debt that the assertion in the editorial was the grossest mockery.[47]

In recognizing the real defeat of the venture and in blaming Robert Owen therefor, these disgruntled democrats came nearer, at least, to the truth than did the loyal son. The New Harmony experiment was characterized by a total lack of a well thought out, consistent program, an inexcusable failure to regulate the quantity and quality of the participants, an absence of wise leadership, and a sheer inability to pay its own way. To be sure, Robert Owen's success as a manufacturer in Scotland was no indication that he could make American backwoodsmen proper exponents of communal life. His motives, despite con-

[47] Brown, *op. cit.*, 106–116, 118–128.

temporary slander, were of the highest. Whether he was to blame for not deeding his estate unreservedly to all who answered his call depends on one's conception of wise philanthropy. Certainly nothing in his previous speeches indicated that Robert Owen was ready to place his land in common ownership, although the precipitate abandonment of the semi-capitalistic Preliminary Society was misleading.

At the very time father and son were insisting that socialism was still in operation about New Harmony, a relapse to individualism was under way. Ten of the so-called communities, comprising at best a few families who had leased land jointly and subscribed to vague principles, were formed by May; but none survived until the next April. Meanwhile the general store passed into the hands of speculators, the wage system was introduced in the local mill, and village lots were sold to private owners. Signboards advertising profit-making ventures appeared. The manufacture of whiskey, prohibited by the community, commenced. In March 1827, and again a month later a large number of families left the scene.[48] Finally, at the end of April, this grim tragedy was followed by a farcical afterpiece in the final break between Robert Owen and William Maclure.

The open clash between these two philanthropists arose from financial difficulties fanned to white heat by mutual irritation at the failure of the experiment. The first rift had appeared in June 1826 when Maclure decided not to give further support to the community. The breach was widened in August when the elder Owen set up schools in opposition to the Education Society; it became irreparable when he threatened to violate that organization's lease.[49] By the spring of 1827 the geologist was criticizing his associate's management, whereas the latter attributed the disaster largely to the inefficiency of the Phila-

---

[48] *New Harmony Gazette*, May 30, 1827, Apr. 23, 1828; Brown, *op. cit.*, 89–96, 120–122; lease to Jonathan Rodgers, Apr. 1, 1827, Embree Papers; *Threading My Way*, 289; Lockwood, *New Harmony Movement*, 156; "Pelham Letters," *loc. cit.*, 415; *Philadelphian*, June 8, 1827.

[49] Maclure to Fretageot, June 9, 20, July 9, 24, Aug. 11, 21, [21?], Sept. 19, 25, 1826, Jan. 3, Feb. 24, 1827, Fretageot Papers.

delphian's teachers. On April 30 Maclure posted a notice that
he was no longer responsible for his colleague's debts. That
same day, knowing Robert Owen was short of cash, he obtained
some of his bonds of indebtedness, transferred them to Say, and
sent the innocent naturalist to Mt. Vernon to demand immediate payment or the arrest of the debtor. The next day the inhabitants of New Harmony were treated to the spectacle of the
squire of Braxfield trying to elude the minions of the law,
while his son William was despatched post haste to the county
seat to sue out a writ against Maclure for failure to meet the
remaining obligations of the Education Society.[50]

Eventually the dispute was settled by arbitration, but by
that time Robert Dale Owen had departed from the Wabash.[51]
Disappointed by the communal fiasco, saddened by the clash
between parent and patron, and left without any immediate
duty at New Harmony, he accepted the invitation of a new
friend to engage in another and more promising venture to aid
mankind. And while the younger Owen is descending the
muddy waters of the Ohio and Mississippi to a place near
Chickasaw Bluffs, it is well to estimate the significance in his
life of this first taste of socialism.

In spite of dissension, uncertainty, and eventual disillusion-
ment, Owen enjoyed his experience at New Harmony. Accommodations were crude and many material comforts were lacking;
but he found a freedom in speech, opinions, and conventions
not possible at Braxfield. Complete religious toleration precluded the sectarian bickering he had known in Scotland; and
the absence of formalism in social relations, he was delighted
to discover, did not lead to immorality. Far from signs of
industrial distress he could discuss calmly and philosophically
with like-minded companions schemes to aid suffering humanity. Good fellowship, among some members at least, was
attained. Frequent dances provided a diversion of which he

---

[50] *New Harmony Gazette*, Aug. 15, 1827; Posey County Circuit Court,
"Order Book," C, 172; Brown, *op. cit.*, 97–98.
[51] Documents dated May 2–5, 1827, Maclure Papers.

was ever fond; and the weekly musicales conducted by Josiah
Warren, inventor and anarchist, long remained a pleasant
memory.[52] Perhaps Owen's autobiography gives a too highly
colored picture of his communal life; certainly it is not a
complete one. But his contemporary writings do reveal an
optimism and faith in progress that even the disastrous experiment could not dampen.[53] He seems, moreover, to have
been a person of great promise; and one friend wrote of him,
"Robert Dale is now and will be a man of a supperior [sic]
mind. The more I am acquainted with him the more I am
convinced of his supperiority." [54]

During his sixteen-month residence at New Harmony, Owen
learned several lessons that governed his subsequent attitude
toward the community system. The social experiment was in
one sense part of his education, a laboratory in which he saw
tested many ideas he had received from his father. Coöperation in theory had promised material abundance with less
work; coöperation in practice had failed to supply even the
bare necessities of life. On paper, manual labor was a healthful employment to be engaged in by all; in fact, it prostrated
those not trained to it. Owen soon discovered that he was in
the latter class. In his first youthful enthusiasm he had volun-
teered to toil wherever another hand was needed, in tearing
down log cabins, sowing wheat, and cooking in the community
kitchen. But when physical exertion brought bodily ills and
culinary efforts drew caustic comments, he recognized the
virtues in a division of labor and turned to the more congenial
occupations of superintendent, teacher, and editor.[55] Others
experienced similar difficulties, and Owen came to believe that
a rational education was a necessary prerequisite to the community system. Man, he felt, must be taught from childhood
to work with his hands, to care for public property as if it were

[52] R. D. Owen to John Mortimer, Nov. 20, 1826, *Co-operative Magazine*,
II, 216–217 (June 1827); *Threading My Way*, 276, 281–282.
[53] *New Harmony Gazette*, Dec. 6, 1826, Feb. 28, Mar. 7, 1827.
[54] Fretageot to Maclure, Mar. 2, 1827, Maclure Papers.
[55] *Threading My Way*, 276–277.

his own, and to regard his fellows as equals, irrespective of birth, nationality, or creed. As a result, after a brief interlude, he turned from socialism to freethought and a scheme of republican education.

In the next quest for a communistic Utopia that appeared on the American scene in the forties, Robert Dale Owen took no part. Espousal of Fourierism might then have hurt him politically, but fear alone did not dictate his course. He no longer accepted the panacea he had learned from his father and which he had so eloquently defended in "Wealth and Misery." As early as 1830 he felt constrained to add a qualifying postscript to that essay. In 1844 he gave an excellent description of the paradox of plenty and scarcity that had come with the Industrial Revolution, but he offered no solution. In his autobiography thirty years later a remedy was still forthcoming, and he then stated that no coöperative enterprise could succeed where equal remuneration was given to all.[56] The end of the New Harmony experiment or, at best, one year afterwards, marked the last date at which the younger Owen could properly be called a socialist. It marked also the termination of the paramount influence upon his life of his father. After 1827 there was a divergence in both the thought and action of the two men that increased with the passing of the years.

[56] R. D. Owen, *Wealth and Misery* (*Popular Tracts*, no. 11, N. Y., 1830), 14–15; "One of the Problems of the Age," *U. S. Magazine and Democratic Review*, XIV, 156–167 (Feb. 1844); *Threading My Way*, 290.

CHAPTER IV

FRANCES WRIGHT

IN THE SPRING of 1827 the future of Robert Dale Owen hung in the balance. With the social experiment at an end, two distinct courses seemed open to him. He might remain at New Harmony and, aided by his father's property, seek his fortune as an individual landowner, helping at the same time to make his residence a distinctive Western village. That was the course chosen by his brother William. On the other hand, he might return to Britain and, while pursuing a mercantile career, gratify his desire to benefit mankind where the need for reform was the greatest. That was the path taken by his father. That Owen followed the example of neither grew out of his friendship for America's pioneer feminist, Frances Wright.

Frances Wright's early life was in many respects similar to Owen's. Born in Scotland in 1795, the daughter of a wealthy, agnostic merchant and a colorless, orthodox mother, she received a good private education amid liberal surroundings. She early renounced revealed religion, published her first book before her twenty-third year, and was patronized, when left an orphan, by such distinguished men as Lafayette and Bentham. Like Owen, a trip to the United States at an impressionable age changed the course of her entire life.[1]

About the time that Robert Dale Owen embarked at Liverpool upon his American adventure, Frances Wright was descending the Mississippi in search of a site for an experiment of her own. A year before, while on her second visit to the New World, she had devised a plan for emancipating the Southern Negroes without loss to the owner, without incurring the dis-

[1] William R. Waterman, *Frances Wright* (Columbia University, *Studies in History, Economics and Public Law*, CXV, no. 1, N. Y., 1924); A. J. G. Perkins and Theresa Wolfson, *Frances Wright, Free Enquirer* (N. Y., 1939).

pleasure of non-participating masters, and without leaving a large, free black population in that section. She intended to set slaves, specially purchased or donated for the purpose, to work under a system of coöperative labor and, after their economical toil had created profits sufficient to extinguish the original debt and pay the cost of future transportation, to settle them in free Africa. To prepare the bondmen for liberty a few philanthropic whites would reside with them on the plantation.[2]

Unlike the Owen enterprise, Frances Wright's Nashoba experiment was conceived on a modest scale. When commenced in February 1826 on a few hundred acres of unimproved woodland along the Wolf River, back of Memphis, it comprised only eight slaves, even fewer whites, and represented an investment of $10,000. Like New Harmony, however, this venture in coöperation proved to be an economic failure, chiefly because the participants were unprepared for the physical labor required. Late in the spring the founder's health gave way, and operations came to a virtual standstill. After a brief but futile vacation at New Harmony, Miss Wright deeded her land and property to ten trustees, one of whom was the younger Owen, to carry on her plan of gradual emancipation.[3] That Robert should have been selected rather than William, whose acquaintance with Frances dated from 1825, may have resulted from the enthusiasm he undoubtedly showed for the ideas of his new friend. Nor would it be surprising if the young reformer had been carried away not only by her vigorous personality but by her striking appearance —

a tall, commanding figure, somewhat slender and graceful . . . a face the outline of which in profile, though delicately chiselled, was masculine rather than feminine, . . . the forehead broad but not high; the short, chestnut hair curling naturally all over a classic head; the large, blue eyes not soft, but clear and earnest.[4]

---

[2] *New Harmony Gazette*, Oct. 1, 1825.　　[3] Waterman, *op. cit.*, 92–110.

[4] *Threading My Way*, 297. Cf. "Diary of William Owen," Indiana Historical Society, *Publications*, IV, 128; Maclure to Fretageot, Aug. 11, 1826, Fretageot Papers.

It was during Miss Wright's subsequent visit to New Harmony in February 1827 that the lives of the two reformers were drawn closer. At that time Owen expressed editorially a perfect agreement with her ideas on slavery. More significant was his unreserved praise for her additional chapters of *A Few Days in Athens*, which were then first published.[5] These chapters contained a bitter attack on all religions and presented a clearer statement of the agnostic position than Owen had yet formulated. Such bold approval caused Frances Wright to tell her admirer that he was one of the few persons with whom she desired to work in the cause of reform. By April there was nothing more Owen could do at New Harmony, and he was ready to go to Nashoba to assist in forming a coöperative community for whites, provided for by the deed of trust.[6]

Whatever hope Owen may have had for communal life in Tennessee was quickly dispelled. On the voyage down the Mississippi Miss Wright became so ill that she had to be carried from Memphis to her settlement in a hammock. At Nashoba Owen found only three whites, Frances' younger sister Camilla, Richesson Whitbey, formerly of New Harmony, and James Richardson, a Scottish physician. The physical setting was anything but attractive. A clearing of a hundred acres of second rate land, worked with indifferent success, three log houses and as many cabins constituted the sole evidence of the hand of man. The crudities of New Harmony were the height of civilization compared with this wilderness.[7]

The discouraging outlook at Nashoba compelled an immediate change of plans. Not only were new members needed for the coöperative experiment but Miss Wright's health required a sea voyage and rest in a cooler climate. When Camilla found it impossible to accompany her sister to Europe, Owen consented to go. It is not unlikely that he had foreseen such a

[5] *New Harmony Gazette*, Feb. 28, Apr. 11, 1827.
[6] *Threading My Way*, 298–299; *New Harmony Gazette*, Feb. 21, 1827.
[7] *Threading My Way*, 303–304; Frances E. Trollope, *Frances Trollope, Her Life and Literary Work* (London, 1895), I, 105–106.

contingency when he left New Harmony. He knew that his
father was about to cross the ocean with the expectation of
returning in the autumn, and the son saw the opportunity to
pay a coincident visit to Braxfield. Thus, in the middle of
May, a scant ten days after his arrival, Owen resumed his descent of the Mississippi to New Orleans, whence the couple
began a tedious two-month voyage. Frances Wright's condition remained critical until she was far out at sea. Her companion improved his leisure by drawing and by writing poor
poetry.[8]

August found Owen in Paris where he spent a pleasant fortnight, marked by a memorable meeting with General Lafayette.
He then crossed to England in a futile attempt to win recruits
for the Nashoba community.[9] All the time, however, he was
irresistibly drawn to Braxfield to see again not only his mother
and sisters but also a fifteen-year-old girl whom he had loved
for about five years. Margaret, whose story as "Jessie" fills a
disproportionate space of *Threading My Way*, had first attracted Owen's notice while he was teaching in the New Lanark
schools. Although the daughter of a mill worker, she was gifted
with high talents and extraordinary beauty. By a curious chain
of circumstances in which the eldest son and the eldest daughter played important roles, Margaret became in March 1823 a
member of the Owen household and was henceforth treated as
one of the family. The young reformer lost his heart completely, loving the child, as he confessed a decade later, with a
truer affection than he was ever likely to hold again.[10] The
American adventure had interrupted this idyl; but on his return
to New Lanark in the summer of 1827, Owen found the girl as
charming as ever. He quickly realized that, if he remained

---

[8] *Threading My Way*, 304; Waterman, *op. cit.*, 112; "Notes on Travel"
(MS.) ; *Free Enquirer*, Aug. 28, 1830.

[9] *Threading My Way*, 304–315; Mrs. Julian Marshall, *The Life and Letters
of Mary Wollstonecraft Shelley* (London, 1889), II, 167–169; Waterman, *op.
cit.*, 122.

[10] *Threading My Way*, 210–238; R. D. Owen to Mrs. Robt. Owen, Aug. 12,
1830, Robert Owen Papers, no. 291.

near her, he would wish to marry. Cold reason, however, told him that she was vain, frivolous, and not entirely sincere. His mother, he discovered, was of a similar opinion; and she objected further to marriage on the grounds of class and age. Thus it was decided that Margaret would remain at Braxfield, for the time being at least, while Robert and his two younger brothers, Dale and Dick, both fresh from three years at Hofwyl, returned with their father to America. What these well born lads hoped to find on the Indiana frontier is not altogether clear, but neither hesitated to seek his fortune in the New World.[11]

Leaving the scene of his boyhood for what was to be the last time, Owen joined his father and Frances Wright in London. There he renewed acquaintances with Rowland Hill and Henry Pickersgill and met for the first time James Mill, George Combe, and John G. Spurzheim. From Spurzheim he obtained an enduring interest in phrenology. Incidentally, contemporary charts of Owen's head showed his organs of benevolence, conscientiousness, and friendship highly developed, while that of wit developed the least of all. During this same London visit Owen may have been introduced to Harriet Martineau and Mrs. Frances Trollope. He saw Mary Shelley on several occasions. The warm friendship between the latter and Frances Wright was shared by Owen, and in the autumn of his life he came to regret that his early manhood had not been influenced by the gentle and sympathetic Mary Shelley rather than the brilliant but impulsive Frances Wright.[12]

Such sentiments regarding Frances Wright were not those of the Robert Dale Owen who sailed from Liverpool aboard the *Consbrook* in November 1827. The friendship formed in the last days at New Harmony had become during the European journey a very real one. It may be, as Owen later asserted, that they were never in love. Certainly Frances Wright seems

[11] *Threading My Way*, 227–229; R. D. Owen to Mrs. Robt. Owen, Aug. 12, 1830, to Robt. Owen, Feb. 21, 1831, Robert Owen Papers, nos. 291, 396.

[12] *Threading My Way*, 342, 350, 331–336, 321–323; Marshall, *op. cit.*, II, 167–179; Mary Shelley to Owen, Nov. 9, 1827, Dec. 30, 1830, Dreer Collection: English Prose Writers, V.

to have been completely absorbed in her experiment.[13] Yet
there can be no doubt that the feelings on both sides were of
the tenderest. Owen admired his friend greatly and from her
company obtained that intelligent feminine association that
he always enjoyed. Miss Wright had an equally high opinion
of her companion and was more than glad to have some
masculine support on which she could depend.[14] What this
relationship meant is perhaps best revealed in a letter to Owen
by Mary Shelley.

Take care of our Fanny, dear Dale — [she said] she is neither so
independent or so fearless as you think. . . . You will say perhaps
that if she confide not in you, the secretiveness is hers — not so —
we must all be sure of sympathy before we confide at all. . . . Inspire a belief in your lively & active interest for her — You are not
in love now — one day you will be again — and the time may come
when in spite of all self-esteem you may fear that you are not loved
in return — Now then practise yourself in such lessons as may
make you *loveable*. . . . Nothing is better calculated to instil sweet-
ness of disposition & that best & most endearing of qualities —
tenderness, than a constant attention to a woman, with whom you are
not in love, yet for whom you have affection and kindness — . . . we
all have in us . . . a desire to find a manly spirit where on [to]
lean — a manly arm to protect and shelter us — The time is perhaps
not far off when Fanny may find in a lover these necessities better
supplied than you can supply them — but till then, no man need
be nearer, dearer, or more useful to her than yourself.[15]

Owen apparently accepted the advice; for shortly afterwards
Frances could write, "Dale arrived, his sweet kind heart
all unthawed, and truly when he left us for Harmony I think
the very last thin flake of Scotch ice had melted from
him." [16]

Leaving his father and brothers in New Orleans, Owen has-

[13] *Threading My Way*, 299. Cf. Frances Wright to Owen, Oct. 2, 1827, Dreer
Collection: English Prose Writers, V.

[14] Frances Wright to Mrs. Robt. Owen, Feb. 9, 1828, Robert Owen Papers,
no. 82.

[15] Mary Shelley to Owen, Nov. 9, 1827, Dreer Collection: English Prose
Writers, V.

[16] Frances Wright to Mary Shelley, Mar. 20, 1828, Marshall, *op. cit.*, II, 180.

tened to Nashoba whither Frances Wright had preceded him a fortnight before. There he found conditions even less promising than in the previous May. Economic failure was apparent. One glance had been sufficient to assure Mrs. Trollope that she had no desire to settle, as she had originally planned, upon the desolate scene. Richardson's unexpected departure had left Whitbey as the sole male white. The former's ill-judged zeal in sending for publication in the *Genius of Universal Emancipation* evidence of his cohabitation with the slaves had, moreover, given the experiment an unenviable reputation. Benjamin Lundy and the other interested Negrophiles had been amazed at this revelation, but Camilla Wright boldly met their protests by endorsing Richardson's action.[17] Of this scandal Owen was probably aware before leaving Europe, but it is unlikely that he anticipated finding on his arrival that Frances Wright had added further fuel to the flames that were already threatening her experiment.

In a long article written at sea while separated from Owen, Miss Wright had again changed the purpose of her colony. Believing that slavery was destined to die from economic waste, she transformed Nashoba into a coöperative community where whites and free blacks would live and work together while their children were educated in common as equals. It was her aim to raise the Negro to the level of the white, thus preparing the way for the eventual amalgamation of the races. As if this bold proposal were not enough, the author attacked at length the American prejudice against color and criticized the existing concept of marriage. In short, Frances Wright issued her Declaration of Moral Independence and dedicated Nashoba as the place where her principles would be carried into practice.[18]

[17] *New Harmony Gazette*, Jan. 30, 1828; Mrs. [F. M.] Trollope, *Domestic Manners of the Americans* (London, 1832), I, 44–45; *Threading My Way*, 359; Waterman, *op. cit.*, 113–119.
[18] "Nashoba. Explanatory Notes, respecting the Nature and Objects of the Institution at Nashoba and of the Principles on which It Is Founded," *New Harmony Gazette*, Jan. 30, Feb. 6, 13, 1828.

The hostility aroused by these notes compelled the author to issue an immediate disavowal for all trustees not then resident at Nashoba.[19] Owen, therefore, can hardly be held responsible for the sentiments expressed, though he undoubtedly agreed with some points. The next manifesto to come out of the Tennessee forests, the first after his arrival, moreover, said nothing about amalgamation but contained still another plan. This one, a virtual admission of the failure of Miss Wright's two previous schemes, made Nashoba a semi-capitalistic colony where the sole communal advantages would be schools in which to train the young for life in a real community of equal property and mutual labor.[20] But even before this change was made public, Owen had returned to New Harmony. Although he continued to speak encouragingly of Nashoba, he had no intention of going back; and within three months Frances Wright also left the scene of failure. On the stubborn soil along the mosquito-infested Wolf River she had learned the lesson taught to Owen upon the Wabash, that not every one was able to endure the physical toil required to establish a cooperative community in the pioneer West. These youthful radicals were now ready to give up that reform and turn their attention to education and intellectual freedom.[21]

On Owen's arrival at New Harmony in March 1828, all traces of the social experiment had disappeared. Early that month the Feiba-Peveli society had entrusted its business to a single manager and afterwards was heard of no more. All the other small communities had failed; and on April 13 Robert Owen addressed not, as he had the previous May, "The Ten Social Colonies of Equality and Common Property" but a "Public Meeting of the Inhabitants of New Harmony." This speech

[19] *New Harmony Gazette*, Feb. 13, 1828; Waterman, *op. cit.*, 128–129.

[20] *New Harmony Gazette*, Mar. 26, 1828.

[21] *Ibid.*; Waterman, *op. cit.*, 130–133. On Feb. 24, 1828 Miss Wright wrote to Jennings, "Cooperation has well nigh killed us all; judge what individual labour would do in your case; you cannot hold the plough, plant corn, or sow cabbages. . . . Reserve yourself for the great, the noble task of fitting the next generation for doing that which we cannot do." *Morning Courier & N. Y. Enquirer*, June 19, 1830.

indicated the new trend of the elder Owen's interests. Little was said of the community system, but the greater part was devoted to the praise of mental liberty and to attacks on the priesthood.[22] The Owenite phase of American socialism was passing.

Concerted efforts to save a part, at least, of the fortune sunk in the New Harmony experiment occupied the Owens during the next months. This attempted salvage was as important to the son as to the father, for upon its success depended his ability to continue the unremunerative life of a reformer. Until then his $50,000 share in the New Lanark mills had assured him an independence, but the low state of parental resources now caused Robert and William to give up voluntarily their stock. In return the manufacturer deeded to his sons jointly some three thousand acres of land and personal effects, worth about $20,000. Most of this property, however, had fallen into the hands of Taylor, Fauntleroy and Company, originally organized as a sort of coöperative community but now an outright commercial enterprise. Although the concern was a financial failure and had violated the terms of its leases, eviction was difficult.[23] Several shrewd local lawyers, themselves interested in land speculation, were associated with Taylor; and the latter played his cards so skilfully that the agreement reached in September was very disadvantageous to the Owens. To get William clear of obligations he had undertaken at his father's request in 1827, the two brothers had to suffer an immediate loss of over $20,000 and the eventual relinquishment of much of the personal property used in the community experiment. So far as Robert was concerned, the settlement was hard but not disastrous. He managed to retain most of his father's real estate and to keep for himself an income, even though a greatly reduced one, that allowed

[22] *New Harmony Gazette,* Mar. 19, Apr. 23, 1828. Cf. *ibid.,* May 30, 1827.
[23] *Threading My Way,* 293–294; Posey County, "Deed Book," E, 95–98. *Ibid.,* 35–36, 36ff, 61–63, 106–107, 114–115; Brown, *Twelve Months in New Harmony,* 83–84; *New Harmony Gazette,* Jan. 23, 1828 (advt.); Taylor, Fauntleroy & Co. Papers, *passim.*

him to continue for a few years more his career as a reformer.[24]

Among the questions that arose in liquidating the affairs of the socialistic venture was the future of *The New Harmony Gazette*. Although established primarily to disseminate the principles of the community system, that paper had not suspended with the general exodus in the spring of 1827, but had been conducted by William Owen during the absence of his father and brother. Upon his return in March, Robert resumed his post as editor, and among the property deeded by the elder Owen to his sons in June was the printing office and the lot on which it stood.[25] No change in policy was announced, but at once a new spirit pervaded the journal. Articles on coöperative communities quite naturally disappeared, but so did those on the Industrial Revolution, labor, and political economy. In their place appeared virulent attacks on sectarianism and the clergy, more than half of Owen's editorials up to the middle of June dealing directly with such topics. If in the spring of 1828 Robert Dale Owen was contemplating a free-thought crusade in the columns of the *Gazette*, it required only the arrival of Frances Wright at New Harmony to confirm his decision.

Frances Wright's zeal for reform had not been dampened by her failure at Nashoba. Although she was unable to establish there, as she had hoped, a journal in which to develop the theories sketched in her "Explanatory Notes," *The New Harmony Gazette* provided a convenient substitute. In June she moved to the banks of the Wabash and purchased a half interest, at least, in that paper. Late in July she and Robert Dale Owen announced, as co-proprietors, a new series that would make the weekly the freest and most independent organ in the nation.[26] It was designed especially to combat the reli-

---

[24] Posey County, "Deed Book," E, 94–95, 99–115; deeds dated Sept. 17, 1828 and W. Owen to J. Fauntleroy, Jan. 5, 1832, Taylor, Fauntleroy & Co. Papers; *New Harmony Gazette*, Sept. 17, 1828 (advt.) ; R. D. Owen to W. Maclure, Sept. 4, 1830, Maclure Papers.

[25] *New Harmony Gazette*, Mar. 19, 1828; Posey County, "Deed Book," E, 95–96.   [26] *New Harmony Gazette*, July 30, 1828.

gious revival of the last two decades. The formation of missionary, tract, and Sabbatarian societies and the sectarian call for a "Christian Party in Politics" that marked those years was at last awakening freethinkers who had been somnolent since the days of Elihu Palmer and Tom Paine.[27]

One center of freethought was New York, where George Houston founded the Free Press Association and in January 1827 began *The Correspondent*. During that year and the next agnostic societies were formed in Philadelphia, Paterson, Woodstock, and Cincinnati. In the West, however, aside from *The New Harmony Gazette*, the real stimulus to agnosticism came from Frances Wright's sensational lecture tour of the Ohio Valley late in the summer of 1828. Before curious crowds she preached the necessity of considering anew all standards in religion, morals, and education.[28] That the younger Owen was influenced by this anticlerical agitation on both sides of the mountains may be admitted; but it is easy to demonstrate that during the four months before his associate left Nashoba, his editorials were already identical in tone with her later addresses. It was to Robert Owen, rather than to Frances Wright or George Houston that the origins, though not the details, of the freethought writings of Robert Dale Owen must be traced.

As Owen surveyed the contemporary American scene in the year of Andrew Jackson's triumph, he felt no native's pride in the great republican experiment. He found the land fraught with evil and unhappiness. He attributed that state of affairs to a mistaken purpose in life, to outmoded standards of morality, and to a religion that fostered and sustained these errors. For Owen the sole end of being was happiness in this world.

[27] G. Adolph Koch, *Republican Religion: the American Revolution and the Cult of Reason* (*American Religion Series*, VII, N. Y., 1933), xv, 275, 281; Waterman, *op. cit.*, 138–148; Ezra S. Ely, *The Duty of Christian Freemen to Elect Christian Rulers* (Phila., 1828), 8.

[28] *Correspondent*, Feb. 17, 24, 1827, June 21, Sept. 20, 1828 *et seq.*, Feb. 2, 1828, Apr. 7, Mar. 31, 1827; *New Harmony Gazette*, Aug. 27, Sept. 3, 24, 1828; Waterman, *op. cit.*, 147–160.

An act that failed to achieve that goal was not virtuous; one that succeeded was right, notwithstanding the teaching of the Bible and the voice of public opinion. To discover what produces happiness, he said, one must observe nature, study one's fellow men, and resort to both reason and experience. Owen's philosophy of free enquiry was taken from two thinkers, poles apart in much of their writings: "Prove all things and hold fast that which is good," and "Error of opinion may be tolerated where reason is left free to combat it." [29]

Upon orthodox religion this child of the eighteenth century turned his heaviest batteries of rationalism, empiricism, and natural law. He asked why so vital a matter as the very existence of God should be left in doubt. He still rejected the conception of an omnipotent deity who permitted evil in the world and then damned his creatures for committing it. He scorned church ceremonies and denied the divine origin of the Scriptures.[30] Owen's quarrel with orthodoxy, however, lay not so much in its theory as in the evils created by its practice. Its teachings, he pointed out, turned men's thoughts to a future life and hindered reformers in their efforts to improve this. Strict observance of the Sabbath deprived the workingmen of normal sports and amusements, encouraging clandestine drinking and gambling. Sectarianism invaded the schools, blocked the advancement of science, and led to unjust discrimination in courts of justice. In the Sabbatarian movement Owen saw a violation of personal liberty; in the central religious organizations, a threat to the nation's freedom. Worst of all was the activity of the clerical profession. In an age when fear and force as motives to well-doing were being abandoned in legal codes and education, they were retained by the ministers of Him who taught that love is the fulfilling of the law.[31]

[29] New Harmony Gazette, Apr. 16, May 14, June 4, 25, 1828; Free Enquirer, Oct. 29, 1828. The following summary is based upon only those articles written before Owen's removal to New York in March 1829.

[30] New Harmony Gazette, Feb. 7, Apr. 25, 1827, Apr. 30, June 4, 1828; Free Enquirer, Nov. 12, 1828.

[31] New Harmony Gazette, Jan. 31, 1827, Apr. 23, 30, May 7, June 11,

In place of Christianity Owen offered his doctrine of scepticism which, although not yet complete, was already developed in its main outlines. The sceptic neither affirmed nor denied the existence of God. He lacked sufficient knowledge for belief and did not feel obliged to seek further evidence. Freed from concern with a future world, he could devote himself to reforming this. Where believers must spend their day of rest worshipping things unseen and unknowable, non-believers could study science and understand the universe about them. Owen denied that scepticism was cold and heartless. He found warmth and pleasure in doing good for its own sake, not for a future reward. In complete mental emancipation he saw the true value of his creed. To those hesitating before the Rubicon that separated orthodoxy and heterodoxy he said, "I have crossed in safety, and found the opposite shore fair and pleasant; a land of freedom and virtue, whence terror is banished, and where tranquillity reigns. He that is a bold swimmer, let him fearlessly attempt the passage. . . . He will become a better, a wiser, and — my experience for it — a happier man." [32]

Unlike many liberals of his day, Owen did not consider freethought as synonymous with mere hostility to Christianity. To him it meant the right to discuss openly all matters pertaining to human happiness, and in this belief he wrote boldly on woman's rights and marriage. He deplored the fashion that confined a lady to a retired, idle existence in which she "must not venture out under Nature's air and sun, lest her lily cheek be tinged with the hue of health, or . . . use her hands, because her taper fingers might lose their pretty form." [33] Owen regarded woman as the social and mental equal of man and urged her, through learning a trade or profession, to become his economic equal. More important, he demanded repeatedly

---

Sept. 17, Oct. 22, 1828; *Free Enquirer*, Oct. 29, Nov. 5, Dec. 10, 1828, Feb. 11, 1829.

[32] "Prossimo's Experience," *Free Enquirer*, Jan. 21, 1829. *New Harmony Gazette*, Apr. 30, 1828; *Free Enquirer*, Jan. 21, Feb. 18, 1829.

[33] *New Harmony Gazette*, Apr. 9, 1828.

that the sexes be governed by the same legal and moral code. As to matrimony, Owen insisted that life-long affection could not be assured by rites or statute. When love died, the law might compel continued wedlock although it engendered discord and strife. Owen opposed such severity and favored separation in all cases except those imperiling the education of the children.[34]

Owen's advocacy at this time of birth control was more the result of accident than design. By the autumn of 1828 he was well aware of the British Neo-Malthusian literature and propaganda; for only a year before, while in England, he had heard his father deny certain allegations made by Richard Carlile on the subject. But the Indiana backwoods was no place to discuss a topic that was too advanced even for the overpopulated, industrial centers of Europe; and while Owen decried the physiologically unsound lives imposed on unmarried people by the existing code of morals, he did not venture to disseminate contraceptive information in the columns of his paper.[35] He had, however, no objections to enlightening his friends and in June lent his copy of the latest work on birth control, Carlile's *Every Woman's Book; or, What Is Love?* to Milo Greenwood, a citizen of New Harmony. A few days later Greenwood asked Owen to republish the essay and to write a prospectus for it; but the latter refused, apparently on the grounds of inexpediency. Soon afterwards a prospectus for Carlile's book was printed without Owen's knowledge on his press, though all information concerning the place of publication was omitted. The sheet was then shown to Owen, who seems to have voiced a mild disapproval of the whole proceeding. Apparently the

---

[34] *Ibid.*, May 2, 1827, Apr. 9, May 28, Sept. 10, 1828; *Free Enquirer*, Dec. 10, 1828, Jan. 7, Feb. 4, 25, 1829.

[35] *New Harmony Gazette*, Sept. 10, 1828; *Free Enquirer*, Feb. 18, 1829; Norman E. Himes, "The Place of John Stuart Mill and of Robert Owen in the History of English Neo-Malthusianism," *Quarterly Journal of Economics*, XLII, 627–640 (May 1928). The account that follows differs materially from the suggestive but not definitive article by the same author, "Robert Dale Owen, the Pioneer of American Neo-Malthusianism," *American Journal of Sociology*, XXXV, 529–547 (Jan. 1930).

complete text was not reissued, for it was never mentioned in the subsequent "exposures." Following Frances Wright's lectures in Vincennes in September, there appeared in the *Wabash Telegraph* an anonymous charge that the prospectus, if not written by Miss Wright, had been published at New Harmony with her partner's knowledge and consent. This accusation compelled Owen to bring the awkward matter before the public.[36]

After stating his version of the incident, Owen gave the reasons for his refusal to republish Carlile's tract. It was the result in part of his own inability to judge correctly the physiological portions of the treatise, in part of the fact that he employed small boys in his printing office, but mainly of the strong prejudice then held by society at large that would destroy the usefulness of such a book. The work itself he approved as dictated "by an honest desire to benefit mankind." In the same editorial Owen alluded to the various editions of the essay, the writings of Francis Place, and the not generally known activity of John Stuart Mill. A month later Owen again praised Carlile for his unflagging efforts in the cause of truth and warned that the coarseness in the Englishman's style did not impair his usefulness. Once again he mentioned *Every Woman's Book* by name, but again declined to discuss the contraceptive methods there outlined.[37]

In the summer and autumn of 1828 a backwoods town in Posey County was fast becoming the most important free-thought center in the United States. Under its new editors the *Gazette* was unquestionably the ablest journal of its kind. Jennings had returned with plans to establish a boarding school employing Pestalozzian methods and inviting the patronage of

[36] *New Harmony Gazette*, Oct. 8, 1828; *Western Sun*, Sept. 20, 1828. The issue of the *Wabash Telegraph* in question has not been located. A contradictory, untrustworthy account of the incident, designed to injure Owen politically, appeared in the *Leavenworth Arena*, Oct. 31, 1839. According to that version, Owen was dissuaded from reprinting Carlile's essay only by a threat to destroy his press.

[37] *New Harmony Gazette*, Oct. 8, 1828; *Free Enquirer*, Nov. 19, 1828.

liberals.[38] Using New Harmony as a base, Frances Wright electrified the Ohio and Mississippi Valleys with her lectures on free enquiry and just knowledge. And to the banks of the Wabash must be traced the earliest recorded approval in America of the Neo-Malthusian movement. The first fruits of the Owen community were not socialism, education, or science but a militant, free discussion of religion, morals, and sexual relations.

Forces were already at work, however, that were to terminate this freethought activity in the West. Early in October there were living together in a state of great confusion and dissatisfaction the four Owen brothers, Frances Wright and her sister, Jennings, D'Arusmont, and his boy printers. Jennings' school had failed to materialize. Miss Wright was eager to resume her lectures. The Owens detested their dependence for printing upon the Frenchman, but they could not resign themselves to do their own work. Eighteen-year-old Richard took this occasion to sow his wild oats, and Robert's stern measures caused his brothers to call him "a hard hearted man." [39] Finally news came from Whitbey at Nashoba that everything there was chaotic. Ostensibly to settle her affairs on the Wolf River, but in reality to extend her liberal crusade, Frances Wright left New Harmony in the middle of October on a tour that was to carry her to New York.

The enthusiastic receptions that greeted her new efforts convinced Miss Wright that her paper should be moved from the isolated Wabash to a more populous section of the Union. Her triumphs in St. Louis, Louisville, and Cincinnati were repeated in Baltimore and New York. She saw in an Eastern city not only a closer contact with the liberal currents emanating from Europe but also larger audiences to crowd the lecture hall and more readers to swell the subscription list. Finding Houston's *Correspondent* in financial difficulties, the feminist decided on

[38] *Correspondent*, June 28, Aug. 23, 1828; *New Harmony Gazette*, July 30, 1828; Posey County, "Deed Book," E, 73-74.
[39] Fretageot to Maclure, Oct. 31, 1828, Maclure Papers. *Ibid.*, Oct. 3, 10, 14, 17, 1828.

January 5 to establish headquarters in Manhattan. Two days later she publicly announced her decision; and before the end of the month, over two hundred new subscribers having been obtained, a New York edition of her journal appeared under the abbreviated title of *The Free Enquirer*.[40]

Owen was not wholly prepared for this news, which reached Indiana late in January. Only a month before, shocked by the increasingly radical speeches of his associate, he had deferred the publication of some pieces and warned her by letter of the injury her boldness might inflict upon the cause.[41] It is highly probable, therefore, that Frances had decided to settle in New York without his previous consent. To be sure, Miss Wright must have believed that he would approve; because she was dependent, as she herself admitted, upon him for editorial assistance.[42] The significance of the incident is that it was the last of a series by which the feminist influenced a life, the future of which had hung in the balance in the spring of 1827. It served to usher in the most radical phase of Owen's career.

Late in February 1829 Owen published the final New Harmony edition of his paper and a couple of weeks later, accompanied by D'Arusmont and his assistants, he ascended the Ohio on his way to a new battle field of reform.[43] His feelings at that time were expressed in one of the last editorials written before his departure. Foreseeing a difficult struggle ahead, he hoped that he would never be led into bitterness and intolerance. He did not agree with Frances Wright "that to call men to a consideration of their own errors and their own sufferings is to attract their hatred." In many cases, he said, "it is to rouse their prejudices, and to gain their ill-will for a time;

[40] *Free Enquirer*, Dec. 10, 1828, Feb. 11, 25, 1829; *Free Enquirer* (N. Y. edn.), Jan. 28, 1829; *Commercial Advertiser*, Jan. 8, 1829; *N. Y. Enquirer*, Jan. 8, 1829; Waterman, *op. cit.*, 163–175.
[41] Fretageot to Maclure, Dec. 19, 1828, Maclure Papers.
[42] Fretageot to Maclure, Feb. 13, 1829, Maclure Papers; Waterman, *op. cit.*, 174.
[43] Fretageot to Maclure, Mar. 13, 1829, Maclure Papers, indicates that Owen had not yet left New Harmony. *The Free Enquirer*, Apr. 22, 1829, gives the date of his arrival in New York as April 11.

but I do not think that those who moderately, and with due deference to the feelings of their fellow creatures, seek to spread knowledge, and remove misery, will be hated, though they may be mistrusted, and perhaps even feared, for the attempt."

I look [he concluded] for years of perseverance and forbearance on our parts, before the public is convinced that we are sincere in our professions; and for years more before they will believe that our principles are just in theory and virtuous in practice. But I trust that I shall always look back upon these years as time well spent, and that I shall be satisfied with the measure of success, small though it may be, which shall reward our efforts.[44]

[44] *Free Enquirer*, Feb. 25, 1829.

CHAPTER V

FREETHOUGHT MILITANT

THE New York to which Robert Dale Owen hastened in April 1829 was a bustling, ambitious city, intent on maintaining its recently won urban hegemony. Its population, numbering 166,000 in 1825, passed the 200,000 mark five years later. Its annual customs exceeded $13,000,000; and its sixteen incorporated banks and fifty-eight packet lines in foreign and domestic service testified to its commercial importance. Ten daily and twenty weekly newspapers were necessary to meet the business and intellectual demands of this young giant. Such a growth, to be sure, was not an unmixed blessing. Immigration brought foreign radicals with materialistic ideals abhorrent to American orthodoxy. Manufactures developed an underprivileged laboring class inconsistent with American democracy. Rapid expansion meant new urban problems of housing, education, and moral correction. The severe winter of 1828–1829 had shown the intense suffering of the less fortunate members of the community. The report of the Magdalen Society in 1831 was to disturb profoundly the complacency of a city that was gaining the world at the cost of its soul.[1]

New York had been purposely chosen as the battle field for reform. In that city were entrenched the most redoubtable forces of organized sectarianism. There no paper dared to advertise a lecture in which the existence of God was questioned. There were located the great bugbears of free enquiry — the American Bible Society with its ever active twenty-eight printing presses, the American Tract Society, an able coadjutor, and

---

[1] Edwin Williams, comp., *The New York Annual Register for . . . 1830* (N. Y., 1830), 143–144, 167, 209–212, 214; John R. Commons and others, *History of Labour in the United States* (N. Y., 1921), I, 12, 170–171; *Free Enquirer*, July 23, 1831; Gilbert H. Barnes, *The Antislavery Impulse, 1830–1844* (N. Y., 1933), 23–24.

the newly formed General Union for Promoting the Observance of the Christian Sabbath. Sometimes independent of but never in opposition to these orthodox auxiliaries were a growing number of humanitarian associations designed to foster temperance, peace, seaman's aid, and prison reform. Even such secular concerns as antislavery, adult lyceums, and manual training schools were largely controlled by men whose philanthropic zeal grew out of a deep religious sentiment. Between the "New York Philanthropists," that pious interlocking directorate in benevolence, and Robert Dale Owen there was a deep gulf.[2] Aside from the unforgivable sin of heterodoxy, Owen's views on private property were distrusted by the aristocratic and middle class liberals, and their fears were not quieted when he became a radical leader of the nascent labor movement. There could be no coöperation between those who sought reform from above and Owen who, whatever may have been his real opinions, talked of reform from below.

Owen arrived in New York without the publicity that had greeted the sensational speeches of Frances Wright. He came not to lecture but to edit *The Free Enquirer*, a three-column weekly quarto, filled mainly with theological discussion but taking some notice of liberal trends in education, the treatment of debtors, the position of women, and other reform movements. With characteristic energy and industry he plunged at once into this work, and his two years as chief resident editor were probably the most active period of a strenuous life. Jennings did nothing but attend to the business end of the paper, and in April 1830 he resigned his partnership to become a leader of free enquiry in Boston.[3] Miss Wright's lecture tours and personal affairs kept her constantly out of New York, and after July 1, 1830, she made practically no editorial contributions. As a result, Owen had more to do, but his journal benefitted. Frances Wright spoke better than she wrote. Her

---

[2] Williams, *op. cit.*, 200, 346; [Theodore Dwight], *The Northern Traveller and Northern Tour* (N. Y., 1831), 3 n. 1; *Free Enquirer*, Dec. 12, 1829; Barnes, *op. cit.*, 17–28.

[3] *Free Enquirer*, May 8, 1830.

style was striking but careless, and in controversy she betrayed signs of dogmatism and egotism. Less effective than his friend on the rostrum, Owen wrote in a careful, engaging manner, with arguments well grounded in fact. His command of words was excellent, and in the most heated discussion he was seldom guilty of want of charity or good temper. As a freethought controversialist Owen was preëminent, and his ability to write persuasively stood him in good stead in later life.

During Frances Wright's prolonged absences Owen twice received editorial assistance. The first came from Orestes Augustus Brownson, later famous as a bold thinker on social problems, a man who began life a Presbyterian and died a Catholic after sampling Universalism, scepticism, Unitarianism, transcendentalism, and other "isms" of his own making. In the autumn of 1829 Brownson had left the Universalist church; and seeking truth "under whatever name it may come," he was persuaded by Miss Wright, then on her way to Haiti, to become a corresponding editor from his home in Auburn. Despite Owen's warm welcome, Brownson's contribution proved negligible, and within a few months he had begun his slow and tortuous drift back to orthodoxy.[4] Of much greater practical value was the acquisition of Amos Gilbert, a Hicksite Friend and former editor of the *Genius of Universal Emancipation*, as an associate. A dull writer, Gilbert proved extremely serviceable as the paper's sole resident pilot during 1832; and although several years Owen's senior, he was one of the latter's best friends in the New York years.[5]

Owen's first efforts were directed toward making his the foremost freethought journal in the nation. In these he was

[4] *Free Enquirer*, Nov. 28, Dec. 12, 1829, Jan. 2, 16, 23, Feb. 6, May 2, 1830; Arthur M. Schlesinger, Jr., *Orestes A. Brownson, A Pilgrim's Progress* (Boston, 1939). Of his defection Owen wrote tolerantly, "Poor fellow! Pecuniary independence is, after all, the bottom of every other in a greater or less degree. A man must live, & he cannot see a wife and children want the necessaries of life. Brownson has both." Owen to Trist, Feb. 23, 1831, Trist Papers, VII.

[5] Owen to Trist, June 8, 1831, Trist Papers, VII; R. D. Owen, "An Earnest Sowing of Wild Oats. A Chapter of Autobiography," *Atlantic Monthly*, XXXIV, 67 n. 1 (July 1874).

eminently successful. Houston's *Correspondent*, financially straitened as early as 1828, found the competition too keen and ceased publication, midst harsh words, the following July. A year later Wooster Beach's *Telescope*, never a great force, was absorbed by the weekly *Sentinel*. In 1831 Abner Kneeland, a close friend of Owen, started the *Boston Investigator* upon its long career, but its early existence was very unstable. Owen's chief rival, the *Delaware Free Press* of Wilmington, lacked both the literary charm and influence of *The Free Enquirer* which, at its height, circulated a thousand copies and maintained forty-four agents in twenty of the twenty-four states.[6]

The next matter to claim Owen's attention was the dissemination of cheap literature for freethinkers. Following the example of Houston and others, he built up an extensive and profitable book business in the years after 1829. Under the imprint of Wright and Owen there appeared inexpensive, stereotyped editions of Holbach's *Good Sense*, Shelley's *Queen Mab*, Paine's *Age of Reason*, and similar standard liberal fare. The same firm published the first American book on birth control, Miss Wright's lectures, a revised version of *A Few Days in Athens*, and Owen's debate with Origen Bacheler. The best articles from *The New Harmony Gazette* and the first volume of *The Free Enquirer* were reissued under Owen's editorship in a series of *Popular Tracts*, to be sold practically at cost. For a time Owen thought to bring out, possibly with the assistance of William Maclure, a set of rational school texts, but the project was abandoned lest he have too many irons in the fire. He did, however, open in July 1831 in the office of *The Free Enquirer* a circulating library, crammed with all the well-known heterodox writings.[7]

[6] *Correspondent*, Dec. 20, 1828, June 27, July 18, 1829; Waterman, *Frances Wright*, 175; Owen to Reuben Haines, Aug. 10, 1830, Maclure Papers; *Free Enquirer*, June 10, 1829, Oct. 29, 1831.
[7] *Free Enquirer*, Aug. 5, 26, Sept. 9, Oct. 31, Dec. 19, 1829, Apr. 24, Oct. 23, Nov. 27, Dec. 4, 25, 1830, Jan. 8, Mar. 5, Apr. 2 (supplement), May 7, 21, 28, July 2, 9, 16, Nov. 26, 1831; R. D. Owen to Robt. Owen, Mar. 27, 1830, Robert

Another concern of editor Owen was the social activity of his local subscribers. The practice of holding Sunday lectures, classes, and debates, begun by earlier freethought groups, was continued with an additional emphasis on science by the followers of Owen and Miss Wright. Even before the former reached New York, Frances had purchased at auction the Ebenezer Baptist Church in Broome Street. After alterations it was reopened in April with a seating capacity of twelve hundred under the name of the Hall of Science. This institution quickly became the chief educational and recreational center in Manhattan for freethinkers, the more so because it contained a library and a dispensary where medical advice was given gratis. On the first day of the week the Hall was in its glory. In front, a book store was open all day, selling the works of Voltaire and Paine under the very eyes of church-goers. Behind, when the weather was fine, a class in gymnastics was held. Within, children and adults heard lectures on astronomy, chemistry, anatomy, and physiology. Usually there were two in the morning, and in the afternoon there was occasionally another. In the evening came the climax, an address by Frances Wright, Owen, Jennings, or some guest. In 1830 these evening talks gave way to debates on popular topics.[8]

As a freethought lecturer Owen gained the experience in public speaking so necessary for his later career. At first he was content to let Frances Wright occupy the rostrum and to speak only in her absence. Thus from April to October he discoursed but three times — on Hofwyl, on coöperative communities, and on the tyranny of public opinion. During the winter of 1829–1830 he appeared more frequently, giving a "course" on the consistency of orthodox religion, on God and the Bible, and on national education. When printed in England,

---

Owen Papers, no. 215; Owen to Trist, Apr. 28, 1831, Trist Papers, VII; "An Earnest Sowing of Wild Oats," *loc. cit.*, XXXIV, 73.

[8] *Free Enquirer* (N. Y. edn.), Jan. 28, Feb. 4, Mar. 11, 25, Apr. 1, 8, 29, May 13, 1829, Sept. 17, Nov. 12, 1831, Apr. 28, 1832; note following the index of volume II (1829–1830); Waterman, *op. cit.*, 176; Owen to Maclure, Sept. 4, 1830, Maclure Papers.

the first of these made a profound impression on the youthful Alfred Wallace. Free enquiry, labor-saving machinery, the French Revolution, and Greek philosophy constituted the staple of other Owen addresses. Many of these were repeated before Kneeland's congregation in Broadway Hall. Wilmington and Philadelphia also heard the reformer in 1829.[9] Early the next year, at the request of many "respectable citizens" he delivered his course at Julien Hall in Boston. Although Frances Wright had created a minor sensation there the previous summer and a complaint against Jennings for blasphemy was to be made three months later, Owen's lectures passed off without any untoward event. The most amusing incident of the trip occurred en route. In the stagecoach an aged matron asked the youngish Owen what preachers he intended to hear in Boston. When he replied that he had time for only the most famous, Lyman Beecher and William Ellery Channing, the well-intentioned lady gravely warned the militant sceptic against the snares laid by the eloquent exponent of Unitarianism.[10]

Although its influence cannot be definitely measured, the Hall of Science is of interest to the historian of religion and adult education. For freethinkers it was a means of acting together and bringing into the open functions formerly kept underground. To be sure, the regular newspapers purposely ignored the proceedings in that abode of Satan; but they were aware of what went on and several travelers have testified to the large audiences that gathered there even in summer.[11] On the other hand, the Hall gave the ignorant workingman a chance to obtain practical knowledge about the world he lived in. In its attempt

[9] *Free Enquirer*, May 6, June 29, July 15, Sept. 3 [2], Nov. 21, Dec. 5, 12, 19, 1829, Jan. 23, 30, Feb. 13, 27, Apr. 3, 24, May 15, 22, Aug. 7, 21, 28, 1830; *Mechanics' Free Press*, Oct. 3, 1829; Alfred R. Wallace, *My Life: A Record of Events and Opinions* (London, 1905), I, 88–89.

[10] R. D. Owen to Mrs. Robt. Owen, Jan. 4, 1830, Robert Owen Papers, no. 176; *Boston Commercial Gazette*, Jan. 7, 1830 (advt.); *Free Enquirer*, Jan. 23, Apr. 17, 1830; Waterman, *op. cit.*, 178.

[11] *Commercial Advertiser*, Mar. 14, Aug. 6, 1829; S. A. Ferrall, *A Ramble of Six Thousand Miles through the United States of America* (London, 1832), 14–16; [James Boardman], *America and Americans* (London, 1833), 62–63; James Stuart, *Three Years in America* (Edinburgh, 1833), II, 13–14.

to diffuse knowledge through scientific instruction and public speaking, in its dependence upon the talents of its own members, and in the general character of its weekly program, Owen's institution resembled the lyceum founded by Josiah Holbrook in 1826. It differed, however, in its constant discussion of religion, or irreligion, its failure to campaign for common schools, and its aloofness from the national organization formed in 1831. It is probably true that lyceum members, in the larger cities at least, were of a higher social stratum than the mechanics attending the Hall of Science. The latter found its real counterpart in similarly named halls that sprang up among the British urban workers in the late thirties.[12]

In one important respect the meetings at the Hall of Science differed from those of the other freethought groups in New York. Despite an elaborate program of activity, no formal order or association was ever constituted. There was no Hall of Science Society, no Hall of Science Party. Then, as throughout his life, Owen opposed organized reform. He realized that more influence could be wielded by such groups but only at the cost of individual thought and action. Some years before Ralph Waldo Emerson resolved a similar problem with regard to antislavery, Owen wrote, "For *practical experiments* . . . men must unite; but there ought to be no association to *support opinions*." [13]

Besides his duties as freethought lecturer, book publisher, and conductor of a weekly gazette, Owen was kept busy in New York, as we shall see, as a labor agitator and chief editor of a daily newspaper. These activities, requiring twelve hours of sedentary work each day, seriously threatened his health. Fortunately Frances Wright had leased before his arrival a commodious country mansion with ten acres of grounds on the banks of the East River, a half mile southeast of Yorkville. Living in what was then beyond the urban area, Owen obtained

---

[12] Cecil B. Hayes, *The American Lyceum, its History and Contribution to Education* (U. S. Dept. of Interior, Bureau of Education, *Bulletin, no. 12, 1932*, Wash., 1932) ; Podmore, *Robert Owen*, II, 469–470.

[13] *Free Enquirer*, Dec. 24, 1831.

his much needed exercise in a ten-mile horseback ride to and from his office in Broome Street. As a further precaution he adopted a vegetarian diet, abstaining from coffee, tea, and spirituous liquors. Like many reformers, Owen's life was an ascetic one.[14]

The nature and intensity of Owen's work appears to have left him little time for recreation or new friends. Frances Wright's radicalism had estranged her well-to-do hosts of 1818, and Owen had nothing in common at this time with such later associates as William Cullen Bryant or John Worth Edmonds. His chief companions were those interested in his reforms, humble mechanics and obscure liberals. The most notable were Kneeland, later victim of a blasphemy trial in Boston, George Henry Evans, future champion of free land, Gilbert Vale, subsequently biographer of Paine and editor of *The Beacon*, and Dr. John Baxter, lecturer in the New York School of Medicine. Before July 1830 the East River home was pleasantly filled by the Wright sisters, D'Arusmont, Jennings, and such distinguished visitors as Robert Owen, fresh from his debate with Alexander Campbell, Josiah Warren, in search of a new Utopia, and David Dale Owen, in quest of a life occupation. After that date, however, Owen was left alone with Dale, who took up painting and drawing; and it was in that period that he blamed his illness on "a hermit's life . . . not very conducive to cheerfulness & that equanimity of spirits which is the basis of good health." [15]

From these New York years dates Owen's life-long friendship with Nicholas P. Trist. Trist, a year Owen's senior, belonged to a group of Virginia intellectuals who watched with

[14] *Ibid.*, May 29, 1830, Jan. 29, Sept. 10, Dec. 10, 1831; Owen to Trist, Nov. 18, 1829, June 2, Aug. 1, 1830, June 8, 1831, Trist Papers, VI, VII; "An Earnest Sowing of Wild Oats," *loc. cit.*, XXXIV, 74; Waterman, *op. cit.*, 177.

[15] Owen to Trist, June 8, 1831, Trist Papers, VII; *Free Enquirer*, July 29, 1829; Will of Frances Wright, dated June 27, 1830, Owen Papers; R. D. Owen to Mrs. Robt. Owen, Aug. 12, 1830, to Robt. Owen, Mar. 27, 1830, Feb. 21, 1831, Robert Owen Papers, nos. 291, 215, 396; "An Earnest Sowing of Wild Oats," *loc. cit.*, XXXIV, 73; William Bailie, *Josiah Warren, the First American Anarchist* (Boston, 1906), 25–29.

delight the liberal religious tendencies manifested in Unitarianism and Universalism. He, however, accepted unreservedly the more advanced ideas of *The Free Enquirer* and as early as November 1828 opened a correspondence with its editors. During the next months Trist contributed anonymously to the paper; but his appointment, first as clerk in the State Department and then as private secretary to President Jackson, made him proceed cautiously. As he wrote to Owen, "I can't be *one* of *you*; & therefore must remain one of the silent herd." Owen agreed that the Virginian must not risk his political position for the cause. He constantly warned him to act discreetly and in September 1830 began to omit his own signature from the letters he sent to Washington. For more than three years these men corresponded without ever having met. To Trist the friendship meant intellectual stimulus and practical advice on educating his children. To Owen it meant more. It was Trist who disseminated his freethought literature among the liberals of the capital and the Old Dominion. It was Trist who taught him national politics and led him to support the Democratic party.[16]

One significant aspect of Owen's activity in New York was the clarification and development of his radical theories through controversy and debate. That consideration had prompted his removal from New Harmony, and soon after his arrival he took the offensive. When his ideas on divorce were criticized by a Washington paper, he promptly but vainly challenged the editor to a formal, journalistic discussion. When the press heralded Alexander Campbell's supposed victory in Cincinnati, Owen invited his father's antagonist to bring his *Christian Baptist* east to the real seat of the war. He constantly appealed to the New York clergy to participate in the Hall of Science debates; and on one occasion he caused an uproar in the Prince Street Universalist Church when, through a misunderstanding,

[16] Trist to Wright and Owen, Nov. 2, 1828; Owen to Trist, Aug. 13, 1829, Aug. 1, Dec. 12, 1830, Feb. 23, Apr. 28, 1831, Trist Papers, VI, VII; *Dictionary of American Biography*, XVIII, 645–646.

he tried to reply on the spot to a sermon.[17] After a time, however, Owen found his orthodox opponents both too numerous and too abusive to please him. The least distinguished he wisely ignored; [18] but with some he engaged in prolonged contests and these last are worthy of passing notice.

To the charge of atheistic bigotry advanced by Menzies Rayner, Universalist editor of the Hartford *Religious Enquirer*, Owen returned the plea of not guilty. The accusation, however, had a wholesome influence in forcing *The Free Enquirer* to provide its readers with some of the standard orthodox rebuttals to agnosticism. From William Gibbons, prominent Hicksite doctor of Wilmington and president of the Delaware Temperance Society came an abusive pamphlet "exposing" Owen's plan to establish anarchy in the land and to substitute for matrimony "a licensed promiscuous concubinage." In refuting these garbled extracts from his own writings, the reformer was compelled to cross swords with Benjamin Ferris, another but better natured Hicksite Friend and historian of colonial Delaware. The resulting letters to Ferris contain the best succinct statement of Owen's views on God, revelation, marriage, and morals. In 1831 the Scotchman had to go over the same ground to convince Thomas Whittemore, noted author and preacher, that the articles printed in his *Trumpet and Universalist Magazine* by Linus S. Everett entitled "The Rise and Progress of Infidelity in America" were misleading and erroneous. The final detailed exposition of Owen's freethought doctrines came in a long debate, not always amicable in nature, in the columns of his

[17] *Free Enquirer*, June 10, July 1, 8, 15, 22, 29, 1829; *Washington City Chronicle*, June 20, 1829.

[18] "Philalethes" [Alexander Greaves], *Reflections on the Statements and Opinions Published in The Free Enquirer Edited by Frances Wright, Robert Dale Owen, and Robert L. Jennings* (N. Y., 1829); Abner Cunningham, *An Address Submitted to the Consideration of R. D. Owen, Kneeland, Houston, and Others of the Infidel Party, in the City of New York* (N. Y., 1833); "An Observer" [W. Young], *Twelve Letters to Young Men, on the Sentiments of Miss Frances Wright and Robert Dale Owen* (Phila., 1830). The last clearly mistakes Owen for his father. *Ibid.*, 24. A similar confusion was apparent in the *Morning Courier & N. Y. Enquirer*, Mar. 12, 1830; *Northampton Courier*, quoted in *The Free Enquirer*, Dec. 3, 1831.

paper with Origen Bacheler, minister, editor, and peace advocate, on the existence of God and the authenticity of the Bible.[19]

The influence of Owen's controversial writings was probably less than he supposed. For the most part they appeared in a radical sheet or fugitive tracts that were not seen by "respectable" citizens. When they did find their way into orthodox periodicals, it was those of the Universalists and Hicksite Friends, themselves considered by many to be dangerous sects. But even if Owen's arguments had been widely read, an essentially Christian nation was certain to reject a creed that ignored the existence of God, reduced Jesus to the rank of a philosophical reformer, denied the revelation and miracles of the Scriptures, and ridiculed the clergy and church ceremony. Yet in so far as Owen and his followers fought against a stricter enforcement of the Sabbath, denounced sectarian influence in public schools, inveighed against the rejection of witnesses in courts of law who did not profess a belief in the Bible, and established a free, if anti-Christian press, they were carrying on the conception of American religious liberty bequeathed by Thomas Jefferson.[20] Jefferson was the idol of these reformers, and the abuse they received differed neither in kind nor degree from that which had been hurled against the author of the Virginia Statute of Religious Freedom.

If Owen's religious writings outran the liberal thought of his day, other matters discussed in *The Free Enquirer* reflected the humanitarian spirit that became a real force in American life about the time Andrew Jackson succeeded to the presidency. The editor's interest in adult education and anti-Sabbatarianism has been noticed, and his agitation for free schools and labor reform is reserved for a later chapter. Owen

[19] *Free Enquirer*, Dec. 12, 1829, Jan. 9, Feb. 6, 27, Apr. 10, 1830. William Gibbons, *An Exposition of Modern Scepticism, in a Letter Addressed to the Editors of The Free Enquirer* (3d edn., Wilmington, 1830), 45; *Free Enquirer*, Nov. 7, 1829, Feb. 6, 13, 20, 27, 1830. *Ibid.*, Feb. 27, Mar. 20, 27, Apr. 3, 10, 17, 1830. *Trumpet*, Feb. 12, 19, 26, Mar. 5, 12, 19, 26, Apr. 2, May 14, 1831; *Free Enquirer*, Feb. 26, Mar. 12, 19, Apr. 2, 9, 16, 1831. *Ibid.*, Jan. 22, 1831 *et seq.*

[20] *Free Enquirer*, Dec. 10, 1828, July 15, Sept. 9, Oct. 31, Nov. 14, 1829, Jan. 2, 30, Mar. 27, July 17, 1830.

had a good if brief word for the abolition of capital punishment
and the crusade for universal peace. He not only opposed imprisonment for debt as a relic of barbarism but demanded that
the law should no longer be resorted to for the payment of
debts. He advised a generation's delay before coöperative
communities be formed on a large scale. Personally abstaining
from all liquor, Owen deplored the extent of intemperance in
the United States and approved the aims of the remedial societies. Slavery he condemned as a blot upon American liberty,
but he had no sympathy for the infant abolitionist organizations. He declared that Garrison's zeal exceeded his wisdom,
and he denied that a Northerner could formulate a solution to
meet actual conditions. Southern excesses after the Southampton uprising in August 1831, however, drew forth more caustic
comments on the peculiar institution.[21]

On no subject were Owen's ideas more misunderstood than
on the rights of women. In the eyes of his contemporaries he
was planning to destroy the institution of marriage, abolish all
ideals of chastity, and make of their wives and sisters common
prostitutes. Yet Owen did no more than advocate logically,
consistently, and indefatigably the liberating measures he had
first broached at New Harmony. He would free woman from
a custom that made her life an intellectual vacuum and from
a fashion that jeopardized the health of her children. He
would provide for her the same educational facilities as for
man and emancipate her from the outmoded disabilities of the
common law.[22] That he finally abandoned his earlier restraint
and discussed the subject of contraception resulted from a
controversy not of his own seeking.

It was Thomas Skidmore, class-conscious leader of the New
York workingmen, who paved the way for the first American

---

[21] *Free Enquirer*, Aug. 26, Sept. 3, [2], 1829, Feb. 6, Mar. 13, May 22, 1830,
May 14, Aug. 6, 27, 1831; *Wealth and Misery (Popular Tracts*, no. 11), 15.
Working Man's Advocate, Mar. 13, 1830; "The Slave," *Free Enquirer*, Feb. 13,
1830; *ibid.*, June 4, Sept. 3, 17, 24, 1831; London *Crisis*, Mar. 16, 1833.
[22] *Free Enquirer*, Aug. 5, Sept. 9, 1829, Jan. 2, 16, 30, Feb. 13, Apr. 17,
Dec. 11, 18, 1830, May 21, 1831.

birth control tract. Ever since Owen had rejected Skidmore's proposal to provide each citizen reaching his majority with an equal amount of land, the latter had sought proof for his belief that Owen's sympathy for labor was false. In July 1830 he felt he had discovered such evidence, first in Owen's suggestion that parents pay a small head tax on each child sent to the new state boarding schools which he wished to introduce and second in his admission, during a journalistic discussion of the population question, that the wage-earner would do well to limit the size of his family.[23] At once Skidmore publicly denounced the suggested limitation as an insult to the poor and the tax as a means of depriving them of their right to have offspring. Gladly did he bring to light a fact overlooked by Gibbons, Everett and other traducers of Owen — the then two-year-old editorial giving a general approval to Carlile's *Every Woman's Book*.[24]

Owen had scarcely corrected the agrarian's misstatements when a more complete publicity was given his earlier praise of Carlile. An anonymous abusive pamphlet printed in full the original article in *The New Harmony Gazette*, called the writer a disciple of Malthus, and accused Robert Owen of introducing contraceptive information into England. It agreed that the son was hostile to the workingman and dared him either to endorse or to repudiate the doctrines of Richard Carlile. Although this tract was inspired by Skidmore, its author was probably George Houston, who was eager to repay Owen for supposed injuries done in the past.[25]

[23] *N. Y. Daily Sentinel*, July 13, 1830; *Working Man's Advocate*, Feb. 13, 1830.

[24] *Friend of Equal Rights*, summarized in *The Free Enquirer*, Aug. 7, 1830, and quoted, in part, in the pamphlet cited in the next note.

[25] *Free Enquirer*, Aug. 7, 1830; *N. Y. Daily Sentinel*, Aug. 11, 1830. [George Houston?], *Robert Dale Owen Unmasked by His Own Pen: Showing His Unqualified Approbation of a Most Obscenely Indelicate Work, Entitled, "What Is Love, or Every Woman's Book." A Work Destructive to Conjugal Happiness — Repulsive to the Modest Mind, Equally of Man or Woman, and Recommending the Promiscuous Intercourse of Sensual Prostitution etc.* (N. Y., 1830), 4, 7–8, 10, 13. Houston's authorship was indicated by the place where the pamphlet was sold, by the similarity to his earlier *Frances Wright Unmasked*

The weapon thus forged by Owen's fellow reformers was quickly seized by his enemies. In July 1830, he had imprudently forwarded to the New York Typographical Society, with whom he had had trouble before, a specimen of typography just received from England. When the members met to consider the acceptance of the gift, one of them read extracts from *Every Woman's Book* and stated that the donor approved its contents. The shocked gathering at once decided to reject the present and gave as a reason, in a letter not then published, the fact that Owen was a scoffer, a foreigner, and a moral incendiary, intent on establishing free intercourse between the sexes. Somewhat taken aback by this intemperate reply, Owen unwisely recounted the main facts of the case in his paper and repeated his qualified approbation of Carlile's work. At once the Typographical Society published its statement in the *Commercial Advertiser*, the editor of which refused to print with it a minority report protesting against the action thus taken.[26]

Owen was now thoroughly aroused. He believed that his alleged endorsement of Carlile was being used by the aristocratic, clerical party solely to injure the cause of freethought, and he felt it keenly that the handle should have been given by another reformer. Honest prejudices entertained by society may have kept him from meeting the challenge of the anonymous pamphleteer, but further silence would imply his approval of both Malthus and Carlile. In short, he felt "baited" into his subsequent course of action.[27] Early in October he began a series of three articles making out the economic and sociological case for Neo-Malthusianism. In the last of these he announced

---

by *Her Own Pen* etc. (N. Y., 1830), on which see *The Free Enquirer*, July 10, 1830, and by the writer's acceptance of the description of himself as "the editor of a late violently anti-christian publication."

[26] *Free Enquirer*, Sept. 25, 1830; *Commercial Advertiser*, Sept. 29, 1830; *N. Y. Daily Sentinel*, Oct. 2, 1830.

[27] Owen to Trist, Dec. 12, 1830, Trist Papers, VII. Of the work Owen wrote, "It seemed to me imperatively called for by the circumstances." R. D. Owen to Robt. Owen, Feb. 21, 1831, Robert Owen Papers, no. 396.

the forthcoming publication of a tract that would treat the physiological aspect of the subject. After some delay there appeared on the first day of December 1830 a seventy-two page pamphlet bearing the author's full name and entitled *Moral Physiology; or, a Brief and Plain Treatise on the Population Question.*[28]

The introductory pages of the treatise explained the reasons for its publication. The author then plunged at once into the heart of his subject, the instinct of reproduction. This he defended as both a means of propagation and a source of pleasure. Upon inquiry he concluded that control of the instinct was possible and desirable, but he did not regard such control as a panacea for the world's ills. Denying that Europe or the United States suffered from overpopulation, Owen rested his case upon the part that contraceptive knowledge would play in improving the quality of the human race, strengthening the marriage tie, and elevating the position of women. Society would benefit from the decrease of celibacy among adults and a decline in prostitution. The poor, relieved of the economic pressure resulting from large families, would be able to give their children a better education.[29]

On turning from the theory of birth control to the practice, Owen showed little concern for objections based on chastity or natural rights. The former he defined in the words of Franklin as "the regulated and strictly temperate satisfaction, without injury to others, of those desires which are natural to all healthy adult beings." [30] Man's natural right to propagate his species should, he thought, be governed by reason. Owen did not consider Malthusian delayed marriages as a solution for the problem at hand. To him they were immoral and impractical, immoral because they increased profligacy, impractical

[28] *Free Enquirer*, Oct. 9, 16, 23, Dec. 4, 1830. The tract, seven inches by four and a half and costing 37¢, contained a frontispiece depicting a mother abandoning her baby before the Foundling's Hospital and exclaiming, "Alas! that it should ever have been born!"

[29] *Moral Physiology* (3d edn., N. Y., 1831), iii–iv, 5, 13–17, 30–42.

[30] *Ibid.*, 70.

because they ran counter to human nature in asking individuals to give up their best years to avert an evil they might not live to see.[31] After sixty pages of such arguments as might well have appeared in *The Free Enquirer*, the author in seven more briefly described three methods of contraception, two of which he abandoned in six months. He noted the advantages and disadvantages of each as to effectiveness and pleasure and invited his readers to communicate to him privately their experience with these checks. He concluded with a few remarks on the dissemination of this information in England by men of irreproachable character.[32]

Owen had foreseen the violent criticism to which he would be exposed by this bold but decently written tract. Upon completing the manuscript, he read the whole in the privacy of his room and then decided, against the advice of all his friends, to give it to the printer. He openly declared, "I desire no reputation that is inconsistent with the authorship of this work. I hold it to be a good work. . . . So long as the world is not prepared to approve its honesty, I can do without the world's approbation." [33] The reception, however, was extremely gratifying. Fifteen hundred copies were sold in five months, and a fifth edition was issued on August 13, 1831. This circulation was attained in spite of the limited number of papers in which the treatise could be advertised. *The Free Enquirer* spoke of it constantly, and the *Boston Investigator* may have done likewise. The New Harmony *Disseminator* listed it among other standard liberal imprints, but there public notice in America seems to have ended.[34] Fortunately much could be done by

[31] *Moral Physiology*, 19, 26–28.

[32] *Moral Physiology*, 61–67, 68–69. The checks suggested were: complete withdrawal previous to emission; use by the female in the vagina of a damp sponge with a ribbon attached; use by the male of a "baudruche" or skin covering. In the fourth edition (N. Y., May 28, 1831), the second and third methods were relegated to a footnote and were later omitted altogether.

[33] *Free Enquirer*, Oct. 23, 1830. *Ibid.*, Oct. 8, 1831; Owen to Trist, Apr. 28, Sept. 26, 1831, Trist Papers, VII, VIII.

[34] Owen to Trist, Apr. 28, 1831, Trist Papers, VII; *Free Enquirer*, Aug. 13, 1831; statement of L. S. Everett, *Trumpet*, Mar. 19, 1831; *Disseminator*, Mar. 12, 19, 26, 1831.

Owen, Trist, and others through private recommendation and distribution.[35]

The praise that the pamphlet received in some quarters was no less gratifying than its circulation. Thomas Cooper, radical president of South Carolina College, commended Owen's boldness in discussing so important a subject and fully approved of his treatment. Trist was delighted and wrote that an acquaintance was profoundly impressed by the benevolence of the author who was, "like other great minds, in advance of the day." Similar encouragement came from Frances Wright in Europe, but she warned her associate not to expect too much in practical results.[36] Even where approbation was not expressed, keen interest was manifested. Judge Henry St. G. Tucker was eager to see the treatise; and the aged Madison declared that, "from the reputed talents & tenets of the author, something may be anticipated well written & out of the trodden circle." [37]

Only two public attacks on *Moral Physiology* appear to have been made at this time. The first came from Linus S. Everett, who found the tract of value in his articles upon the immorality of infidels. Everett carefully avoided a description of the contents, restricting himself to generalities and such characterizations as "a mean, disgusting, and obscene book, filled with arguments that would disgrace the tenants of a brothel." [38] Equally abusive but more significant was a pamphlet by Thomas Skidmore, published about June 1831. Skidmore's method was ingenious. With Owen's knowledge he reprinted in identical format the fourth edition of *Moral Physi-*

[35] Owen to Trist, Dec. 12, 1830, Feb. 23, 1831, Trist Papers, VII; *Free Enquirer*, Mar. 26, 1831.

[36] Cooper to Owen, Dec. 12, 1830, Dreer Collection: Physicians; Owen to Trist, Apr. 28, Sept. 26, 1831, Trist Papers, VII, VIII; *Free Enquirer*, Mar. 5, Oct. 8, 1831.

[37] J. A. G. Davis to Trist, Nov. 7, 1830; Madison to Trist, May 5, 1831, Trist Papers, VII.

[38] *Trumpet*, Mar. 19, Apr. 2, 1831. Like Origen Bacheler, Everett may have sneered at the tract without having read it. Cf. *Free Enquirer*, July 9, 16, 23, 1831.

ology, adding only a title page of his own, extensive footnotes, and a long conclusion. In these additions he reasserted that birth control was an insult to the poor, publicized his own reform panacea, and sought to discredit Owen in the eyes of the workingman. He denied that contraceptive practices were desirable; for if the worker limited the size of his family, he would be forced by the competitive system to subsist on lower wages. On the contrary, the agrarian argued, an increased population would benefit the laborer by enabling the manufacturer to sell to him more cheaply. But Skidmore was less concerned with economic theory than his depiction of Owen as the leader of the "sponge party" in America. Although called an "aristocratical, sophistical, *self-contradictory*, contemptible Jesuit," Owen did not lose his equanimity or sense of fair play. He printed the full title of the pamphlet in *The Free Enquirer*, admitted an explanatory letter to his columns, and placed the work in his circulating library. He briefly denied that birth control would lower industrial wages, and he declared that Skidmore's essay "will do its author no good, and me no harm." [39]

The immediate influence of *Moral Physiology* was seen in the publication in January 1832 of *Fruits of Philosophy*, the second known American tract on birth control. Its author, Dr. Charles Knowlton, a materialistic thinker of Massachusetts, had not only read Owen, but had lifted bodily with slight change in wording and scant acknowledgment the sociological and economic arguments for contraception. Its subtitle, however, suggests a different appeal, while the writer's interests insured a different approach. Where more than half of Owen's essay

[39] Thomas Skidmore, *Moral Physiology Exposed and Refuted. Comprising the Entire Work of Robert Dale Owen on That Subject with Critical Notes Showing Its Tendency to Degrade and Render Still More Unhappy than It Is Now, the Condition of the Working Classes, by Denying Their Right to Increase the Number of Their Children; and Recommending the Same Odious Means to Suppress Such Increase as Are Contained in Carlile's "What Is Love, or Every Woman's Book"* (N. Y., 1831), 13, 15–17, 23, 27, 30–32, 34, 36, 44, 51, 67, 70, 72–73, 75, and, especially, 51, 72; *Free Enquirer*, June 25, July 2, 9, 1831; Owen to Trist, Apr. 28, 1831, Trist Papers, VII.

was concerned with the social aspect of the population question, only a tenth of Knowlton's discussed that matter. The doctor, on the other hand, devoted more than half his work to a description of the vital organs and treated equally the subject of conception and contraception. Knowlton's treatise, first published anonymously, contained an additional check of great importance and corrected a physiological detail on which Owen was in doubt.[40]

Owen's position as the first American writer on birth control has now been recognized by students of the social sciences. He is entitled to a similar rank in the history of eugenics.[41] To what extent his tract influenced contemporary thought is more debatable. The paucity of public criticism suggests both ignorance of the work in conservative circles and a realization that vehement attacks would afford additional publicity. Where some obscure later writers, like A. M. Mauriceau, leaned heavily on Owen's treatise, John Humphrey Noyes denied that his superficially analogous male continence was in any way indebted to Owen's theories.[42] It is probable, however, that *Moral Physiology* enjoyed a fair circulation for its day; and its name, if not its contents, was spread by the tactics of Owen's political opponents. In later years it was advertised in the leading American and British freethought periodicals and occasionally in regular newspapers. At least a dozen editions were printed before Owen's death in the United States and an equal number in England. Since the author took out no copyright and thus received no royalties, we are forced to depend upon his own guess that it had circulated from 50,000 to 60,000 copies by 1874.[43] The greatest demand for it, how-

[40] Charles Knowlton, *Fruits of Philosophy; or the Private Companion of Young Married People* (2d edn., Boston, 1833), 127–135. Cf. *ibid.*, 20–21 with *Moral Physiology* (3d edn., N. Y., 1831), 32–33. Knowlton's additional check was the use of a chemical solution and syringe.

[41] *Encyclopaedia of the Social Sciences*, XI, 517–518; Norman E. Himes, "Eugenic Thought in the American Birth Control Movement 100 Years Ago," *Eugenics*, II, 3–8 (May 1929).

[42] Himes, *Medical History of Contraception*, 260–285; J. H. Noyes, *Dixon and His Copyists* (Wallingford, 1871), 34.

[43] "An Earnest Sowing of Wild Oats," *loc. cit.*, XXXIV, 77.

ever, came immediately after his decease when the English
Society for the Suppression of Vice unsuccessfully prosecuted
Knowlton's tract but won a similar action against Owen's. The
publicity given by these trials made possible an increased distribution of Owen's essay and its successor; and to the contraceptive information thus disseminated has been attributed,
by some writers, the decline in the British birth rate during the
last half century.[44]

Moral Physiology was the most temperate, refined, and readable of the nineteenth century tracts on birth control.[45] Published in an age of prudery, it subjected its author to violent
criticism, often political in nature, throughout his life. Never
again did Owen openly advocate Neo-Malthusianism; but although the temptation was often great, he did not repudiate
his early treatise. The work represents, perhaps, the best example of Robert Dale Owen's militant freethought. Yet in
1830 the anathemas that were hurled at his head were not
primarily the result of *Moral Physiology* nor even of his un-
concealed agnosticism. They resulted from his participation in
the first organized activity of labor in New York.

[44] Himes, *op. cit.*, 238–259; *National Reformer*, 1876–1877, *passim*; *The Queen v. Edw. Truelove, for Publishing the Hon. Robert Dale Owen's "Moral Physiology"* (London, 1878). Both Himes, "Charles Knowlton's Revolutionary Influence on the English Birth Rate," *New England Journal of Medicine*, CXCIX, 461–465 (Sept. 6, 1829) and Robert E. Riegel, "The American Father of Birth Control," *New England Quarterly*, VI, 489–490 (Sept. 1933) attribute a declining birth rate to increased knowledge of contraception.

[45] George J. Holyoake, *Sixty Years of an Agitator's Life* (London, 1892), I, 112.

CHAPTER VI

EDUCATION FOR THE WORKERS

THE formation of a central city organization of wage-earners in Philadelphia in 1827 marked the real beginning of the American labor movement. Before that date trade association and trade activity had been well known, but it remained for the growth of American manufactures after the depression of 1819 and the increasing stratification of national society in those years to give rise to an expression of class solidarity that transcended single trades and extended to the workingmen as a whole. The distinctive demand of the subsequent agitation was "equal citizenship" — a termination of political, economic, and social disparities that belied the immortal Declaration of Jefferson. In particular, the industrial worker demanded shorter hours of labor, higher wages, cheaper forms of justice, a lien law, and, above all, better educational facilities for his children.[1]

It was not until April 1829, a few days after Owen had arrived from the West, that the New York mechanics followed in the path of their Philadelphia brethren. In two preliminary meetings the wage-earners not only appointed a Committee of Fifty to safeguard the ten-hour day but resolved that every workingman who did not own real estate was entitled to a decent existence by society. Although class discrimination lay at the root of labor's grievances, its program of reform appealed beyond the landless mechanic to every liberal who placed the rights of person before the rights of property. For Robert Dale Owen, reared in the shadow of Scotland's model factory, the appeal was attractive; and his first editorials written in the East manifested a revived interest in industrial problems.[2]

---

[1] Commons and others, *History of Labour in the United States*, I, 11-12.
[2] *A Documentary History of American Industrial Society* (J. R. Commons and others, eds., Cleveland, 1910), V, 146-148; *Free Enquirer*, May 6, 1829.

A summer of comparative calm, during which Owen strongly urged the formation of an independent labor party, was broken on October 19 by a gathering of radical workingmen in the Wooster Street Military Hall.[3] The Committee of Fifty's report and the resolutions there adopted hotly denounced paper money, banks, monopolies, and the tax exemption of ecclesiastical property. The existing distress was attributed to the unequal distribution of land; and it was incautiously suggested that there could be no true reform "until a revolution takes place, such as shall leave behind it no trace of that government which has denied to every human being an equal amount of property." Although the meeting had a good word for republican education and agreed with Owen that the wage-earner should be represented at Albany by members of his own class, it was inspired less by the doctrines of *The Free Enquirer* than by Thomas Skidmore and his recently published book, *The Rights of Man to Property*! [4]

The interest that Owen quite naturally took in its proceedings immediately proved embarrassing to the nascent labor movement. At the meeting of October 19 Owen was accidentally chosen secretary to the consternation of the committee, which had selected another and less notorious person. Thus the radical resolutions attacking private property and the clergy went forth under Owen's signature and were promptly attributed by the conservative press to his influence. Recognizing the latent danger of associating his heterodoxy with a political party, Owen promptly published a letter disclaiming all responsibility for either the calling or the proceedings of the Military Hall gathering, and he renewed his earlier criticism of Skidmore's plan, popularly known as agrarianism.[5] The charge of complicity, however, would not down. On three subsequent occasions Owen felt compelled to make a public dis-

---

[3] "Cause of the People," *Free Enquirer*, Aug. 19, 26, Sept. 3 [2], 9, 1829.
[4] *Morning Courier & N. Y. Enquirer*, Oct. 23, 1829; *Free Enquirer*, Mar. 20, 1830.
[5] *Commercial Advertiser*, Oct. 23, 26, 1829. Cf. *Free Enquirer*, Aug. 26, Oct. 31, 1829.

avowal, and on another he sent to his father for insertion as "New York Correspondence" of the London *Times* a careful distinction between his program and that of Skidmore.[6] The canard, moreover, was effective. Never again did Robert Dale Owen act publicly as a member of the new Working Men's Party.

Disappointed but not discouraged by the incident, Owen sought another way to aid labor's cause. Through the Association for the Protection of Industry and for the Promotion of National Education, formed by Frances Wright the previous month and officered by the leaders of the Hall of Science, he began to demand free boarding school instruction for the children of the workers. Three nights before the legislative election, the same evening the Committee of Fifty was meeting elsewhere, the Association assembled in Military Hall and endorsed unreservedly this educational scheme called state guardianship.[7] A daring action followed. Led by Owen and Jennings, the meeting repaired to Masonic Hall, where dissatisfied Democrats and remnants of the disorganized Adams-Clay faction had gathered in an attempt to present a united front against Tammany. As soon as, almost before, that group had adjourned, Owen's followers gained control of the hall and adopted the same radical resolutions passed in Wooster Street. This capture of the old parties by the workingmen was both asserted and denied according to the politics of the paper concerned, but most were willing to dismiss the incident as the work of the "deluded followers of a crazy atheistical woman." [8] Since Owen had as secretary signed the Wooster Street resolutions, his name once more appeared in connection with the new labor movement.

[6] *Courier & Enquirer*, Nov. 20, 1829; "To the Conductors of the New York Periodical Press," *Free Enquirer*, Nov. 28, 1829; *Daily Sentinel*, Apr. 28, 1830; R. D. Owen to Robt. Owen, Mar. 27, 1830, Robert Owen Papers, no. 215; *Times*, May 1, 1830.

[7] *Evening Journal*, Nov. 2, 1829.

[8] *Commercial Advertiser*, Oct. 31, 1829. Cf. *Courier & Enquirer*, Oct. 31, 1829; *Evening Post*, Oct. 31, 1829; *Daily Advertiser*, Oct. 31, 1829; *Journal of Commerce*, Oct. 31, 1829; *Working Man's Advocate*, Oct. 31, 1829; *Free Enquirer*, Nov. 7, 1829; Stuart, *Three Years in America*, II, 13–15.

Despite this last minute excitement the three-day November election began quietly. On the first day the Democratic organ was more concerned with a split in its own ranks than with the "workies," and that evening a conservative paper declared that the canvass "seems to excite less interest than almost any preceding one we remember." [9] On the next day Tammany resorted to a ruse. Under the pretense that the "Infidel Ticket," opposed to the rights of property and headed by Wright, Owen and Jennings was sweeping all before it, its editor implored the people to vote for any respectable party. A political ally took up the cry of alarm and sagely hinted that the best way to defeat Fanny Wright was to unite behind the regular Democrats. This panic-stricken pose was maintained on the third day. [10] The result was a complete Democratic triumph over the other parties. The surprise, however, came in the election of a Working Men's candidate to one of the eleven Assembly seats and an average poll by his colleagues of six out of twenty-one thousand votes. [11]

The emergence of the workingmen as a real force in New York City politics delighted Owen but did not satisfy him. Almost at once he began to discuss the steps necessary to insure complete success. [12] Certain shortcomings, such as weak nominations and injudicious resolutions, were beyond his control. His own heterodoxy and association with the New Harmony experiment, responsible for much of the post-election abuse showered upon the new party, he felt the mechanics must endure; for they had many agnostics in their ranks. [13] Thus at a meeting on December 29 the laborers followed Owen in officially repudiating Skidmore's agrarianism, and during the next month they seemed willing to pursue a policy of complete toleration. [14] The real

[9] *Courier & Enquirer*, Nov. 2, 1829; *American*, Nov. 2, 1829.

[10] *Courier & Enquirer*, Nov. 3, 4, 1829; *Evening Post*, Nov. 3, 4, 1829.

[11] *Daily Advertiser*, Nov. 9, 1829; Commons, *op. cit.*, I, 239–241.

[12] *Free Enquirer*, Nov. 14, 1829.

[13] *Evening Post*, Nov. 5, 14, 1829; *Courier & Enquirer*, Nov. 9, 13, 1829; *Journal of Commerce*, Nov. 10, 1829; *Commercial Advertiser*, Nov. 12, 13, 14, 1829. *Free Enquirer*, Nov. 14, 1829.

[14] *Evening Journal*, Jan. 14, 23, 1830; *Working Man's Advocate*, Feb. 6, 1830.

problems, as Owen saw them, were first, to establish a press
that could organize, rally, and defend the wage-earner, and
second, to devise a simple, popular program on which all workers could unite. To the solution of these problems Owen turned
his indomitable enthusiasm and unflagging industry.

Unlike their Philadelphia brethren, the New York workingmen had no newspaper of their own until the very eve of the
November election. In the preceding months *The Free Enquirer*, true to its liberal principles, had stood in the breach,
reporting meetings and printing significant documents.[15] Its
notorious heterodoxy and the comparatively small space it could
devote to politics, however, made necessary a journal devoted
solely to the interests of labor. Such a one was *The Working
Man's Advocate* which appeared on October 31. Its editor,
George Henry Evans, later famous as a land reformer and at
this time a close friend of Owen, had agreed to place republican
education before agrarian equality. Although he did valiant
work, Evans' efforts did not answer the need. As a weekly,
his paper could hardly cope with the host of Jackson and Clay
dailies; as a foreign-born agnostic, he, like Owen, exposed the
party to the charge of atheism and encouraged the plea of
nativism.[16]

The establishment of a daily labor organ was hastened by
the party's strong showing in the legislative election. First
the *Morning Herald* began to show more liberal tendencies.
Of greater import was the abandonment by the *Evening Journal*
of its benevolent neutrality. Hitherto that little known paper,
begun early in 1829 and circulating chiefly in the upper wards,
had printed accounts of workers' meetings but had refrained
from editorial approval of their cause. In November, however,
it offered constructive criticism, not unlike Owen's, and openly
defended the mechanics from the frequent charge of infidelity
and agrarianism.[17] Until the end of 1829 it pursued an honest,

[15] *Free Enquirer*, Apr. 29, May 6, Aug. 19, Sept. 6, 23, 30, Oct. 7, 1829.
[16] *Dictionary of American Biography*, VI, 201–202; *Commercial Advertiser*,
Nov. 11, Dec. 10, 1829.
[17] *Evening Journal*, Oct. 14, 21, Nov. 2, 9, 14, 19, 28, 1829.

tolerant course and refused, though sorely tempted, to increase
its circulation by attacking Owen, Evans, and other sceptics
among the wage-earners. It even printed advertisements of the
Hall of Science. Its editor, however, frequently disavowed any
connection with that organization; and his successor in 1830
belonged to a group within the party that hated Owen as much
as Skidmore.[18]

Even before the *Evening Journal* had entered its claim as
the spokesman of the Working Men's Party, proposals were
issued for another labor daily. The newcomer at once encountered obstacles. Those papers already friendly to the cause
proved hostile to this rival and hinted at a plot to divide the
laboring class. Promise of financial backing was suddenly withdrawn when the proprietors refused to support the Sabbatarian
crusade. Notice that the venture was, therefore, being abandoned brought Owen to the rescue.[19] Unable to offer pecuniary
assistance of his own, he persuaded Camilla Wright to advance
a sum probably exceeding $3,000. The proprietors, themselves
mere journeymen printers, pledged their office for the loan; and
Owen secured Miss Wright against loss with a mortgage on
his New Harmony property.[20] This timely aid permitted plans
for publication to proceed but also caused the resignation, presumably because of the paper's now infidel origin, of two experienced journalists engaged the previous December as editors.
In desperation the proprietors announced that they would conduct their own journal, but that task was beyond their ability.[21]
In the end, therefore, the position that the original editors,
James G. Brooks and Edward V. Sparhawk, could hardly have
filled to the satisfaction of humble mechanics fell unexpectedly
to one of more zeal and of equal talent, to Robert Dale Owen.

For more than a year after its appearance on February 15,

[18] *Ibid.*, Nov. 9, 14, 17, 28, 1829; Commons, *op. cit.*, I, 248.
[19] *Working Man's Advocate*, Dec. 12, 19, 1829, Jan. 16, 1830; *Courier &
Enquirer*, Feb. 5, 1830. Cf. *Evening Journal*, Dec. 21, 23, 24, 1829; *Morning
Herald*, Dec. 25, 1829.
[20] Owen to Maclure, Sept. 4, 1830, Maclure Papers; Owen to Trist, Feb. 23,
1831, Trist Papers, VII; Waterman, *Frances Wright*, 208 n. 1.
[21] *American*, Feb. 11, 1830; *Courier & Enquirer*, Dec. 30, 1829, Feb. 12, 1830.

1830, Owen was the chief editor of *The New York Daily Sentinel*. Although he had previously given Evans some assistance in running the *Advocate*, the reformer probably did not intend to do more than get the new journal started; for the departure of Jennings and Miss Wright was soon to thrust upon his shoulders complete direction of *The Free Enquirer*. Editorial skirmishing, however, proved so enjoyable to him that his withdrawal was postponed month after month. Evans himself joined the staff in June when *The Working Man's Advocate* merged with the weekly edition of the *Sentinel*. Owen's connection was further prolonged by the precarious financial position of the paper during all of 1830 and the early part of 1831. In fact, it was Owen who sought monetary aid from William Maclure and to please the latter suggested that Thomas Say be made the chief editor. Nothing came of either the plea or the suggestion, for the entomologist was not interested and his patron had long been irked by a belief that *The Free Enquirer* had stolen his ideas. All the time Owen had to do his best to conceal his position from the public lest the paper's circulation suffer from the heterodoxy of its pilot. For once he gave up his practice of signing editorials, and he scrupulously stayed out of the *Sentinel* office. He even delayed revealing his work to his father and to Trist and then gave the information under pledge of strictest secrecy.[22] Despite these precautions, many contemporaries suspected his activity.[23]

Complete control of a labor daily gave Owen an excellent medium in which to discuss the second problem confronting the

[22] R. D. Owen to Robt. Owen, Mar. 27, 1830, Feb. 21, 1831; to Mrs. Robt. Owen, Aug. 12, 1830, Robert Owen Papers, nos. 215, 396, 291; Owen to Trist, June 2, Nov. 1, 1830, Feb. 23, 1831, Trist Papers, VI, VII; "An Earnest Sowing of Wild Oats," *Atlantic Monthly*, XXXIV, 77–78 (July 1874). Frances Wright to Maclure, Jan. 3, 1829 [1830]; Owen to Maclure, Sept. 4, 1830; Fretageot to Maclure, Oct. 2, 13, 1830, Maclure Papers; Say to Owen, Oct. 12, 1830, Dreer Collection: Scientists, III; Maclure to Fretageot, Feb. 20, Mar. 22, Apr. 3, Sept. 15, Oct. 20, Nov. 24, 1830, Fretageot Papers. *Daily Sentinel*, June 1, 5, Sept. 17, 1830, Jan. 1, Feb. 15, Aug. 5, 1831.

[23] *Courier & Enquirer*, May 20, 1830; [Houston?], *Robert Dale Owen Unmasked by His Own Pen*, 5–6; Skidmore's letter in *The Free Enquirer*, Oct. 2, 1830.

workingmen, the formulation of a platform. Ever since the New Harmony fiasco Owen had regarded improved educational facilities as a prerequisite to all reforms; and his opinion was strengthened when he discovered in New York that the community system was, for the moment, "a sort of bugbear." [24] Following the lead of the more original Frances Wright, he began during the summer of 1829 to sketch a system of boarding schools open without charge to all the children of the state. By November his agitation had become incessant, and he had formulated a creed, delightful in its vagueness.

I believe [it read] in a National System of Equal, Republican, Protective, Practical Education, the sole regenerator of a profligate age, and the only redeemer of our suffering country from the equal curses of chilling poverty and corrupting riches, of gnawing want and destroying debauchery, of blind ignorance and of unprincipled intrigue.

By this, my creed, I will live. By my consistency, or inconsistency with this, my professed belief, I claim to be judged. By it I will stand or fall.[25]

Feeling that the issue of reublican education had not been presented clearly to the voters in the legislative election, Owen repeatedly urged the new party to place it at the head of its demands. He did not wish the workingmen to strive for too many things at once but rather concentrate on the measure which he believed "would do more to reform the abuses that pervade this country than any other." [26] The December meeting of the Working Men's Party declared in favor of tax-supported schools and appointed a sub-committee to draw up some suitable plan. Unfortunately that body prolonged unduly its deliberations, and doubt arose among the mechanics as to what republican education meant. Prompted by an exhaustive report of the Philadelphia wage-earners in which the existing

[24] R. D. Owen to Robt. Owen, Mar. 27, 1830, Robert Owen Papers, no. 215.

[25] *Free Enquirer*, Nov. 7, 1829. See also "Cause of the People," *ibid.*, Aug. 19, 26, Sept. 3 [2], 9, 1829.

[26] R. D. Owen to Mrs. Robt. Owen, Jan. 4, 1830, Robert Owen Papers, no. 176; Owen to Trist, Feb. 3, 1830, Trist Papers, VI.

pauper, common, and high schools were scored as inadequate, Owen decided to lead public opinion not follow it.[27] Early in April 1830, with but slight foreshadowing, there appeared anonymously in the *Sentinel* his six essays on "Public Education."

In a republican system of education as conceived by Robert Dale Owen the state would become the guardian of all its children. It would provide them with equal food, clothing, and instruction and lodge them in boarding schools maintained at public expense. The existing regime of day schools was deemed unsatisfactory because the pupils spent their idle hours in environments that varied according to the wealth of their parents. Equality was to be the keynote of the new order, and nowhere more so than in the curriculum. Each student was to receive instruction not only in reading, writing, and arithmetic but also in history, modern languages, chemistry, drawing, and music. In addition, each was to be trained in agriculture and one useful trade so that he could, if necessary, earn a living with his hands. This combination of literary and manual education, it was hoped, would inculcate in all alike an appreciation of the dignity of labor and thus go far to eliminate the stratification of American society.[28]

Despite its bold departure from American scholastic tradition, Owen's scheme of republican education met with considerable favor. Such a reception was all the more surprising since the author expected to pay for the costly boarding schools not through the products of the pupils but by taxation, a method nowhere widely accepted. Nevertheless the six essays were copied in full into sixteen papers, were approved by many more,

[27] *Evening Journal*, Jan. 2, 6, 1830. *Ibid.*, Jan. 25, 1830; Utica *Mechanics' Press*, quoted in the *Daily Sentinel*, Mar. 29, 1830; Report of the Tenth Ward, Mar. 29, 1830, *Working Man's Advocate*, Apr. 10, 1830; *Mechanics' Free Press*, Feb. 20, 27, 1830.

[28] *Daily Sentinel*, Apr. 8, 9, 10, 12, 13, 14, 1830. Evidence of Owen's authorship appears in Owen to Trist, Sept. 9, 1830, Trist Papers, VII; *Crisis*, Dec. 29, 1832; New Harmony *Indiana Statesman*, Feb. 11, 1843. The essays were twice circulated in pamphlet form, once anonymously, once under Owen's name. *Free Enquirer*, Sept. 11, 1830 (advt.); N. Y. *Beacon*, June 22, 1839 (advt.).

and were soon followed by a similar series in the *Evening Journal*. Even in rural districts they were kindly noticed.[29] For more than a month no important criticism seems to have been made in liberal circles. Yet, in the end, these essays paved the way for a disastrous schism within the ranks of labor, a schism that shattered all hopes to ameliorate the condition of the industrial worker through political action.

Partisan considerations in the last analysis lay behind this fatal division. Ever since the November election had revealed the potentialities of the recently enfranchised wage-earner, members of the inchoate conservative groups had flocked to the labor standard, hoping to build upon its democratic base an effective opposition to the dominant Jackson forces. As early as the meeting of December 29 control of the Working Men's Party had passed into the hands of politicians who had voted another ticket eight weeks before.[30] Now it so happened that those men conducted the *Evening Journal* and tended to look with disfavor upon the rival *Sentinel*. They were not pleased when Owen's six essays gave that paper wide publicity, and they were genuinely alarmed when its editor, aided by Evans, tried to force the state guardianship plan upon the party's subcommittee on education.[31] Undoubtedly there were many mechanics to whom Owen's militant scepticism was abhorrent; and there were others, especially master journeymen, who feared he was another Skidmore. Even the most tolerant may have been pained by Owen's undue emphasis on boarding schools as the single worth-while labor reform,[32] and very few would have denied that his notorious radicalism was embarrassing the cause. But it is doubtful whether the real workingmen repudiated his leadership because guardianship required a broad use of the

[29] Owen to Maclure, Sept. 4, 1830, Maclure Papers; *Working Man's Advocate*, May 15, 1830. *Disseminator*, June 27, 1830; *Western Sun*, Aug. 14, 1830; *Shawneetown* (Illinois) *Gazette*, quoted in the *Daily Sentinel*, Aug. 30, 1830.
[30] Commons, *op. cit.*, I, 259.
[31] "What the Times Require," *Daily Sentinel*, May 3, 1830; *Working Man's Advocate*, Apr. 17, 1830.
[32] "*Without a State System of Education and guardianship* . . . our cause is scarcely worth supporting." *Daily Sentinel*, May 3, 1830.

taxing power or because they regarded it as a plot to spread infidelity through the land, establish anarchy, force year-old children from their mothers' arms, and paralyze the militia system.[33] Those were, rather, appeals by which seasoned politicians hoped to win conservative support for the young labor party.

The first signs of a rift came in the middle of May, 1830. Irked by Owen's rejoicing, if not boasting, in both his papers that guardianship had been endorsed by all labor periodicals, the *Evening Journal* indignantly denied that it favored his "peculiar notions." At the same time it praised a letter from one "Americanus" who denounced guardianship, "one of the wildest fancies that ever entered the mind of a visionary fanatic," as an infringement of parental rights and a covert attack on marriage. Shortly thereafter the conservative workingmen were further aroused by the approval of Owen's plan at a ward meeting through the questionable tactics of a proprietor of the *Sentinel*.[34] James Gordon Bennett chose the opportune moment to fish in troubled waters by confusing state guardianship with agrarianism and asserting that Owen edited the *Sentinel*. These events caused the latter to adopt a more conciliatory policy, and on May 21 he declared that the plan outlined in the six essays could be changed in its details. This bid for peace came too late. That same evening the sub-committee on education, after nearly five months of investigation, abandoned on the spur of the moment its original intention to stick to generalities and submitted an intemperate, ill-considered report.[35]

[33] *Evening Journal*, May 14, 1830, *Boa Constrictor*, both quoted in the *Daily Sentinel*, May 17, July 28, 1830.

[34] *Evening Journal*, May 14, 1830, quoted in the *Daily Sentinel*, May 17, 1830; *Working Man's Advocate*, May 15, 22, 1830. *Address of the Majority of the General Executive Committee of the Mechanics and Other Working Men, of the City of New York* (N. Y., 1830), 4. Evidence that the *Evening Journal* reversed itself in May 1830 must depend on the statements of its opponents, for no file of that paper after March has been located.

[35] *Courier & Enquirer*, May 20, 1830; *Daily Sentinel*, May 21, 1830; statement of Paul Grout, a member of the Committee, *ibid.*, June 12, 1830.

That document, the immediate cause of the split in the Working Men's Party, praised the principle of republican education but denied that any satisfactory scheme had yet been devised. Its greater part consisted of a scathing condemnation of a minority report, based largely on Owen's essays for attempting to fasten deism on the labor movement. Several mechanics' journals were rebuked for seeking to forestall public opinion on the question of free schools, and Owen was virtually read out of the party by being placed in the same class with Skidmore. Although a third of its members were absent, the General Executive Committee of the workingmen decided to act that night and by a margin of five votes accepted the majority report.[36]

A reaction set in at once. Owen's followers, and probably many others who deemed the attack on personalities uncalled for, convened a meeting five days later at the North American Hotel of all friends of the workingmen. There the rival factions came to blows in scenes compared by the conservative press to "the revolutionary assemblages of the Parisian mob." [37] For the moment the Owenites were victorious. The report of May 21 was censured, and its supporters removed from the General Executive Committee of the party.[38]

The breach thus opened was widened during the succeeding weeks. Outside of New York all labor journals except the *Mechanics' Free Press*, the *Delaware Free Press*, and Orestes Brownson's showered abuse on Owen who continued to champion his plan.[39] In New York each group formed its own executive committee and tried to speak in the name of the united

[36] *Daily Sentinel*, May 24, 1830.

[37] *Courier & Enquirer*, May 28, 1830; *Evening Post*, May 27, 1830; *Commercial Advertiser*, May 27, 1830.

[38] *Working Man's Advocate*, May 29, 1830.

[39] Albany *Farmers', Mechanics', and Workingmen's Advocate*, June 12, 1830; *Troy Farmers' Register*, printed in the *Daily Sentinel*, May 31, 1830; Commons, *op. cit.*, I, 260. See also the *American Spectator*, June 19, 1830; *Southern Review*, VI, 1–31 (Aug. 1830); *Mechanics' Free Press*, May 29, 1830; *Delaware Free Press*, quoted in the *Daily Sentinel*, July 1, 1830; Le Roy *Genesee Republican*, quoted in the *N. Y. Sentinel and Working Man's Advocate*, July 17, 1830. *Daily Sentinel*, May 28, June 7, 8, 9, 10, 11, 1830.

party. In the middle of June the *Evening Journal* wing met in order to condemn as irregular the proceedings at the North American Hotel. The blame for the split was placed upon Owen and Skidmore who were accused of seeking to reverse the supposed repudiation of their leadership by the party the previous December. Guardianship was denounced as a revival of the New Harmony community system; and since its advocates secretly desired to subvert all civil and social institutions, they were spurned as unworthy of political fellowship. One week later the *Sentinel* faction assembled and reaffirmed the usual labor principles, including the right of private property and religious freedom. Although state boarding schools were not specifically demanded, a tax-supported educational system was insisted upon. This group attributed the discord to politicians who sought to control the party for the benefit of the conservative, anti-Jackson element.[40]

The political results of the labor schism were first revealed in the Fifth Ward aldermanic election, held early in July. Only three men took the field, one supported by the Democrats, one by the *Sentinel* wing of the Working Men's Party, and one by a coalition of the *Evening Journal* faction and the old Adams-Clay forces. In an exciting canvass, featured by a repetition of Tammany's electoral ruse and an abusive handbill against the community system, the coalition candidate was victorious.[41] Owen, however, was jubilant; for despite factional strife, his choice had received fifty more votes than had been cast for the successful workingman in the November election. Greater triumphs seemed assured. To his mother he wrote that his name was then as widely known in America as his father's was in

[40] *Address of the Majority of the General Executive Committee of the Mechanics and Other Working Men, of the City of New York; Address of the General Executive Committee of the Mechanics and Other Working Men of the City of New York, Read at a General Meeting of the Working Men, Held at the West Chester House, Bowery, June 21* (N. Y., 1830).

[41] *Commercial Advertiser,* July 9, 14, 15, 1830; *American,* July 15, 1830; *Daily Advertiser,* July 16, 1830; *Daily Sentinel,* July 15, 1830; *To the Mechanics and Working Men of the Fifth Ward, and Those Friendly to Their Interests.*

England, that he and Frances Wright had as much political influence in the state as any other single individual.[42]

The gubernatorial campaign that followed in the next few months rudely shattered Owen's dreams of political power and gave conclusive proof that the May schism among the workers had been suicidal. Late in July, as a result of pressure from other state papers, the warring factions in New York talked of consolidation; but mutual distrust led ultimately to still greater estrangement.[43] In August both groups sent representatives to the state convention of workingmen at Salina. That body, to Owen's disgust, refused to seat the *Sentinel* delegates and then proceeded to nominate two irregular Democratic politicians who withdrew a month before the election in favor of the Anti-Masonic candidate. Owen's followers at once brought forth their own nominees, whereas the *Evening Journal* joined in a "United Interest Ticket," called by some the National Republicans, and supported by Clay men, Anti-Masons, and conservative mechanics.[44] The canvass in the city was no less bitter than it was important. Owen played the role of a party leader, summoning his cohorts to the polls through the columns of both his papers. The outcome was an overwhelming victory for the Democrats, who secured 10,000 votes. The best that Owen's group could average was 2,000, whereas the coalition of conservatives and adherents of the *Evening Journal* obtained 7,000. It was evident that new party lines in New York City had been drawn, and that an independent labor organization could play but a negligible role. The *Sentinel* wing of the workingmen fought on until 1834, but with their merger in that year with the Democrats the movement turned from political action to trade unionism.[45]

[42] *Daily Sentinel*, July 15, 1830; *Free Enquirer*, Sept. 4, 1830; R. D. Owen to Mrs. Robt. Owen, Aug. 12, 1830, Robert Owen Papers, no. 291.

[43] *Daily Sentinel*, July 17, 23, 28, 1830.

[44] *Ibid.*, Aug. 28, Sept. 7, 1830; *Journal of Commerce*, Nov. 1, 1830; *Commercial Advertiser*, Oct. 30, 1830; Commons, *op. cit.*, I, 265–268.

[45] *Daily Sentinel*, Nov. 1, 1830; *Free Enquirer*, Oct. 30, 1830; *Daily Advertiser*, Nov. 8, 1830; Commons, *op. cit.*, I, 268–270.

In the summer of 1829 Robert Dale Owen had urged the mechanics of New York to seek equality of citizenship with their recently won ballot. Slightly more than a year later, as a result of divergent ideologies and tactical blunders, that venture lay wrecked on the shoals of dissension. In the gubernatorial election neither Tammany nor the coalition manifested fear of Fanny Wright, Bobby Owen, or agrarianism. On the contrary, the former inveighed against Anti-Masonry, while the latter's goal was the ousting of the Regency.[46] But though it no longer appeared as a threat to party stability, the Working Men's proved to be a liberalizing force. For all his public utterances that the mechanics would of themselves effect reforms, Owen hoped for no more. From the labor movement, he told Trist, he expected indirect results in the form of changes that ordinary men in public life would ignore if not urged upon them by popular demand. Some progress of that sort was evident in the early thirties. In New York a mediocre lien law was enacted, imprisonment for debt abolished, and the onerous militia duties modified. Private contributions to school societies increased, and it may well be that the triumph of tax-supported public institutions in Pennsylvania in 1834 was made easier by the agitation of the Philadelphia and New York mechanics for equal, republican education.[47]

Owen's chief contribution to the early labor movement was his scheme of state guardianship. In his six essays he revealed the shortcomings of the common schools and fought doggedly those who opposed placing public instruction on a firm, tax-supported basis. Drawing upon his own experience at New

[46] *Courier & Enquirer*, Oct. 27, 28, 29, Nov. 2, 3, 1830; *Journal of Commerce*, Oct. 26, 1830; *American*, Oct. 28, 29, 1830; *Commercial Advertiser*, Oct. 23, 29, 1830.

[47] Owen to Trist, Mar. 16, 1830, Trist Papers, VI; *Daily Sentinel*, Apr. 27, 1831; Frank T. Carlton, "The Workingmen's Party of New York City: 1829–1831," *Political Science Quarterly*, XXII, 415 (July 1907); Dixon R. Fox, *The Decline of Aristocracy in the Politics of New York* (Columbia University, Studies in History, Economics, and Public Law, LXXXVI, N. Y., 1919), 359; William O. Bourne, *History of the Public School Society of the City of New York* (N. Y., 1870), xxii.

Lanark, Hofwyl, and New Harmony, he demanded a broad
curriculum that would include industrial and agricultural training. To be sure, his plan for state boarding schools was rejected as alien to American traditions; and other of his suggestions, notably the use of manual labor for indigent students, did
not receive a fair hearing until brought forward under orthodox
auspices.[48] Yet our modern educational system, with its dependence on heavy taxation, its emphasis on vocational training,
and its increasing attention to proper environmental conditions, has followed in many respects the course charted by
Robert Dale Owen one hundred years ago.

Upon the more immediate problems of the workingmen
Owen's influence was both good and bad. Through *The Free
Enquirer* he gave the cause an early and much needed publicity. Through his editorial and financial assistance a true
labor daily was established. That paper continued to be published after the 1830 debacle and remained true to the wage-
earner even while becoming more Democratic on national issues.
Owen was among the first to advise political action and among
the first to repudiate agrarianism. But political methods failed,
and agrarianism was associated as much with the name of
Owen as of Skidmore. Owen's militant scepticism and former
connection with the New Harmony experiment made him a
questionable ally for a party already radical for its day. His
premature elaboration of and insistence upon state guardianship were equally damaging; for however benevolently the plan
was conceived, it was politically very vulnerable.

The influence of Owen's participation in the early labor movement was not confined to New York. His editorials were frequently copied and commended by the leading mechanics'
journal in Philadelphia.[49] Although Anthony Morris had been
propagating the gospel of Fellenberg since 1827, it was Owen's
description of Hofwyl, given in a lecture at the Hall of Science

---

[48] *Daily Sentinel*, June 16, 17, 1831; Bennett, *History of Manual and Industrial Education to 1870*, 182–192; Barnes, *Antislavery Impulse, 1830–1844*, 38.

[49] *Mechanics' Free Press*, Aug. 15, 29, Sept. 5, 12, 19, 26, Dec. 5, 1829, Jan. 23,
Mar. 27, Apr. 17, 24, May 1, 8, 15, 22, Aug. 21, 1830.

in June 1829, that was copied verbatim into the important report
on manual training submitted by the workingmen of the Quaker
City early in 1830.[50] Owen's six essays on republican education
received widespread notice and discussion. In the Eastern cities
they circulated as a pamphlet, and in New Harmony a town
meeting ordered their printing for distribution throughout the
state. Yet the fact that that gathering continued to advocate
the common school system despite its praise of the essays suggests a limited acceptance of the boarding institution feature in
rural districts. The Hoosiers, for instance, had a real need for
the labor of their family; and, as Madame Fretageot sagely
remarked, "The farmer thinks that if his children are put to
school, they will raise less corn." When Owen returned to the
Indiana environment, he, too, abandoned his boarding school
plan.[51]

In the advocacy of republican education, as in his militant
freethought, Owen clearly established his claim to the title of
an American reformer. Except for a loss of faith in coöperative
communities as a panacea for the ills of an industrial society,
and a less sanguine belief in the rapidity of human progress,
he did not differ very much in the New York years from the
young man who had come to the United States in 1825.[52] Residence in the cosmopolitan East served to develop, confirm, and
disseminate more widely his earlier ideas. The new environment, it is true, did bring contributions of its own. If Owen
had remained at New Harmony, it is unlikely that *Moral*

[50] *Ibid.*, Aug. 15, 29, 1829, Feb. 20, 27, 1830; Joseph J. McCadden, *Education in Pennsylvania, 1801–1835, and Its Debt to Roberts Vaux* (Phila., 1937),
59–63.
[51] *Disseminator*, July 20, 27, 1830; *Free Enquirer*, Aug. 21, 28, 1830; Fretageot to Maclure, Aug. 23, 1830, Maclure Papers. *Handbill III. To the Voters of
Posey County* [July 1836], mounted in "Political Memoranda"; *Indiana Statesman*, Feb. 11, 1843.
[52] In the autumn of 1831 Owen wrote, "I am not over sanguine as to the
effect that this volume may produce. . . . The time is past with me — the early
age of enthusiasm — when I dreamed of thousands of converts, and imagined
that what seemed self-evident to me must therefore so also seem to all my
fellow-creatures." *Discussion upon the Authenticity of the Bible between Origen
Bacheler and Robert Dale Owen* (London, 1853), 2.

Physiology would ever have appeared; certainly the six essays on republican education would never have been written. From the New York years dates Owen's excellence as a writer, controversialist, and public speaker. During that time he adopted political principles that wore well for a quarter of a century. The change from the life of a reformer was yet to come. When it came, it stemmed in thought from advancing age and in action from a different milieu. After that change had come, Owen never again exhibited the ardor or the independence of these early years. But independence brought notoriety, and Owen's reputation as an atheist and a radical died slowly. Many times in his later career he had reason to regret his earlier ultraism, and in the sunset of his life the New York years quite naturally seemed "an earnest sowing of wild oats."

CHAPTER VII

MARRIAGE

LATE in October 1831, before a Hall of Science crowded to capacity, Owen gave a "farewell address" on the influence of the clerical profession. In repeating his earlier strictures on the priesthood and predicting that those agents of orthodoxy would not long survive, he spoke with a moderation and want of animosity seldom before in evidence. After redelivering the lecture in Tammany Hall and again in Wilmington, the reformer boarded the Albany steamboat on November 10 and began the first leg of a long delayed journey to New Harmony.[1]

More than a year before, Owen had known that private business would compel a visit to Indiana. The large estate left by Robert Owen to the management of his eldest sons had not been successfully developed and was barely meeting expenses. In getting clear of his entanglements with Taylor, Fauntleroy and Company, William Owen had drawn upon the financial assistance of the Wright sisters, and his brother felt obliged to look after his associate's interests.[2] For his own part, in severing editorial and business connections with the *Sentinel* a few months before, Owen had suffered along with Frances Wright a loss of some $3,000. Although he still retained "a bare competence," he felt the need of obtaining a larger annual income from his Western property.[3] His mother's death the previous spring, moreover, necessitated a trip to England, and the acquisition of Amos Gilbert as editor was undoubtedly made with that absence in mind. In April 1831 Phiquepal D'Arusmont,

---

[1] *Free Enquirer*, Oct. 29, Nov. 5, 12, 1831, June 9, 16, 1832.

[2] Owen to Maclure, Sept. 4, 1830, Maclure Papers; Wm. Owen to R. D. Owen, [Aug. 1830?], Owen Papers; "New Harmony Estate in Acc't with Robert Owen," [Jan. 1832], Stone Papers; R. D. Owen to Robt. Owen, Mar. 27, 1830, Robert Owen Papers, no. 215.

[3] Owen to Trist, Sept. 26, 1831, Trist Papers, VIII.

who was to marry Frances Wright on his return to Paris, had arrived in New York to conclude such arrangements as would enable Owen to suspend the business which had become too much for him alone, leave the paper in Gilbert's hands, and, after visiting Harmony, take his well earned and much needed vacation in Europe. Not until July, however, had the readers been informed of the forthcoming change.[4]

Owen was still too much of a propagandist to proceed directly and silently to the Wabash. In order to spread the gospel of freethought he made frequent stops as he passed through New York State. At Hudson he combatted the effects of a recent Methodist revival. In Albany his words left a deep impression on the youthful Horace Seaver, later editor of the *Boston Investigator*. At Ithaca Owen met for the first time Orestes Brownson, already well along on his return to orthodoxy. Lectures in Buffalo and Cleveland were equally well received, and the sceptic was delighted to discover that not only was heterodoxy becoming widely tolerated but in some places agnostics and deists outnumbered professing Christians. In Ohio an early cold spell abruptly terminated river travel, and Owen was forced to make the trip beyond Cincinnati on horseback without further addresses on the virtues of free enquiry.[5]

Upon his arrival in New Harmony Owen set about to estimate and improve the financial position of his family. The property of the father and sons was valued at $140,000, but no income was being received from it. In fact the estate was in debt, and its books could be balanced only by collecting other money owed it. The reformer placed his own possessions at $16,500, but its true worth rested upon the prompt disposal of surrounding lots and farms to independent small holders. During January and February Robert and William sold land and houses to the value of $5,000. With characteristic enthusiasm

[4] Owen to Trist, June 8, 1831, Trist Papers, VII; Frances Wright to Robt. Owen, Mar. 26, Nov. 11, 1831, Robert Owen Papers, nos. 457, 445; *Free Enquirer*, July 9, Aug. 27, Sept. 17, 1831.

[5] *Free Enquirer*, Nov. 19, 26, Dec. 3, 10, 17, 24, 31, 1831, Jan. 7, Feb. 4, 18, 1832.

the former talked of the great improvements that were soon to be effected in the town. He hoped that many of his liberal friends in the East would remove to New Harmony. The possibility that Frances Wright and Owen's sisters might settle in the village was mentioned, and it was rumored that the editor of *The Free Enquirer* himself would, within a year, abandon his journalistic post in New York in order to develop his Indiana property.[6]

Behind this intention to make New Harmony his permanent home lay the fact that Owen had fallen in love. It was not strange that in his thirty-first year he should think of marriage. Nothing in his freethought writings precluded such a step, and his associate had already taken it. Ever since boyhood Owen had been accustomed to female company. In New York it had been provided by the Wright sisters whose departure in July 1830 had left "a terrible blank . . . just such a blank — the worst of all — which the loss of intelligent female society always leaves, & which nothing else can effectually replace." [7] There is no evidence that Owen's platonic friendship for Frances Wright had ever turned to true love, although it is possible. More probably, as his later writings suggest, he had come to hold a real affection for the gentler and more feminine Camilla. She, in turn, seems to have reciprocated and remembered Owen generously in her will.[8] In any case, events in 1831 entirely altered the situation. In February Camilla took sick at Paris and died. The tragic circumstances of her death — coming

[6] "Rough Estimate of New Harmony Real Estate, January 1832," "R. D. & Wm. Owen in a/c Current with Robt. Owen," "List of R. D. Owen's Property [Jan. 1832?]," "Sales Effected in New Harmony, Jan. & Feb. 1832," Owen Papers; "New Harmony Estate in Acc't with Robert Owen," Stone Papers. Owen to Trist, Feb. 12, 1832, Trist Papers, VIII; A. Maclure to W. Maclure, Feb. 3, 1832, Maclure Papers; Lucy Say to M. D. Fretageot, Jan. 5, 1832; Maclure to Fretageot [Mar. ?], 1832, Fretageot Papers.

[7] Owen to Trist, Aug. 1, 1830, Trist Papers, VII.

[8] *The Debatable Land* (N. Y., 1872), 350–351, 434, 438 n.; "An Earnest Sowing of Wild Oats," *Atlantic Monthly*, XXXIV, 78 (July 1874); "How I Came to Study Spiritual Phenomena," *ibid.*, XXXIV, 584 (Nov. 1874). The description there given fits Camilla Wright. See also Sarah E. L. Taylor, ed., *Fox-Taylor Automatic Writing, 1869–1892* (Minneapolis, [1932]), 256; Perkins and Wolfson, *Frances Wright, Free Enquirer*, 306, 308–310.

when complete recovery appeared likely — so prostrated her sister that she postponed indefinitely her return to America. When in the summer of 1831 Owen learned what he may have already foreseen, that Frances had married D'Arusmont, whom he disliked, it was evident that the home on the banks of the East River would soon be but a pleasant memory.[9]

Soon after the Wrights had left New York, Owen wrote, "I am very lonely at present," and he contemplated gloomily a solitary winter. By the following February he was "fairly tired of vegetating here alone" and "fighting the battle single-handed."[10] At such a time his thoughts reverted to the family circle across the sea. To his mother he revealed his most inward feelings in a letter worthy of quotation not only for the light it throws upon his character but also for the joy it brought to a maternal heart soon to be stilled forever. After referring to his prominence in New York politics and to the turbulent life of a reformer, he continued,

All this is very foreign to my character, which always was, & still is, a quiet, domestic — almost indolent one. Did I not believe that my presence here is useful, & that it gives impetus to the cause of practical democracy & education, I wd. willingly exchange the bustle for the quiet of retirement. . . . I have, I think, neither so much ambition nor so much perseverance as my father. . . . I am willing to do something — nay a great deal for the public . . . but I am not willing to . . . make myself the public's slave. . . . I am surprised, considering the variety of scenes I have gone through in the last four years, that I am . . . so little changed. . . . They say the world corrupts young men. I see it often does; but I feel, that instead of corrupting, it has done me good. I do not see that I have lost any thing but my inexperience & a considerable portion of my good opinion of mankind. . . . I believe I have as little deceit, dishonesty of any kind, vicious habits or worldly excesses in my character & habits at this moment as I ever had in my life. I mention this — at the expense of modesty — as a proof how powerful early habits &

[9] Frances Wright to Robt. Owen, Mar. 26, 1831, Robert Owen Papers, no. 457; Waterman, *Frances Wright*, 229–231.

[10] R. D. Owen to Mrs. Robt. Owen, Aug. 12, 1830, to Robt. Owen, Feb. 21, 1831, Robert Owen Papers, nos. 291, 396; Owen to Trist, Nov. 1, 1830, Feb. 23, 1831, Trist Papers, VII.

impressions are. How much of those I owe to you, my dr. mother, I shall never forget.[11]

In his loneliness Owen spoke also of Margaret in whose welfare he still took a deep interest. He admitted that he had loved her more tenderly, perhaps, than he might ever love another and that even now he had only conquered his feelings, not lost them. But at a distance he could judge her character dispassionately, and he had no desire to marry her.[12] His father, however, misinterpreted these reflections and late in 1830 made some proposal apparently looking forward to the marriage of his eldest son with the daughter of a mill hand. For such disinterestedness Owen was duly thankful; but with a logic that even the great socialist could not fail to comprehend, he replied,

My own feelings speak even more strongly than you do, in her [Margaret's] favor; but my judgment demurs. . . . I fear — very much fear — she is not *perfectly* sincere. You will say, how *could* she be so? But *if* she is not so, it matters not that we can easily explain *how* that trait in her character was formed. I cannot trust my happiness for life in the hands of one in whose sincerity I have not *perfect* confidence. The venture is too great.

Turning to the less "fastidious" William who had also been attached to Margaret, Owen continued, "I believe he cd. be satisfied & happy with her. . . . He does not, like me, look for all but perfection in a woman. He has not seen, I know, as much of female intellect as I. His standard is fixed far lower; & perhaps, so much the better for him." [13]

It was in such a frame of mind that Owen found himself during his last months in New York attracted by Mary Jane Robinson, daughter of one of the *Sentinel's* supporters. Born in Connecticut in 1813 of Puritan stock, Mary had passed her childhood in Virginia. In 1828 Mr. Robinson moved to New

---

[11] R. D. Owen to Mrs. Robt. Owen, Aug. 12, 1830, Robert Owen Papers, no. 291.

[12] *Ibid.*; R. D. Owen to Robt. Owen, Feb. 21, 1831, Robert Owen Papers, no. 396.

[13] R. D. Owen to Robt. Owen, Feb. 21, 1831, Robert Owen Papers, no. 396.

York City to continue his moderately successful mercantile business, and it was there that both father and daughter became interested in the freethought movement. At the age of sixteen, the latter was one of the few women to hear all of Frances Wright's original lectures at the Park Theater. She proved to be a constant attendant at the Hall of Science where she met her future husband. After hearing him speak, she confided to her sister that, although he was the ugliest man in the world, she would marry him or no one. For a while Owen's semi-isolated life kept them apart, and it was only in the last three weeks before he left for the West and she for Petersburg that they came to know each other intimately.[14]

Owen realized but slowly that he was in love. At first he regarded Mary as a mere child, for she was twelve years his junior. Some of her traits, however, were especially calculated in those days to arouse his approval and admiration. At a time when he was subsisting on milk and water, bread and biscuit, rice and barley, she adopted a vegetarian diet. At a time when he was preaching that women before marriage should become financially independent, she was mastering, to the amusement of her family, a trade. Perhaps it was her bold endorsement of *Moral Physiology* that caught Owen's fancy most.[15] Certainly it was her character and intellect that Owen appreciated, for she had very few European accomplishments. Indeed, as he wrote to Trist, she is "neither pretty nor interesting looking. . . . I am not sure that in twenty-four hours' acquaintance you will find much to like in her. But . . . hereafter . . . you will distinguish the jewel in the rough casket." Modestly but correctly he added, "Neither of us happen to have beauty to boast of." So far as we can reconstruct, Owen at this time

[14] Owen to Trist, Feb. 12, Mar. 20, 1832, Trist Papers, VIII; Mary J. Owen to R. D. Owen, Sept. 14, 19, 1832, Stone Letters; *New Harmony Register*, Aug. 26, 1871; manuscript memoir of Owen written in 1886 by his daughter, Rosamond Dale, in the English Collection.

[15] R. D. Owen to Robt. Owen, Mar. 27, 1830, Robert Owen Papers, no. 215; Owen to Trist, Mar. 20, 1832, Trist Papers, VIII; Mary Owen to R. D. Owen, Sept. 14, 19, 1832, Stone Letters.

was below medium height. His lips were thick, his nose was prominent, and his forehead high. His voice was unmusical. In his blue eyes, fair hair, and sandy complexion one could already see a striking resemblance to his father, a resemblance that increased as the years passed.[16]

"The good sense apparent in every letter" received from Mary while he was in the West tipped the scale in her favor. When Owen contracted to build a house in New Harmony, his secret became generally known. To Trist he wrote that he would marry if he were accepted, and late in February 1832 he ascended the Ohio to learn his fate.[17] After two lectures in Cincinnati, during one of which a stone was hurled through a window in the hall, he hastened on to Petersburg. At Mary's suggestion he remained there several days as a guest before receiving an answer in order that the young couple might come to know each other better. During this brief courtship both exchanged detailed accounts of their early lives; and the conscientious rationalist confessed to his future bride that at a former period he had loved another more engrossingly, though not better, than he now loved her. Within a week, however, Owen was accepted and plans were being made for a wedding in New York. After lingering in Petersburg until late March in order to enjoy the Virginia spring, the happy pair set out together for Washington.[18]

It was in Washington where he and Mary stopped "just to see the lions" that after three years of intimate correspondence Owen first met Trist. In deference to his friend, whom he had repeatedly cautioned against any public handshaking with a heretic, Owen omitted his customary freethought lecture and went sightseeing instead. He filled more than two printed pages

[16] Owen to Trist, Feb. 12, Mar. 20, 30, 1832, Trist Papers, VIII; *Free Enquirer*, Dec. 31, 1831.

[17] Owen to Trist, Feb. 12, 1832, Trist Papers, VIII; Mary Owen to R. D. Owen, Sept. 14, 1832, Stone Letters. Lucy Say to Fretageot, Jan. 5, 1832, Fretageot Papers; A. Maclure to W. Maclure, Feb. 3, 1832, Maclure Papers.

[18] *Baptist Weekly Journal of the Mississippi Valley*, Mar. 9, 1832; *Free Enquirer*, Mar. 31, 1832; Owen to Trist, Mar. 20, 23, 24, 30, 1832, Trist Papers, VIII.

of his paper with a description of the capital, then "rather a scattered aggregation of buildings than a regular town." He inspected both Houses of Congress and through Trist, who had been private secretary to the president, was received in audience by Andrew Jackson. Thus did the reformer properly visit the seat of the government whose citizen he had finally become the previous summer.[19]

On Thursday afternoon, the twelfth of April, Robert and Mary were wed in the Robinson home. The ceremony was performed strictly in accordance with Owen's advanced ideas on marriage and religion and with his then economical scale of living. None of the thirty guests was dressed specially for the occasion; and some, like Amos Gilbert, had been invited but a half hour before. No clergyman was present.[20] By signing a legal form that was attested by the whole gathering, the young couple entered into the bonds of matrimony without promises, prayers, or benedictions. With the propagandist still strong within him, Owen could not refrain from writing on the morning of the nuptials the following statement, intended, however, for the eyes of only his intimate friends:

> This afternoon I enter into a matrimonial engagement with Mary Jane Robinson. . . . We contract a legal marriage, not because we deem the ceremony necessary to us, or useful . . . to society; but because, if we became companions without a legal ceremony, we should either be compelled to a series of dissimulations which we both dislike, or be perpetually exposed to annoyances, originating in a public opinion . . . we do not perceive the utility of unnecessarily braving. We desire a tranquil life in so far as it can be obtained without a sacrifice of principle.
>
> We have selected the simplest ceremony which the laws of this state recognize, and which . . . involves not the necessity of calling in the aid of a member of the clerical profession; a profession . . . we do not recognize, and the influence of which we are led to consider injurious to society. The ceremony, too, involves not the necessity

---

[19] Owen to Trist, Feb. 12, 1832, Trist Papers, VIII; *Free Enquirer*, May 12, 1832; Posey County Circuit Court, "Order Book," E, 233.

[20] Gilbert's description, *Free Enquirer*, Apr. 21, 1832.

of making promises regarding that over which we have no control, the state of human affections, in the distant future. . . .

Of the unjust rights which, in virtue of this ceremony, an iniquitous law tacitly gives me over the person and property of another, I cannot legally, but I can morally divest myself. And I hereby distinctly and emphatically declare, that I consider myself, and earnestly desire to be considered by others, as utterly divested, now and during the rest of my life, of any such rights; the barbarous relics of a feudal and despotic system, soon destined . . . to be wholly swept away. . . .

I put down these sentiments on paper this morning, as a simple record of the views and feelings with which I enter into an engagement, important in whatever light we consider it. . . .

Beneath her husband's signature Mary wrote, "I concur in these sentiments." [21]

For a whole month longer Owen tarried in New York attending to business. Amos Gilbert was to be left again in charge of the paper, aided by weekly contributions from his itinerant chief. To save money the Hall of Science had been sold in the previous autumn, and in May the subscribers of *The Free Enquirer* transferred their social activities to Concert Hall on Broadway.[22] Early that month Owen delivered there an optimistic opening lecture. Already he had noticed on his Western trip the spread of heterodoxy. Now he commented at length upon other indications of human progress; the decline of superstition, the relinquishment of force, and the diffusion of useful, scientific knowledge among the plain people. He predicted a bright future for mankind; and to reformers he held out the consolation, "Men may be sacrified . . . [but] the human race will still survive, will still improve; each coming day richer in knowledge than its predecessor, and every succeeding generation wiser and happier than the last." [23]

On May 16 the Owens, accompanied by Mary's sister and

[21] *Free Enquirer*, June 2, 1832. Gilbert published the statement on his own responsibility during Owen's absence.

[22] *Ibid.*, Nov. 5, 1831, Apr. 28, May 5, 19, 1832.

[23] *Free Enquirer*, Apr. 28, 1832; *Address on the Hopes and Destinies of the Human Species* (London, [1840?]), 16.

Henry D. Rogers, later distinguished as a geologist, sailed for London on the packet-ship *Hudson*. Rogers, who had recently resigned a professorship at sectarian Dickinson College and was then contributing to *The Free Enquirer*, was only one of the excellent company that made the slow and stormy crossing speed by for the happy Owen.[24] The reformer studied navigation, wrote for his paper, and argued interminably on politics and religion with a high Tory, Anglican minister. At Portsmouth he left the party and hurried on to London by land. To one accustomed to the bad roads and endless forests of the American West, the macadamized turnpikes and carefully trimmed landscape of the island kingdom proved a welcome sight. But it was the temper of the nation rather than its beauty that caught Owen's attention. The great Reform Bill had just passed, and the quiet loyalty and orthodoxy that he remembered from his last visit were replaced by excitement and bold inquiry. The calmness with which people discussed the possibility of a revolution made the American think that Europe was soon to be the "New World" and afforded further basis for his optimistic faith in human progress so eloquently expressed before leaving New York.[25]

Many changes had taken place in the Owen family circle since Robert's brief visit to Scotland five years before. Margaret had married. In 1829 his father had severed connections with the New Lanark mills, and shortly afterward Braxfield was given up. Mother and daughters lived for a while at Allen Bank, Hamilton, while the elder Owen centered his activity in London. In October 1830 Ann, who had been partly responsible for bringing Margaret into the household, had passed away; and in the spring Mrs. Owen followed her to the grave. Upon his arrival in England, Owen learned that Mary, his youngest sister, had also died. Jane, the sole surviving daughter, was teaching at the new Association of the Industrious Classes,

---

[24] *Free Enquirer*, May 5, 12, June 2, 9, 16, 23, 30, 1832; *Dictionary of American Biography*, XVI, 94–95.

[25] *Free Enquirer*, Aug. 11, 18, 25, Sept. 1, 1832.

opened on Gray's Inn Road by her father for the benefit of the urban laborers. For Robert Owen at sixty-one was still engrossed in the amelioration of the human race. He had recently commenced *The Crisis*, a small weekly paper; but his chief interest was a labor exchange to which workers could bring their products and receive credit for other goods in proportion to the time they had devoted to the manufacture of their own article.[26]

London is at its prettiest in June, and the young newlyweds spent a delightful month there before continuing to France to join the D'Arusmonts. It was Mary's first visit to England and sightseeing was the order of the day. Comments on the National Gallery, the British Museum, and the theaters and parks filled her letters to Amos Gilbert. Her husband, on the other hand, wrote on current events. He visited Carlile in prison, lectured before his father's society, and participated in its debates. Then, late in July, the original party, except for Jane in the place of Rogers, crossed the Channel by way of Guernsey, Jersey, and St. Malo. France, too, presented a pleasing picture to the friends of liberalism; and seeing the early stirrings of the nation under its bourgeois king, Owen prophesied the speedy establishment of a republic.[27]

At Passy, outside of Paris, Owen found Frances Wright living happily with her husband and daughter. The travelers passed an enjoyable few weeks in that quiet retreat, and it was there that the two reformers finally decided to give up the journalistic enterprise begun four years earlier in *The New Harmony Gazette*. Behind that decision was the fundamental fact that the interests of each lay elsewhere. Camilla's death, a long illness, and the birth of her baby had for some months past completely silenced Frances' voice and pen; and D'Arusmont's opposition made it appear at the time that they would never be heard again. The founder of Nashoba had herself written

---

[26] Podmore, *Robert Owen*, II, 392–394; Robert Owen Papers, *passim*; *Threading My Way*, 230; *Free Enquirer*, Sept. 22, 1832.

[27] *Free Enquirer*, Sept. 1, 8, 22, 29, Oct. 6, 20, 1832; *The Crisis*, June 16, 23, 1832.

only a few months before, "We have all sacrified too much of our worldly ease in attempts to better human society." [28] Owen also felt that his previous exertions entitled him to devote his attention to personal matters. Marriage had increased his financial responsibilities and he could no longer spend his time exclusively in the non-remunerative business of reform. The value of his New Harmony property would depend largely on the supervision he gave to it. Perhaps, too, he was averse to exposing Mary to the torrent of abuse that was the lot of a freethought editor. Two years before, he had told his mother that whenever he thought he could be spared from the struggle, he would leave it. Now, he informed his subscribers in a letter dated August 17, that time had come. The main object of the paper, the establishment of a press free to discuss every topic pertaining to human happiness, had been achieved; and since others could continue the work thus begun, the original conductors felt at liberty to retire to private life.[29]

In taking this abrupt and unexpected leave of his readers, Owen divulged his future plans. With the assistance of his oldest brother he hoped to make New Harmony an attractive Western village and a center of American liberalism. Private property, not communism, would prevail; but the inhabitants might coöperate to form schools, reading rooms, and public lecture courses. Owen stated further that Madame D'Arusmont would move with her family to Indiana in the following spring and that the East River home would be reëstablished on the Wabash. For the present Mary was to remain at Passy to obtain the cultural benefits of a winter in France; while he returned to America, as he was pledged to do, to settle the business affairs of himself and others.[30]

[28] F. W. D'Arusmont to Robt. Owen, Nov. 11, 1831, Robert Owen Papers, no. 445; Waterman, *op. cit.*, 230–231, 238–239.

[29] R. D. Owen to Mrs. Robt. Owen, Aug. 12, 1830, Robert Owen Papers, no. 291; *Free Enquirer*, Oct. 13, 1832.

[30] *Free Enquirer*, Oct. 6, 13, 1832; R. D. Owen to Mary Owen, Sept. 17, Oct. 3, 1832, Stone Letters.

Fortunately for Owen's peace of mind, chance nullified this proposed separation from his bride. Despite pressure from his father to assist in the labor exchange venture and a tempting opportunity to disseminate his freethought writings among the English workers, Owen embarked dutifully but sadly at Gravesend early in October. Twice, however, the boat was forced back by Channel storms; and then, contrary to all assurances, the captain sailed while Owen had gone to London on an errand. As that was the last vessel that could reach America before ice had closed the Ohio, the reformer joyfully agreed to abandon his transatlantic crossing.[31] The incident is not without interest, for Owen's letters written at the time reveal that he was not debating with himself the mere question of remaining abroad a few months. He was thinking of making England the scene of his life's work. New Harmony, he argued, offered a more independent and adventurous career, one in which success rested solely upon his own efforts. London afforded more intellectual stimulus, more opportunity to engage in humanitarian enterprises, and a more healthful climate in which to raise a family. In spite of his recently obtained citizenship and in spite of Mary's known preference for America, Owen could not decide whether he wished the winds to blow him across the sea or delay him. He felt that if he remained in London that winter, he would never settle permanently in the United States.[32]

Under the new arrangement Mary left Passy at once to join her husband, and together they lived at Robert Owen's home in Burton Crescent. The son promptly took a salaried position as secretary of the Association of the Industrious Classes and editor of *The Crisis*.[33] It does not appear that he became superintendent, as his father had wished, of the Exchange Bazaar; and it was just as well that he did not. After a promising few months the undertaking rapidly declined, entailing eventually

[31] R. D. Owen to Mary Owen, Sept. 10, 16, 17, Oct. 3, 1832, Stone Letters. Cf. Jane D. Owen to Mary Owen, Sept. 29, 1832, Stone Letters.
[32] R. D. Owen to Mary Owen, Oct. 3, 9, 1832, Stone Letters.
[33] R. D. Owen to Mary Owen, Oct. 16, 1832, Stone Letters.

a great loss upon its sponsor.[34] Owen, however, was busy enough with his other duties. Like the Hall of Science, the Association held regular lectures and debates, as well as social functions. For a time the Owen family monopolized the rostrum. The father usually spoke Sunday evenings on topics of current interest; but when he was spreading his gospel elsewhere, the eldest son served as substitute. Dale, who had abandoned art for chemistry, commenced with Henry Rogers a series of popular lectures on scientific subjects; and Robert followed with others on physical geography. With some members of the Association the latter formed a Social Missionary and Tract Society and became its president. With others he established a National Political Council which circulated his anonymous tract, *The Anatomy of Taxation*.[35]

Owen's heaviest work came in the conduct of *The Crisis*, a weekly reform journal begun the previous April. Before he assumed control in November, its contents had been confined chiefly to reports of meetings and Robert Owen's writings with very little original matter or comment on current developments. Under its new pilot *The Crisis* quickly showed marked improvement. The brilliant, short editorial piece, sparkling with epigrammatical phrases and bristling with provocative points, was introduced. For more than five months Owen wrote every one of those articles, touching on such varied matters as the progress of the labor exchange, the course of liberalism in France, and the success of manhood suffrage in America.[36] Many essays were copied from *The Free Enquirer*.[37] As a result Owen gave the paper a more controversial and anti-theological tone, but he never lost his sense of fairness. He attacked the various attempts to strengthen the Sabbath laws, the brutal policy of the government in Ireland, and the newspaper stamp duties which he called "taxes on knowledge." His heaviest

---

[34] Podmore, *op. cit.*, II, 408–417; *Crisis, passim.*

[35] *Crisis*, Dec. 15, 22, 1832, Apr. 13, 27, 1833; Francis Place to Owen, n. d., mounted in "Political Memoranda."

[36] *Crisis*, Nov. 10, 24, Dec. 1, 1832, Jan. 12, 19, 26, 1833.

[37] *Ibid.*, Nov. 17, 24, Dec. 1, 8, 22, 29, 1832, Jan. 5, 26, Mar. 16, 23, 30, 1833.

blows, however, were reserved for the indirect taxes for which he urged the substitution of a graduated property levy.[38]

Such leisure as remained Owen improved by supervising English editions of his freethought writings. The Rational Library printed as its first two numbers his speech on the "Hopes and Destinies of the Human Species" and his "Address on the Influence of the Clerical Profession." The six essays on republican education were circulated as a pamphlet.[39] More important were three reissues of *Moral Physiology*. Upon his return from Passy, Owen learned that Francis Place, father of British Neo-Malthusianism, had read the treatise and wished to speak with him. At an interview on September 15 Place apparently gave the work his emphatic approval and asked the American to correct the text, before his departure, for a new edition of 3,000 copies. The elder Owen warned his son of the danger in such a course and advised against it. The latter, however, declared that he wished no reputation inconsistent with the tract and went ahead with his plans.[40] In October an unauthorized sixpence edition, printed while Owen was in France and corrected by a friend, was published by James Watson. A month later the revised version, requested by Place and costing a shilling, appeared under the imprint of James Brooks. It was dedicated, though her name was not mentioned, to Mary; and in the foreword the author declared that as a husband, he could no longer be accused of wishing to destroy marriage.[41] During the winter the reformer received communications which caused him in another edition issued in April to cast some doubt on the wisdom of the check recommended. As an alternative he suggested, curiously enough, Carlile's method, previously condemned by himself as ineffectual, and

---

[38] *Ibid.*, Nov. 3, Dec. 8, 1832, Feb. 2, 23, Mar. 2, 9, 23, 30, Apr. 13, 1833.

[39] *Ibid.*, Oct. 13, Dec. 29, 1832.

[40] Place to Robt. Owen, Aug. 4, 1832, Robert Owen Papers, no. 564; R. D. Owen to Mary Owen, Sept. 16, 1832, Stone Letters. Place to Harriet Martineau, Sept. 8, 1832, Place Papers, speaks less highly of the treatise.

[41] *Crisis*, Oct. 27, Nov. 3, Dec. 8, 1832; *Moral Physiology* (8th edn., London, 1832), i, iii.

passed over the more recent one of Knowlton.[42] Despite this eleventh-hour hesitation, Owen continued to emphasize the necessity for some limitation on population; and his oft-reprinted tract, together with its advertisement in *The Crisis*, gave an important impetus to Neo-Malthusianism in England.

The London winter proved to be a pleasant interlude rather than a vital influence in Owen's life. In the spring he resumed his interrupted journey to America and did not cross the Atlantic again for twenty years. The chief result of his visit was the exalted place he obtained among British secular leaders. For the first and last time the Owens, father and son, were actively associated as equals in reform labors; and in the next generation men like Holyoake and Bradlaugh held their names, for a time, in equal esteem. Owen seems to have been his father's favorite, and the latter cherished fond hopes that in the future his eldest son would return to England to carry on the work.[43] Robert had won, too, the admiration of many Owenites, and his subsequent career in America received much publicity in English freethought circles. The tracts of the New York period were reprinted more frequently abroad than at home and gained for him the title of the best early writer on coöperation.[44] Less aware than their American brethren of the growing conservatism of Owen's middle years, British secularists were deeply shocked by his later religious views, and the cry of apostasy was as loud on one side of the Atlantic as on the other.

On April 19 Owen and his party left London and a few days later boarded the *Hannibal* at Portsmouth for a stormy voyage to New York.[45] Six months in England had not made him wish, as he had feared, to live there permanently. Although urgent business now called the reformer across the ocean, there

---

[42] *Crisis*, Nov. 3, 1832; *Moral Physiology* (10th edn., London, 1833), 50 n., 63–64. This additional note did not appear in all subsequent editions.

[43] R. D. Owen to Mary Owen, Sept. 10, Oct. 16, 1832, Stone Letters.

[44] *Crisis*, Apr. 27, 1832; *The Works of George Petrie* (London, [1841?]), 5; George J. Holyoake, *The History of Co-operation in England* (London, 1875–1877), I, 175–176.

[45] *Crisis*, Apr. 20, 27, 1832; Owen to Trist, June 2, 1833, Trist Papers, X.

is no evidence of his intention to return. The indecision of the previous autumn had disappeared. Financial prospects in New Harmony had brightened while those in London had darkened. In the latter the Exchange Bazaar was ominously approaching disaster; in the former the Owen brothers were given in trust all of their father's American property. With that vast estate Robert hoped to build a sound economic base for his contemplated intellectual paradise on the Indiana frontier. Although Frances Wright had already decided not to remove to New Harmony, Owen did not manifest great regret. Dale and Jane were returning with him, and the latter intended to make her home in the New World if she found it to her liking. In November Trist had written from Washington that his family would join the Owens on the Wabash, and it was hoped that Amos Gilbert and John Baxter would do likewise.[46]

In New York Owen hastened to conclude the business connected with his paper and the book store. At Tammany Hall he bade a final farewell to his old followers and early in July left for the West.[47] Even upon his departure the journalistic scene he had known was changing. A few days before the *Daily Sentinel* had published its last number. In September a former proprietor, Benjamin H. Day, was to initiate the era of the penny press. Horace Greeley had arrived from Vermont in 1831; and James Gordon Bennett, freed from the *Courier and Enquirer*, would soon begin his *Herald*. In 1833 there was a lull in the freethought movement. At Wilmington the *Delaware Free Press* had failed for want of support, and the *Boston Investigator* was threatened with the same fate.[48] The Hall of Science leaders were scattered, Frances Wright in Europe, Kneeland in Boston, and Gilbert in Pennsylvania. Jennings had dropped out of sight. Baxter, Evans, and Vale remained; but within a year the first moved west and within three the second retired, broken in health, to his New Jersey farm. The agnostic

---

[46] Posey County, "Deed Book," F, 260–264; R. D. Owen to Mary Owen, Sept. 17, 27, 1832, Stone Letters; Owen to Trist, Feb. 13, 1833, Trist Papers, IX.
[47] *Free Enquirer*, June 22, 1833.
[48] *Free Enquirer*, July 13, 1833.

debates in Concert Hall lost their old intellectual quality and descended to mere "noise, gesticulation and cant." Under Henry D. Robinson, its new pilot, *The Free Enquirer* discarded all sense of fairness toward orthodox opponents, and an inferior style and typography paralleled its editorial decline. It was suspended temporarily in 1834 and in the following May came to a not unexpected end.[49]

For Owen, removal from New York brought to a close a definite period in his life. It may be too much to say that after 1833 he no longer deserved to be called a reformer, but it is a fact that after that date he was seldom an active participant in the multifarious humanitarian crusades that mark our middle period. Owen was ever the child of his surroundings, and in the next two decades his ties with old associates in the East were to snap, one by one. In the years that were to come his thought and action were influenced by a new environment, one not so congenial to a radical reformer, that of the democratic, individualistic, and self-assertive West.

[49] E. W. Carpenter to Trist, Feb. 11, 1833, Trist Papers, IX; N. H. Hill, comp., *History of Knox County, Ohio* (Mt. Vernon, O., 1881), 194; *Working Man's Advocate*, Mar. 16, 1844. Gilbert left *The Free Enquirer* in October 1832.

PART II
THE WESTERN DEMOCRAT

CHAPTER VIII

VILLAGE LIFE IN THE WEST

NEW HARMONY in August 1833 showed few signs of prosperity. Age was beginning to take its toll of the poorer Rappite structures, and not many new homes had been built in their place. Eighteen months before, Owen himself had praised the town in public but had spoken privately of disorder and neglect. Little population had flowed into the village since the post-community exodus, and the census of 1830 numbered the inhabitants at 626. Most of the talented participants in the social experiment had moved away. Maclure, Troost, and Madame Fretageot were gone, never to return. Tiebout had died, and Neef had retraced his steps to Louisville. Say and Lesueur, as well as William and Richard Owen remained; but the untimely death of the great entomologist was only a year off. In social and intellectual activities there had been a marked decline. No good school existed, and the weekly *Disseminator* had ceased publication. The dramatic corps and the mutual instruction society likewise appear to have been discontinued. With socialistic Utopias a thing of the past, the residents of New Harmony revealed more and more their Western environment — their absorbing interest in crops, speculation, politics, and drink. In short, the village, lacking trade advantages and handicapped by a name that offended decent society, had relapsed into the mediocrity and the crudity of that semi-isolated backwoods region which lay behind the fast advancing frontier.[1]

The adjustment to this environment by a temperate, intellectual, and well born yet radical reformer was one of the finest

[1] *Free Enquirer*, Feb. 25, 1832; Owen to Trist, Feb. 12, 1832, Trist Papers, VIII; [John Scott], *The Indiana Gazetteer or Topographical Dictionary* (2d edn., Indps., 1833), 65; Maximilian, Prince of Wied, *Travels in the Interior of North America* (*Early Western Travels, 1748–1846*, R. G. Thwaites, ed., Cleveland, 1905), XXII, 163–197.

achievements of Owen's middle years. This success came partly from his own extraordinary versatility and adaptability and partly from a deep-seated tolerance that permitted him to ignore surface shortcomings and reach the basic, sterling qualities of human kind. Even in the first few busy weeks while he made preparations for his wife's arrival, Owen showed a willingness to meet his future townsmen more than half way. The decision of the D'Arusmonts to remain in France had put a temporary end to his plans for erecting a new home, and he set about to convert an old Rappite dwelling on the eastern edge of the village. He would have preferred to live, like Richard, on the ridge of hills to the south; but business required a location nearer the town. Owen's spirits ran high as he praised Harmony's natural beauty, jested about the difficulties of getting work done promptly in the backwoods, and related how one farmer had sold him a crib because he had thought that the newcomer was the man most likely to need such an article.[2] To his absent spouse Owen thus humorously described his daily routine:

I am as well as you have ever known me. I am most hospitably entertained at Rosebank & grow fat upon it. I generally rise about five o'clock; & . . . have the pleasure of a mile's ride to breakfast. Rich[d's] breakfast hour is six exactly. After breakfast we usually sit chatting for about an hour; (you shall get me out of this bad habit as soon as you arrive.) Then I mount Mamaluke & gallop him to town to superintend, & lend a hand to the various alterations & emendations by which I endeavor to make an auld house look amaist as weel as new! This, with an interlude of feeding & watering my horse, listening to some backwoodsman's long story who "guesses he'll try to make a trade with me for a quarter . . . if I'll sell cheap;" or perhaps riding three or four miles into the woods with him, to look at the land, or other episodes of a similar character, fill up the time until 12, when Rich[d] dines; &, by that time, what with working & riding I generally have gotten me a famous appetite, as you no doubt wd. devoutly believe cd. you see me at table. Then . . . I set out again on my trusty charger to see that things are all going straight.

[2] R. D. Owen to Mary Owen, Aug. 1, 7, 18, 21, 1833, Stone Letters; Owen to Trist, Feb. 13, 1833, Apr. 30, 1834, Trist Papers, IX, XI.

. . . Today I am going to paint our bedsteads. I return at 6, & at 8 I generally set out for my town abode, there to retire to a solitary chamber & to meditate, my own dear Mary, on her who will soon — would that it were tomorrow! — enliven its solitude.[3]

One unpleasant problem remained to be solved before Owen could settle down to his rustic life. That was a $11,000 debt owed by William and himself to Frances Wright and for the collection of which D'Arusmont had come to New Harmony. Most of this obligation, perhaps all, had been incurred when William in 1830 finally got rid of all ties binding him to the Taylor-Fauntleroy fiasco.[4] To give D'Arusmont sufficient security the brothers proposed to mortgage some of the land just received from their father; but at the last moment they discovered that, since it was held in trust, such a procedure was not possible. Both Robert and William were reluctant to encumber their own property; and it was only after the Frenchman had threatened to place the matter in the hands of a lawyer that another agreement was reached. This settlement, involving the payment of eight per cent interest for fifteen years, led, however, to strained relations; and when Frances Wright returned to America in 1835 she did not visit New Harmony.[5]

At the end of September Mary, together with Jane and Dale, reached the Wabash; and with her arrival terminated the delightful, intimate, and revealing correspondence that had passed between the young couple during their two separations. Enough can be gleaned, however, from that source and others to depict Owen as a husband and father during his early married life. His honeymoon had been one of complete joy. The letters written from Indiana showed not only a glowing optimism but also a dry, engaging humor that seldom came to light again

[3] R. D. Owen to Mary Owen, Sept. 1, 1833, Stone Letters.

[4] R. D. Owen to Robt. Owen, Mar. 27, 1830, to Mrs. Robt. Owen, Aug. 12, 1830, Robert Owen Papers, nos. 215, 291; R. D. Owen to Mary Owen, Oct. 3, 1832, Stone Letters.

[5] Posey County, "Deed Book," F, 250–255, 264–265, 282–284; O, 527–529. A. Maclure to W. Maclure, Oct. 1, 1833, Maclure Papers. The explanation given in Waterman, *Frances Wright*, 238–239, seems inadequate; for Owen's actions there mentioned occurred before his visit to Passy in 1832, at which time his relations with his partner were as cordial as ever.

until late in his public career. Not the least source of his satisfaction was the development of his wife from a timid, un-
worldly girl to an independent, thoughtful woman, capable of
acting in emergencies and sensibly advising her more experienced husband. While in New York, with Robert a thousand
miles away, Jane fell a victim to the cholera epidemic; and
although already with child, Mary nursed her sister-in-law
through a grave, delirious illness.[6] Even at this early period
she acted as a curb upon her husband's undue enthusiasm and
won from him the compliment, "If I had a wife as hasty &
precipitate as myself I know not what I shd. do." [7]

After all he had written on marriage, rationalism in his
marital relations was to be expected from Owen. The statement penned on the morning of his wedding had embodied his
oft-published ideas on life-long affection. This air of detach-
ment led him to petty criticisms that kept Mary in constant
fear because she felt they were so just.[8] When, however, the
husband saw that his wife felt she loved more than she was
loved, he became remorseful. In an important letter given to
self-analysis Owen admitted that he had always set too much
store on the exterior qualities of grace, manner, and beauty.
He begged his bride to remember that, if they were not perfectly suited to each other, they were more so than most people.

Let us then [he wrote], ever bear and forbear. Let us not expect
what cannot be, nor idly lament any thing we cannot change. Shd.
my affections ever seem to you unstable, easily attracted, excited by
fancy or governed by caprice, do not forget, my love, that there are
yet some redeeming points to my character. . . . And underrate not
the influence of your character on mine. Oh believe, that should I
ever love others more, I shall love none better than you. I shall love
none more chastely, more worthily, even if more warmly. And is not
that affection best worth having, wch. is founded on knowledge of
character, on esteem of virtue . . . ? [9]

---

[6] Owen to Trist, Feb. 12, 1833, Trist Papers, IX; Mary Owen to R. D. Owen,
Aug. 8, 13, 1833, Stone Letters.
[7] R. D. Owen to Mary Owen, Aug. 21, 1833, Stone Letters.
[8] Mary Owen to R. D. Owen, Sept. 16, 1833, Stone Letters.
[9] R. D. Owen to Mary Owen, July 25, 1833, Stone Letters.

Thus early did Owen describe his own character. Throughout his life he sought the company of fashionable yet intellectual women, and protracted absences from home on state affairs made it impossible for him and Mary to repeat the intimacy of these first years. But a strong love based on mutual esteem and need never ceased. In all the bitter, unfounded personal attacks made during Owen's long public service, there was no mention of unfaithfulness to his wife.[10] What Robert wrote to Mary in July 1833 continued to be true until that hot August day, thirty-eight years later, when high on Maple Hill behind the village they had both loved so well, he conducted the funeral ceremony of his own beloved wife — "I owe whatever man can render to woman: & that debt of love, so life remain to us, shall be paid." [11]

In *The Free Enquirer* Owen had theorized on the duties and obligations of parents. Now that he was faced with the actual problems, he conscientiously applied his earlier writings to practice. To Trist he reflected,

Are we not bound, when we are about to give birth to sentient creatures, who, but for our voluntary act, wd. never have been called into existence, to consult their future happiness in preference to our own? . . . If there be any moral obligation, any natural responsibility in the world, it is, in my view, the obligation of the giver of life to make that life, to the full extent of his ability, happy. It seems to me highly immoral to confer life, except with such a resolution.[12]

Some two months after reaching New Harmony, Mary gave birth to a large, handsome girl who was christened Florence Dale. The rational husband had insisted on a name at once cultivated, euphonious, and uncommon. The young couple quickly instituted a Spartan regime of light clothes, frequent exercise, and daily baths. A more elaborate program based upon

[10] Four years after his wife's death a story of Owen's faithlessness appeared, but it was immediately denied by his daughter. *Cincinnati Commercial*, July 14, 19, 1875. Mistakes as to time and place are enough to brand the report as fallacious.

[11] R. D. Owen to Mary Owen, July 22, 1833, Stone Letters.

[12] Owen to Trist, Apr. 30, 1834, Trist Papers, XI.

Robert Owen's educational theories was mapped out for subsequent years. At four months the child seemed perfect in
health and conduct, "a fat, laughing, healthy chubby faced infant, with large bright blue eyes, what phrenologists call a
mathematical forehead . . . and as lively as a cricket: in
short just such a marvellous child as all first children are — to
their parents." [13] In the summer of 1834, however, the baby
was stricken and died before completing her first year. Of the
grief felt by the agnostic parents nothing is known, for Owen
made no mention of it in his letters of that date which survive.
But in the Maple Hill cemetery today the curious will find a
flat, weather-worn, stone slab on which is inscribed:

Ephemera all die at sunset; and no insect of this class ever sported
in the rays of the rising sun. Happier are ye, little Human ephemera!
Ye play only in the ascending beams and in the early dawn; and in
the eastern light, ye drink only the first sweet draughts of life; hover
for a little space over a world of freshness and blossoms, and then
fall asleep in innocence ere ever the morning dews are exhaled.[14]

One delightful feature of Owen's life in New Harmony was
the extraordinarily close relations existing between the brothers
and sisters and their families. It is not improbable that during
1833 and 1834 Jane and Dale lived with the newlyweds; and
the former, free until her marriage from the household chores
that burdened the less sophisticated and talented Mary, co-
operated with Owen in various literary and recreational undertakings.[15] Of the brothers William was then, as always, closest
to Robert. He was more handsome and more given to commercial affairs, but the tradition that he was the best business
man of the four is not well founded. All were equally bad.
Dale was absent from New Harmony part, and Richard most,

---

[13] Owen to Trist, Apr. 30, 1834. Cf. Owen to Trist, Aug. 13, 1829, Trist
Papers, VI, XI; R. D. Owen to Mary Owen, Sept. 29, 1832, Stone Letters.

[14] The name was preserved in another daughter born early in 1836. Later
children included Julian Dale (1837), Ernest Dale (1839–1845), Rosamond
Dale (1846), Ernest Dale (1850).

[15] Owen to Trist, Apr. 30, 1834, Trist Papers, XI; Jane D. Owen to Robert
Owen, Oct. 2, Dec. 25, 1834, *New Moral World*, Feb. 28, 1835.

of the three years after 1833. The former was studying at the Medical College in Cincinnati, but his life work was to be in the field of geology. He, too, was good-looking and possessed an even-tempered, attentive, and studious nature. Dick had married in 1828, but after his first wife's death he moved to Cincinnati. There he worked in a brewery until he returned to New Harmony in 1836 to take up farming. Of all the Owens he was the most high-spirited.[16]

In 1835 Jane married Robert Henry Fauntleroy, a handsome and able civil engineer from Virginia. Two years later a triple wedding joined William with Mary Bolton, daughter of a participant in the social experiment, and Dale and Dick with the daughters of Joseph Neef. Owen's new sisters were, he wrote,

as amiable girls as I have almost ever met with. William's wife is the least & the cleverest; Dale's is the most steady & quiet; & Richard's is the loveliest and prettiest. . . . They are not what would be called in England accomplished . . . though they all sing, all dance beautifully & two of them play well on the piano: but their manners are good; for the backwoods particularly good. . . . Richard's wife would be admired for her ladylike appearance, even in fashionable society.[17]

Many a pleasant evening must have been passed in the old Rappite homestead as this large gathering sat before an open fire discussing local crops and politics, reading the latest reform scheme of their father in England, criticizing Dale's newest paintings, or listening to one of Robert's translations of Schiller. Undoubtedly family musicales were held, with Jane at the harp, William at the violin, Richard at the cello, and one of the young wives accompanying on the piano. The moral in-

[16] R. D. Owen to Mary Owen, Oct. 16, 1832, Stone Letters; R. D. Owen to Robt. Owen, May 26, Sept. 29, 1834, *Crisis*, July 19, 1834, *New Moral World*, Feb. 14, 1835; Richard Owen to Robt. Owen, Oct. 3, 1834, Robert Owen Papers, no. 711; R. D. Owen to Richard Owen, Mar. 17, 1836, Neal Letters; *Dictionary of American Biography*, XIV, 116–117.

[17] R. D. Owen to Robt. Owen, May 15, 1837, Robert Owen Papers, no. 889; Nora C. Fretageot, "The Robert Dale Owen Home in New Harmony," *Indiana History Bulletin*, I (extra no. June 1924), 15.

fluence of this talented and sports-loving group was long remembered with gratitude by the children of that day.[18] The
Owens never made the most of the economic opportunities
afforded by their father's property, and financially their lives
were undistinguished; but they did succeed by personal charm,
tact, and intelligence in making their Western village a more
cultured and sociable place in which to live.

Aside from family matters, Owen's primary concerns during
his first years in Indiana were improving the physical and intellectual character of the little village, making a living, and
finding an outlet for his boundless energy. The first of these
problems he attacked at once. Thanks to his initiative there
occurred in the spring of 1834 a general movement to repaint
houses, whitewash fences, and convert vacant lots into gardens.
A subscription was raised to repair streets, construct sidewalks,
provide drains, and build a new road, flanked by a canal, to
the ferry landing a quarter of a mile distant. At the same time
Mary and Jane so successfully broke down a ridiculous class
feeling then existing that a visitor a few years later commented
upon the democratic spirit at the various town functions.[19]

During that same spring a village lyceum was formed to
replace the long since defunct Society for Mutual Instruction.
Owen was the leading spirit and first president of this New
Harmony Institute. The constitution was probably of his making. He donated the building in which the meetings were held,
acted as moderator at the weekly debates, and delivered two
series of regular lectures. Mary and Jane were also active
participants; and Dale, who was just beginning to fit up his
laboratory, may have given some scientific talks. At first the
Institute was a phenomenal success, boasting over one hundred
members and drawing to its monthly social gatherings people
from Mt. Vernon and Princeton. In less than a year, however,

[18] Francis D. Bolton, "Autobiography" (MS.).
[19] Owen to Trist, Apr. 30, 1834, Trist Papers, XI; R. D. Owen to Robt.
Owen, May 26, Sept. 29, 1834, *Crisis*, July 19, 1834, *New Moral World*, Feb.
14, 1835; *Disseminator*, July 19, 1834; Mrs. John Baldwin to W. Maclure,
Aug. 19, 1839, Maclure Papers.

the requirement of dues began to cause trouble, and during 1835 and 1836 the organization steadily declined. But before it passed out of existence, the New Harmony Institute had inculcated a spirit of good fellowship in the village and had revealed the value of coöperative study. Shortly after its demise the idea was revived under the auspices of William Maclure in the Workingmen's Institute which still exists today.[20]

Even more important than facilities for adult education was a proper provision for instructing the youth. The elaborate system of schools projected during the social experiment had never advanced far beyond the paper stage, and Maclure's post-community efforts had met with a similar lack of success. In 1832 the inhabitants subscribed $400 and the Owens were prepared to contribute the necessary land and buildings in a desperate attempt to locate the county seminary, a mixed institution for elementary and secondary students, at New Harmony; but Mt. Vernon captured the prize. The ostensible reason for that decision was that the land offered was held in trust, but it is quite possible that the local officials feared that benefits of the improvement would accrue chiefly to "two great Aristocratic landholders," Robert Owen and William Maclure.[21] The gift thus rejected Owen promptly placed at the disposal of the district school, an elementary institution provided for by state law but dependent upon local authorities for its management and support. Once again the reformer was disappointed. The school never functioned properly; and Amos Gilbert, who had been expected to come West to take charge, failed to put in an appearance.[22]

[20] *Disseminator*, July 19, Aug. 2, 9, 1834; *Free Enquirer*, Sept. 7, 1834, Jan. 4, 11, 1835; R. D. Owen to Robt. Owen, May 26, 1834, *Crisis*, July 19, 1834; Mary Owen to R. D. Owen, Nov. 6, 1834, Stone Letters; Manuscript list of members, dated Mar. 1, 1836 (LWI). T. J. de la Hunt, comp., *History of the New Harmony Workingmen's Institute* (Evansville, 1927).

[21] W. Maclure to M. D. Fretageot, [Mar. ?], 1832, Fretageot Papers; A. Maclure to W. Maclure, Oct. 1, 1833, Maclure Papers.

[22] A. Maclure to W. Maclure, Oct. 1, 1833, Maclure Papers; R. D. Owen to Robt. Owen, May 26, Sept. 29, 1834, *Crisis*, July 19, 1834, *New Moral World*, Feb. 14, 1835; R. D. Owen to H. D. Robinson, July 6, 1834, *Free Enquirer*, Sept. 7, 1834.

The most ambitious of all of Owen's educational schemes was the stillborn New Harmony Manual Labor College. That type of institution was being regarded with more and more favor by liberals of all shades, and as early as August 1834 Owen sought the assistance of William Maclure. Despite grandiose dreams of making Thomas Cooper president, he won the support of the sceptical younger Maclure. In February the state legislature approved a charter for the college; and in the next summer Owen, soon to be elected president, addressed a printed circular to his former followers in the East appealing for financial aid. Although the advantages of an industrial and agricultural training in a healthful, inexpensive residential village, boasting of two libraries and a chemical laboratory, were glowingly set forth, the public response was feeble. The Owen brothers had offered to bestow upon the college property worth $5,000 as soon as a contingent fund of $10,000 had been subscribed, but not a tenth of that sum was ever raised.[23] Local hostility did not impede donations, for most of the near-by papers noticed the scheme favorably. Rather the enterprise was conceived on too vast a scale. In the Western country day schools were difficult to organize; and there was no demand for more costly boarding institutions, literary or agricultural. Owen's project suffered also from a lack of the cohesive religious spirit that was so instrumental in founding schools in the wilderness; in fact it was quickly set down as an abode of infidelity. By 1836 its sponsor was already losing interest; and in the end, the net result of his agitation was to draw a few liberals to the Wabash and attract the attention of others who hoped that a new communal experiment might be commenced there.[24]

[23] A. Maclure to W. Maclure, Aug. 14, Dec. 8, 1834, Maclure Papers; *Disseminator*, Dec. 6, 1834, Feb. 28, May 9, 1835; *Circular Addressed to the Friends of Liberal Education in General and to the Former Readers of The Free Enquirer in Particular* (n. p., n. d.); *Beacon*, June 5, 1841.

[24] *Disseminator*, May 9, 1835; Corydon *Investigator*, Oct. 19, 1835; *Evansville Journal*, cited in *ibid*. *Trumpet*, Nov. 21, 1835. A. Maclure to W. Maclure, Feb. 15, 1836. Wm. Amphlett to Maclure, Feb. 16, 1838, Maclure Papers; Lewis Masquerier to Robt. Owen, Feb. 6, 1836, Robert Owen Papers, no. 770.

In its failure to establish decent schools, elementary, secondary, or collegiate, New Harmony was neither better nor worse than the majority of its neighbors. But aside from the mutual instruction society, it did boast of two other undertakings not then common in other Hoosier villages of similar size. One was the weekly *Disseminator* which, when it was revived in June 1834, was the only periodical in Posey, Vanderburg, or Gibson counties. The cultural significance of the newspaper in the days before the cheap magazines, the cinema, and the radio should not be underestimated. Equally important was the renewed activity of the Thespian Society, founded in 1828. Enthusiasm for amateur dramatics ran high in 1834, and a climax was reached early the next year as a contemporary letter indicates.

The whole town [wrote one citizen] is agog in getting up the play of William Tell. R. D. Owen is as much Interested in it as if the fate of the Republic depended on it and everything is ransacted to find the proper costumes of by gone days. Mrs. Owen, Jane & William and all are to take part. Rehearsal has been taking place at the Hall & at R. D. Owen's House for nearly a month past altho the Play is not to be acted till 28 feby. . . . Mr. Leseur [sic] has been engaged and is still in Painting some new Scenery for the occasion. . . . The people from far & near are coming. . . . The president of the Bank at Evansville . . . & the Cashier who is a musical man is to take part. . . . They are trying to get Mr. Neef into the orcastra. . . .[25]

Heralded by flattering notices in neighboring towns, the piece made such a success that it had to be repeated a month later. Thereafter theatricals which were frowned upon as immoral in most Western communities became a regular part of New Harmony's social life, and the excellence of the performances was commented upon by travelers.[26]

Owen's active participation in all of the town's public functions did not completely dissipate his restless energy. Quite in-

[25] A. Maclure to W. Maclure, Dec. 29, 1834, Maclure Papers.

[26] *Disseminator*, Feb. 28, 1835; *Evansville Journal*, quoted in *ibid.*, Feb. 7, 1835; New Harmony Thespian Society, "Minutes" (MS.); *New Harmony Register*, Jan. 3, 17, 31, 1874. *Beacon*, Oct. 21, 1837.

tentionally he kept his pen busy; for, as he told Trist, during "some years past I have spent so much time in writing for the press that to have a literary undertaking in hand has become almost a habit with me. It is a habit which I see not the use of breaking myself of. . . ."[27] Thus after 1832 he contemplated several projects: a biography of Galileo, a romance centered about Bartolomé de las Casas, the Apostle of the Indies, a simple essay on manners, and a more elaborate work on American national traits and political institutions.[28]

Unfortunately the topic he finally settled upon was much less happy than any of the foregoing. An excellent prose writer, gifted with a fund of anecdote, Owen might well have expanded the letters he had written for *The Free Enquirer* while on his travels in 1831 and 1832 into a valuable picture of America in the age of the common man. He had shown himself to be a shrewd observer in citing incessant attention to "party politics and prices current" as a distinctive American characteristic. He had not confused civility with a want of servility, and he had manifested a friendly appreciation of the independent qualities of the Western backwoodsmen.[29] To describe such a people would have been worth while. But by wandering into the field of poetry for the purpose of portraying Indian character and illustrating the possibilities in historical dramaturgy, Owen succeeded in writing a tragedy which, after obtaining a brief notice in its day, has long since been relegated to obscurity.

In choosing the theme of Pocahontas, Owen's motives were didactic, and he proceeded along scholarly lines. Therein lies the drama's greatest fault as literature. So strict was his historical accuracy that he created only two imaginary characters, both of secondary importance. Every principal event in the tragedy may be found in Captain Smith's own narrative, and even authentic speeches and charters were fitted into Eliza-

---

[27] Owen to Trist, Apr. 25, 1834, Trist Papers, XI.
[28] "Notes on Galileo" (MS.) ; Owen to Trist, June 23, July 9, 1833, Apr. 25, 1834, Trist Papers, X, XI; R. D. Owen to Mary Owen, Sept. 4, 1833, Stone Letters.
[29] *Free Enquirer*, Dec. 24, 31, 1831, Jan. 7, Feb. 18, 1832.

bethan blank verse. In each case the author supported incidents, utterances, and mention of aboriginal customs by copious
notes.[30] The two dramatists who had previously written on
the theme had been bothered by the fact that the natural climax,
the rescue of Smith by Powhatan's daughter, came early in the
story. In *Pocahontas, or the Settlers of Virginia* (1830) George
W. Custis had abandoned all chronology and had made the
deliverance the finale of his drama. James N. Barker's *Indian
Princess* (1809) had preserved the order of events but had
added a second rescue at the end.[31] Owen not only retained the
original sequence but refused to invent any new facts. "I have
preferred," he explained, "making what I could out of the
genuine materials before me; rather at the expense . . . of its
chances of popularity in representation." He coveted a reputation for accuracy in national portraiture rather than for fer-
tility in poetical ingenuity.[32]

During his leisure moments in the winter of 1835–1836
Owen completed his research on Indian character and embodied
it in a five-act tragedy in poetry and prose. Eighteen months
later it was printed in New York under the pseudonym of "A
Citizen of the West" as *Pocahontas: a Historical Drama in
Five Acts; with an Introductory Essay and Notes.* The author's
opinion, expressed in the foreword, that it was "a useful work,"
worthy of perusal, will hardly be accepted by the modern
reader.[33] The action is too drawn out and deficient in dramatic
effect. The character delineation is moderately successful
though better suited to a novel than a play. The poetry has no
lofty passages, but its blank verse may have been appreciated
by a generation raised on Shakespeare. The best lines are found
in a ballad, the words of which were altered from a poem of
Felicia Hemans to fit an old Scotch air.

[30] *Pocahontas: a Historical Drama in Five Acts* (N. Y., 1837), 21–22. Cf.
ibid., 183.
    [31] Arthur H. Quinn, *A History of the American Drama from the Beginnings
to the Civil War* (N. Y., 1923), 139–140, 272.
    [32] *Pocahontas*, 21, 222.
    [33] R. D. Owen to Richard Owen, Mar. 17, 1836, Neal Letters; *Pocahontas*, 20.

'Tis home where'er the heart is,
  Where'er its living treasures dwell;
In cabin or in princely hall,
  In forest haunt or hermit's cell.

'Tis bright where'er the heart is:
  Its fairy spells have pow'r to bring
Fresh fountains to the wilderness,
  And to the desert vernal spring.

'Tis free where'er the heart is,
  Nor rankling chains, nor dungeon dim
Can check the mind's aspirings,
  The bounding spirit's pealing hymn.

The heart gives life its beauty,
  Its warmth, its radiance, and its power,
Is sunlight to the rippling stream,
  And soft dew to its drooping flower.[34]

Whatever its merits may be, *Pocahontas* should not be classified as a literary contribution of the West. The careful preparatory research was not typical of that region. The Indians portrayed were those of the frontier of 1607, not those of the Black Hawk War. Only in his praise of American forests and in his characterization of Captain Smith as a good democrat did Owen reflect the environment in which he wrote.[35] In one quotable passage a spirit of Manifest Destiny appeared.

Albeit this land conceal not, in her bosom,
Rich mine of gold, or bed of orient pearl;
Albeit Arabia's perfumes breathe not out
From her primeval forests; nor Cathay's
Odorous spices load her green savannahs;
Yet she is blessed with better riches — such
As make a nation prosperous and great:
With soil, as rich as India's self can boast;
Forests, might build a navy for the world;
And noble rivers, an untaxed highway,

---

[34] *Pocahontas*, 74. Cf. *ibid.*, 219 n.
[35] *Ibid.*, 160–162; Ralph L. Rusk, *The Literature of the Middle Western Frontier* (N. Y., 1926), I, 425.

Down whose wide-spreading waters, in rude craft,
The wealth of provinces may safely glide.
A sun, that's warm and bright; a territory,
That stretches from the tropic to the pole.
Needs but the hand of industry, and here
Cities may rise, shall rival Europe's marts,
And States spring up, shall, one day, bear away
The palm of greatness from the Eastern World.[36]

The anonymous publication of *Pocahontas* in October 1837 brought forth lavish praise from James Brooks, editor of the lately established *New York Daily Express*. Brooks, himself a writer of merit, reviewed the tragedy in a leading editorial and declared it to be "an honor to the country, and to American literature." He commended its style as reminiscent of Shakespeare and expressed astonishment that so chaste a work could have come out of the West. Brooks's encomiums might have been more restrained if he had known that the author was the former associate of Frances Wright, whose renewed appearance on the lecture platform in New York was then the subject of scathing attacks in his paper.[37] Other Eastern editors lauded the sterling qualities of the play, and these tributes were eagerly seized upon by political journals in the West, where the dramatist's identity was quickly discovered. Partisan applause engendered partisan criticism, and Owen's adaptation of the Hemans poem exposed him to the charge of plagiarism.[38] In general, however, transmontane commentators regarded the tragedy with sectional pride. The most significant fact of all was that *Pocahontas* attracted enough attention to secure for its author a literary reputation, often exaggerated to be sure, at the very time he was embarking upon a career of public service.[39] That renown was not without value in an age when

---

[36] *Pocahontas*, 55.

[37] *Daily Express*, Oct. 10, 1837. *Ibid.*, Oct. 18, 19, 20, 24, 1837.

[38] *N. Y. American*, Oct. 14, 1837; *Boston Investigator*, Oct. 27, 1837. *Indiana Democrat*, Oct. 25, Dec. 26, 1837; *Logansport Herald*, Dec. 14, 28, 1837, Jan. 4, 1838.

[39] Louisville *Enquirer*, Feb. 17, 1838, mounted in "Political Memoranda"; *Indiana Statesman*, Aug. 30, 1845.

Western politicians were widely regarded as demagogic ruffians, more adept with the bowie knife than with the quill.

As a theatrical production *Pocahontas* was never a success. Its first performance in New York City on February 8, 1838, was damned by bad acting and worse stage management. There is no record of any subsequent revival.[40] A year later the drama was produced under the crudest possible conditions in Indianapolis by William Lindsey's professional company. Early in 1839 the troupe repeated the performance at Logansport and probably at Peru and Ft. Wayne.[41] Tradition states that the tragedy was put on by amateur groups in both the Hoosier capital and New Harmony.[42] Owen himself never had great faith in his work as a dramatic masterpiece; and it is unlikely that he ever desired, except in the vagaries of an unbalanced mind near the close of his life, to have it staged again. *Pocahontas* was his first and last venture into the field of poetical drama. Yet it is of interest if only to illustrate his extraordinary versatility. Of the four books he had published by 1837, one was a descriptive outline of his father's schools, one a pioneer treatise on birth control, one a scholastic controversy on the reality of God and the authenticity of the Bible, and the last an historical tragedy in blank verse.

The one remaining aspect of Owen's village life to be considered is the prosaic business of making a living. In this instance his many efforts to make New Harmony a progressive Western settlement coincided with self-interest, for his economic status depended on the rapid occupation of the land in and about the town. For that reason he constantly advertised local advantages in Eastern and English papers, and he did his

---

[40] *Beacon*, Feb. 10, 1838; George D. Odell, *Annals of the New York Stage*, IV (N. Y., 1928), 200; Quinn, *op. cit.*, 273.

[41] Reminiscent account of Austin H. Brown, quoted in the *Indianapolis Star*, Jan. 15, 1921. Local histories disagree on the date of Lindsey's performance. My conclusion is based on Owen's reference to the troupe in his letter, signed "Tullius," in the *Indiana Democrat*, Dec. 22, 1838 and the notice in the *Logansport Herald*, Feb. 14, 1839.

[42] Jacob P. Dunn, *Greater Indianapolis* (Chi., 1910), I, 460–461; *New Harmony Register*, Jan. 10, 1874.

part in organizing the Posey County Agricultural Society and the New Harmony Jockey Club. The Owen brothers derived jointly income from rentals on their father's estate and together they embarked on various speculative and commercial enterprises. One of these was a $6,000 investment in Josiah Warren's new rapid printing press. Another of Robert's special hobbies at this time was the raising of mules and fine horses for sale in the New Orleans market.[43]

Upon his return to New Harmony in 1833 Owen hoped that a few years hence would see him financially independent. The general prosperity that preceded the speculation and subsequent panic of 1837 gave substance to these hopes. The rising price of produce had by 1833 almost doubled land values in four years, and this rise was sustained after a brief decline in 1834. Trade on the Wabash became heavier, and the younger Maclure wrote that people were not only getting out of debt but also showing a disposition to buy land.[44] Expectations stirred by these signs were raised further when it became evident that a state-wide system of canals, railways, and good roads was to be constructed. Owen was not oblivious of the growing sentiment for internal improvements. In the spring of 1835 he began to purchase lots at Evansville, where property was to increase in value four hundred per cent in eighteen months, thereby giving the Owen brothers a $7,500 profit over a three-year period. Hoping for a similar boom at Mt. Vernon, Owen continued to speculate extensively.[45] Neighbors began to doubt his

[43] *Crisis*, Sept. 29, 1832; *New Moral World*, Feb. 14, Dec. 5, 1835; *Free Enquirer*, Sept. 7, 1834; *Disseminator*, July 19, 1834. *Ibid.*, Sept. 19, Oct. 3, 1835; [Walter R. D. Owen], *A Glimpse of the Early History of New Harmony* (Evansville, 1898), 10–15; Owen Papers, Maclure Papers, *passim*. For the financial relations of Robert Owen and sons see Posey County, "Deed Book," G, 35–39; M, 394–400; Robt. Owen to R. D. Owen, June 10, 1837; R. D. Owen to Robt. Owen, Sept. 4, 1837, Owen Papers; R. D. Owen to Robt. Owen, May 15, 1837, Sept. 18, 1844, Robert Owen Papers, nos. 889, 1338.

[44] R. D. Owen to Mary Owen, Aug. 7, 9, 19, Sept. 4, 1833, Stone Letters; R. D. Owen to Robt. Owen, Sept. 29, 1834, *New Moral World*, Feb. 14, 1835; *Disseminator*, May 30, 1835; A. Maclure to W. Maclure, May 26, Dec. 7, 1835, [Feb. 5, 1836?], Maclure Papers.

[45] R. D. Owen to Richard Owen, Mar. 17, 1836, Neal Letters; "Statement of the Owen Bros., 1837-8-9," "Papers Connected with . . . Mount Vernon En-

business competency, but he remained confident. In March 1836 he was thinking of paying off the entire debt to the D'Arusmonts, and to his brother he confided, "We are *getting on*." [46]

At that very moment the development of New Harmony, and with it Owen's economic security, were being seriously threatened. In January 1836 the much discussed plan for internal improvements became law, and to the dismay of Owen and his friends no public work was allotted to Posey County. Not only was New Harmony to be left without the necessary means of communication with other parts of the state; but the improvement of the Wabash, along which Owen's property lay, was to be subordinated to the construction of a rival canal passing through the adjacent counties of Pike, Gibson, Warwick, and Vanderburg. The people of Posey were faced with a discouraging increase in taxes for projects which would not directly benefit them. The law of 1836 was, in fact, a challenge to the leading citizens of New Harmony; it was the immediate cause of Owen's entrance into state politics. In one sense, his venture into public affairs may be regarded as another of his many efforts, noticed in this chapter, to make New Harmony a distinctive Western village.

The years from 1833 to 1836 mark the transition to the second major period of Owen's life. It was in these years that he came to know and love the Western people whom he so ably served for two decades. Upon the ruins of his father's exotic community that had not been, and never could have been, an integral part of Hoosier society, he sought to build a progressive town along lines acceptable to public opinion but with an intellectual and liberal spirit all of its own. Some success had crowned his efforts. The disorder and idleness that had followed in the wake of the disastrous social experiment gave way to enterprise and enlightenment. New Harmony never lost its

---

largement," and indentures dated May 22, 1835, Mar. 24, Apr. 7, June 2, July, Aug. 10, 1836, Apr. 5, 1837, Owen Papers.

[46] A. Maclure to W. Maclure, Feb. 15, 1836; A. E. Fretageot to Maclure, Sept. 12, 1836, Maclure Papers; R. D. Owen to Richard Owen, Mar. 17, 1836, Neal Letters.

reputation for learning; and when David Dale Owen began his work, it became an outpost of science as well. Not all of Owen's expectations were fulfilled, to be sure, in these years. But even if he had established a manual labor college or had collected a circle of freethinkers on the Wabash, he could never have led an idle, retired life. Some work, literary, journalistic, reform, even scientific perhaps, would have absorbed his restless spirit. As it was, the internal improvement issue turned his attention to politics, and political advancement became the predominant interest of his middle years. Even when, a quarter of a century later, he sought privacy to study a new religion, the national crisis of secession demanded his services anew; and Owen's public career did not end until ten years before his death.

CHAPTER IX

STATE POLITICS

THE Indiana law of 1836 was not an isolated phenomenon upon the American scene. Ever since the close of the second war with England there had been a growing demand for better facilities of transportation. Among the states New York had led the way with her Erie Canal, and a decade later Ohio broke ground for the first of her public works. The Hoosiers were not immune to this universal enthusiasm for internal improvements; and their acceptance in 1826 and 1828 of two federal land grants for projects connecting the Ohio and the lakes provided an entering wedge for a state-wide system of their own. After eight years of lobbying and log-rolling a powerful bi-partisan bloc appropriated in January 1836 $10,000,000 for eight major works designed for national utility while benefitting sectional interests. In the populous and wealthy southeastern corner of Indiana a canal was to follow the Whitewater Valley between Lawrenceburg and Cambridge City. The Wabash and Erie Canal, for which the grant in 1828 had been made, was to be extended south of Lafayette to Terre Haute. A railroad was to bear in a northwesterly route from Madison to Lafayette by way of Indianapolis; and a second one, or a macadamized road, was to run in the same general direction only through the counties to the south, connecting Jeffersonville and Crawfordsville. A modern turnpike was to be laid upon the old stagecoach route from Vincennes to New Albany. An appropriation was made for the improvement of the Wabash, and a survey authorized for a future canal or railway from Ft. Wayne to Michigan City. The most daring and expensive enterprise of all, however, was the Central Canal that would begin on the upper Wabash and enter the Ohio at Evansville. This work, to be linked by cross-cut waterways with the Whitewater and the Wabash and Erie

Canals, was to follow river routes south to Indianapolis, parallel the White to its forks, and then cut overland to Evansville.[1]

The "Mammoth Bill" of 1836 undoubtedly represented the demands of the people of Indiana. All groups favored improvements in the abstract, and when criticism arose, it came mainly from those counties not directly benefitted. Such a one was Posey, and it was there that Owen took the lead in protesting against the details of the proposed system. For the chief purpose of procuring for his county its share of the public works he decided to enter politics and late in March 1836 announced his candidacy for the lower house of the legislature. Although he was at once lauded as the champion of education, Owen's own contemporary statement, as well as the conduct of his campaign, showed that his real interest was in internal improvements.[2] His very first act was to write to the state administrative board recommending the survey of an alternative route for the Central Canal that would both benefit Posey and save the people of Indiana $300,000. Shortly thereafter, under the pseudonym of "Tullius," he penned three widely copied letters entitled "Indiana's Great Work," the really first critical discussion of the recently enacted law. The system, he concluded, would never be abandoned, nor did he desire such a step. To add new works, he believed, was financially dangerous; to leave some counties unprovided for was politically dangerous. Minor revision in the interest of economy and justice was Owen's solution in the spring of 1836.[3]

Having taken his stand on the foremost issue of the hour, Owen next placed his political principles before the electors. In the first of three handbills issued during May and June, he

[1] Logan Esarey, "Internal Improvements in Early Indiana," Indiana Historical Society, *Publications*, V (Indps., 1912), 41–102.

[2] *Disseminator*, Mar. 26, 1836; *Evansville Journal*, quoted in *ibid.*, Apr. 16, 1836. Owen's contemporary statement, found in his scrapbook "Political Memoranda," contradicts the later, idealistic assertion that he desired to effect certain reforms, given in the untrustworthy "Recallings from a Public Life. Western People and Politicians Forty Years Ago," *Scribner's Monthly*, XV, 258 (Dec. 1877).

[3] *Disseminator*, May 28, 1836; Indianapolis *Indiana Journal*, June 11, 25, July 23, 1836.

tackled boldly two objections raised against his candidacy; his foreign birth and his wealth. Then, as always, Owen's reply to partisan nativism was that America was his country by choice, not by chance. As to his riches, he pointed out that all his property lay in Posey so that any vote made in Indianapolis to aid himself would benefit his constituents as well. In his second handbill he described his plan to alter the route of the Central Canal and dwelt upon the advantages such a change would bring to the county. In the last he pledged his allegiance to the Democratic party and outlined its tenets as he understood them.[4] It is not altogether surprising that the propertied Owen should have opposed the cohorts of Webster and Clay. Trist was staunch Jacksonian; and such diverse figures as Robert Owen and Orestes Brownson regarded the Democrats as the exponents of reform. The *Daily Sentinel* had supported their policies; and while its editor, Owen had written an article that was copied into the national organ on the theme, "the world is governed too much." [5]

In a spirited canvass that drew forth more votes than the subsequent presidential contest, Owen won a decisive and not unexpected victory. His opponents were James R. E. Goodlet, the able and persevering late president of the circuit court, and Kenner Crallé, an honest and plain farmer. No issues seem to have divided the candidates; and Owen owed his success to diligent campaigning, his appeal to the Board of Internal Improvements, his "Tullius" letters, and to a lavish but legitimate use of his own money to obtain public works for the county. He was forced to combat an abusive pamphlet containing extracts from *Moral Physiology* with suggestive comments by Goodlet. Acting boldly, Owen placed every copy of his treatise that he could find in the hands of respectable citizens for examination and in a fourth handbill in July denied the licentious character of the work. He declared that the tract had been

---

[4] These handbills are mounted in "Political Memoranda."

[5] Owen to Trist, Apr. 28, 1831, Trist Papers, VII; Robt. Owen to Martin Van Buren, May [?] 20, 1833, Robert Owen Papers, no. 641 (copy?); *Daily Sentinel*, Apr. 4, 1831.

written in self-defence and was better suited to England than America, yet he was ready to justify its contents at any time or place other than a political meeting. Goodlet's tactics met with little success, and Owen's majority mounted to the largest ever obtained in a Posey legislative election up to that time.[6]

Shortly after Owen's triumph enthusiasm in New Harmony for internal improvements reached its climax. Spurred by the speculative sentiment that followed in the wake of the Mammoth Bill, its leading citizens arranged an extensive and widely advertised sale of farm lands and town lots. In the public notices the wildest prophecies regarding the future of the region were indulged in. Of Chainville, an isolated spot on the river nine miles south of New Harmony, it was said that "eligibly situated at the foot of . . . the first rapid . . . it bids fair from its advantageous location to become the Louisville of the Wabash Valley." It was there that Owen envisaged the beginning of the last portion of the Central Canal that was to unite at Mt. Vernon the waters of Lake Erie with those of the Ohio. Even stolid Alexander Maclure was moved to write,

Many think we have caught the Land Mania the rage of the day. . . . I am . . . not at all averse to making some excitement so as to induce people to come here examine and judge for themselves for I am of opinion we have here local advantages which very few Places in the State possess. . . .[7]

This sale, coinciding with the annual fair and the Jockey Club races, gave New Harmony a thrilling few days in October; and it was with high hopes of obtaining for his county the public works that would make these expectations a reality that Owen late in the following month saddled his horse and began the long ride northward to the state capital.

[6] The result was: Owen, 775; Goodlet, 250; Crallé, 201. On the election see Owen's notes in "Political Memoranda"; *A Candidate's Defence against a Base Accusation*, mounted in *ibid.*; A. E. Fretageot to Maclure, Mar. 29, Sept. 12, 1836, Maclure Papers. Owen had subscribed $200 for the proposed canal survey and had loaned the state $300 for a turnpike survey, ordered but not appropriated for by the legislature.

[7] *Vincennes Saturday Gazette*, Oct. 1, 1836; A. Maclure to W. Maclure, Oct. 18, 1836, Maclure Papers.

Indianapolis in 1836 was only beginning to lose its title of "the capital in the wilderness." Less than twenty years had passed since the first pioneer located on its site; and despite the removal of the state government thither in 1825, its population a decade later numbered but 3,500. The town boasted of no important manufactures, suffered from want of good roads and navigable water, and supported papers that barely deserved the name of state party organs. Yet at no time before the arrival of the iron horse was there more excitement and hope than in 1836. The Mammoth Bill meant much to the infant capital. Situated as it was at the junction of the proposed National and Michigan Roads, the Madison and Lawrenceburg railways, and the Central Canal, its inhabitants were already dreaming of their future as the "Railroad City."

On Monday, December 5, 1836, the Twenty-First Session of the General Assembly of Indiana met in the recently completed Doric capitol. After a week occupied in preliminary organization, during which Owen was placed on the Committee of Education, the lower house turned to the all absorbing question of public works. The last election had left the powerful bi-partisan internal improvements bloc with a majority of more than thirty; and its leaders, triumphant after a difficult struggle, opposed all modification of the original act lest the sectional balance therein attained be destroyed.[8] Their position was outlined in Governor Noah Noble's message. Indiana, it said, had staked her fortune upon a law long discussed and passed at the behest of the people. To meet the large debt that would be incurred by the program the state had just received a windfall in the form of the federal government's distribution of its surplus revenue. Something might be done to placate the disaffected counties; but since construction had been begun on every project, there was no retreat that was either safe or honorable.[9]

[8] *Indiana Journal*, Aug. 20, 1836.
[9] Indiana General Assembly, *House Journal*, 21st Session (1836–1837), 19–20, 25–28 (Dec. 6). By an act of June 23, 1836 Congress provided for the distribution among the several states of the surplus revenue then in the United

These words convinced Owen that his original plan to revise the law of 1836 and alter the route of the Central Canal was futile. Tacking on a different course, he supported a bill which, because it was smaller than the previous year's was familiarly called the "calf." Its purpose was to provide improvements for those counties hitherto neglected. The first "calf" bill was referred to a select committee; and on December 19 Owen reported an amended version appropriating a little less than $2,000,000, a fifth of the former grant, in small amounts for county turnpikes, new surveys, and subscriptions to private enterprises.[10]

This report initiated a bitter four-day debate during which Owen spoke twice. His maiden effort, abounding in historical allusions and aptly chosen phrases, set forth the necessity and justice of the bill. Half the counties, he asserted, would derive no substantial good from the law of 1836; and their representatives must now either obtain additional works or curtail the tax burden that would fall upon their constituents. The majority hastened, in response, to scotch this uprising. No law, it was argued, could directly benefit every county; but that of the previous year had at least created a unified system, whereas the present one was a catch-all. One member dragged the abortive New Harmony experiment into the debate; while his colleagues assailed the proposed change as excessive in cost, inconsistent in principle, and designed to destroy the progress already made. Owen spoke a second time but in vain. On December 22, in an almost full house, the "calf" was overwhelmingly rejected; and it was thus decided early in the session that there would be no wholesale additions to the act of 1836. Four weeks later a veto of Owen's special bill for a clay turnpike in Posey revealed a similar opposition to the inclusion of new single works in the system.[11]

States Treasury. It was thought at first that Indiana would receive $1,500,000. Indianapolis *Indiana Democrat*, Nov. 16, 1836.

[10] *House Journal*, 21 Sess., 97; *Indiana Democrat*, Dec. 23, 1836.

[11] *House Journal*, 21 Sess., 103, 265 (Dec. 22, Jan. 17); *Indiana Democrat*, Dec. 23, 27, 1836; *Indiana Journal*, Dec. 27, 31, 1836, Jan. 4, 7, 21, 25, 1837.

These defeats left Owen in a difficult position. He seemed unable to aid his county in any way. With their large majority the system men, as they came to be called, bade fair to sweep all before them, including the disposal of the surplus revenue. Already Owen had on several occasions expressed his willingness to finance the "calf" bill with that gift.[12] But in an attempt to score some triumph in the general rout, he boldly reversed his stand, opposing its use for internal improvements and seeking to divert at least a part to the support of public schools, a matter in which his constituents had shown interest.[13] At first Owen's eloquent speech of January 11 praising the benefits of education fell on deaf ears. Six days afterwards a bill was reported reserving the interest on the surplus revenue for the payment of the debt being created by the public works program.[14]

At this juncture Owen resorted to a successful stratagem. Perceiving a division among the majority between those who would place the surplus revenue in bank stock and those who would distribute it among the several counties, he instructed his followers to vote against first one proposition and then the other always with the purpose of preventing the passage of either. Out of the deadlock created by these tactics arose a compromise between Owen and Joel Vandaveer that placed all of the federal money in the hands of the counties but allotted a third of the interest to the Common School Fund. On January 23 this bill passed an astonished House and then was so amended in the Senate as to give half of the interest to education. Much as Owen preferred that amendment, he stood loyally by the compromise until Vandaveer, losing his nerve, himself violated the agreement. That step left Owen free to support the Senate version which, after another struggle, became law.[15]

[12] *Indiana Democrat*, Dec. 23, 27, 1836.

[13] *Indiana Democrat*, Jan. 13, 1837.

[14] *Ibid.*; *House Journal*, 21 Sess., 273.

[15] *House Journal*, 21 Sess., 325–327, 406, 411 (Jan. 23, 30, 31) ; *Indiana Democrat*, Jan. 24, 31, Feb. 8, 1837; *Indiana Journal*, Feb. 1, 1837; Owen's notes in "Political Memoranda." See also Harlow Lindley, ed., "Robert Dale Owen and

By skilful tactics and wise concession Owen had won a victory that brought satisfaction to his constituents and credit to himself. In later years, when the system of 1836 had broken down under its own weight, leaving its authors in disrepute, Owen could boast of having saved something from the whirlpool of disaster. By a fortuitous chain of circumstances he had diverted to the only means of supporting the Hoosier public schools not one third, as he had proposed, not a half, as the Senate demanded, but two thirds of the federal surplus revenue.[16] But although Owen deserves credit for his efforts, it should be remembered that he might never have become, at that time, a benefactor of Indiana education if the internal improvements party had not rejected his "calf" bill.

In spite of his failure to secure for Posey a share in the public works program Owen could count his first term in the legislature a success. No member had come nearer to extending the original system, and none had been more influential in passing the annual revenue bill which imposed an honest pay as you go policy.[17] The cause of schooling had benefitted from his presence; and several reform bills, to be discussed later, had been brought forward. Owen's ability was promptly recognized. At home he was praised for his eloquence and perseverance, and regret was expressed that he had not been in the legislature when appropriations for improvements were more liberally made. At the capital he was regarded as the leader of the anti-system group, and to him fell the honor of delivering the patri-

Indiana's Common School Fund," *Indiana Magazine of History*, XXV, 52–60 (Mar. 1929).

[16] The sum originally expected was $1,500,000. This was reduced to $1,100,000 of which the first two installments were given to the Common School Fund. When the federal government withheld the fourth payment, education had received $573,502 of the $860,254 distributed. W. A. Rawles, *Centralizing Tendencies in the Administration of Indiana* (Columbia University, *Studies in History, Economics and Public Law*, XVII, no. 1, N. Y., 1903), 56–59.

[17] *Indiana Journal*, Jan. 21, 1837. *Ibid.*, Feb. 18, 1837; *Indiana Democrat*, Feb. 8, 1837; *House Journal*, 21 Sess., 431–432 (Feb. 1). Owen's estimate is in *To the Citizens of Posey County* [Apr. 10, 1837], mounted in "Political Memoranda."

otic Eighth of January oration.[18] On this record Owen sought
reelection; and although compelled by the death of Mr. Robinson to be absent from New Harmony much of the spring, his
triumph was never in doubt. Crallé, his chief opponent, avoided
the public meetings where Owen was advocating a policy of
classification, that is, limiting the financial risk by completing
only one or two of the major works at a time. Instead he sought
political capital by spreading false rumors and exposing his
rival's alleged immorality. His tactics, however, proved fruit-
less. In a somewhat lighter vote than the previous year, Owen
was reelected by a greater majority and with a larger percentage
of the total votes cast.[19]

The foremost issue in the Twenty-Second Session was classification. Until then that policy had been thrust aside partly because it was thought unnecessary but mostly because the Board
of Internal Improvements contained at least one member actively interested in each project. During his first term Owen
had voted for a resolution favoring classification but only
after the failure of his "calf" bill. In the spring of 1837 the
matter was discussed before the people, and the election of
David Wallace in August as governor was everywhere interpreted as a repudiation of the proposal.[20] Encouraged, however,
by retiring Governor Noble's remarks on "the evident impolicy"
of completing all the works simultaneously, the classifiers revived the idea early in December 1837. With the scales of
self-interest fallen from his eyes, Owen then stepped forward
at last as a determined and indefatigable champion of retrench-
ment. A startling speech in which he placed the actual cost of the
program of 1836 at $25,000,000 instead of the $10,000,000 an-

[18] A. E. Fretageot to Maclure, Feb. 9, 1837, Maclure Papers; *Indiana Democrat*, Jan. 6, 13, 1837; *Indiana Journal*, July 28, 1838, a review of the past
two sessions.

[19] The result was: Owen, 757; Crallé, 301; Edson, 23. *Beacon*, Sept. 2, 1837;
Owen's notes in "Political Memoranda"; *A Few Explanations from a Candidate*,
mounted in *ibid.*

[20] *House Journal*, 21 Sess., 292–293 (Jan. 19). *Indiana Democrat*, Mar. 5,
Apr. 12, 26, May 3, 31, June 7, 1837; *Indiana Journal*, Apr. 15, 22, 29, May 13,
June 3, 1837. *Ibid.*, Aug. 26, 1837.

ticipated was partly responsible for the astonishing ballot on December 13. Although the gubernatorial canvass had supposedly settled its fate, classification was defeated by only four votes.[21]

Emboldened by this moral victory, Owen's group continued its fight to save the credit of the state. Discarding the scheme of classification because of the sectional antagonisms it necessarily aroused, the members sought instead to alter the character of the more expensive works while leaving the system as a whole intact. Owen quickly pointed out the path that these modifiers, as the minority came to be called, were to take. In a widely circulated speech on January 15, 1838, he substantiated with statistics his earlier assertion that the system would ultimately cost $25,000,000; and he proposed to transform part of the Madison and Lafayette Railroad into a less expensive macadamized turnpike. This innovation the House accepted, but his other changes the system men refused to grant.[22] They resisted all attempts to reduce the size of the unwieldy Board of Internal Improvements or to limit by law its expenditures for any one year. They ignored Owen's plea that a twenty-cent ad valorem property tax was necessary to keep the state's books balanced; and in the Senate the ten-cent levy, specifically reserved by the House for public works, was halved to accord with the previous year's impost.[23]

Since their reforms had been blocked in both branches of the Assembly, the modifiers took their case to the people. At a large meeting held in the Hall of Representatives on the day before the legislature adjourned, Owen read an address reviewing the attempts made during the session to secure economy in administration and repeating word for word his own speech on the alarming condition of the state's finances. This document,

[21] *House Journal,* 22nd Session (1837–1838), 15, 17, 35, 63–64, 70, 75–76 (Dec. 5, 6, 11, 12, 13). The vote of 51–47 is to be contrasted with that of 63–29 on Jan. 19, 1837. Owen's speech is found in a clipping from the *Indiana Democrat* of December 1837, mounted in "Political Memoranda."

[22] *House Journal,* 22 Sess., 278–279, 551 (Jan. 15, Feb. 2); *Indiana Democrat,* Jan. 19, 1838.

[23] *House Journal,* 22 Sess., 299–300, 759 (Jan. 17, Feb. 17); *Indiana Democrat,* Feb. 9, Mar. 9, 1838.

adopted and signed by forty-eight members of both parties, did not urge the abandonment of the system but rather a prudent -retrenchment in carrying it to completion.[24] Modification thus became the issue for 1838; and Owen, now fully recognized as its champion, was reelected, as all had expected, though by a greatly reduced plurality.[25] Elsewhere in the state the Whigs triumphed, but the domination of the system men was so threatened that in September the Democratic organ advanced Owen's name for the speakership. The choice met with some approval, and late in November Owen agreed to become a candidate.[26] At the last minute, however, he stepped aside in favor of a Whig modifier only to see the internal improvements bloc reelect the presiding officer of the previous year.[27]

Modification of the system of 1836 along the lines marked out in the last session was Owen's chief concern during his third term. His earlier prophecies regarding the precarious state of Hoosier finances, so bitterly impugned when made, had proved to be only too true; and even Governor Wallace in his annual message betrayed slight signs of apprehension. In the House the speaker gave Owen's group control of the select committee raised to frame a new modification bill.[28] Owen's draft, presented on January 2, was bitter medicine for the system men to swallow, and it led to three weeks of stormy and violent debate during which the outcome was always in doubt. On one occasion a fisticuff between George H. Proffit and Samuel Judah caused an immediate adjournment after which a general scuffle ensued.[29] In the end it was Owen's perseverance and

[24] *Indiana Democrat*, Feb. 23, 1838.

[25] *Indiana Journal*, Mar. 3, 1838. See Owen's notes in "Political Memoranda"; John Beal et al to Maclure, Apr. 22, 1838; Amphlett to Maclure, July 5, 1838, Maclure Papers. The result was: Owen, 798; Arza Lee, 518.

[26] *Indiana Journal*, Aug. 25, 1838; *Indiana Democrat*, Aug. 29, 1838. *Ibid.*, Sept. 5, 1838. *Disseminator*, Oct. 4, 1838; Terre Haute *Wabash Enquirer*, Oct. 7, 1838; *Mt. Vernon Courier*, quoted in the *Indiana Democrat*, Oct. 10, 1838.

[27] Owen's letter in the *Indiana Democrat*, Dec. 8, 1838; *House Journal*, 23rd Session (1838–1839), 5 (Dec. 3).

[28] *House Journal*, 23 Sess., 18–20 (Dec. 5); *ibid.*, 9 (Dec. 4).

[29] *Ibid.*, 192–198. *Investigator*, Jan. 24, 1839; Lawrenceburg *Political Beacon*, Feb. 2, 1839.

wily legislative maneuvering rather than his brilliant, widely copied speeches that carried the day. Although once rejected, he brought up his bill a second time and on three successive days framed three different amendments to a disputed section. On January 23 his tenacity was rewarded; and amid the applause of crowded galleries, the Modification Act, almost identical with Owen's original proposal, passed by a large majority.[30] The triumph of the revenue bill a few weeks later marked the final acceptance of the demands of the representative from Posey. The same House that a year before had refused his plea for a property tax of twenty cents or more now hastily levied one for thirty cents in order to bolster the faltering credit of the commonwealth.[31]

After a difficult struggle lasting more than two sessions, the administration of Indiana's public works program was placed on a sound basis. Classification was virtually adopted. Annual expenditures were limited, a small executive board was established, and the ruinous policy of borrowing to pay interest prohibited. Although his course was not altogether consistent — at various times he advocated revision, addition, caution and change — Owen deserves more credit for the result than he has heretofore received.[32] His speech of January 15, 1838, was among the first to show with facts the real cost of the system; his parliamentary tactics, beginning with the Madison Road Bill and ending with the Modification Law, were characterized by wisdom, resolution, and fearlessness. Modification, unfortunately for the state, came too late. In August 1839 work on all projects had to be suspended for want of funds. Partly as a result of poor management, partly as a result of hard times, but

---

[30] *Indiana Democrat,* Jan. 12, Feb. 28, 1839; *House Journal,* 23 Sess., 300, 325–330, 339, 355 (Jan. 17, 21, 22, 23); *ibid.,* 358–359; *Leavenworth Arena,* Jan. 31, 1839.

[31] *House Journal,* 542–543 (Feb. 12); *Indiana Democrat,* Feb. 20, 1839.

[32] Esarey, "Internal Improvements in Early Indiana," *loc. cit.,* makes no mention of Owen's work. Owen himself later subordinated this achievement to his activity in education and woman's rights. "Western People and Politicians Forty Years Ago," *loc. cit.* In 1852 he still believed it better to spend $11,500,000 on eighty counties than $10,000,000 on forty. *Indiana State Sentinel,* Apr. 26, 1852.

chiefly as a result of having embarked on an undertaking far beyond her means, Indiana faced bankruptcy and in the next years gained a most unenviable reputation in the financial centers of the world.

The curb placed upon a reckless, ill-digested program of internal improvements and the unexpected addition to the Common School Fund were Owen's most important achievements in his three years as a legislator. Other matters attracting little notice at the time, however, deserve brief mention as the first steps in his later work. Foremost among these were his attempts to obtain for married women greater control of their own property. Such a reform had been frequently advocated in *The Free Enquirer* and had served as a topic for debate in the New Harmony Institute. Early in 1835 an incident in his village gave Owen fresh proof that an unjust provision of the common law gave husbands complete command of their wives' possessions.[33] Yet in the legislature Owen acted conservatively. In his first term he merely inquired into the expediency of adopting Louisiana's civil code on the subject and introduced a bill that permitted women about to marry to retain their chattels by means of a previous contract. There was nothing mandatory about the proposal and it did not extend to real estate.[34] The next year he reported an act to alter the common law so far as it applied to the property rights of married women, but leave to print was not even granted.[35] In his last session Owen left the question untouched. The reform evoked no popular enthusiasm among the Hoosiers, and similar indifference prevailed elsewhere. Neither Chancellor Kent nor Supreme Court Justice Story, to whom Owen sent copies of his bill, were willing to endorse the suggested change; and when Ernestine L. Rose petitioned the New York legislature in 1836 on the same subject, she could obtain the signatures of only five women.[36]

---

[33] *Disseminator*, Jan. 31, 1835.

[34] *House Journal*, 21 Sess., 118, 397 (Dec. 26, Jan. 30); *Indiana Democrat*, Feb. 8, 1837. A printed copy of the bill is mounted in "Political Memoranda."

[35] *House Journal*, 22 Sess., 312–313, 575 (Jan. 19, Feb. 8).

[36] Kent to Owen, June 1, 1837; Story to Owen, July 29, 1837, mounted in

Closely allied to the injustice perpetrated by the common law upon married women was that which denied to the widow of an intestate the greater portion of her husband's possessions. Under the existing Indiana statutes the wife received but a third of his real and personal property, the former during her lifetime only; while the rest descended to the children, grandchildren, parents, brothers, and others more remote of kin. But on this matter, too, Owen did not proceed as a radical innovator. He did not insist uncompromisingly upon a change, but waited until the old law of descent came before him and another, acting as a sub-committee to revise the statutes of the state. He then proposed to give the widow two thirds of the husband's personal property and one third of his real estate in fee absolute. At the outset the House seemed hostile to the idea, which was described by one delegate as a subtle plot "to subvert the whole system of society"; but after a warm debate in which Owen spoke eloquently in behalf of the unrepresented fairer sex, the committee report, only slightly amended, was carried by acclamation.[37] The omission of this enlightened law from the revised code five years later compelled Owen to do the work over again in 1851 and 1852.

The only other step taken by Owen at this time in woman's behalf did not stamp him as a radical reformer. To Indiana's already liberal divorce law he merely added one more cause for separation, habitual drunkenness for two years.[38] Later in the century when the Hoosier state had become a haven for unhappy husbands and wives throughout the nation, Owen was wrongly accused of being responsible for its lenient statutes; and despite his denials the misconception has persisted even in scholarly books of the present day.[39]

"Political Memoranda"; *History of Woman Suffrage* (Elizabeth C. Stanton, Susan B. Anthony, Matilda J. Gage, eds.), I (N. Y., 1881), 98–100.

[37] *House Journal*, 22 Sess., 235, 522 (Jan. 9, 30); *Indiana Democrat*, Feb. 23, 1838; undated article in *ibid.*, mounted in "Political Memoranda"; "Western People and Politicians Forty Years Ago," *loc. cit.*, XV, 262.

[38] *House Journal*, 22 Sess., 235, 669 (Jan. 9, Feb. 10).

[39] Owen's letters in the *Family Visitor*, May 17, 1849; *N. Y. Daily Tribune*,

Except for his adroit handling of the surplus revenue, Owen was not in these years an outstanding champion of Indiana's public schools. To be sure he defended more than once that initial victory, he attended the Education Conventions that were held each winter at the capital, he made futile attempts to obtain funds for the State Library, and he began his distinguished service as trustee of the infant university at Bloomington. His apt statement that "The world is governed too much and educated too little" became a standard resolution at local Democratic gatherings.[40] Yet the fact remains that during these years Owen and his colleagues failed to organize an efficient free school system. An excessive decentralization in administration was permitted to continue; and an earlier measure, allocating certain state taxes to the support of elementary institutions, was repealed in 1837 without any violent protest by the former editor of *The Free Enquirer*. An attempt made in his last term to improve conditions was lost in the Senate.[41] This educational failure, it is true, may be explained by the universal craze for internal improvements which cast all other tax-supported enterprises in the shade, but the fact that it can be explained does not conceal the reality of the shortcomings.

To humane legislation, as to common schools, the General Assembly during Owen's tenure gave scant notice. Social consciences are less easily stirred in pioneer settlements; and even where enlightenment reigns, the means with which to act are usually wanting. It should be remembered, too, that in 1836 the Perkins Institution was in its infancy and Dorothea Dix

---

Mar. 5, 1860; "An Earnest Sowing of Wild Oats," *Atlantic Monthly*, XXXIV, 76 (July 1874). Cf. *Dictionary of American Biography*, XIV, 119; Arthur C. Cole, *The Irrepressible Conflict, 1850–1865* (*A History of American Life*, A. M. Schlesinger and D. R. Fox, eds., VII, N. Y., 1933), 171–172.

[40] *House Journal*, 23 Sess., 110, 188–189, 281–282 (Dec. 14, Jan. 1, 16); *Beacon*, Mar. 23, 1839. *Indiana Journal*, Jan. 21, 1837, Jan. 5, 12, 1839; *Indiana Democrat*, Jan. 5, 1838. *House Journal*, 23 Sess., 67 (Dec. 11). Indiana General Assembly, *Local Laws, 1837–1838*, 296. *Indiana Statesman*, Feb. 10, 1844.

[41] *House Journal*, 21 Sess., 431–432 (Feb. 1); *ibid.*, 23 Sess., 414–426, 603 (Jan. 29, Feb. 14); *Indiana Journal*, Feb. 16, 1839; Rawles, *op. cit.*, 28–34, 61–62.

had not begun her crusade. The most that Owen did was to introduce one resolution to abolish capital punishment and another to prohibit the use of solitary confinement, the last being an indirect criticism of the famous Pennsylvania system of penology. Neither proposal became law, nor did the recommendations of a general report by Owen and others in 1839 on the treatment of the insane. As a matter of fact, every one knew that the state in its existing financial straits would never levy taxes for benevolent institutions, and effective action had to await the removal of the incubus of internal improvements.[42]

The three years after 1836 are of importance in Owen's biography quite apart from his successes or failures in the legislature. They mark the beginning of the ascendancy of the politician over the reformer. In this new role Owen did not renounce his liberal philosophy or bow on every occasion to party exigencies. But life in a new environment and the conservatism that came with age brought an end, publicly at least, to the extreme notions and bold expressions of the New York years. In answering an attack upon his alleged radicalism, Owen himself confessed

that, some eight or ten years ago, I was somewhat ultra in my notions of moral and political reform, I am free to admit. A man who thinks for himself and is good for anything, is, in early youth, almost necessarily an ultra-reformist. In that fresh and sanguine season, the warm conviction of what ought to be, often precludes the calm observation of what is. As one advances in years, one is gradually led to the unwelcome conclusion, that it is far easier to detect than to correct errors, and to distinguish deficiencies than to supply them. One becomes less confident in one's own wisdom and more deferring to usage and experience. . . . I am not sure that we are much better or happier for this worldly wisdom; yet it cures us, at least, of dogmatic self-sufficiency, and we lose our relish for propagandism.[43]

To his new career Owen brought certain assets and certain liabilities. Awkward gestures and a rasping voice prevented his

---

[42] *House Journal,* 21 Sess., 92 (Dec. 17); *ibid.,* 23 Sess., 227, 337, 349–350 (Jan. 8, 22, 23); *Indiana Journal,* Feb. 9, 1839.

[43] Owen to the editor, Jan. 22, 1838, Washington *Madisonian,* Jan. 30, 1838.

being a great orator; yet his carefully prepared speeches, crammed with pertinent facts, embellished with literary quotations, and delivered in a persuasive manner, were remarkably effective. Their argumentative qualities reflected his experience as a controversialist just as their felicity of expression betrayed his training as an editor. For bills in legislative hall and resolutions in party caucus Owen's pen was invaluable.

At a time when the talents of Western editors were measured by their virulent abuse of political opponents and the credence that any glaring misrepresentation could obtain, Owen's radical past left him exceedingly vulnerable. The social experiment at New Harmony was not then regarded with pride by Hoosiers, and the doctrines preached in *The Free Enquirer* were not calculated to find favor among a people predominantly Methodist, Baptist, and Presbyterian. It was unnecessary for many copies of his gazette or of *Moral Physiology* to find their way west of the mountains; mere mention of the titles was enough to incriminate Owen. Often a judicious selection was made by one paper, copied by a dozen others, and then filed away to be dragged forth at each ensuing election.[44] Early in his political career Owen showed himself extremely sensitive to such personal attacks, and he was quick to answer these canards in long public letters of denial or explanation.[45]

In spite of partisan editorial sniping the people of Indianapolis were convinced, after three winters, that Owen was no dangerous radical, harboring principles inimical to everything

---

[44] The quotation most frequently used came from the Bacheler debate where Owen argued that if he believed the Biblical statement that all power was of God, he must necessarily believe all the Revolutionary patriots were consigned to hell. He added that he did not believe that, but partisan editors ignored the proviso and called his argument an insult to all true Americans. *Free Enquirer*, Oct. 15, 1831. Jacob P. Dunn, *Indiana and Indianans* (Chi., 1919), I, 459, has stated without evidence that *Moral Physiology* circulated widely among the Hoosiers. The present writer agrees with Milton Gregg, a contemporary critic of Owen, that the treatise would have been little known in Indiana if its title had not been repeatedly mentioned by politicians. *Madison Daily Tribune*, June 10, 1851.

[45] *Logansport Herald*, Dec. 28, 1837; *Indiana Democrat*, Feb. 23, Nov. 28, 1838; *Political Beacon*, Oct. 27, 1838; *N. Y. Express*, Jan. 30, 1838.

decent and good. During that period he won a wide circle of friends in both political camps. Significantly enough, he was on the best of terms with Governor Noah Noble, the father, if any one may so be called, of the system of 1836.[46] While at the capital Owen first met many of his future Congressional colleagues: Joseph A. Wright, the typical self-made man of the West; independent, outspoken John Pettit; and Andrew Kennedy, the eloquent but boisterous blacksmith. The redoubtable Jesse D. Bright was still unheard of, but during the session of 1839 Owen sat near Joseph Lane, not yet raised to heroic proportions by the Mexican War. All in all, the more worldly and talented Scot found much to admire and respect in the Hoosier farmer-legislator. He probably disliked the religious zeal and prudish hypocrisy of many of his new associates, but he acted in the words of the poet he was then so fond of quoting,

> Shall I ask the brave soldier who fights by my side,
> In the cause of mankind, if our creeds agree?
> Shall I give up the friend I have valued and tried,
> If he kneel not before the same altar with me?
> From the heretic girl of my soul shall I fly,
> To seek some where else, a more orthodox kiss?
> No! Perish the hearts and the laws, that try
> Truth, valor, or love, by a standard like this! [47]

With the emergence of new interests and new friendships came a corresponding decline in old. While in the legislature, Owen made no contribution to liberal periodicals and outwardly severed all connection with the freethought movement in the East. In 1839 he was made an officer of the United States Moral and Philosophical Society, but he took no part in its proceedings. Vale, Kneeland, and the latter's successor, Horace Seaver, did not choose to notice publicly this growing aloofness. On the contrary, they pointed with pride to the political progress

---

[46] Owen to Noble, Nov. 12, 1836; N. Noble to Catherine Noble, Apr. 24, 1836, Noble Papers; Owen to Catherine Noble, Jan. 19, 1840, Valette Smith Collection.

[47] *Indiana Democrat*, Jan. 19, 1838. Cf. *N. Y. Daily Sentinel*, Apr. 8, 1830; *Free Enquirer*, Dec. 31, 1831.

of an agnostic and continued to reprint, advertise, and sell his early writings.[48] But with Frances Wright came the final rupture of a once beautiful friendship. The few weeks at Passy in 1832 was probably the last occasion that the two met; and after the adjustment of the debt by D'Arusmont the next year, even direct correspondence was broken off.

Late in 1836, when Owen was launching his career upon the stormy sea of politics, Frances resumed her freethought agitation as a lecturer and associate editor of the *Boston Investigator*. Shortly thereafter Owen wrote privately to Kneeland, Vale, or some other journalistic friend in the course of which he asked about his former partner, adding by way of explanation that a misunderstanding between himself and another, not Madame D'Arusmont, had caused a lapse in their correspondence. In some way the letter was seen by the subject of the inquiry, who interpreted it as a veiled attack upon her husband. With her usual impetuosity, she printed a signed editorial rebuking Owen for making a private matter public and saying,

Mr. Owen is well aware, that not one act, but a course of action, brought, but too fully and too painfully, to my knowledge, forced upon me the conviction that his principles were not my principles; and that, consistently with a rule of conduct . . . which he (Mr. Owen) knows me to have followed in cases somewhat similar to his own, I interrupted at once and forever, all intercourse with him. From that time forward all such communications as business might necessitate, have been conducted solely by my husband; between whom and Mr. Owen there has never been any misunderstanding. . . . If there should be aught in the above observations displeasing to Mr. Owen, he will admit that they have been forced from me.[49]

This unexpected castigation brought evident pain to Owen, for he could not admit it had been called for. He felt that he had done nothing to warrant a public reprimand by one for

---

[48] *Beacon*, Oct. 12, 1839, Jan. 6, 1840. *Ibid.*, Sept. 2, 1837, Dec. 22, 1838, Mar. 23, June 22, 1839, July 11, 1840. *Boston Investigator*, Mar. 2, 1838, Jan. 11, Mar. 27, 1839.

[49] *Boston Investigator*, Mar. 10, 1837.

whom, apparently, he still retained cordial feelings.[50] At once he wrote to Kneeland denying he had overstepped any line of propriety and explaining that his original inquiry had been made in a private letter, addressed to an editor in his private capacity.[51] With regard to the sentence that had aroused Madame D'Arusmont's ire, he said,

a remark more charitable, less calculated to offend, I can hardly imagine, expressed in a private letter, too, never published, and never, of course, intended for publication. My former co-editor dissents from my opinion. That is very natural. We are all poor judges in our own case. . . . But she *publishes* her dissent. Reflection cannot, I think, fail to produce in her naturally strong and discriminating mind the conviction that this was an error. . . . Even under the veil of a private letter, my heart acquits me of having said one uncharitable word. I might be in error, as every man may, in my conception of the causes that produced alienation. If I could believe that I was, it would not cause me to think better of one, who may yet live to recognize and regret the deep injustice she has done me.[52]

Never in her unfortunate married life nor in the last unhappy years when she was separated from both her child and her husband did Frances recognize any injustice done her former admirer and associate. The breach was never healed.

As Owen completed his third winter at Indianapolis, he had little reason to regret the choice that had substituted the life of a politician for that of a reformer. His three terms in the legislature had been a success; and in a fourth, as author of the Modification Act, he might well be elected speaker. Even higher honors, such as a seat in Congress, might be attained the next August. Already George H. Proffit, whom he had bested on several occasions in the House, had announced himself as the Whig candidate in Owen's district; and no prominent Democrat had come out in opposition. For the moment,

[50] R. D. Owen to Richard Owen, Mar. 17, 1836, Neal Letters.
[51] Mme. D'Arusmont had said that Owen's inquiry had been addressed to the office of a public journal. Kneeland himself may have been at fault. See his comments on the incident in the *Boston Investigator*, May 5, 1837.
[52] *Boston Investigator*, May 5, 1837.

however, Owen resisted temptation. In view of his growing family and his waning business fortunes, his private affairs required immediate attention; and in an address to his constituents he declined to run for either the national or state legislature.[53] The customary partisan pæans that greeted this declaration of temporary retirement must have convinced Owen that political advancement was for him but the matter of a few years.[54]

[53] *Indiana Journal*, Mar. 16, 1839; Amphlett to Maclure, Mar. 9, 1839, Maclure Papers.

[54] *Wabash Enquirer*, Mar. 27, 1839; *Dearborn County Democrat*, Mar. 28, 1839.

CHAPTER X

NATIONAL POLITICS

WHEN in the spring of 1839 Owen announced his return to private life, he had reached a decision that was both intelligent and imperative. There is no reason to believe that it was insincere. Still under forty, he had risen rapidly and further political advancement could hardly be jeopardized by a momentary withdrawal. The need for some attention to his disordered finances was unanimously voiced by Maclure's correspondents in New Harmony.[1] Although those opinions were not altogether impartial, their general correctness is confirmed by the fragmentary records of Owen's business dealings. The land boom along the Wabash, hoped for in 1836, had not materialized; and the depression that began the following year had embarrassed several speculative ventures of the Owens. Despite a $7,500 profit in Evansville lots and the receipt for an investment of $20,000 from their father, the brothers in their collective enterprises lost $2,550 annually in 1837, 1838, and 1839.[2] Owen's earlier hopes of economic independence were rapidly fading, and in later life he ruefully admitted that he and his brothers had neither known how to develop Western property nor applied themselves steadily to business pursuits.[3]

Despite earlier statements to the contrary, Owen became on June 3, 1839, the Democratic candidate for Congress from the First District of Indiana. This sudden reversal, executed only eight weeks before the August election, was occasioned by the

[1] A. Maclure to W. Maclure, July 14, 1837, May 11, 1839; Amphlett to Maclure, Oct. 9, 1838, Mar. 9, Apr. 10, 1839; Mrs. J. Baldwin to Maclure, Jan. 14, 1840, Maclure Papers.

[2] "Statement of the Owen Bros., 1837-8-9," Owen Papers.

[3] R. D. Owen to Robt. Owen, Sept. 18, 1844, Robert Owen Papers, no. 1338; *Threading My Way*, 296.

unexpected withdrawal of James G. Lockhart who had already taken the field.[4] Although Owen may not have been so reluctant as he appeared to place party above personal demands, it is certain that the erstwhile reformer did not realize the disadvantages under which he was to labor. The depression had placed the Van Buren men on the defensive; while the Whigs, who had barely lost the district two years before when they were badly divided, were now united and confident. Their standard bearer had opened his campaign in April and had already attracted many independent voters. Lockhart's mysterious retirement enabled the opposition to charge dictation and corruption.[5] The Democrats were further hampered by having but one newspaper, established only late in May, with which to combat the onslaught of the four local Whig journals. Most serious of all was the task Owen faced of convincing in the short time at his disposal the people of ten other counties what he had already proved to the citizens of Posey — that he was not a dangerous radical but a sane, liberal, constructive legislator.

One hundred years ago in Indiana, when the radio was undreamed of and the telegraph had not come into even occasional use, when no important railroad lines existed and a twenty-five-mile carriage journey in bad weather might take the greater part of a day, when the newspapers appeared but weekly and compressed all the news on to one page in four, when many people could not read and still more could not afford to subscribe to the local gazette, election methods were very different from what they are today. It was then the custom for the candidates to speak together almost daily during the two months before the August election. These meetings were usually scheduled in advance; their sites were rarely more than fifteen or twenty miles distant. Since the rivals traveled together on horseback, they could stop to talk briefly before small groups where no

[4] *Leavenworth Arena*, June 13, 1839.
[5] *Ibid.*, June 13, 20, 1839; *Indiana Journal*, Aug. 26, 1837, June 1, 1839; A. E. Fretageot to Maclure, June 17, 1839, Maclure Papers.

previous appointment had been made. Although Saturdays found the antagonists at the Court House of the county seat, the other five speeches of the week might be made at a cross-roads' store, in a field where the farmers were at work, or deep in a forest glade. Two hours of speaking by each man was the minimum, and often a rebuttal was required. This practice of stumping may have produced loquacious Congressmen from the West, but it also made possible a more intelligent use of the ballot by poor and illiterate backwoodsmen.[6]

Owen's campaign for Congress was his first taste of stump speaking on an extended scale. In June he and his Whig rival, the volatile George H. Proffit, met in Posey and the adjacent counties of Vanderburg, Warrick, Gibson, and Pike. In the following month they worked their way eastward until on the last Saturday before the election they addressed the people at the old state capital of Corydon. On this tour Proffit had a decided advantage. Some of the places he had visited once or twice before; everywhere Owen was making his first appearance. At the same time the Whig candidate was the better orator, his loud, clear voice and winning manners being ideally suited to open air gatherings.[7] Proffit's abilities were best suited to the stump; Owen's to a legislative chamber. The former resorted to wit and humor, the latter relied on facts and logic. The two men had clashed consistently in the Assembly at Indianapolis, and each knew the strength and weakness of the other.

The political issues dividing the contestants were not many. In state affairs there was a wide gap, Owen having been a modifier and Proffit a system man. In the national arena, however, Proffit did not advocate extreme Whig tenets. He glossed over the tariff in silence. He denied that his party was pledged to restore the bank and dismissed the monster as a dead issue. His blows were directed chiefly against the Sub-Treasury Act and the alleged dishonesty of Democratic office-holders.

[6] N. Y. Globe, June 29, 1847; Owen, Beyond the Breakers, 101–106.
[7] O. H. Smith, Early Indiana Trials and Sketches (Cinn., 1858), 359.

Owen fought mainly on the defensive, trying to justify the Van Buren administration *in toto*.[8]

Personal rather than political matters dominated the campaign of 1839. Even before Owen had become a candidate, the Democratic state organ had so roundly attacked Proffit's moral and religious traits that the later virulent assaults upon the former editor of *The Free Enquirer* were not altogether unjustified.[9] On the Whig side the prime source of vituperation and scurrility was a small clique of Evansville lawyers, Robert Evans, Amos Clark, and W. T. T. Jones, whose hatred of Owen dated from either the community experiment or the unsuccessful attempt to eliminate Evansville as the terminus of the Central Canal. These men received valiant assistance from local editors, who did not hesitate to reprint parts of *Moral Physiology* in their columns, from intolerant clergymen to whom Owen's freethought was anathema, and from several determined ladies who openly campaigned for Proffit in the supposed interest of orthodoxy and morality. One Malinda Miller won fleeting fame by warning her Democratic spouse that a vote for Owen constituted a just cause for divorce.[10]

The defamatory barrage laid down by the Evansville group was climaxed by a libellous handbill issued behind Owen's back on the eve of the election. This document, which differed in degree rather than in kind from other contemporary detractions, was ostensibly the work of Benoni Stinson and Jesse Lane, two politically ambitious clerics; but the best evidence suggests that many others had a hand in its composition.[11] Its main object was to "expose" Owen's licentious character

[8] *Indiana Democrat*, July 10, 1839; *Leavenworth Arena*, July 11, 25, 1839.
[9] *Indiana Democrat*, May 1, 29, 1839; *Leavenworth Arena*, June 6, July 4, 1839; *Indiana Journal*, July 6, 1839.
[10] *Indiana Journal*, Aug. 24, 1839. Neither issue of the Corydon *Investigator* or the *Leavenworth Arena* reprinting *Moral Physiology* has been located, but their existence is attested by journals of both parties. See the *Leavenworth Arena*, July 18, Aug. 1, 1839; *Indiana Democrat*, July 24, 1839; Owen's post-election statement in *The Beacon*, Oct. 19, 1839.
[11] J. J. Chandler to Elisha Embree, Feb. 7, 1849, Embree Papers; J. P. Elliott, *A History of Evansville and Vanderburg County* (Evansville, 1897), 361.

by detailing, with gross distortions and inaccuracies, his role in the New Harmony community, his war on orthodoxy in New York, and his advocacy of birth control. All the doctrines that the radical reformer had once espoused were attributed to the Democratic candidate of 1839. What upset Owen's customary equanimity as it had not been upset since Skidmore's attack on his Neo-Malthusianism was the manner in which the enemy operated. Although printed at Evansville while he was still at hand to answer its slander, the handbill was not distributed until after he had begun his tour to the eastward. So skilfully was it circulated that Owen was not aware of its existence until three days before the polls opened. Such tactics were typical of what neutral observers described as "the most violent party election ever known here." [12]

The first Monday in August brought disaster to the Van Buren standard-bearer. Owen made a splendid showing in the eastern counties which he had visited last but trailed badly in the west where the virus of the Stinson-Lane circular may have sapped his strength. Even the strongly Democratic Posey gave its son but a bare plurality. Proffit's triumph was a decisive one, his lead mounting to 779 votes. So while the Whigs of Corydon burned tar barrels in celebration and his own family dolefully held a ball scheduled in anticipation of victory, Owen's cup of disappointment was filled to overflowing. In his first bid for Congress he had been badly beaten and in a year when his party was generally successful in both its national and state tickets.[13]

The Owen-Proffit contest had aroused interest within and

[12] Amphlett to Maclure, July [Aug.] 10, 1839, Maclure Papers. Neither the handbill nor the issue of the *Evansville Journal* in which it was printed have been located; but see a similar, if not identical, "Short Exposition of the Moral, Religious, and Political Principles of Robert Dale Owen," *Leavenworth Arena*, July 25, 1839. Owen's account of the incident is in *The Beacon*, Oct. 19, 1839 and Owen to Trist, June 30, 1840, Trist Papers, XVI; his opponents' in the *Leavenworth Arena*, Oct. 31, 1839.

[13] *Indiana Journal*, Sept. 7, 1839; *Wabash Enquirer*, Aug. 30, 1839; Mrs. Baldwin to Maclure, Aug. 19, 1839, Maclure Papers. The vote stood, Proffit, 6,008; Owen, 5,229.

without the state, and many divergent explanations were offered for the result. The Democrats declared that it was not a Whig victory but one of "bigotry, intolerance, and hypocrisy." Some of their rivals hailed it as a moral triumph; others, as a rebuke to Van Buren. Freethinkers saw in the outcome the insidious influence of orthodoxy. Gilbert Vale thought an erroneous conception of *Moral Physiology* was to blame and took advantage of the occasion to print a new edition. An observer at New Harmony regarded Owen's lavish campaign expenditures and exorbitant ambition as the chief stumbling blocks to his success. The loser himself attributed his defeat to the Stinson-Lane handbill; and Proffit, after he had broken three years later with the Clay faction, acquiesced in that estimate.[14]

Beneath these conflicting opinions and rationalizations lay certain basic reasons for Owen's defeat. Thanks to an earlier start, a more numerous press, abler allies, and superior stumping, Proffit had placed his case before the electors more effectively. He had retained the allegiance of even those, like Amos Clark, who detested him.[15] Owen had been unable to make capital out of his more enlightened record in the state legislature. National issues played a larger part in the canvass than the defeated Democrats liked to admit, and Owen was compelled to defend an administration which, in the "Pocket" at least, was unpopular, as the next year was to show. It is unlikely that Owen's notoriety as a radical reformer was ever the primary cause of his political setbacks, but it must be admitted that his past affected him most adversely in 1839.

Although the religious and moral issues did not sway the voters so much as the disappointed Owen believed, their intrusion into the canvass was none the less significant. It afforded conclusive proof that no matter how efficient a legis-

[14] *Wabash Enquirer*, Aug. 16, 1839; quotations in the *Leavenworth Arena*, Sept. 12, 1839; *Wabash Courier*, Aug. 17, 1839; *Boston Investigator*, Aug. 28, 1839; *Beacon*, Sept. 21, 1839; Amphlett to Maclure, July [Aug.] 10, Sept. 26, 1839, Maclure Papers; Owen to Trist, June 30, 1840, Trist Papers, XVI; *Indiana Statesman*, Nov. 12, 1842.

[15] Clark to Noah Noble, Aug. 17, 1839, Noble Papers.

lator Owen might become, how tactful an attitude he might adopt toward the orthodox, or how far he might go to explain, justify, and retract, his earlier writings would always be a political bugbear to him. It was evident that in every subsequent election he would labor under the handicap of virulent personal invective. The danger was that his own party, fearing his vulnerability, might refuse him another Congressional nomination. If that fear were translated into action, then his hopes for political advancement that had burned so brightly the previous spring would soon be extinguished. To prevent such a possibility from becoming a reality was for him the vital problem raised by defeat.

After a month of reflection and inquiry Owen resolved that problem. Despite financial exigencies and the wisdom of letting passions cool, he decided to return to the political arena. To the electors of the district he issued a long address, explaining his recent canvass and rationalizing his decision into a belief that he was battling for the right of private judgment in public life.[16] Yet in his heart of hearts Owen probably realized that it was the aid he might render his party in the forthcoming presidential contest rather than any abstract principle he might uphold that would most facilitate Congressional nominations in the future.

As a result of this important decision Owen spent the next twelve months immersed in the swirling tides of national politics. His first care was to mend fences at home. His ringing post-election circular reestablished his prestige in the district, and editors at Paoli and New Albany insisted that he be renominated in 1841. In October 1839 he addressed the Floyd County Democratic Convention on state and national issues, an address he was careful to distribute throughout Indiana.[17] At the same time several newspapers urged his candidacy for governor the next year on the grounds that he had "bared his

[16] Printed in part in *The Beacon*, Oct. 19, 1839.

[17] Paoli *True American*, Oct. 11, 1839, mounted in "Political Memoranda"; *Wabash Enquirer*, Nov. 8, 1839; Owen to M. R. Southard, Dec. 12, 1839, Southard Papers.

bosom to the malicious shafts of *religious fanaticism*, and suffered political martyrdom. His blood," it was said, "cries aloud upon the Democratic party for redress." The Whigs took this gubernatorial boom seriously, but its beneficiary soon scotched it by publicly declaring that he "probably" would not accept the nomination if offered it.[18] Nevertheless Owen played an important role in the Democratic State Convention held at Indianapolis in January 1840. There he delivered the address to the people that defined the issues for the presidential contest, and there he was chosen as the Van Buren elector in the First District with the specific task of waging another strenuous campaign.[19]

Accordingly Owen took the field late in April in behalf of the state and national candidates. He spoke several times in the Bloomington area and then addressed an important gathering at the capital. At the end of June he set out with John W. Payne, the Whig elector, on a tour of the First District, covering much the same ground as he had the previous year. In September he went round the circuit a second time, worked his way northward through Sullivan and Monroe counties, and then swung homeward via the more westerly towns of Greencastle, Terre Haute, and Vincennes.[20]

One other interesting aspect of Owen's activity in 1840 was his attempt to mold public opinion through the newspapers. The lack of a strong Democratic press in the western part of the First District had been a severe handicap to Owen in his Congressional canvass, and in the few months after his defeat he repaired that deficiency by helping to set up at Evansville the *South-Western Sentinel* in charge of Jacob Page Chapman, one of the talented brothers then editing the *Wabash Enquirer*

[18] *Wabash Enquirer*, Sept. 27, 1839; *Indiana Journal*, Oct. 5, 1839; *Indiana Democrat*, Dec. 5, 1839.

[19] *Indiana Democrat*, Jan. 9, 14, 1840; *Wabash Enquirer*, Jan. 22, 1840; Owen to Trist, June 30, 1840, Trist Papers, XVI.

[20] *Bloomington Post*, May 1, 8, Sept. 25, Oct. 9, 1840; *Wabash Enquirer*, May 28, Sept. 16, 28, Oct. 10, 17, 1840; Indianapolis *Semi-Weekly Journal*, May 20, 1840; *Leavenworth Arena*, June 25, Sept. 3, Oct. 15, 1840; *Western Sun*, Sept. 20, Oct. 17, 1840.

at Terre Haute.[21] With this organ at his disposal the Democratic elector wrote during the summer months an extensive series of fifteen articles on national topics. Designed to introduce reason and honesty into a campaign of emotion and evasion, these articles conclusively proved that the former editor of *The Free Enquirer* had lost none of his old journalistic ability.[22]

The year 1840, however, was ill-suited to Owen's overlong and highly rational disquisitions. His untiring energy on the stump similarly proved unavailing. Indiana was still a Whig state and Harrison, a local idol, had already bested Van Buren there in 1836. Thus with a log cabin as a hull, hard cider as cargo, and a coon as mascot, the good ship *Whiggery*, propelled by a veritable gale of songs, huzzas, and empty words, sailed majestically on, carrying to the highest office in the land a man of undisputed bravery, experience, and personal integrity, but one whose future policies were shrouded from Democrats and Whigs alike. For months the Hoosier state was dotted with giant barbecues, while its staid newspapers printed tremendous woodcuts of the gallant general sitting on a cider keg by the open door of a log cabin. In November Harrison swept to victory, carrying every Congressional district in the state, the First by a startling margin of 1,100 votes.[23]

In spite of the complete rout of the Democrats in Indiana, Owen had not lost all by his year's efforts. His ceaseless activity had made him a valuable party worker and had wiped away the stain of his defeat in 1839. He had become favorably known through his writings and speeches in other parts of the commonwealth, an important asset in future Senatorial elections. He had proved his willingness to labor for the cause when the

---

[21] *Beacon*, Oct. 19, 1839; Amphlett to Maclure, Sept. 26, 1839, Maclure Papers; *Wabash Enquirer*, Nov. 8, 1839; *Indiana State Sentinel*, Mar. 4, 1846.

[22] No complete file of the *South-Western Sentinel* has been located. Reprints of Owen's articles are in the *Western Sun*, June 27, July 4, 11, 18, 25, Aug. 1, 8, 15, 22, 1840; *Wabash Enquirer*, Aug. 26, Sept. 16, Oct. 14, 21, 1840; *Indiana Democrat*, Oct. 2, 1840.

[23] *Indiana Journal*, Nov. 28, 1840.

outlook was gloomy and when there was no immediate personal reward at stake. Now he could retire gracefully to attend to private affairs, leaving a credit balance in his favor on the Democratic ledger. And he did so with a clear recognition of that debt by the party organ at the state capital which asserted, "Mr. Owen has probably done more for the cause of Democracy than any other man in Indiana. . . . We hope the Democracy . . . will not forget him who does not forget them." [24]

Owen's subsequent retirement from public life was more apparent than real. To be sure he held no office and undertook no campaign in 1841 and 1842 but remained quietly at New Harmony occupied with business, family, and local matters. Yet he kept in touch with old colleagues, made occasional political speeches, and saw his name advanced rather prominently for United States Senator in the autumn of 1842.[25] It is not altogether unlikely that Owen found the opportunity convenient to lie low until the political skies had brightened. And it is well that he did. The Whig tide that had swept the state in 1840 did not ebb until after the Congressional elections held prematurely the following spring. With Owen declining to run, Lockhart took the field in the First District, only to be buried under an avalanche of Proffit votes. To the conquest of all branches of the state government made the previous year the Whigs now added six of the seven Hoosier seats in Congress. The early summer of 1841 marked the nadir of Democratic fortunes in Indiana, and at that time Jacob Page Chapman gave up an apparently hopeless battle and suspended publication of the *South-Western Sentinel*.[26]

Eighteen months later the picture was completely changed. In the state the Democrats were staging an impressive recovery. Paced by the *Indiana State Sentinel*, the new party organ established at the capital by the Chapman brothers in July 1841, they

[24] *Indiana Democrat*, Oct. 9, 1840.
[25] *Indiana State Sentinel*, Oct. 11, Dec. 7, 1841; *Indiana Statesman*, Aug. 19, 1842.
[26] *Leavenworth Arena*, Jan. 21, 1841; *Indiana Democrat*, May 26, 1841; *Western Sun*, July 10, 1841 (advt.).

captured the lower house in that year, won control of the legislature in 1842, and promised a vigorous gubernatorial contest in 1843.[27] In the First District the skies had also cleared. The popular Proffit had broken with the Clay men on the bank issue, and his renomination by the Whigs was impossible. A new Democratic paper, edited by Alexander Burns, Jr., and dedicated to the political advancement of Robert Dale Owen, had been begun in Evansville and was soon to move to New Harmony. By withdrawing from the Senatorial race in 1842 in the interest of party harmony, the former radical further strengthened his claim to the Congressional candidacy in 1843. As a matter of fact, there was never much doubt that he could have the nomination if he desired it. At first, however, Owen demurred, even going so far as to say he did not wish to run; but at the District Convention held at Jasper on April 10, 1843, he was unanimously chosen. The prompt acceptance that followed left him in the strong position of having been, apparently, drafted for the race.[28]

The canvass of 1843 was among the most strenuous Owen ever undertook. Between late May and early August he spoke at more than sixty public meetings in the district. Yet the task was a pleasant one, for at last everything seemed to be going right. Off to an early start, Owen carefully distributed a well prepared address *To the Electors of the First Congressional District of Indiana* in which he proclaimed protection to be the chief issue and scored the Whigs for breaking their promises of 1840. His opponent, John W. Payne, upheld the Act of 1842; and thus, in contrast to four years before, the contest saw a full debate of party principles, the tariff, the currency, and internal improvements. At the same time, and again in contrast to 1839, there was no revived religious hysteria. Payne waged a gentlemanly battle; and with Evans, Jones, and Clark dead or living elsewhere, with Stinson's political ambitions

[27] *Indiana Journal*, Aug. 11, 25, 1841; Aug. 17, 1842.
[28] *Indiana State Sentinel*, Nov. 8, 15, 1842. Owen to J. P. Chapman, Aug. 20, 1842, *ibid.*, Sept. 30, 1842. *Ibid.*, Nov. 22, 1842, Apr. 25, 1843. *Indiana Statesman*, May 13, 1842, Feb. 4, 25, Apr. 22, 1843.

crushed, ·and Owen possessed of a capable press, there was little opportunity for the Whigs to repeat the underhand tactics of the past.[29]

The first Monday in August found Owen again at Corydon, this time undisturbed by fears of secret circulars. The result of his well conducted campaign was highly gratifying. When the official vote was tabulated, he led by a margin of 577, an overturn of 1,942 ballots in two years. This excellent showing, an admirable personal achievement, was not, however, an isolated victory. The Hoosier election of 1843 was rightly called by the Chapmans a "revolution." For the first time since statehood, Indiana's executive chair and General Assembly were in the hands of the Democrats. In addition, where two years ago that party had won but a single Congressional seat, it now captured eight out of ten.[30]

Once again the outcome in the First District occasioned a variety of comment. The Democrats attributed the tremendous change of popular sentiment to a repudiation of the Whig political principles. William H. Chandler of *The Evansville Journal*, Owen's arch foe, regarded the causes as local in character, mainly an apathy among the voters; while other Whig editors deplored the triumph of atheism and "universal concubinage." Freethinkers like Burns saw religious liberty in politics vindicated. Some truth may be found in these explanations. Political rather than personal issues dominated the canvass. Owen made an eloquent plea for a Congressman's right of private judgment. Chandler did notice a lessened interest, for many of his former subscribers were reading the *Indiana Statesman* and voting accordingly.[31] There is little doubt, moreover, that by 1843 Owen had become a better campaigner; whereas Payne,

[29] On the campaign see Owen's circular, cited in the text; the files of the *Indiana Statesman*, *Indiana State Sentinel*, and *Indiana State Journal*; *The Evansville Journal*, Aug. 10, 24, 1843; R. D. Owen to Robt. Owen, Aug. 15, 1843, *New Moral World*, Nov. 11, 1843.

[30] *Indiana State Sentinel*, Aug. 15, 1843; *Indiana State Journal*, Aug. 30, 1843. The vote stood, Owen, 6,659; Payne, 6,082.

[31] *Indiana Statesman*, Aug. 19, Sept. 9, 16, 1843; *Evansville Journal*, Aug. 10, 24, 1843; *Louisville Weekly Journal*, Sept. 6, 1843.

for all his sterling qualities, lacked the fire and eloquence of Proffit. Some weight, finally, must be given to the general Democratic trend, not only in Indiana but in the nation at large.

Four years after experiencing bitter defeat Owen had reached his goal. The hopes for political advancement, burning so brightly in the spring of 1839 and well-nigh extinguished by the debacle of that summer, had now become a reality. "The upstart, foreign demagogue and disorganizer," the man who "would disgrace the gallows," had won a seat in the national legislature.[32] It was in a cheerful mood that Owen sat down to write his father the latest news of his sons in the New World — of Dale's progress as a geologist, of Richard's success as a sheep farmer, and of his own election. He assured his agnostic sire that on religion he had taken a tolerant yet independent stand. "That I should have succeeded," he concluded,

heretic and foreigner as I was, by the largest Democratic majority ever obtained in this district, may be to you, my dear father, some assurance . . . that I have been able to inspire my fellow citizens with some confidence in my integrity and ability, and to build up among them a reputation which I hope my acts as Congressman may still increase and confirm.

Quickly checking any trace of boastfulness, he added, simply, "Thus a new career, I trust it may be of usefulness, is opened to me." [33]

[32] R. M. Evans in the *Leavenworth Arena*, Oct. 31, 1839; *N. Y. Times*, July 24, 1839.
[33] R. D. Owen to Robt. Owen, Aug. 15, 1843, *New Moral World*, Nov. 11, 1843.

CHAPTER XI

MANIFEST DESTINY

The American people in 1843 were in a buoyant, optimistic, expansionist mood. Ever since independence they had regarded themselves as a chosen race, destined by their successful development of free institutions to uplift the Western World. During most of their national existence they had been content to serve as a beacon light for the oppressed of all lands, to spread democracy by example, by remote control as it were. Recently, however, there had arisen a widespread belief that the United States had a more immediate mission to perform, to become an active rather than a passive champion of liberty, to cast its republican mantle over the entire continent. This belief was fed by a fear that the European monarchies were intriguing to establish a balance of power in the New World. These exponents of Manifest Destiny had no conscious desire to propagate their faith by the sword, no selfish wish to create a dependent empire. Convinced that man could live most happily under the American constitution, they sought simply an area extensive enough for working out the great republican experiment. As one enthusiast put it,

More, more, more! will be the unresting cry, till our national destiny is fulfilled, and "the whole boundless continent is ours." Texas, Oregon, California, Canada, yes, all, all are sooner or later to be embraced within the ever-widening circle . . . of free and independent States, bound together in . . . a common pursuit of the Great American idea of the free development of humanity to the best and highest results it may be capable of. . . . For this great destiny . . . we want — or we shall want by and by — the whole, and nothing short of the whole.[1]

[1] *N. Y. Morning News*, Feb. 7, 1845. See Julius W. Pratt, "The Ideology of American Expansion," *Essays in Honor of William E. Dodd* (Avery Craven, ed., Chi., 1935), 335–353; Albert K. Weinberg, *Manifest Destiny* (Balt., 1935), *passim*.

Owen's election to Congress coincided with the breaking of this new wave of expansionist sentiment against the boundaries established after the second war with England. In particular, both the Oregon and Texas problems were ripe for solution. Both had a complicated past that can only be summarized here. In two important treaties negotiated in 1818 and 1819 the United States had fixed its northern limits at 49° and its southern at a zigzag line that began at the mouth of the Sabine and terminated along the 42nd parallel. To obtain these metes and bounds American diplomats had been forced to renounce the territory between the Sabine and the Rio Grande, claimed by this nation under the Louisiana Purchase, and to accept, in view of conflicting titles, joint occupation with England of the Oregon country, that region lying between 49° and 54° 40′ and between the mountains and the Pacific.

During the next quarter of a century these territorial settlements were undone by the steady westward march of the American pioneer. In the Southwest Mexico's liberal land policy attracted many immigrants to Texas; and when the inevitable clash between divergent civilizations occurred, an independent republic resulted. In the Northwest the American trapper was succeeded in the thirties by the New England missionary and finally by the boisterous backwoodsman of the Mississippi Valley frontier. It was this last element that challenged the long-standing domination in the Willamette and Columbia valleys of the Hudson's Bay Company and which might have precipitated another armed conflict if the officials of that company had not decided to move their main post to Vancouver Island. By the summer of 1843 both problems were being thrust before the American people, Oregon by a series of popular conventions in the West which declared our rights to 54° 40′ to be "unquestionable," Texas by rumored Anglo-French intrigues looking toward the abolition of slavery and the erection of a permanent barrier to the southward expansion of the United States. In October diplomatic negotiations were begun almost simultaneously to terminate joint occupancy in the Northwest and to bring the Lone Star republic into the federal union.[2]

Texas and Oregon played no part in the Democratic revolution of 1843 in Indiana. In the Owen-Payne contest, as in the state at large, the tariff was the chief issue, and little or no reference was made to territorial extension. Yet scarcely two months after his victory Owen had decided that the Oregon question would and ought to occupy much attention in the approaching session. In a public letter, printed for his constituents and widely copied in the Eastern press, he declared that the time had come to assert our just claims and to take possession of the territory without bloodshed before the Hudson's Bay Company, profiting by joint occupancy, made peaceful penetration impossible. These remarks Owen supplemented with a lecture at New Harmony in which he described the value of the disputed region, a value often denied, and strongly urged an immediate settlement with the British government. The Whigs at once ascribed political motives to the new Congressman's activity; but the fact remains that, whatever his motives, Owen was leading public opinion in his district, not following it.[3]

If before his departure from New Harmony Owen had begun to breathe the spirit of Manifest Destiny, he became soon after his arrival in Washington one of its most ardent devotees. The leading expansionists of the Twenty-Eighth Congress that convened in December 1843 came from the West, and it was these with whom Owen was most readily thrown into contact. Since Congressional wives were still the exception rather than the rule in the national capital, the Indianan took up bachelor's quarters at Mrs. Mattingly's on Pennsylvania Avenue just below Third Street. All the members of this "mess" lived beyond the mountains. One was the son-in-law of the late Lewis F. Linn, long a champion of Oregon in the upper house.

[2] An adequate summary is in Samuel F. Bemis, *A Diplomatic History of the United States* (N. Y., 1936), ch. XIII, XVI.
[3] *Indiana Statesman*, Oct. 21, 28, 1843; *Evansville Journal*, Nov. 16, 1843.

ROBERT DALE OWEN, ABOUT 1850

The ablest were the two Ohio Senators, William Allen and Benjamin Tappan, the latter being a brother of the New York philanthropists against whom Owen had inveighed a dozen years before. Most, however, like Andrew Kennedy and John Pettit, fellow Hoosiers, or John B. Weller of Ohio were the boisterous and bumptious type whom the Eastern Whigs so liked to satirize. It was, it must be admitted, a rather crude group, talented in only a limited sense, and one into which the intellectually inclined and well born Scot would have had difficulty fitting if it had not been for his decade of conditioning in the Indiana backwoods.[4]

After a month devoted to organization and trivialities, the House got down to the serious business of the session. Since it was Democratic in complexion and the Senate was still controlled by the Whigs, there was no chance for tariff reform; and as most commentators had predicted, expansion was pushed to the fore. Owen quickly revealed the policy he planned to pursue. In his annual message Tyler had kept silent on the negotiations for the annexation of Texas, but had recommended the extension of American laws over the Oregon country and the erection of military posts along the main routes of travel to it.[5] That was the procedure Linn had vainly pressed upon Congress for almost a decade, but to Owen it did not seem to meet the problem squarely. On January 4, therefore, he offered a joint resolution requesting the president to give England, in accordance with the Convention of 1827, notice that the joint occupation of Oregon would be terminated at the end of twelve months. Although criticized by the Whigs as a move to break off the very negotiations that the United States in October had requested Great Britain to commence, Owen's proposal was lauded by the Democratic press as the only practical solution of the problem. The conservative Committee on Foreign Affairs, however, did not agree with Blair and Bryant; and after a three-

[4] *Congressional Directory for the First Session of the Twenty-Eighth Congress of the United States of America* (Wash., 1843–44).
[5] James D. Richardson, *A Compilation of the Messages and Papers of the Presidents* (Wash., 1897), IV, 257–263.

week delay, it reported that in view of the transfer of diplomatic discussions from London to Washington then taking place, it was inexpedient to act at that time.[6] Yet Owen's motion, the first of its kind presented in either house during the session, proved to be the method by which the boundary dispute was finally put into a train of settlement.

As author of the resolution thus summarily rejected, Owen rose to reply in what was properly his maiden speech. He denied that his suggestion was untimely and warned that there could be no solution until "we assume an attitude more independent than has hitherto characterized our proceedings relative to Oregon." To give the year's notice would, he believed, convince England of our earnestness. While the joint occupation remained, the United States could not legally grant land titles in the Columbia Valley. Yet already the great migration was in full swing, never to be checked. When, the Indianan concluded,

you can whistle back the mountain eagle in his upward flight to the sun; when you can arrest, by a word, the wild horse of the prairie in his mad career; when you can quench, in the bird of passage, that instinct which bids her be up and away to the regions nature designed for her, — then, then only, expect to set up mete or bound short of the broad Pacific, a barrier to the restless enterprise of the West. Oregon is our land of promise. Oregon is our land of destination. . . . Two thousand American citizens are already dwellers of her valleys. Five thousand more — ay, it may be twice that number — will have crossed the mountain passes before another year rolls around. While you are legislating, they are emigrating; and whether you legislate for them or not, they will emigrate still.[7]

With this peroration a new exponent of Manifest Destiny emerged.

As an attempt to reverse the decision of the committee, Owen's speech was a failure. The House displayed no inclination to engage in a general debate on the subject; and

[6] *House Journal*, 28th Congress, 1st Session, 164, 280; *North American*, Jan. 6, 1844; Washington *Globe*, Jan. 4, 1844; N. Y. *Evening Post*, Jan. 8, 1844.

[7] *Congressional Globe*, 28 Cong., 1 Sess., Appendix, 86–88 (Jan. 23, 24, 1844).

during the remainder of the session no "notice," not even the fortification bill that the president requested, was passed. As a step, however, to arouse public interest in the question and to gain personal credit the Hoosier's maiden effort was eminently successful. Almost forty papers reprinted his words in full, and within three days 21,000 pamphlet copies had been sold. Owen's was the first address of the new Congress to be published in its entirety by the two Democratic journals in New York, and it appeared twice in the national party organ.[8] The agitation thus begun was continued by Owen and other Westerners through the presentation of memorials and petitions and helped pave the way for the inclusion at the Democratic Convention in Baltimore of the resolution for the "re-occupation of Oregon."

Unlike the Oregon question, Congress had little occasion to discuss Texas until the very eve of the presidential campaign. Up to mid-March the secrecy of the negotiations, the latent antislavery sentiment in the North, and the impossibility of legislating before the diplomats acted had kept the matter in the background. Some bold spirits desired to link Texas and Oregon into a single expansionist measure, but the first steps in that direction were voted down on March 25.[9] As a matter of fact, even in the West, editors like Burns and the Chapmans were eager to let the Texas issue alone lest it redound unfavorably to their candidate, Martin Van Buren.[10]

Owen, too, was a Van Buren man. Ever since his entrance into politics he had fought for the squire of Lindenwald. Yet being at the capital, he could read more expertly the political skies than could his friends at home. He realized that the younger men in the party wanted expansion to be the issue in 1844 and, that if they obtained their wishes, Van Buren's Texas

---

[8] Princeton *Democratic Clarion*, Aug. 28, 1847; *N. Y. Herald*, Apr. 27, 1844. *Evening Post*, Jan. 30, 1844; *N. Y. Plebeian*, Feb. 3, 1844. *Globe*, Jan. 24, 25, Feb. 9, 1844.

[9] *House Journal*, 28 Cong., 1 Sess., 662–663.

[10] *Indiana State Sentinel*, Mar. 28, 1844; *Indiana Statesman*, Dec. 2, 1843, Mar. 30, 1844.

letter would make him unacceptable. Owen hesitated long before publicly opposing his old chief, yet he was reluctant to lose the tide that might sweep him into the inner circle of the new party leaders. Thus on the one hand, he refused to sign a card subscribed to by every other member of the Indiana delegation declaring that, if Van Buren were nominated, Clay would be elected. On the other hand he wrote an open letter to *The Globe* under his old pseudonym "Tullius," criticizing extremists in both the pro-Texas and anti-Texas ranks. Cautiously he admitted that the United States had the right to annex the region up to the Rio Grande, but he insisted that the Baltimore Convention alone could decide whether annexation would become a party principle.[11]

Owen's conciliatory letter was more important in foreshadowing his future course than in calming the turbulent seas of the Democracy. It attracted little attention in Washington; and at home it was not recognized until his friends, Burns and the Chapmans, had further committed themselves against immediate annexation.[12] A fortnight after the incident, on May 21, the Hoosier finally obtained the floor of the House for the first "set speech" in that chamber on the burning issue of the hour. In this eloquent yet carefully documented address, delivered just one week before the Democratic Convention assembled, Owen made his position crystal-clear. The United States, he asserted, had both a duty and a right to annex Texas at once and up to the Rio Grande. The duty arose from the pledge given in 1803 and not impaired in 1819 to provide free institutions for the Texans. The right was conferred by international law whereby one nation might negotiate with a government that had won its independence and maintained it for several years. In thus advocating immediate annexation Owen declined to become an apologist for the South's peculiar institution. He criticized Calhoun's unfortunate reply to Pakenham and lifted the Texan question out of a slavery setting and

[11] *Globe*, May 6, 8, 1844.
[12] *Indiana Statesman*, May 11, 18, 1844; *Indiana State Sentinel*, May 16, 1844.

placed it on the high ground of national policy. The Indianan clearly reflected the spirit of Manifest Destiny when he dismissed possible Mexican retaliation thus, "What is the real danger? Much, I admit, of inkshed and bluster; some perhaps of predatory bands . . . none, if we may judge from the past, of any war that a couple of regiments of good Kentucky riflemen could not terminate in a fortnight."[13]

Of all the speeches that Owen made during his first session in Congress, that on the burning question of Texas won him the greatest prestige within his party.[14] It was an opportune effort, timed to influence both the Democratic platform and the vote on Tyler's treaty of annexation. Owen spoke before crowded galleries; and although Robert J. Walker, the apostle of expansion, was defending the pact before closed doors in the upper chamber, many Senators attended the more dramatic proceedings in the House, remarking ruefully, "You are taking the shine off from us."[15] Applause constantly interrupted the Indianan; and the speech was widely hailed as the best of the session, one commentator going so far as to say it was the ablest given in either house during the last two years. Even the Van Buren journals were impressed, and the Hoosier editors quickly swung into line behind their popular Representative, eloquent proof that once again Owen was leading, not following, public opinion.[16] Partisan as such evidence admittedly is, it does help us to understand the esteem in which Owen was held by many of his contemporaries.

On May 27, amid confusion and uncertainty, the discordant hosts of the Democracy assembled in Baltimore to choose their presidential candidate. Selected as a delegate from Indiana more than a year before, Owen refused to leave his Congressional post even though legislation was at a standstill.[17] By

[13] *Cong. Globe*, 28 Cong., 1 Sess., Appendix, 696–701.

[14] *Mohawk Courier*, quoted in the Washington *Union*, May 2, 1845.

[15] *N. Y. Journal of Commerce*, May 23, 1844.

[16] *N. Y. Herald*, May 24, 1844; *Richmond Enquirer*, May 24, 1844; *Madisonian*, May 22, 1844. *Evening Post*, May 23, 1844; *Plebeian*, May 28, 1844. *Indiana State Sentinel*, June 6, 1844; *Madison Courier*, June 29, 1844.

[17] *Indiana State Sentinel*, Jan. 11, Oct. 24, 1843.

means of the newly installed Morse telegraph, however, he was able to learn instantly of the nomination of James K. Polk and of the resolution favoring the "re-occupation of Oregon and the re-annexation of Texas," a result that was bound to please the author of the "Tullius" letter.

In the middle of June the House finally adjourned, its last weeks being devoted mostly to political claptrap. Although denounced by John Quincy Adams as "the most perverse and worthless . . . that ever disgraced this Confederacy," the first session of the Twenty-Eighth Congress was a memorable one for Owen.[18] Despite a failure to obtain a much desired local law, despite frequent Whig allusions to his foreign birth and youthful radicalism, he had, thanks to his espousal of Manifest Destiny, risen high in the ranks of the party. It is safe to say that no other House Democrat received more favorable publicity during the winter and spring, and the House at that time contained such worthies as Douglas, Ingersoll, Cave Johnson, Andrew Johnson, Cobb, Rhett, Slidell, and Hamlin. Owen's speeches in pamphlet form had obtained a greater average circulation than those of any other Congressman.[19] Nationally he was coming to be recognized as one of the most promising of the younger Representatives. At home his work was fully recorded by the *Indiana Statesman*, and frequent letters printed therein under his own name kept his constituents fully informed of his plans and his achievements.[20]

Upon his return to New Harmony Owen at once cleared the decks for a new campaign. Having given an account of his stewardship, he sought to enlighten the electors on the virtues of Texan annexation, a subject which, he said, "from its novelty is but imperfectly understood." In July he stumped his district for Polk, climaxing his efforts with an address at a monster mass meeting in Madison. He declined, however, to visit in Septem-

[18] *Memoirs of John Quincy Adams* (C. F. Adams, ed., Phila., 1874-1877), XII, 57.

[19] R. D. Owen to Robt. Owen, Sept. 18, 1844, Robert Owen Papers, no. 1338.

[20] Cf. *Indiana Statesman*, Oct. 21, 1843; Jan. 6, 27, Feb. 3, 17, Mar. 2, Apr. 27, May 4, June 15, 1844.

ber the northern part of the state. With Texas, the tariff, and nativism as the chief issues, the Hoosier Democrats, despite an unexpected setback in August, carried the commonwealth for Polk by some 10,000 votes, clearly indicating that the revolution of the previous year had not yet been checked.[21]

Late in November 1844, accompanied by his septuagenarian father, who was visiting America for the first time in fifteen years, Owen returned to Washington. With the Whigs determined to use their control of the Senate to block all Democratic measures,[22] the "lame duck" session promised little constructive legislation. Owen and other Western expansionists were eager to execute the Baltimore resolution on Texas and Oregon; but the Democratic triumph had been differently interpreted within the party and some members wished to await Polk's inaugural for a clear statement of policy.

Tyler's last annual message gave the expansionists plenty of encouragement. He was especially eager to annex Texas before March 4, and that question, therefore, took precedence over Oregon. In its early stages the debate called forth the best speakers of both parties. Robert Winthrop stated the Whig position, and Owen was expected by the supposedly independent *New York Herald* to make the ablest annexationist speech of the session in reply.[23] The Indianan's effort of January 8 was designed, in effect, to dispose of the usual objections raised by the opposition to the annexation of Texas. Once again he denied that the measure was a slaveholders' conspiracy. He saw no constitutional obstacle to the acquisition of territory by joint resolution. He did not view with apprehension the extension of our national boundaries, for his Democratic philosophy taught that as a people became more enlightened, the province of legislation contracted. In his opinion the United States could spread the blessings of liberty over the whole North American conti-

[21] *Indiana Statesman*, June 29, July 13, 20, Aug. 17, Sept. 7, Oct. 5, 1844; *Indiana State Sentinel*, Oct. 24, 1844; *Indiana State Journal*, Aug. 10, 17, Nov. 30, 1844.
[22] *Courier & Enquirer*, Nov. 30, 1844.
[23] *N. Y. Herald*, Jan. 7, 1845; *Cong. Globe*, 28 Cong., 2 Sess., 27.

nent without injury to its free institutions. Finally the ex-
reformer did not believe that annexation meant war. On the
contrary, he felt that inaction would only encourage the Mexican generals to carry their threatened butchery across the Rio
Grande. "Boldly, then," he concluded,

and without reserve, let us meet the question. Let us annex Texas
at once. The liberal portion of the world will approve, the rest will
acquiesce; and, in ten years, the wonder will be, not that Texas
has settled quietly down into an integral portion of our confederacy;
but that men should ever have been found, so blind to the interests
of their country, as to oppose her annexation.[24]

In none of his Congressional speeches was Owen so carried
away by the buoyant optimism of the hour as in this second on
the Texan question. He failed to foresee not only that annexation would lead to war but also that victory in that war,
while inevitable, was not the matter of a few weeks or "a
couple of regiments of good Kentucky riflemen." Too easily
did the Hoosier accept the prevalent theory that to disperse
slavery over a larger area was to hasten emancipation in the
Border States. Most questionable of all was his assertion
that the province of legislation grew smaller as an intelligent
population extended its boundaries. This line of reasoning,
which Owen had already elaborated in a magazine article, was
promptly criticized by the Whigs.[25] Yet despite these shortcomings the address was lavishly praised by Democratic editors,
and it became at once the most heavily subscribed for oration
yet made during the session. Success, moreover, followed in its
wake. On January 25 a joint resolution to annex the Lone Star
Republic passed the House.[26]

In an honest attempt to carry out the second branch of
the Baltimore resolution, the House leaders turned at once to the
Oregon question. Spurred on by the recent election and by the

[24] *Cong. Globe*, 28 Cong., 2 Sess., Appendix, 98–102.
[25] *National Intelligencer*, Jan. 25, 1845. Cf. "The Province of Legislation,"
The Democratic Monthly Magazine and Western Review, I, 31–37, 112–120, 219–
228 (May, June, July 1844).
[26] *Indiana Statesman*, Feb. 1, 1845; *House Journal*, 28 Cong., 2 Sess., 264–265.

apparent popularity at home of the policy, the Westerners manifested an interest, even a belligerency, that had been absent
when Owen had broached the subject a year before. Once again
the Indianan wished before taking further steps to give England notice that joint occupancy would end in a year. His
colleagues were not so diplomatic, however; and in a burst of
enthusiasm the House combined the "notice" with an act to
fortify and legislate for the disputed region, a combination that
the Whigs supported in order to make the Oregon measure un-
palatable to the upper chamber.[27]

One other matter remained before the Democratic expansionists were satisfied. On February 13, 1845, Owen made a
report on appropriations for Iowa and Florida, and six days
later a bill admitting those territories to statehood was passed.[28]
Upon the Whig Senate now rested this important program of
territorial extension. By the slender difference of two votes that
body, influenced partly by Tyler's special message, partly by
inertia, and partly by politics, declined to consider the Oregon
bill. The joint resolution on Texas, however, met a different
fate, being adopted by an equally slight margin. When news
of Tyler's approval was read in the House on March 1, applause
rang through the chamber; and when it was added that the
Senate had agreed to admit Iowa and Florida as states, cries
of "Good! that makes 29 stars" were heard.[29] Two days later,
as the House was about to adjourn *sine die*, Owen reported
favorably on Asa Whitney's petition for a grant of public lands
to aid the construction of a railroad from Lake Michigan to the
Pacific. Although no specific plan was recommended by the
committee, Owen stated that it had found nothing impractical
about the project. On the contrary, he said, a transcontinental
railway might well divert the carrying trade of China and the
East Indies from its existing channels to the great benefit of

[27] *House Journal*, 28 Cong., 2 Sess., 319–322; *Cong. Globe*, 28 Cong., 2 Sess.,
222. Cf. *ibid.*, 29 Cong., 1 Sess., 206.
   [28] *House Journal*, 28 Cong., 2 Sess., 341–342, 379–380.
   [29] *Senate Journal*, 28 Cong., 2 Sess., 220, 238 (Feb. 27, Mar. 3); *Cong. Globe*,
28 Cong., 2 Sess., 386.

the American people.[30] Such was the Manifest Destiny of the day.

To Owen the second session of Congress seemed as satisfactory as the first. Most of the problems in which he was interested had been solved to his liking, and on those that had not he had taken a stand that coincided with the views of a majority of his constituents. In the short space of one term he had become a national figure. His career was glowingly described by the party organ; and when Francis P. Blair sent Andrew Jackson a list of young Democrats for Polk to consider as cabinet possibilities, he wrote that "Owen of Indiana is a man of high talent and power."[31] No offer was forthcoming, but the rising Western Democrat felt free to advise the incoming administration on its dispensation of patronage among the New York papers. Still further favorable publicity, national in scope, was obtained by a vigorous open letter answering Horace Greeley's strictures on Indiana's default on her state debt, a letter that convinced many, in the East at least, that the most promising and talented Hoosier Representative was Robert Dale Owen.[32]

Despite this progress Owen's renomination was not yet a settled fact when he reached New Harmony in April 1845. Rotation of office was still a Democratic dogma, nowhere more so than in the West; and notwithstanding the incumbent's excellent record, there were some who wished him to step down. Owen loyally played the rules of the game and dutifully presented his claims to the District Convention at Rockport on May 6. There he was unanimously selected for another term, and his past achievements were lavishly praised.[33]

Owen's third Congressional canvass was the easiest he ever

[30] *Reports of the Committees*, 28 Cong., 2 Sess., no. 199.

[31] *Union*, May 2, 1845; Blair to Jackson, Jan. 3, 1845, *Correspondence of Andrew Jackson* (J. S. Bassett & J. F. Jameson, eds., Wash., 1926–1933), VI, 357.

[32] Owen to R. J. Walker, Mar. 18, 1845, N. Y. H. S. Autograph Collection. *N. Y. Tribune*, Dec. 13, 1844, Feb. 1, 1845; N. Y. *Sun*, quoted in the *Indiana State Sentinel*, Apr. 10, 17, 1845.

[33] *Indiana Statesman*, Feb. 8, 15, 22, Mar. 8, 22, May 24, 1845.

undertook. Whig fortunes in the "Pocket" were at a low ebb, not unlike those of the Democrats in 1841 when Owen declined to run. The opposition was unable to enlist the services of its strongest candidate, and it sorely lacked a winning issue. Payne had been beaten on the tariff in 1843 and Texan annexation was already a *fait accompli*. A bold stand on Oregon, to be sure, was popular in the West, but the Democrats had already pre-empted that position. For a time editor Chandler thought he had a valuable weapon in Owen's delay in obtaining a much desired local law, and he taunted his rival, saying, "If the canal bill should not pass at this session, Mr. Owen may 'hang his harp upon the willows' — he goes back to Congress no more. This the Statesman knows, and . . . dreads the result. . . ." [34] But the canal bill did pass, depriving Chandler of his thunder and enhancing Owen's prestige.

The campaign of 1845, then, lacked both clearcut issues and dramatic interest. Owen made a careful canvass, depending chiefly on his record; while his opponent, George P. R. Wilson, a mediocre local politician, had a little to say on everything without ever pressing an attack home. Even on Texas the incumbent escaped unscathed. Neither Wilson nor Chandler insisted that war with Mexico was inevitable; neither was disposed to deplore in a district largely composed of Southern upland stock the impetus that annexation would give to slavery. [35] In desperation the Whig press resorted to personalities. Owen's superior education and alleged wealth was contrasted with his rival's humble background, the implication being that Wilson understood better the needs of the common man. Robert Owen's current radical activity in England and America was played up to embarrass his son. The *Louisville Journal* published a new "exposition" of writings by the former editor of *The Free Enquirer* and earnestly begged those

[34] *Evansville Journal*, Mar. 6, 1845. See also Samuel Frisbie to Elisha Embree, May 12, 14, 1845, Embree Papers; *Evansville Journal*, May 22, 29, 1845.
[35] This conclusion is based on the files of the *Indiana Statesman, The Evansville Journal*, and other local newspapers. Neither candidate issued a circular.

who profess to be Christians . . . to read the extracts from his writings, and then support him for office if they can. . . . How a Christian can vote for Owen and then dare to lift his thoughts to that Being, whose existence Owen disbelieves, we cannot understand. It is high treason against Heaven. . . .[36]

The Democratic tide and Owen's political invulnerability proved too strong for this essay in religious hysteria. On August 2 the erstwhile reformer won handily by more than a thousand votes. In four years he had erased a 1,365 Democratic deficit in the district, substituting in its place a plurality of 1,005.[37]

The force of environment has seldom been better exemplified than in the modification it wrought upon the thought and activity of Robert Dale Owen. Ten years of conditioning in the democratic West had transformed an alien, well born critic of our institutions into an eloquent exponent of Manifest Destiny. In his new milieu he had become adept on the stump, had grown tolerant of the foibles of his fellow men, and, most of all, had glimpsed the West's vision of a great expanding republic. Thanks to his decision of 1836 he had found an outlet for his boundless energy, and within a decade his natural talents had raised him high in the ranks of his party. As a spokesman of territorial extension he had come by 1845 within striking distance of the great goal of his middle years, a seat in the United States Senate. Expansion, however, was not to be for him an unmixed blessing; and in the next years his political progress was threatened by the perplexing problems of the first fruits of Manifest Destiny — a crisis in Anglo-American relations, a war with Mexico, and a violent resurgence of the slavery controversy occasioned by the disposition of the lands to be won in that war.

[36] Quoted in the *Indiana Statesman*, June 14, 1845. See also *The Evansville Journal*, July 10, 17, 1845.

[37] *Indiana Statesman*, Sept. 6, 1845. The vote stood, Owen, 7,336; Wilson, 6,331.

CHAPTER XII

THE OREGON CRISIS

BEFORE returning to Washington to face the problems raised by expansion, Owen made a second bid for the United States Senate. In the autumn of 1845 the "Pocket's" Representative was an outstanding candidate for a seat he had coveted as early as 1839 and for which he had been prematurely suggested three years before. From various parts of the state came demands that his unquestionable talents be transferred to the upper chamber. As in 1842, however, his chances were virtually destroyed before the caucus met. It so happened that one of his initial supporters, the Lawrenceburg *Beacon*, unwittingly involved his candidacy in an internecine struggle then raging among Hoosier Democrats with the result that the over-cautious Owen in a well-intentioned but unnecessary public letter offered to withdraw from the Senatorial race whenever it would promote party harmony. This statement was quickly distorted by interested factions into a declaration that the Congressman would not, under any circumstances, allow his name to be used.[1]

By early December the Owen boom had collapsed. Since his injudicious letter in September no important editor had come out in his favor. Being a national official, Owen lacked both the local patronage and the state-wide contacts possessed by his chief rivals, Governor James Whitcomb and Lieutenant-Governor Jesse D. Bright. Even his closest friends were discouraged. "You are aware," wrote Joseph Lane from the state capital on the eve of the election,

that I prefer Mr. Owen to any man in the State, whether he can get the nomination is doubtful. His warm and good friends from the

[1] *Political Beacon*, Aug. 14, 1845; Owen to the editors, Sept. 7, 1845, *Indiana State Sentinel*, Sept. 20, 1845; *Madison Courier*, Sept. 27, 1845. Cf. Owen to M. R. Southard, Dec. 16, 1839, Southard Papers.

pocket is afraid to give him up for fear we loose the district. I am however willing to Risk the district if we can get him in the Senate. . . . The U. S. Senate would be *the* place for Mr. Owen's Towering intilect.[2]

Lane's fears were only too well founded. Owen lacked strength among the rank and file of the state legislators, and in the caucus the next day he made the poorest showing of the leading candidates. Once more the desired post eluded him, going instead to Jesse D. Bright who was thus launched on one of the most brilliant and fascinating political careers of any ante-bellum Hoosier.[3]

Before Owen's Senatorial aspirations had been again crushed in disappointment, the new session of Congress had commenced. Life in the national capital during the coming winter promised to be brighter for him; for to the companionship of his father, again returned to America, was to be added that of Mary. The prevailing custom that kept the wives of the lawmakers away from Washington had not, during his first term, bothered the Indianan very much. Intent upon establishing his name in the political firmament, he had thrown himself into his public duties with such industry that he found little time for ordinary recreation. But the Congressional "mess" which made politics a twenty-four-hour-a-day preoccupation, which fanned the fierce partisanship of the period by preventing Democrat and Whig from meeting in social circles could hardly please the cultured and gregarious Owen for long.[4] Thus it was with relief that he grasped the opportunity afforded by the tragic death of his younger son to take his wife eastward and reward her for the many solitary winters she had spent since 1836.

Robert and Mary engaged rooms at a boarding house on Pennsylvania Avenue, near Third Street, where five other

[2] Lane to Alex. Burns, Jr., Dec. 4, 1845, Burns Papers.

[3] *Evansville Journal*, Dec. 11, 1845; *Indiana Statesman*, Dec. 12, 1845. The vote in the caucus was said to have been: Bright, 24; Whitcomb, 18; Chamberlain, 12; Law, 8; Owen, Wright, and others, scattering.

[4] Alex. Mackay, *The Western World; or, Travels in the United States in 1846–47* (London, 1849), I, 180–181.

Democratic Congressmen and their families lodged. Unlike the mess-mates of the first session all these, except Henry St. John of Ohio, came from the East. In contrast to the alleged ruffian-ism of Kennedy and Pettit, Robert P. Dunlap of Maine, Jacob S. Yost of Pennsylvania, Orville Hungerford and George Rath-bun of New York formed such a respectable group that one correspondent jocularly termed it a "religious mess." "Robert Dale Owen," he wrote, "is the *archer* of the establishment. He 'didn't used to be' so pious, but now he is a pattern of exemplary Honorables." [5] As at Indianapolis, Owen dissipated all pre-conceived ideas among strangers of his character by his tact, sincerity, and gentlemanliness. Even his severest critic ad-mitted that "in private life . . . he is amiable, courteous, honest, decent — in short, the very reverse of his public opinions." A more friendly pen wrote of him

As a public man he is without concealment; as a companion and friend he is frank, vivacious, and instructive. He is a great walker, and will give you every day an hour's exercise that will strain your ancles or try your corns.[6]

Except for ex-Governor Dunlap of Maine, with whom he lived again the following winter, Owen found his closest friends outside the boarding house. More than a decade had passed since he had urged Nicholas Trist to join a proposed intellectual retreat on the Wabash, and during much of that time Trist's absence from the country had caused a break in the formerly intimate correspondence. Now, however, the two were thrown together, for really the first time, in a setting that neither could have foreseen in the hectic days of *The Free Enquirer*. In August 1845 Trist returned to Washington in the important post of Chief Clerk of the State Department, and in the trying months of the Oregon crisis and the early part of the Mexican War he and Owen were frequently together. It was Trist's drawing room, enlivened by Mrs. Trist and her charming daugh-

[5] N. Y. *Sun*, June 8, 1846.
[6] *North American*, Jan. 10, 1845; *Mohawk Courier*, quoted in *The Union*, May 2, 1845.

ter, that remained the Indianan's most pleasant recollection of social life at the capital.[7]

When Owen arrived in Washington late in 1845, Anglo-American relations had reached a crisis. Two years before when he had first introduced his notice to terminate the Convention of 1827, the diplomatic seas were comparatively unruffled and the people relatively unconcerned. Now the negotiations begun in October 1843 had ended in failure, and popular opinion on both sides of the Atlantic was aroused. The British were incensed by Polk's inaugural assertion that American rights in Oregon were "clear and unquestionable," and they were determined not to be bullied into surrender. On the other hand, the administration organ in Washington shortly before Congress met insisted on "THE WHOLE OF OREGON OR NONE." West of the mountains Burns was crying that 54° 40' "is ours, and we must have it." The Chapmans declared that, if war was avoidable only at the expense of republican institutions on the Pacific Coast, "then LET IT COME." A contemporary proclaimed as his motto, "Peace, if practicable — war, if necessary." [8]

Behind this jingoism lay the Democratic victory of 1844 and the bold policy of James K. Polk. Like Owen, the president was convinced that the Oregon controversy should be liquidated, immediately and definitively, and for more than a year after his inaugural gave the impression that he would demand all of the province. To be sure, in July 1845, because of the action of his predecessors, the chief executive felt constrained to divide the disputed area at the 49th parallel; but he seemed little disappointed when Richard Pakenham, the British minister, tartly rejected the proposal without referring it to Westminster. Accordingly Polk withdrew the offer and in his annual message of 1845 recommended the extension of American laws over the settlers in Oregon, the erection of forts and stockades

[7] Owen to Trist, Mar. 20, 1849, Trist Papers, XXXIII.

[8] *Union*, Nov. 6, 1845; *Indiana Statesman*, Nov. 29, 1845; *Indiana State Sentinel*, Nov. 15, 1845; Indianapolis *Indiana Democrat*, Nov. 28, 1845.

along the strategic routes to it, and, most important of all, the passage of a notice to terminate joint occupancy of that region. To a friend the president declared,

The only way to treat John Bull was to look him straight in the eye; that I considered a bold & firm course on our part the pacific one; that if Congress faultered or hesitated in their course, John Bull would immediately become . . . more grasping in his demands.[9]

Such a bold course did not, it is true, frighten the British into concessions. It did convince the English government that an immediate settlement must be made, though whether that settlement would be one of peace or war was not clear until the very end.

Spurred on by presidential declarations and expansionist sentiment at home, most Western Democrats quickly committed themselves to a settlement at 54° 40'. Owen, who had been among the first to advocate formal cessation of joint occupancy, now found himself among the moderates. His first speech during the crisis, that of January 3, 1846, contained none of the belligerent fanfare that had become the fashion of the hour. It defended Polk from the extremists who were criticizing the July offer to compromise at 49°. On the other hand, it rejected the Whig solution of arbitration. A second way out, continuance of the agreement of 1827, Owen also opposed since that arrangement had already enabled the Hudson's Bay Company to prevent even a single American citizen from settling north of the Columbia River, the chief area in dispute. A firm assertion of our rights, the Indianan believed, would dispose England to compromise; and he proposed to prove at a later date that a just compromise should be drawn not, as the British wished, at the Columbia River but at the 52nd parallel.[10]

The moderation shown by Owen was not in evidence when the

---

[9] Richardson, *Messages and Papers*, IV, 395–397; *The Diary of James K. Polk* (M. M. Quaife, ed., Chi., 1910), I, 155 (Jan. 4, 1846). Hunter Miller, ed., *Treaties and Other International Acts of the United States*, V (Wash., 1937), 5–101, has the best summary of the diplomatic negotiations.

[10] *Cong. Globe*, 29 Cong., 1 Sess., 135–136.

general debate began two days later. For five long weeks an endless cannonade of words on war and peace, occupation and arbitration, Manifest Destiny and national honor rent the air until the earlier crowds in the galleries began to thin and the vacant benches on the floor deprived the House of its quorum. There was little chance to contribute anything new to the discussion, most of the speeches repeating the preceding ones with monotonous regularity. Even the Western Whigs climbed on the expansionist bandwagon; their bellicosity reflected the fact that beyond the mountains the 54° 40′ spirit was burning at white heat. The Indiana legislature instructed its Congressional delegation to combat any compromise that would yield an inch of American soil, while the Democratic convention in that state opposed any umpirage for the question save at the cannon's mouth.[11]

Late in the debate, but under rather dramatic circumstances, Owen made his second and more important speech on the Oregon question. Being tardy for the appointment, he entered a chamber buzzing with anticipation; and without even taking his seat, he threw off his cloak and began speaking at once. He first pointed out that no boundary south of the 49th parallel could be considered. To accept less would deprive the Americans of the valuable harbors of Puget Sound so necessary for their future trade with the Orient. The Indianan next sought to prove that by the Nootka Convention of 1790, the very document on which Great Britain rested her diplomatic claims, and by contemporary interpretations of it, the United States had the sole and undisputed title to all territory south of 49½°. From this proposition he easily inferred that a just compromise fell not at the 49th but at the 52nd parallel. In concluding, the erstwhile reformer neither wished nor feared war, but appealed to Congress to stand behind the president.

No temporizing policy [he said] befits the present crisis, nor can avail to avert its dangers, if with any it be rife. Firmness, neither

[11] *House Journal*, 29 Cong., 1 Sess., 393 (Feb. 13, 1846); *Indiana Democrat*, Jan. 13, 1846.

boastful itself, nor yet moved by the boasts of others, becomes us as an independent nation. And in such firmness is to be found the best promise, at last, of permanent, because honorable, peace.[12]

Owen's resort to the Nootka Convention to strengthen American claims north of the Columbia brought him more credit, he believed, than any of his earlier speeches in Congress. Hailed as the single novel contribution to the tedious Oregon debate, the interpretation was accepted by three later speakers and several party papers.[13] One result, however, the Indianan had not foreseen. By concentrating on the indisputable American title south of $49\frac{1}{2}°$ and upon the justice of a compromise at the 52nd parallel, he aroused the ire of the extremists. As Hoge of Illinois later remarked, a man who spent an hour justifying claims to $49\frac{1}{2}°$ could not have had much faith in our right to $54° 40'$.[14] Being a Westerner, Owen felt the necessity of keeping his record on expansion clean and at once prepared a corrected version of his remarks for general circulation. By changing the wording in three places and by inserting one new paragraph, the Hoosier reached the conclusion that south of $49\frac{1}{2}°$ the title of the United States was uncontestable, that $52°$ was a proper compromise, and that by the Nootka Convention American claims really extended beyond $54° 40'$.[15]

The significance of Owen's address lies not in the changes provoked by Hoge but in its essentially moderate tone. This moderation grew out of a realistic appreciation that the actual area in dispute lay between the 49th parallel and the Columbia River, the view now generally held by historians. Owen knew that England had never proposed terms essentially better than the river-parallel boundary. He knew also that on five occasions she had refused to accept any compromise at approxi-

[12] *Cong. Globe*, 29 Cong., 1 Sess., Appendix, 146–151 (Jan. 28); *Evening Post*, Jan. 30, 1846.
[13] Owens to Burns, Feb. 20, 1846, Burns Papers; *Courier des Etats Unis*, Feb. 3, 1846, translated in the *Indiana State Sentinel*, Feb. 18, 1846. *Cong. Globe*, 29 Cong., 1 Sess., Appendix, 225, 324, 416; *Evening Post*, Jan. 31, 1846.
[14] *Cong. Globe*, 29 Cong., 1 Sess., 208 (Jan. 30, 1846).
[15] Cf. *ibid.*, 29 Cong., 1 Sess., 270, 272 with Appendix, 147, 149, 150.

mately 49°. His speeches show that he knew too that, on the basis of occupation, British claims to the disputed triangle were the stronger. Forty-nine, on the other hand, would give the United States what it really wanted, good harbors on the Pacific. Without admitting that he hoped for nothing more than an equitable division, Owen resorted to the ingenious interpretation of the Nootka Convention to bolster his country's claims where they were weakest.

After no less than seventy speeches on the subject, the Oregon debate came to a welcome close on February 9. By a vote of three to one, including a majority of the Whigs and all but sixteen Democrats, the "notice" was engrossed, and it passed without a roll call. In the final form the clause requiring that it be given "forthwith" was omitted, and a proviso was added to the effect that the resolution was not intended to interfere with negotiations for an amicable settlement.[16] These changes did little to weaken the original measure; and thus, almost two years after. Owen had made his first futile attempt, an almost unanimous House voted to end the joint occupancy that had existed since 1818 in the Oregon country.

Unfortunately for a prompt disposal of the problem, the Senate required another two months' debate before acting. During February and March the crisis grew more serious. The protracted discussion in the upper house kept the nation in constant apprehension of war. The disclosure that Polk had twice refused arbitration led to one scare; reports of an increase in British armaments precipitated another. New fears were raised late in March by the executive's recommendation that Congress strengthen the country's defences. About the same date one of Owen's colleagues wrote publicly to the Chapmans that an outbreak of hostilities was likely.[17]

The aged Robert Owen chose this critical moment to under-

[16] *House Journal*, 29 Cong., 1 Sess., 367–368; *Cong. Globe*, 29 Cong., 1 Sess., 350.

[17] *National Intelligencer*, Feb. 13, 1846; *Diary of James K. Polk*, I, 241–243 (Feb. 21, 23); Richardson, *op. cit.*, IV, 426–428. *Indiana State Sentinel*, Apr. 1, 1846.

take a self-appointed mission of peace. For some time the old philanthropist had watched with natural dismay the rising tide of chauvinism that threatened to engulf his nation and that of his son. On several occasions he broke into print on the subject; and late in March, in his most important article, he urged a settlement along the 49th parallel with Vancouver Island and free navigation of the Columbia for ten years being reserved to Great Britain.[18] This realistic suggestion was shorn of its force, however, by the manner of its presentation, a manner characteristic of the elder Owen and not unlike that of a Medieval Pope issuing a Bull to an expectant Christendom. Then early in April, without encouragement from the Polk administration but not unnoticed by the press, the former squire of Braxfield sailed for home to intervene personally at Westminster in behalf of compromise.[19]

Although he must have known that for the last quarter century his father had been without influence in British government circles, Owen did not discourage the impractical journey. From the slight evidence available, it appears that after his January speeches the Indianan became even more convinced that the boundary would eventually be drawn along the 49th parallel. Whether he knew that late in February the president was informing his minister in London and leading Democratic Senators that, if Pakenham proposed 49° as a compromise, he would submit the offer to the upper house for advice is not certain. At that time, however, he was informing Burns to prepare sentiment at home for such a contingency.[20] On the eve of his father's departure, Owen forwarded a copy of a speech by Webster in which the Massachusetts statesman precluded any settlement below 49°. If the British were not persuaded by such an authority, wrote the Indianan, "neither would they be persuaded though one rose from the dead." Owen warned that public opinion which had settled down on the 49th parallel

---

[18] *Union*, Mar. 24, 1846. Cf. *ibid.*, Jan. 10, Feb. 4, 1846.

[19] Podmore, *Robert Owen*, II, 588–590; *Union*, Mar. 28, 1846; *National Intelligencer*, Mar. 30, 1846; *N. Y. Herald*, Mar. 31, 1846.

[20] Owen to Burns, Feb. 21, 1846, *Indiana Statesman*, Mar. 7, 1846.

"will soon settle away from it again, if that which ought to be done is not done quickly." [21]

Robert Owen was properly impressed and urged compromise on the cabinet at Westminister. As might have been expected, however, nothing came of his personal intervention. Prime Minister Peel declined to see him, and Lord Aberdeen, Minister for Foreign Affairs, granted him but a single interview. Although he cited his son as the authority for many of his statements, the Welsh reformer was brusquely informed that he brought no information not possessed by Her Majesty's government and "that no public advantage would arise from Mr. Owen's authorized interference in the matter." [22]

While the elder Owen was vainly cooling his heels at Whitehall, his son was participating in the final disposition of the Oregon question. On April 16, 1846, the House resolution was passed by the Senate, so amended as to be unrecognizable. Instead of a "notice" being required of the president, the matter was now left to the discretion of that officer. The measure which Polk had envisaged as a blunt statement terminating joint occupancy was now enacted in the pacific hope

that the attention of the governments of both countries may be the more earnestly and immediately directed to renewed efforts for the amicable settlement of all their differences and disputes in respect to said territory.[23]

Owen, as we have seen, was no 54° 40′ die-hard. Only a day before the House turned to the Senate's handiwork he helped to persuade his chamber to be moderate on some other Oregon legislation.[24] The amended "notice," however, he considered vacillating and unsatisfactory. On a visit to the White House on the evening of April 17, he rejected the president's argument that any "notice" would do and declined to heed the executive's

[21] R. D. Owen to Robt. Owen, Apr. 1, 1846, Robert Owen Papers, no. 1456.
[22] Robert Peel to Robert Owen, May 13, 1846, Robert Owen Papers, no. 1456 and enclosures therein.
[23] *House Journal*, 29 Cong., 1 Sess., 684.
[24] *Cong. Globe*, 29 Cong. 1 Sess., 688.

plea to let well enough alone.[25] As soon as the Senate version was read in the House the next morning, Owen jumped to his feet and proposed two changes, one to strike out the discretionary clause, the other to substitute the words "speedy adjustment" for "amicable settlement." He then moved the previous question. With debate thus shut off, the House accepted his amendments and then repassed the resolution by a large majority.[26] The Hoosier's peremptory action was denounced as belligerent by newspapers of both parties, but the ensuing vote in the Senate was close enough to justify his course. Nevertheless the upper chamber did decide by a margin of eight votes to stand firm. After that decision Polk again brought pressure on the lower house to yield lest the necessity of appointing a conference committee enable the more pacific Senate to block all legislation on the subject.[27]

Once more Owen disregarded presidential wishes. Realizing more clearly than the chief executive that the belligerent popular branch would never back down unless at least a gesture of mutual concession were made, the Indianan again took the initiative. As soon as word of the Senate action had been received, he moved the appointment of a committee of free conference. Because of a point of order, no vote was reached before the day's adjournment; and that night, April 20, Polk again expressed displeasure at the course being pursued by his followers. Nowise deterred the House next morning accepted the motion. As members of the conference committee Speaker Davis of Indiana chose Charles J. Ingersoll, chairman of the Committee on Foreign Relations, Henry W. Hilliard, a Southern Whig who favored a discretionary "notice," and Owen himself. In the Senate, where the ultra-expansionists were purposely passed over, two Whigs and a Southern Democrat were selected. When their names were read in the House, the irre-

[25] *Diary of James K. Polk*, I, 335–336.
[26] *House Journal*, 29 Cong., 1 Sess., 684–686.
[27] *National Intelligencer*, Apr. 20, 1846; *North American*, Apr. 20, 1846; N. Y. *Sun*, Apr. 23, 1846. *Senate Journal*, 29 Cong., 1 Sess., 252. *Diary of James K. Polk*, I, 340–341.

pressible Kennedy could not help giving vent to his disappointment by saying, "What a hell of a committee that is."[28]

As things turned out, Owen's policy, rather than the president's, proved the more effective. By its action the Senate had
given the lower chamber the alternative of a conciliatory resolution or a final disagreement. The latter body could now
recede with dignity, and its appointees were too moderate to
fail to do so.[29] On the evening of April 22 Owen brought to the
White House the welcome news that an agreement had been
reached, an agreement which would be, he predicted, acceptable
to all parties. On the next day the Conference report, almost
identical with the original Senate resolution, passed both houses
by large majorities. It is not without interest that, when the
cry of "Fifty-four forty" was resounding at home, the only
Democrat from the Old Northwest in either branch to support
this measure, so vital for the prompt liquidation of the Oregon
controversy, was Robert Dale Owen.[30]

The Senate "notice" proved to be the final number in the
combination which was to unlock the door barring the way to a
pacific settlement of the boundary dispute. For some time past
Minister Louis McLane had been writing to his government
that the British would take no steps until Congress enacted the
president's recommendations.[31] By May 15, when word of
the resolution of April 22 was received, all the other elements
were prepared. By then the Hudson's Bay Company, realizing
that profitable fur trapping along the Columbia River was at
an end and fearful of the new boisterous American settlers from
the Mississippi Valley frontier, had moved its main post from
that river to Vancouver Island, thus destroying the last British
excuse for insisting upon the area between the Columbia and
49°. By then Lord Russell, disturbed by internal dissension

[28] *N. Y. Herald*, Apr. 23, 1846. *House Journal*, 29 Cong., 1 Sess., 696, 700–
701 (Apr. 21). *Diary of James K. Polk*, I, 341. *Senate Journal*, 29 Cong., 1
Sess., 256.
[29] *Charleston Mercury*, Apr. 23, 1846.
[30] *Diary of James K. Polk*, I, 347.
[31] *Ibid.*, I, 344, 418 (Apr. 22, May 23).

among the Whigs resulting from Palmerston's bellicose foreign policy, had given Peel the political truce necessary to make the Oregon surrender. By then Aberdeen had skilfully won popular support for that surrender by propaganda, while at the same time the economic forces that effected the repeal of the Corn Laws tended to promote international coöperation and good will. Convinced by the Senate's conciliatory wording that the United States would receive favorably a new proposal, Aberdeen despatched on May 19 a final offer, the terms of which were substantially those rejected five times before by his own nation. In Washington Polk submitted the project, as he had planned, to the Senate for counsel, and on June 12, 1846, that body advised acceptance. Six days later the treaty was ratified.[32]

The Oregon settlement inevitably drew forth criticism from extremists on both sides. The Whigs accused Polk of having claimed 54° 40' solely for political purposes, whereas the Democrats from the West blamed him for taking less than the whole. To Owen, however, the treaty brought satisfaction. It vindicated the wisdom of the policy urged by him in 1844, and he was sufficiently realistic to appreciate the extent of England's surrender. He had been cautious enough, too, not to commit himself irretrievably to 54° 40'. On August 6 some remarks of John Quincy Adams stung him into a defence of the pact, and he asserted,

I say, frankly, so far from being ashamed . . . of the boundary we have obtained . . . I should be glad to have the terms . . . incorporated, in the very words of the treaty, in the first section of this bill. . . . In view of these various offers of compromise [1818, 1823, 1826, 1843, 1845], I say, that men who have looked calmly and dispassionately over the whole ground, must have come long

[32] Frederick Merk, "The Oregon Boundary and the Pioneers," *American Historical Review*, XXIX, 681–699 (July 1924); "British Party Politics and the Oregon Treaty," *ibid.*, XXXVII, 653–677 (July 1932); "British Government Propaganda and the Oregon Treaty," *ibid.*, XL, 38–62 (Oct. 1934); "The British Corn Crisis of 1845–46 and the Oregon Treaty," *Agricultural History*, VIII, 95–123 (July 1934). The treaty divided the region at 49°. Vancouver Island and free navigation of the Columbia for ten years were retained by Great Britain.

since to the conclusion, if Great Britain, departing from pretensions to the Columbia river as a boundary — pretensions stoutly maintained for a quarter of a century — did, at last, offer to us the very line we had five times offered to her, that public opinion of the world would not permit us to reject it.[33]

Nor after he had met with political reverses did Owen regret the solution. In an extended review of the whole question a year later, he showed that impartial observers had called the treaty the most humiliating surrender ever made by a British government. Rejection of the pact by the United States would have inevitably led, Owen believed, to a needless and perilous war.[34]

[33] *Cong. Globe,* 29 Cong., 1 Sess., 1203.
[34] *Democratic Clarion,* Aug. 26, 1847.

CHAPTER XIII

POLITICS AND REFORM

BEFORE the Oregon crisis had reached its pacific denouement, Congress was confronted with actual hostilities on another front. Under the aegis of Manifest Destiny Texas had been annexed despite Mexico's blunt warning that such an act would mean war. Whether the conflict was hastened and made unavoidable by Mexican perversity and braggadocio or by presidential recklessness and intrigue is a matter upon which historians are not yet agreed; but while Owen was engrossed in problems relating to the Northwestern boundary and to James Smithson's bequest, signs of imminent danger multiplied. The Indianan was not blind, as some editors later charged, to these portents; but believing Polk's policy the correct one, he gave the administration his full support. There is no reason to believe that at any time, even thirty years later, he dissented from the presidential dictum:

after repeated menaces Mexico has passed the boundary of the United States, has invaded our territory and shed American blood upon the American soil. . . . War exists, and notwithstanding all efforts to avoid it, exists by the act of Mexico itself.[1]

In the first warm glow of patriotic enthusiasm Congress responded readily to the executive's appeal for war supplies. At Indianapolis a similar unanimity prevailed as Democrats and Whigs joined in declaring that the people of the West would support without distinction of party a war involving national honor.[2] After this initial outburst, however, harmony gave way to discord. The militancy of the united Whig minority that

[1] Richardson, *Messages and Papers*, IV, 442. "Recallings from a Public Life. II. Texas and the Peace of Guadalupe Hidalgo," *Scribner's Monthly*, XVI, 868–878 (Oct. 1878).

[2] *Indiana State Journal*, May 20, 1846.

fought to the last ditch every proposal of the administration even remotely connected with the Mexican War has seldom been equalled in Congressional annals. Incessant moral, personal, and partisan criticism characterized the debates. Patriots felt their country was guilty of bullying, humanitarians deplored the extension of slave territory, demagogues exaggerated the cost of the struggle. Most of all, politicians feared that a glorious victory would benefit the party in power. Thus the waste of national treasure, the hardships of the poor volunteers, and the suffering of widows and orphans formed the staple of countless speeches as Whig orators in both houses sought to convince the nation that the war was both unholy and unjust.

Early in January 1847, when Whig obstructionist tactics were at their peak, Owen rose to defend the Democratic record. He first insisted that the annexation of Texas was amply justified by international law and that the war was traceable not to Polk's military maneuvers but to Mexican politicians who, having aroused national prejudices and animosities, feared to receive the new American envoy. The peace terms, Owen believed, must cede sufficient Mexican soil to satisfy old claims and indemnify the United States for the cost of the war. Specifically, he had in mind a boundary running along the Rio Grande and the 32nd parallel to the Pacific, with Lower California being included in the cession. Thus the Hoosier stood half way between the Whigs who opposed further territorial extension and the extreme Democrats who would acquire all Mexico.[3]

Toward the exasperating Whig minority Owen was more tolerant than Polk. He would reprove no man who, honestly believing his country to be in the wrong, criticized the administration, even though such criticism nerved the foe and prolonged the war. But he would denounce as an enemy of civilization those politicians who, with an eye to 1848, were willing to sacrifice the nation's blood upon the "prostituted altar of party." To dispose Mexico to peace, he concluded,

[3] *Cong. Globe*, 29 Cong., 2 Sess., 106–110 (Jan. 4).

She must see us united, harmonious, conscious of the justice of our cause, ready to put forth all our strength. Then, and thus, may she be brought to terms. Then, and thus, may this appeal to arms, the last, I trust, in which America shall ever be forced to engage, come to a close; and the period at last arrive, when we may turn our swords into ploughshares, and study war no more.[4]

For the remainder of his second term in Congress Owen maintained that position. Generally speaking, he gave consistent and loyal support to the Democratic administration. To many reformers and old associates on both sides of the Atlantic who did not appreciate the environment in which he had been living for more than a decade, his course was disappointing, to some even treasonous. A still greater surprise awaited them when Polk's attempt to obtain peace caused to flare up anew, after a quarter century of compromise, the divisive question of slavery.

Before August 1846 slavery had played little part in Owen's political career. Upon the few occasions he had touched the subject, he had reflected his early training and contemporary environment. Although a youthful admirer of Thomas Clarkson, Owen had never been a rabid antislavery advocate. He regarded the institution as a great moral evil, but neither in the columns of *The Free Enquirer* nor as a Representative from southwestern Indiana did he betray any sympathy for the Garrisonians or the Lane Seminary rebels. At Indianapolis and at Washington he joined in rebukes to abolitionists who were bringing pressure on Congress to interfere with slavery in the states, though he did help John Quincy Adams rescind the "gag rule." In his speeches on Texas he expressed the belief that gradual emanicipation, in the Border States at least, was only a few years distant and that economic factors would eventually cause human bondage to disappear.[5]

[4] *Ibid.*, 109.
[5] Indiana General Assembly, *House Journal*, 23d Session, 177–178 (Dec. 31, 1838) ; *Journal of the House of Representatives of the United States*, 28 Cong., 1 Sess., 11–12, 479–480 (Dec. 4, 1843, Feb. 26, 1844) ; *ibid.*, 28 Cong., 2 Sess., 10–11 (Dec. 3, 1844) ; *Cong. Globe*, 28 Cong., 1 Sess., Appendix, 699 (May 21, 1844) ; *ibid.*, 28 Cong., 2 Sess., Appendix, 100–101 (Jan. 8, 1845).

The determination of James K. Polk to obtain a generous slice of Mexican soil at the conclusion of the war brought the erstwhile radical reformer face to face with the question of extending slavery into the federal territories. With characteristic realism the chief executive understood that no Mexican president or general could sign a treaty ceding the northern provinces unless plentifully supplied with money. Following Jefferson's precedent of 1803, Polk requested from Congress on August 8 an appropriation sufficient to cover the preliminary steps in making peace.[6]

Saturday the eighth was extremely hot and muggy, a typical August day in Washington. As if realizing that the capital was no fit place for human beings at such a season, Congress had set its final adjournment for the following Monday. To the usual frantic excitement attendant upon the close of a long, seven-month session was now added the president's mysterious request for money. Bewildered and suspicious, the lawmakers discussed the proposal over their meal during the afternoon recess. With Owen were two fellow lodgers, Dunlap and Yost, and David Wilmot who had sat almost directly behind the Indianan during the session. Wilmot, the only Pennsylvania Democrat to vote for the Walker Tariff, expressed fear lest the sum sought by the executive would be used to acquire new slave states and thus destroy the balance so zealously guarded since 1820. He felt obliged, therefore, to offer an amendment prohibiting slavery in any territory obtained by the two-million-dollar appropriation which had been reported to the House just before the recess. Owen at once demurred. While sympathizing with Wilmot's ultimate aim, he declared that to place in a peace measure a reference to such a controversial subject would defeat the very end the president sought. Wilmot recognized the danger but, unlike the Hoosier, determined to place principle before expediency. After dinner, without Owen's aid,

[6] *Diary of James K. Polk*, II, 50–51, 56–59 (July 26, 30, 31, Aug. 1, 1846); Richardson, *op. cit.*, IV, 459–460.

the Pennsylvanian and other antislavery Democrats drew up the proviso that has since borne Wilmot's name.[7]

The ensuing debate on the Two Million Bill was one of the most interesting in which Owen ever participated. The last evening of the session attracted many visitors of both sexes to the capital as well as such prominent personages as Buchanan, Bancroft, and General Scott. Wilmot's amendment barring slavery from all territories acquired with the appropriation under discussion, introduced soon after the House reconvened, caused the empty benches to fill at once and the Representatives to compete eagerly for the opportunity to speak. With great difficulty Owen obtained the floor, the first Democrat of the Old Northwest to do so. Talking slowly and emphasizing every word, he warned that a denial of the president's request would be interpreted by the world as an expression of our intention to whip a weaker neighbor into submission. In reply to repeated questions from the Whig side of the chamber, Owen declared he was willing to purchase a suitable boundary, not fight for it. Peace was now the main desideratum; for the optimistic Hoosier, ignoring the imminent sectional conflict over slavery, insisted that, once the Mexican imbroglio were removed, there would be no more dangers on the political horizon.[8]

After a heated discussion, the Wilmot Proviso was added, by an 83 to 64 vote, to the Two Million Bill. Since the poll was taken by tellers in the Committee of the Whole, most commentators failed to notice that Owen was one of the few Representatives from the free states to join the opposition. Although the peace bill was thus burdened with what he considered an extraneous matter, Owen voted for its ultimate passage. On the following Monday, however, an eleventh-hour filibuster in

[7] Wilmot's account is summarized in Charles B. Going, *David Wilmot, Free Soiler* (N. Y., 1924), 134–135, and is corroborated by Owen's version of the dinner conversation in a letter printed in *The Democratic Clarion*, Sept. 18, 1847.

[8] *Cong. Globe*, 29 Cong., 1 Sess., 1216; *N. Y. Herald*, Aug. 11, 1846.

the Senate by "Honest John" Davis of Massachusetts killed the measure, leaving the question for settlement by the short session.[9]

This short session saw the sectional clash over slavery reach an acrimony unequalled in Congress since 1820. Owen took no part in the furious debates that raged in the House, but he was again faced with the problem of voting for or against a new Wilmot Proviso. His decision was consistent with his past action. When the measure was first before the House in February 1847, he voted against the slavery restriction as a separate proposition, but for the peace bill as a whole when his opposition had once more proved unavailing. The Senate, however, declined to accept the amendment, returning Polk's appropriation to the lower branch with the antislavery section eliminated. On March 3 the House again voted on the matter, and for the third time in seven months Owen cast his ballot in a manner that might cause him to be regarded as a defender of the peculiar institution. On this occasion, at last, he proved to be in the majority; and to the surprise and chagrin of the abolitionists, the House repassed an appropriation for peace negotiations without the Wilmot Proviso.[10]

With victory once again snatched from their grasp, extremists in the North gave full vent to their disappointment. "Slavery Triumphant" screamed the nation's most widely circulated paper. Many journals placed the names of those men from the free states who had voted against the proviso in a box, bordered by heavy, black lines and entitled "Betrayers of Freedom." In such a box stood the name of Robert Dale Owen. There, too, appeared that of Stephen Arnold Douglas as well as both Indiana Senators and two other Hoosier Representatives.[11]

[9] *Cong. Globe*, 29 Cong., 1 Sess., 1217, 1220–1221; *House Journal*, 29 Cong., 1 Sess., 1284–1286. Cf. Owen's later statements in the *N. Y. Tribune*, Mar. 18, 1847; *Democratic Clarion*, Sept. 18, 1847.

[10] *House Journal*, 29 Cong., 2 Sess., 346–350, 501–505; *Senate Journal*, 29 Cong., 2 Sess., 252–253.

[11] *N. Y. Tribune*, Mar. 4, 1847. *Ibid.*, Mar. 8, 9, 1847; *Liberator*, Mar. 12, 1847. See also, *N. Y. Express*, Feb. 18, 1847; *Indiana State Journal*, Mar. 3, 1847; *Evansville Journal*, Mar. 11, 1847.

ROBERT DALE OWEN AT THE CLOSE OF THE INDIANA YEARS

In some cases, enraged antislavery papers went beyond the bounds of both decency and sanity. In a much copied article a correspondent of Greeley's *Tribune* attempted to show "How It was Done." He attributed the vote of each opponent of the Wilmot Proviso to some bit of executive patronage. In Owen's case it was alleged to be a promise of the diplomatic mission to Brazil, an appointment ostensibly denied at the last moment because Polk disapproved of *Moral Physiology*.[12] Owen wisely ignored the silly allusion, but he grasped the opportunity to explain publicly a course that had astonished his liberal friends in both America and England. To Horace Greeley he wrote late in March,

It is not in accordance with your usual candor to suffer a correspondent to impute not only baseless but absurd motives to public men. . . . It so happens that I voted, session before last, precisely as I did last session. It happens, farther, that I never, in my life, applied for any office in the gift of the Government. . . . A little common sense . . . might have suggested to your correspondent that a sincere and earnest desire to place in the President's hands the probable means of peace, might cause an upright man to vote against the introduction into a peace bill, of a clause, which every one knew must, if persisted in, defeat it; no matter how much opposed that man might be to domestic institutions, which the progress of improvement must soon sweep away. He merits not the name of a Statesman, who seeks an object, however just, with a disregard of all considerations of time or place.[13]

Thus did Owen reconcile politics and reform on the slavery issue.

Paradoxical as it may seem, in an age distinguished by innumerable crusades to aid the common man, a member of Congress found it difficult to participate in reform movements. In politics it was dangerous to be associated publicly with the lunatic fringe, and Owen's radical record in the past made him exercise more than ordinary caution. Then, too, the philosophy

[12] *N. Y. Tribune*, Mar. 13, 1847. Cf. Washington, *National Era*, Mar. 25, 1847; *Liberator*, Mar. 26, 1847.
[13] *N. Y. Tribune*, Mar. 18, 1847. Cf. *National Era*, Apr. 8, 1847; *Democratic Clarion*, Apr. 10, 1847; *N. Y. Globe*, Mar. 19, 1847.

of the day, as well as the practice, decreed that government should be confined to a few functions and not touch the daily life of the individual. The true arena for the reformer in politics was the state legislature. There, and there only, could laws be passed to abolish imprisonment for debt, to secure property rights to married women, to curb intemperance, and to improve facilities for education.[14]

A freethinker in Congress had little opportunity to attest his zeal for religious liberty. Only one item in that connection worthy of mention came up during Owen's tenure. That was a proposal to stop governmental appropriations for chaplains officiating in the national legislature. Thanks to the persistency and fearlessness of Owen's Presbyterian colleague, John Pettit, a resolution to accomplish that purpose was introduced at the beginning of each session. Though roundly abused by his hypocritical colleagues as an infidel at war upon Christianity, Pettit stuck to his guns. As to Owen, he remained aloof from the debates, in which Frances Wright's name was bandied about. On three occasions when the resolution was rejected he was not compelled to record his vote. On a fourth, however, he answered nay to the proposal that "Chaplains shall look to members of the two houses of Congress for their compensation; and that the United States shall not be liable for their salaries or any part thereof." [15] Certainly the former editor of *The Free Enquirer* did not show up too well on that slight test of his liberalism.

In social reform as on the chaplain issue Owen acted with caution. He was more justified in this case, perhaps; for the

[14] Other purely political issues, not mentioned in the text, in which Owen took an interest were the tariff, in which he argued for a drastic reduction of duties, the Independent Treasury, which he helped to reestablish, internal improvements on which he took a strict constructionist stand, the public lands, whose prices he hoped to scale downward by a graduated system, and local problems such as grants from the public domain to complete the Wabash and Erie Canal.

[15] *Cong. Globe*, 28 Cong., 1 Sess., 464 (Mar. 30, 1844); *House Journal*, 28 Cong., 2 Sess., 7–8 (Dec. 2, 1844). *Ibid.*, 28 Cong., 1 Sess., 56; *ibid.*, 29 Cong., 1 Sess., 72, 464.

panacea of the hour, coöperative communities, had long since been rejected by him. He recognized, to be sure, the evils which the Fourierists sought to eradicate and in February 1844 contributed to the *Democratic Review* an article on the steadily diminishing reward received by labor. But in discussing this "Problem of the Age," the Indianan added nothing to what he had said twenty years before in "Wealth and Misery"; and now he omitted the crux of his earlier piece, the solution of the problem. Yet this slight essay helped sustain Owen's reputation as a liberal and won plaudits from two such different men as Van Buren and Greeley. Albert Brisbane read it "with the greatest satisfaction" and begged the author to contribute to the *Phalanx*. He asked Owen for his candid opinion of Fourier's doctrines.[16]

What the Western Democrat had to say about Fourierism has not survived, for his next writings dealt with a less controversial subject, the proper scope of legislation. In these Owen argued strongly for *laissez-faire* in government. He portrayed the futility of trying to curb freedom of thought by law and developed the thesis, discernible in subsequent Congressional speeches, that as a people grow more intelligent and civilized, the need for new laws diminishes. These essays, like the first, were safe; they contained nothing Owen had not said earlier in *The Free Enquirer* or *Daily Sentinel*.[17] Yet again they drew praise from such liberally inclined Democrats as Van Buren, Bryant, and James Kirke Paulding. The last thought the Indianan's articles excellent, marred only by a childlike faith, natural enough in a son of Robert Owen, in the miracles to be wrought by the magic word "progress." To the author he wrote,

I hope you will have an opportunity of bringing your views on the subject . . . before Congress ere long: though I fear they will have

[16] "One of the Problems of the Age," *U. S. Magazine and Democratic Review*, XIV, 156–167. Owen to Van Buren, June 15, 1844, Van Buren Papers, LI; *N. Y. Tribune*, Apr. 11, 1844; Brisbane to Owen, Mar. 28, 1844, Dreer Collection: American Prose, I. See also, *Evening Post*, Feb. 7, 1844; *Daily Plebeian*, Feb. 9, 1844.

[17] *Ante*, 186 n. 25.

little effect. . . . If you will permit me to advise, be moderate at first, and deal with one subject at a time. . . . Truth never bursts open the door, but knocks softly. . . . It is of great consequence to know where we are going, before we set out; and my suggestion to you is, never as a Legislator, or Philosopher, to lay down a principle without following it out through all its consequences. In doing this, I have nine cases in ten, found that two roads leading in exactly opposite directions brought me to precisely the same point at last.[18]

By keeping to the middle of the road, as advised by Paulding and in accordance with his own interests, Owen gave offence to at least one old associate. In 1836 George Henry Evans, sick in body and discouraged by his inability to keep alive a radical daily in New York City, had retired to a farm in New Jersey. There he regained not only his health but also the agrarian philosophy that he had learned from Thomas Skidmore in 1829 but which he had subordinated at that time to the educational theories of Owen and Frances Wright. Declaring every citizen had an inherent right to a piece of land, Evans brought forward a proposal for allowing actual settlers to stake out for their own immediate use portions of the public domain. Gathering a group of followers that included many of the old Working Men's Party into a National Reform Association, Evans began in March 1844 a new series of the *Working Man's Advocate*. Quite naturally he turned to his former co-editor, already becoming an important figure in the national legislature, for assistance in promoting his ideas. As early as January 1844 Owen had introduced a petition from Evans to dispose of Oregon lands free to settlers, and five months later he presented a formal request for a general homestead law.[19]

Offering memorials in Congress and openly advocating freedom of the public lands meant two different things to Owen, as Evans quickly discovered. Ever since the failure of the New Harmony experiment Owen had doubted the efficacy of

---

[18] Paulding to Owen, Jan. 6, 1845, Dreer Collection, American Prose, VI. Cf. Paulding to Van Buren, Dec. 20, 1844, Van Buren Papers, LII.

[19] *Working Man's Advocate*, Mar. 16, May 11, June 8, 1844; *House Journal*, 28 Cong., 1 Sess., 217, 1069 (Jan. 12, June 11, 1844).

curing social ills by giving individuals equal bits of real estate, and among his property-conscious constituents the panacea of the National Reformers excited little interest. Owen recognized that cheap Western lands provided a potential safety-valve for industrial America; but he did not labor the point, going no further than recommending a graduation of sale prices. To a member of the National Reform Association who had requested his aid, public or private, in advancing Evans' plans, the Hoosier replied,

Each man can only do a certain amount of good in this world. In attempting too much, he often fails in that which he might actually accomplish. In all the questions which came before Congress, I have taken . . . that side which I considered to be in accordance with just principles of human rights. If, so far as I have gone, I have gone right, that is something; even if it should be thought I have not gone far enough.[20]

In short, the Western Democrat declined to march under Evans' banner.

Although disappointed by Owen's middle of the road policy, Evans did not divulge the identity of his correspondent, whose letter he printed. He held his peace until Owen's advocacy of a bill giving Indiana 800,000 acres of the public domain in order to complete the Wabash and Erie Canal seemed to indicate hostility, not indifference, to free homesteads. In an extended editorial headed "Robert Dale Owen" Evans regretfully placed his old friend among the enemies of republican institutions and human rights. He even went so far as to repeat the false Whig charges that Owen's championing of the Canal Bill resulted from a desire to benefit his own private property. Another member of the old Working Men's party agreed, in a public letter, that Evans had just cause for suspicion.[21]

Such grave charges, made by former friends, could not be

[20] "A Voice from Congress," *Working Man's Advocate*, June 8, 1844. The writer's name was not given, but Owen's authorship is suggested by internal evidence and Evans' description of the correspondent. See also, *Democratic Review*, XIV, 167.

[21] *Working Man's Advocate*, Mar. 8, 15, 1845.

ignored. In a detailed explanation of the Canal Bill, Owen publicly denied that it would encourage land speculation or that it would benefit him personally. He thought the measure a good one and pointed to memorials signed by 17,000 persons as an unanswerable justification for his vote. Evans replied that a Representative's obligation to his constituents did not extend to the support of so infamous an act, but he said nothing more regarding Owen's motives. In fact, he even expressed the hope that the Western Democrat would yet assist the National Reformers.[22] In this last, however, he was disappointed. Owen voted against Evans' wishes not only on the land question but on Whitney's petition for railroad subsidies, the tariff, the Mexican War, and the Wilmot Proviso.[23] During the Twenty-Ninth Session of Congress the National Reform Association ceased to send its petitions to Owen. Silently, without further ado, another thread with the past snapped.

One interesting aspect of Owen's attempt to reconcile party politics and social reform concerned his relations with his father. Many changes had taken place since Robert Owen and son embarked twenty years before on their American adventure. The latter was nearing the zenith of his powers, whereas the former's active influence was largely at an end. In England a new generation had arisen to carry on the work of socialism and coöperation, while the founder lapsed into theories that became progressively more hopeful, more visionary, and more impractical. Nor did his three winters spent in America from 1844 to 1847 serve any useful purpose. Yet with a filial respect that was ever one of his most admirable traits, Owen gave sympathetic assistance to his sire's vague efforts. He introduced his father to party leaders, circulated his socialistic tracts under the franking privilege, and apparently never protested against any radical action that might bring political embarrassment

---

[22] Owen to the editor, Mar. 19, 1845, *Young America*, Mar. 29, 1845. *Ibid.*, Mar. 29, Apr. 12, 1845.
[23] *Ibid.*, June 28, 1845, Mar. 6, 1847; *Working Man's Advocate*, May 18, 1844.

upon himself.[24] This attitude was the more praiseworthy; for, as we shall see, father and son had drifted far apart in their ideas on social amelioration.

To many Americans of that generation and the next Robert Dale Owen seemed a greater man than his father. With his life work done and senility upon him, Robert Owen became to the men of the forties and fifties an intolerable bore. On one occasion the irate John Quincy Adams noted in his diary that the former squire of Braxfield "mesmerized me for . . . an hour and a half with his lunacies about a new organization of society" and upon another "he went over the same preamble that I had heard from him twenty-seven years ago in London, which he afterwards crowded upon me year after year here . . . and from which I have hoped for the last fifteen years, that this country was forever delivered." Compared in influence to the Representative from Indiana, declared one commentator, the father was "a harmless driveller." [25] The current interests and work of the two men were eloquently contrasted on the first page of *The Daily Union* for December 5, 1846. Except for advertisements there was nothing but two long articles by the Owens. The one signed by Robert Dale Owen was entitled a "Report of the Organization Committee of the Smithsonian Institution." The one over the name of Robert Owen bore the heading, "A Few of the Innumerable Reasons for an Immediate Entire Change of the Existing System of Society in the United States, in Europe, and over the World."

Despite his comparative conservatism on the reforms of the hour, the younger Owen never completely lost his reputation as a radical. His literary contributions and his outspoken denunciation of nativism reinforced his claim to liberalism.[26]

---

[24] Robert Owen to J. E. Smith, Dec. 28, 1844, *New Moral World*, Feb. 22, 1845; R. D. Owen to Robt. Owen, Aug. 20, 1847, Robert Owen Papers, no. 1508. Cf. *N. Y. Herald*, Dec. 10, 1844.

[25] *Memoirs of John Quincy Adams*, XII, 117, 120 (Dec. 6, 11, 1844); *North American*, Jan. 10, 1844.

[26] *Cong. Globe*, 28 Cong., 1 Sess., Appendix, 380–381 (Apr. 24, 1844); *ibid.*, 29 Cong., 1 Sess., 71 (Dec. 17, 1845); *Madison Courier*, Aug. 17, 1844.

Freethinkers continued to read his earlier writings in their journals, and between 1839 and 1846 at least three American and four English editions of *Moral Physiology* appeared. Handbills advertising these were said to have been circulated in Washington to annoy him.[27] Party editors wishing to discredit the rising Western Democrat continued to depict him as a blasphemous, wild-eyed disorganizer. Even Robert Owen helped to create a false impression in England by saying unjustifiably, "He is gradually coming to see the practical measures as I view them, and will one day or other prove serviceable to the great cause in which we are all engaged." [28] Robert Dale Owen was yet to strive diligently to aid suffering mankind but not along the lines envisaged by his father in 1845.

[27] *N. Y. Tribune*, Aug. 23, 1847.
[28] *North American*, Jan. 26, Mar. 28, 1844, Jan. 10, 1845; *Courier & Enquirer*, July 14, 1846. Robert Owen to G. A. Fleming, Mar. 31, 1845, *New Moral World*, May 10, 1845.

CHAPTER XIV

THE SMITHSONIAN INSTITUTION

DURING his Congressional years Owen made one strenuous effort to aid the common man. That was his work as legislative proponent and Regent of the Smithsonian Institution. Today we think of that worthy organization as learned rather than popular, helpful to the student rather than to the layman. But a century ago there were those who dreamed of and battled vainly for a different use of the fortune left the United States "to found at Washington, under the name of the Smithsonian Institution, an establishment for the increase and diffusion of knowledge among men." One of these dreamers and fighters was Robert Dale Owen.

By 1843 fourteen years had passed since James Smithson's death and five since the United States had obtained his bequest of $508,318.46. During that half decade not a single American had been made wiser by Smithson's generosity for the simple reason that Congress could not decide what kind of an "establishment" should be created. Some people wanted a national university of graduate standing, though they could not agree whether it should embrace divinity, medicine, and law or just the sciences and the humanities. Some wanted an agricultural experiment station, others a botanical garden, still others, an art gallery. There were those who favored the founding of a popular periodical of useful information, like the English *Penny Magazine*. John Quincy Adams advocated a national observatory; whereas Richard Rush suggested an organization that would coöperate with the government in its scientific work, correspond with learned societies abroad, print monographs based on exhaustive research, and offer lectures by noted educators. Still another proposal was to use the bequest for the

National Institute, a scientific society founded in 1840 at the capital, which possessed no endowment of its own.[1]

During his first winter at Washington Owen took no visible interest in the problem of the Smithsonian legacy. Although he became a corresponding member of the National Institute, he did not participate in its much publicized meeting of April 1844, designed to promote the campaign to merge that body with the non-existent Smithsonian.[2] At that time the young Congressman was too busy winning laurels with speeches on Oregon, Texas, and the tariff to attend to a matter in which his constituents had no interest. It was not until his return to the capital in December 1844 that the Western Democrat began his efforts to enact James Smithson's will into law. It was probably his liberal friend and former "mess-mate" Benjamin Tappan who called his attention to the subject; for only a few days after his arrival, Owen was writing to Van Buren, requesting permission to use the ex-president's name as Director in the Smithsonian bill that the Ohio Senator intended to introduce early in the session.[3]

On December 12, 1844, Tappan presented his plan for increasing and diffusing knowledge among men. His measure provided for an agricultural college, chemical laboratories, scientific cabinets, and popular lectures. Great emphasis was placed on the application of science to the everyday life of the common man.[4] Tappan's highly utilitarian scheme proved very unpopular, at least among those who could register their views in Congress or had access to the columns of the leading newspapers. In the Senate the chief foe was Rufus Choate who insisted, without good authority, that Congress had already decided not to use the legacy for an educational institution. While

---

[1] George B. Goode, ed., *The Smithsonian Institution, 1846–1896* (Wash., 1897), 1–41. See also Owen's speech of Apr. 22, 1846, *Cong. Globe*, 29 Cong., 1 Sess., Appendix, 467–471.

[2] *Third Bulletin of the Proceedings of the National Institute for the Promotion of Science* (Wash., 1845), especially 408, 455–460.

[3] Owen to Van Buren, Dec. 11, 1844, Van Buren Papers, LII.

[4] William J. Rhees, ed., *The Smithsonian Institution: Documents Relative to Its Origin and History, 1835–1899* (2 v. Wash., 1901), I, 276–280.

willing to accept a few minor items in the Ohioan's proposal, the brilliant Whig orator from Massachusetts eloquently urged an entirely different project, the expenditure of $20,000 annually to build a national library, equal in quality if not in quantity to any in the world. The Senator deplored the lack of great collections in the United States, the absence of which, he thought, justified the taunts so frequently made by foreigners of our cultural backwardness. He felt that a Smithsonian Library would not only increase knowledge effectively but also wipe away the stigma of inferiority.[5]

Thanks to Choate's stirring appeal to patriotic pride and to the prevalent fear that a national university would waste money on expensive professorships, the library plan won immediate and widespread approval. Neither Tappan's followers, who thought it undemocratic, nor the friends of the National Institute, who regretted the lack of attention to science, could prevent its passage in the Senate. Owen was equally disappointed. So long as $20,000, almost the entire annual income, was to be used for the purchase of books, there would be little money left for functions that would more directly diffuse knowledge.[6] In order to obtain a juster compromise between the conflicting views, Owen drew up a substitute measure to present to the House.

Given Owen's previous experience in the East in educating adult workingmen through cheap tracts and popular lectures, and given his first-hand acquaintance with the backward state of agricultural and common school instruction in the West, the new bill was certain to be more democratic and lay more emphasis on the diffusion of learning than that of the aristocratic Choate. The sections dealing with finances and administration were taken from Tappan's draft, as were provisions for scientific cabinets and horticultural experiments. The significant alteration came where the preamble of the Senate draft declared

[5] *Cong. Globe*, 28 Cong., 2 Sess., Appendix, 62–65 (Jan. 8, 1845). Cf. *National Intelligencer*, Dec. 25, 27, 1844, Jan. 3, 1845.

[6] *Cong. Globe*, 28 Cong., 2 Sess., 106–107, 115–117, 179 (Jan. 8, 9, 23, 1845). The bill was printed in the *National Intelligencer*, Jan. 24, 1845.

that "an ample and well-selected public library" was a most effectual way to increase and diffuse knowledge. To this Owen added a coördinate statement that "judiciously conducted common schools" were equally important in achieving that end. The Indianan then reduced the yearly expenditure on books from $20,000 to $12,000 and authorized the appointment, among others, of a professor of common school instruction. Another important addition provided for the occasional publication by the Institution at cost price of essays, pamphlets, or magazines for the dissemination of useful scientific knowledge.[7]

The ensuing failure in the House of Owen's amended bill was due chiefly to John Quincy Adams. Although the measure had apparently the approval of both Choate and Tappan and although a special evening meeting was arranged for its consideration, it was postponed and finally, on the last day of the session, cast aside by the obstructionist tactics of the testy ex-president. Adams confided exultingly to his diary that he had defeated "a swindling Smithsonian bill"; but the press, without distinction of party, blamed him for his action.[8] As *The Globe* remarked, Old Man Eloquent's own plan had been rejected four times, yet he would not assent to any scheme not original with himself. The statesman's own writings reveal the jealousy and suspicion with which he regarded the efforts of other men. To Robert J. Walker, staunch friend of the National Institute, he described Owen's "absurd amendment" and the desperate attempts made by the Indianan and others "to force the bill upon the House in its last agonies *and the selfish purposes transparent through their motions.*"[9] To be sure, Adams still hoped to see an institution established; but at the next session

---

[7] Owen's bill of Feb. 10, 1845 was printed in *The Daily Globe*, Feb. 21, 1845.

[8] *House Journal*, 28 Cong., 2 Sess., 449, 563; *Cong. Globe*, 29 Cong., 2 Sess., 331, 395; *National Intelligencer*, Feb. 24, Mar. 6, 1845; *N. Y. Herald*, Mar. 5, 1845. See also *Memoirs of John Quincy Adams*, XII, 177; *Globe*, Feb. 21, 1845; *National Intelligencer*, Feb. 22, Mar. 4, 1845; *N. Y. Tribune*, Mar. 5, 1845; *Evening Post*, Mar. 5, 1845.

[9] *Globe*, Mar. 5, 1845; *Memoirs of John Quincy Adams*, XII, 199. The italics are mine.

he was to discover that, either because of his own peevish envy or because of the more energetic and conciliatory tactics of another, his assistance was no longer indispensable. With Tappan, Choate, and Walker gone from the Senate, the initiative fell to the lower house; and the leadership there was provided not by John Quincy Adams but by Robert Dale Owen.

Late in the summer of 1845 Owen prepared for another attempt to enact Smithson's bequest into law. From his brother Dale, an able draftsman, a trained student of chemistry and medicine, and one of the nation's outstanding geologists, he obtained interior and exterior sketches for the building of the future institution. He probably discussed, too, with his brother Richard the latter's proposal, published five years before in the *South-Western Sentinel*, to use the legacy to found a national normal school.[10] Returning to Washington, Owen early in December introduced a new bill which, at his request, was referred to a select committee of which he was named chairman. Favorable press notices from both parties gave reason to hope that success was at hand. The Whig national organ, for instance, was delighted to see the matter brought up at the beginning of the session "under the auspices of so influential a member." Only the correspondent of *The North American*, who had previously ridiculed the work of Tappan and Walker, tried to arouse prejudices against the measure.[11]

As the only bill embodying his ideas unmodified by any necessity for compromise or conciliation, Owen's draft of December 1845 is worthy of close examination. By its provisions $242,129 (the interest accruing on the original sum transmitted in 1838), or a part thereof, were to be used to enclose grounds suitable for agricultural and horticultural experiments and to

[10] R. D. Owen to D. D. Owen, Aug. 15, 1845; D. D. Owen to R. D. Owen, Oct. 10, 1845, copies of which are in the Library of the Workingmen's Institute. See also R. D. Owen to Robt. Owen, Oct. 10, 1845, Robert Owen Papers, no. 1394; *New Moral World*, Aug. 7, 1841.

[11] *House Journal*, 29 Cong., 1 Sess., 137 (Dec. 19); Owen to Burns, Dec. 19, 1845, Burns Papers; *National Intelligencer*, Dec. 20, 1845; *Union*, Dec. 19, 1845; N. Y. *Sun*, Dec. 19, 1845; *North American*, Dec. 12, 1845.

erect a plain building capable of housing laboratories, lecture rooms, scientific cabinets, and a library. The institution was to be governed by an unsalaried committee comprising the vice-president of the United States, the chief-justice of the Supreme Court, three Senators, three Representatives, and seven citizens at large. The real executive, however, was to be a superin-tendent, appointed by the Committee of Managers.

The important part of Owen's draft was the section which definitely abandoned the compromise with Choate's bill. In February 1845 Owen had declared that a large library and efficient public schools were the best means of adding to and disseminating learning. Now, in December, he asserted that "the most effectual mode of promoting the general diffusion of knowledge is by judiciously conducted common schools," while "knowledge may be essentially increased among men by insti-tuting scientific researches, and generally, by spreading among the people a taste for science and the arts." Thus Choate's annual expenditure for books, cut from $20,000 to $12,000 in February, was now reduced to $5,000. A normal school of graduate rank was provided for, and emphasis was placed upon popular instruction and experimental research. Drawing once again upon his New York experience, Owen authorized the publication and sale of magazines and cheap tracts.

for the dissemination of information among the people, *and espe-cially works in popular form on agriculture and its latest improve-ments, on the sciences and the aid they bring to labor, manuals explanatory of the best systems of common school instruction, and generally tracts* illustrative of objects of elementary science and the rudiments of history, chemistry, astronomy, or any other department of useful knowledge; *also they* [the Managers] *may prepare sets of illustrations, specimens, and apparatus, suited for primary schools.*[12]

Owen's further democratization of the Senate bill of the pre-vious session was not fully approved by the committee to which it was referred. Adams strongly opposed the section dealing

---

[12] Rhees, *op. cit.*, I, 322–326. The italics are mine and indicate the additions to a similar section in Owen's bill of Feb. 1845.

with agricultural experiments and the national normal school. With George P. Marsh of Vermont, to whom fell the mantle formerly worn by Choate as champion of a big library, he sought to restore the $20,000 annual appropriation for books; but only a $5,000 increase could be obtained. One important victory for the ex-president, however, was an amendment investing the Board of Managers with all the powers, duties, and liabilities of a corporation. This change, which Owen disliked and which was to cause more protest in the House than any other provision, succeeded only because Sims, a Calhoun man, voted for it against his true convictions in order to make the entire act unacceptable to the Southern Democrats.[13]

Consideration of Owen's measure in the House awaited the disposition of the Oregon resolution. The Indianan finally opened the debate on April 22, 1846, with a detailed history of the bequest. He defended his own bill as incorporating most of the features suggested in the past for the new institution. He attacked Choate's scheme as contrary to Smithson's intentions and, because of the large sum allotted to books, fatal to any scientific activity. A huge library at Washington he regarded as aristocratic, designed for a few local or wealthy bibliomaniacs. In his opinion the money could be most advantageously utilized to remove inequalities among its citizens, especially inequality of education. A national normal school, supplementing but not replacing those in the several states, would do much to further uniform teaching. "I hold it to be a democratic duty," said the Hoosier, "to elevate . . . the character of our common school instruction. I hold this to be a far higher and holier duty than to give additional depth to learned studies, or supply curious authorities to antiquarian research." In the improvement of primary education, the advancement of agriculture, and the stimulus to scientific experiments Owen saw useful features of his bill. But even more important to him was the fact that it benefitted the people as a whole.

[13] *Memoirs of John Quincy Adams*, XII, 239–240, 245–247 (Jan. 30, Feb. 13, 20, 1846).

Sir [he concluded], over the entire land must the rills from this sacred fountain freely flow. . . . To effect permanent good . . . we must reach the minds and the hearts of the masses; we must diffuse knowledge among men; we must not deal it out to scholars and students alone, but even to Tom, Dick, and Harry; and then . . . "they will become Mr. Thomas, and Mr. Richard, and Mr. Harry." . . . The ancient masters realized not these truths. With the millions they had no sympathy. . . . Thanks to the stirring spirit of progressive improvement, all this, in our age, is changed. By modern teachers the people are spoken of, spoken to, care for, instructed. To the people the characteristic literature of the day is addressed. . . . The people govern in America. . . . As we value wise government . . . let the schools of the people, and the teachers who preside in these schools, and the system that prevails in these schools, be our peculiar care. We can not reform the world, no, nor provide instruction for a great nation, by any direction given to half a million dollars. But something, even in such a cause, may be effected by it — something, I devoutly believe, that shall be felt all over our broad land. The essential is that, if little we can do, that little be well done, be done faithfully, in the spirit of the trust, in the spirit of the age, in a spirit not restrictive, not exclusive, but diffusive, universal.[14]

Owen's democratic appeal, very appropriate in the age of the common man, passed unheeded. A few speakers in the subsequent four-day debate did stress the popular aspects of the institution, some demanding even a manual labor school and free lectures throughout the nation.[15] But the great majority rejected the plan for diffusing the benefits of the bequest among the masses. Owen's draft was criticized by those who desired a national library, by those who were horrified at the idea of Congress creating a corporation, by the extreme constitutionalists who wished to return the legacy to England, and by those who wanted to postpone all legislation until the original fund, invested in worthless Michigan and Arkansas bonds, was recovered. This last group was led by Adams, who in 1844 had inconsistently proposed to borrow the missing capital from the Treasury, and included Andrew Johnson who had already launched a demagogic attack on the Military Academy at West

[14] *Cong. Globe*, 29 Cong., 1 Sess., Appendix, 471.
[15] *Cong. Globe*, 29 Cong., 1 Sess., 475.

SKETCH OF THE PROPOSED SMITHSONIAN INSTITUTION: VIEW FROM THE NORTHEAST

Point.[16] Whether Owen's prominence in championing the bill retarded its progress was a matter on which commentators could not agree, but at least one editor and his Washington correspondent professed to believe that the proposed measure was a diabolical plot to spread Fourierism throughout the land.[17]

The general hostility manifested towards Owen's draft made modifications inevitable. The voting on April 29 resulted in a victory for the "big library" advocates. Owen's most novel contribution, the national normal school, was badly beaten. A substitute measure, drawn up by Owen's friend William J. Hough of New York would have met a similar fate if the provisions for professorships, experimental research, and the publication of cheap tracts had not been eliminated. When the Committee of the Whole finished its work, Owen's bill had been shelved and Hough's substitute burdened with a section appropriating $25,000 annually for books, a sum exceeding even that demanded by Choate the previous year. Owen was thus confronted with the unhappy alternative of voting for a measure he obviously disliked or, by opposing it, of delaying for another year, at least, the execution of the will of the English philanthropist. To his credit, the Indianan did not hesitate. Turning to a fellow member, he declared his intention to support the amended version. This he did, and by a margin of seven ballots the House for the first time passed an act establishing a Smithsonian Institution.[18]

In the Senate procrastination was the chief obstacle to success. Although reported with some changes by a committee early in June, the measure was not considered, despite promptings from the press, until two days before adjournment. Even then it was immediately laid aside lest debate over the changes

[16] *Ibid.*, 714, 719–720, 736, 739, 741; Rhees, *op. cit.*, I, 332.

[17] N. Y. *True Sun*, Apr. 24, 1846; *N. Y. Herald*, Apr. 24, 1846; *North American*, Apr. 24, 25, 1846.

[18] *House Journal*, 29 Cong., 1 Sess., 736–738; *Cong. Globe*, 29 Cong., 1 Sess., 749. *Evening Post*, Aug. 22, 1846. An analysis of the poll shows little except that more than a quarter of the House did not vote.

consume valuable time. As the body assembled on the very last day of the session, however, the alert George Evans, a Whig from Maine, moved that the bill be taken up and the Senate's amendments disagreed to. The motion was accepted; and quickly, almost unexpectedly, the long desired act passed.[19]

The complete triumph of Choate's plan was apparent in the law creating the Smithsonian Institution. Every vestige of an educational establishment had disappeared. Nothing was said concerning lectures, obligatory scientific research, or the publication of cheap tracts. The only well defined purpose of the Institution was the formation of a library, and for that almost the entire annual revenue might be used.[20] Yet the refusal of the House to accept Owen's favorite proposals does not deprive him of all claim to being a founder. In form, phraseology, and certain details the statute was his or, better, his and Tappan's. Probably no act specifying too minutely the functions of the establishment could have satisfied a majority in Congress, and the main problem in 1846 was to get some bill passed. Thus it is Owen's chief credit that the very first session in which he acted as legislative steersman, the subject received a more complete hearing, both in committee and on the floor of the House, than ever before.[21] Without Owen some law would have eventually been enacted. That it came in the year that saw the tariff revised, the Independent Treasury reestablished, the Oregon boundary settled, and the Mexican War begun was in a large part the result of the Indianan's courtesy, tact, and perseverance. Although political opponents rejoiced at the defeat of his supposedly "visionary scheme," Owen's true service was recognized both in Congress and in the press. And that service was rewarded by his appointment

[19] *Senate Journal*, 29 Cong., 1 Sess., 320, 519 (June 1, Aug. 10); *Cong. Globe*, 29 Cong., 1 Sess., 1205 (Aug. 7). Cf. *N. Y. Morning News*, June 24, 1846; *N. Y. Journal of Commerce*, June 26, 1846; *Evening Post*, June 30, 1846.

[20] *United States Statutes at Large*, IX, 102–106.

[21] Owen to Burns, Jan. 24, 1846, *Indiana Statesman*, Feb. 7, 1846; *Memoirs of John Quincy Adams*, XII, 235, 239, 245, 247, 250. Cf. *ibid.*, XII, 26, 27, 29, 32, 34, 41.

as one of the three Regents of the Institution from the House of Representatives.[22]

Three weeks after the end of the long eight-month Congressional session, Owen was again in Washington to take up his new duties. At noon on an exceedingly hot seventh day of September, 1846, he and twelve other Regents assembled in the General Post Office Building, closed the doors to all visitors, and sat for some hours discussing the vague instrument with which they were to increase and diffuse knowledge among men. Owen quickly proved to be one of the most industrious and influential of the governors. He was placed on an Executive Committee of three entrusted with control of the Institution's finances. He was made chairman of a sub-committee raised "to digest a plan to carry out the provisions of the act." He probably had as much as any other one man to do with the final selection of the site of the new organization, the Mall between Twelfth and Fourteenth Streets. When the Regents turned to the problem of a Smithsonian building, Owen was ready with the plans drawn up by Dale the previous summer. This design, together with an earlier one by Robert Mills, was referred to Owen and four others who were authorized to take steps "for the erection of buildings fulfilling all the conditions . . . in the law organizing this institution." Accordingly, Owen and two of his colleagues made a tour late in September of the important Eastern cities, examining public edifices, consulting prominent architects, and inquiring into proper construction materials, styles, and methods of heating, lighting, and ventilation. Owen kept a daily record of this investigation and submitted it as an appendix to a subsequent report.[23]

[22] *North American*, May 1, 1846. Cf. *Cong. Globe*, 29 Cong., 1 Sess., 748; *ibid.*, Appendix, 851; *N. Y. Journal of Commerce*, June 26, 1846; N. Y. *Sun*, Aug. 13, 1846; Washington *Saturday Evening News*, Aug. 15, 1846; *Evening Post*, Aug. 22, 1846. *House Journal*, 29 Cong., 1 Sess., 1306 (Aug. 10).

[23] *The Smithsonian Institution: Journals of the Board of Regents, Reports of the Committees, Statistics, etc.* (W. J. Rhees, ed., *Smithsonian Miscellaneous Collections*, no. 329, Wash., 1879), 1–20; *Diary of James K. Polk*, II, 120, 124–125, 264–265, 272–273, 284; *National Intelligencer*, Sept. 8, 1846; *N. Y. Herald*, Sept. 9, 1846. According to Mr. H. W. Dorsey, Chief Clerk of the Smithsonian Institution, Owen's journals were probably destroyed in the fire of 1865.

In the important task of selecting a permanent Secretary, Owen played an equally prominent role. Since the scope of the Institution's activity was still undetermined and since the Regents were necessarily a transitory and untrained group, the success of Smithson's bequest might depend largely on this choice. Owen realized that fact and wrote in his first report that

the office of Secretary must . . . be regarded, not as one to be filled by any man capable to act as recording clerk, or to receive with politeness, the visitors of the Institution . . . but as an office on the due administration of which the executive efficiency of our Institution at home and its reputation abroad, mainly depend. . . .[24]

Among the applicants for the position were Francis Markoe, Jr., Corresponding Secretary of the National Institute, Charles Pickering, late Chief Zoologist of the United States Exploring Expedition to the South Seas, and John Romeyn Brodhead, subsequently historian of the state of New York.[25] Owen's choice seems to have been Joseph Henry, distinguished for his research in physics and then professor at the College of New Jersey, or at least a man of similar caliber. Before the election took place he suggested that the future Secretary "possess qualifications of a professor of the highest standing" (thus excluding Markoe, Pickering, and Brodhead) and then formally resolved that he be a man "capable of advancing science and promoting letters by original research." Other evidence, less trustworthy, also indicates that Owen and his friends preferred the Princeton scholar.[26] On December 3, therefore, amid universal expressions of satisfaction, Henry was elected by the Board of Regents.[27]

[24] "Report of the Organization Committee," Dec. 1, 1845, printed in *The Union*, Dec. 5, 1846.

[25] Markoe to Peter Force, Aug. 13, 18, 1846; John R. Bartlett to Force, Sept. 3, 1846, Force Papers, XXI; Markoe to Samuel G. Morton, Feb. 15, 1847; Pickering to Morton, Sept. 7, 1846, Morton Papers. Baltimore *Sun*, Dec. 1, 1846.

[26] "Report of the Organization Committee," *Union*, Dec. 5, 1846; *Smithsonian Institution: Journals*, 11. Robert Owen's *Millennial Gazette*, May 15, 1858; Trist to Robley Dunglinson, Dec. 27, 1846; [Trist] to the editor of the Baltimore *Sun*, Dec. 2, 1846, Trist Papers, XXIII.

[27] *Smithsonian Institution: Journals*, 12. *N. Y. Journal of Commerce*, Dec. 7, 1846; *N. Y. Tribune*, Dec. 7, 1846; *North American*, Dec. 14, 1846.

Even before Henry's selection Owen had submitted, as requested by his colleagues, a plan to carry out the law creating the Institution. The vague provisions of the charter and a general misapprehension by the public at large as to the purpose of the establishment made the document both necessary and important. Owen's report of Dec. 1, 1846, followed the same broad, democratic lines as his earlier bills and speeches. While fulfilling every specific requirement of the statute, it reintroduced certain items previously eliminated by Congress, such as the permanent professorships, the experimental farms, and the conservatories, as well as several sweeping statements reminiscent of the much disliked national normal school. It is difficult to escape the conclusion that Owen was trying to reverse in the smaller committee the defeats he had suffered in the legislature the previous April.[28]

Owen's plan of organization met the same fate in the Board of Regents as had his earlier bill in Congress. It was too democratic. On the very day that Henry entered upon his new duties, it was returned to the committee. When it reappeared a month later, still under Owen's name, the conservatories, botanical gardens, and farms were eliminated; all mention of a permanent faculty was omitted; and the references to the interest which the Institution was to take in "the theory and practice of public education" were reduced from three to one. The sections dealing with the building, the museum, the scientific cabinets, and the art gallery were left largely as Owen had designed. The completely equipped chemical laboratory, probably the suggestion of David Dale Owen, was retained, though not under the supervision of a regular professor. The plan for lectures outside of the capital was greatly restricted. The chief additions to the report consisted of specific methods of increasing and diffusing knowledge. The former was to be accomplished by awarding annual premiums for original papers and by grants to scholars for definite research projects. Knowledge was to be disseminated by brief, popular publications, similar

[28] "Report of the Organization Committee," *Union*, Dec. 5, 1846.

to those of the English Society for the Diffusion of Useful
Knowledge, by annual reports containing a record of the year's
discoveries and inventions, and by free lectures. The last were
to emphasize the physical sciences, the useful arts, agriculture,
and public education.[29]

This revised report, together with a series of resolutions
by Rufus Choate, also a Regent, became the basis for the
operations of the Smithsonian Institution during its first years.
Several men deserve the credit for the result. Choate had
successfully removed all semblances of a national university
but had not founded the great library he so desired. Henry was
responsible for the specific methods of increasing and diffusing
knowledge. Owen's contributions were the chemical laboratory, the provision for cheap publications, and the definition
of the type of lectures to be delivered. These last were described in words identical to those in his bill of December
1845. The compromise character of this revised report of
January 1847 was seen in the accompanying resolutions which
made permanent appropriations from the annual income.
Each year the sum of $15,000 was to be used for the purchase
of books, the maintenance of the museum, and the payment of
half of Henry's salary. The remainder, or slightly more than
that figure, was to go for publications, premiums, lectures, and
the other half of the Secretary's stipend. In brief, it was a
compromise in which Owen, Choate, and even Henry for the
time, felt constrained to acquiesce.[30]

All through the short session of his second term Owen spent
much, perhaps too much, of his time on Smithsonian affairs.
With the plan of organization decided upon, his chief interest
became the Institution's future home. Having already helped
to select the site, he now proved instrumental in choosing the

[29] *Smithsonian Institution: Journals*, 24. It was published as the *Report of
the Organization Committee of the Smithsonian Institution: with Resolutions
Accompanying the Same, and Adopted by the Board of Regents: also the Will
of the Testator, the Act Accepting the Bequest, and the Act Organizing the Institution* (Wash., 1847).

[30] *Union*, Feb. 11, 1847.

style of the building, a late Norman design by James Renwick, Jr., architect of the Grace Church in New York City. In January 1847 the Indianan wrote the resolution by which the Board of Regents confirmed the choice and was promptly named chairman of the committee to supervise the construction.[31] Despite concurrent Congressional duties Owen met with his colleagues more than thirty times during the next two months, receiving, fortunately, valuable assistance from Robert Mills, who was appointed superintendent, and David Dale Owen, who donated his services.[32] At the same time the Hoosier Representative served on other sub-committees, wrote two public letters suggesting a more central location for the new Institution, and finally was entrusted by the Regents with the preparation of a brief treatise intended to explain the style and the details of the proposed edifice.[33]

While Owen was absorbed in these matters, the infant Institution was being subjected to a barrage of criticism. These incessant attacks, hitherto ignored by historians, clearly foreshadowed the explosion of 1854 and 1855. A beginning was made by Renwick's unsuccessful competitors who considered themselves inadequately remunerated by the Regents for their architectural services. When a remonstrance to those officers proved futile, David H. Arnot published a short pamphlet accusing the Board in general, and its sub-committee in particular, of gross favoritism, excessive parsimony, and barbaric taste.[34] Nothing came of the demagogic blast, but other complaints were not slow in appearing. In Congress the constitutional right of Senators and Representatives to serve as Regents was questioned, and an attempt was made to prevent the

[31] David H. Arnot, *Animadversions on the Proceedings of the Regents of the Smithsonian Institution in Their Choice of an Architect* (N. Y., 1847), 10–11; *Smithsonian Institution: Journals*, 20–21, 25, 28–30, 33 (Jan. 20, 25–28, Feb. 5, 1847).

[32] *Smithsonian Institution: Journals, passim.*

[33] *Ibid.*, 30, 32, 602 (Jan. 28, Feb. 5, Mar. 6, 1847); *Union*, Feb. 11, 13, 15, 1847; *National Intelligencer*, Feb. 22, 24, 1847.

[34] Arnot, *op. cit.*, 10–15; *National Intelligencer*, Feb. 24, 1847 (advt.); *Smithsonian Institution: Journals*, 31–32.

Treasury from paying any money to the Institution until the war was ended. In the press it was inaccurately asserted that the governors were violating the charter by refusing to report to the national legislature and by spending part of their funds on a building. In Washington a rumor that convict labor was to be used in constructing the edifice aroused the local working-men to protest.[35]

As so often happened, these unfounded criticisms stung the sensitive Owen into a public reply.[36] But there is no evidence that in the spring of 1847 the Indianan regretted the time he had devoted to the Smithsonian Institution. Nor did he betray any disappointment that his wishes had not been followed to the letter. He was probably satisfied by the realization that, up to that time, no other individual had more influenced the development of the Institution. Certainly no other Regent had been more industrious. If the work had dealt with a subject in which his constituents were not vitally interested, it had, at least, won him new friends, even among political opponents. It had helped him, moreover, to become a national figure.

By the spring of 1847 Owen was more widely and more favorably known than he had ever been as a reformer. The party press in Washington and New York gave the Western Democrat excellent publicity, and the editor of the national Whig organ became a close friend as a colleague on the Board of Regents. In England his eloquence and ability were noticed, while in the national capital his presence was eagerly sought at both popular meetings and literary gatherings.[37] With the Polk administration he stood high enough to obtain within a short time three family appointments: Robert Fauntleroy as astronomer on the Coast Survey, Richard Owen as captain of

[35] *House Journal*, 29 Cong., 2 Sess., 117, 237. *North American*, Feb. 13, Apr. 14, 1847. *N. Y. Tribune*, Jan. 18, 1847; *N. Y. Herald*, Jan. 21, 1847; *Evening Post*, Jan. 29, 1847; *N. Y. Express*, Feb. 13, 1847.
[36] Owen to the editor, Apr. 19, 1847, *Evening Post*, Apr. 20, 1847.
[37] *N. Y. News*, Nov. 8, 1845; *Plebeian*, Feb. 5, 1845. *New Albany Weekly Ledger*, Nov. 6, 1850; London, *Reasoner*, July 1, 1846. *National Intelligencer*, Mar. 23, Apr. 3, 6, 1846, Feb. 8, 11, 12, 1847.

infantry, and David Dale Owen as director of the geological expedition in Wisconsin.[38]

As Owen took his seat in the train in April 1847 for a long delayed return to Indiana, he could feel well satisfied with his progress in public life. Politically, he had risen high in a short time. Socially, Washington with his wife and father at his side had been extremely pleasant. Intellectually, he had found in the Smithsonian Institution an outlet for his liberal and cultural interests. The future seemed equally bright. It was not unreasonable to hope for reelection. No other Representative from the "Pocket" had ever won such fame on the national scene. His district had become more and more Democratic in its complexion, and the Whigs there lacked an experienced candidate. And with the prestige gained by a third successive election might he not hope to attain at last the prize he so ardently desired, a seat in the United States Senate?

[38] R. D. Owen to Robt. Owen, Apr. 9, 1847, Robert Owen Papers, no. 1450; Owen's explanation in *The Democratic Clarion*, Sept. 25, 1847.

CHAPTER XV

DEFEAT

FOUR years of uninterrupted success had made Owen careless. Upon his return to New Harmony in April 1847 he exhibited none of the political sagacity that had marked his earlier triumphs. With charges of neglect and overweening ambition current, with Burns and the *Indiana Statesman* silent for more than a year past, with the Whigs united and his own party discordant, extreme caution was imperative. Yet in spite of those facts, in spite of the obvious dissatisfaction with the war among some of his constituents, in spite of Democratic defeats the previous year in New York, Pennsylvania, Kentucky, and Ohio, in spite, finally, of a prolonged absence from the district, Owen failed adequately to describe in print the achievements of his second term. As a result of this oversight, he left himself extremely vulnerable to the false accusations and the one-sided accounts of his Congressional actions that were spread broadcast by his opponents.

The spearhead of the attack was the Whig standard-bearer, Elisha Embree, a Methodist lawyer of Princeton who had formerly served in the state legislature and who had just completed a ten-year term as president judge of the local circuit court. Less gifted than Proffit but infinitely abler than Payne or Wilson, Embree was the most methodical, tenacious, and calculating rival Owen ever faced. His campaign tactics were simple yet extraordinarily clever. Hoping to attract Democrats disgruntled by the incumbent's fourth nomination for Congress and seeking to turn to account the tremendous popularity in the "Pocket" of Zachary Taylor, whose political affiliations were still unknown, Embree posed as a non-partisan candidate who would serve all factions and seek to elevate to the presidency the hero of Buena Vista. On such questions as the tariff, the status of slavery in the federal territories, and the expediency of voting supplies to continue the war, the judge carefully hedged. It was no part of his plan to contrast himself with his more talented opponent but rather to align Owen's personality against Taylor's. The former was to be portrayed as a British aristocrat, a notorious infidel, and an inveterate spoilsman, who ignored the needs of the common soldier, wasted his time on a useless Smithsonian Institution, and, worst of all, voted at the president's bidding to deprive gallant Whig generals of their high command.[1]

Although the excessive cost of the war, the valiant exploits of Zachary Taylor, and the pitiable lot of widows and orphans constituted the chief staple of Embree's speeches, the Hoosier's record in Congress did not escape close scrutiny. Three matters were singled out for special criticism and distortion. One was an early vote against a poorly drawn bill to increase the pay of the volunteer, a vote that was amply justified but so easily misrepresented that all through the canvass the Western Democrat was depicted as the enemy of the poor soldier.[2] Similarly Owen's sudden approval, after three times opposing, of an act to create a lieutenant general superior to Scott and Taylor was given undue emphasis and construed to mean that the Representative of the First District followed orders from the White House rather than the dictates of his own conscience. When this ostensible truckling to the executive was coupled with the bountiful patronage that the Owen family received early in 1847, the Whigs were able to build up a plausible case of bargain and corruption. It made little difference that Owen had later championed salary increases for the army, had several times refused to comply with Polk's wishes, and had suggested no one for appointments who was not well qualified.

---

[1] Although neither candidate issued a circular, the sources for the canvass are full. Three sets of notes for speeches, two of them identical, are in the Embree Papers, as well as numerous letters by local politicians suggesting campaign tactics. The Embree notes correspond with his speeches reported in *The Democratic Clarion*, June 12, 26, July 10, 1847. A complete file of that paper and of the Evansville *Tri-Weekly Journal* from June 9 to July 10, 1847 have been examined.   [2] *Evansville Journal*, July 10, 1847.

What stuck in the mind of the average Hoosier farmer, who cleared perhaps a couple of hundred dollars a year, was that his Congressman and his Congressman's brothers received together $8,500 annually from the federal government.[3]

Since the approval or disapproval of Robert Dale Owen was the issue before the voters, it was inevitable that his free-thought writings should be taken from the shelves of the Whig editors where they had been gathering dust since 1845. Embree's very real spiritual feelings probably made him loathe his heterodox opponent, but he was not blind to the possibility of exhorting co-religionists among the Democrats to desert their leader. Long before such problems as the war and patronage had arisen, Embree was discussing with friends "the proper mode of attacking Owen" and had formulated a plan by which "he might be beaten . . . without any great sacrifice of time or money." This method, later described as "arduous and disagreeable," was called to the judge's attention again on the eve of the canvass, and in the following weeks was carried into effect by the simple means of having Embree read on the stump selected passages from *The Free Enquirer*.[4] It is doubtful whether these agnostic sentiments, worn threadbare since 1836, greatly shocked the electors, but they did cause their author rather stupidly at public meetings to waste valuable time in explanation that more profitably could have been allotted to other matters.

On Monday the second of August, with Owen's victory generally conceded, the Hoosiers went to the polls. The bitter and stormy campaign had brought much discomfiture to the Democrat, but with the district having given his party more than a thousand plurality for two successive years few questioned his invincibility.[5] The unexpected, however, happened. With

---

[3] *Evansville Journal*, June 24, 26, July 8, 1847.

[4] Samuel Frisbie to Embree, May 12, 1845, May 15, Aug. 14, 1847, Embree Papers; *Democratic Clarion*, June 26, July 10, 1847; *Evansville Journal*, July 7, 1847.

[5] L. Q. de Bruler to Embree, Apr. 24, 1847, Embree Papers; *N. Y. Tribune*, June 16, 1847; *Indiana State Journal*, June 29, 1847.

dissatisfied Democrats, independent voters, and anti-war men flocking to the Whig standard, Owen's tremendous majority of 1845 rapidly melted away; and Embree swept to victory by 391 votes, the most stunning political upset of the decade in Indiana. Members of both parties were dumbfounded, and few took pains to conceal their surprise. In the East, where the press had first announced a Democratic triumph, the astonishment was the greatest.[6] The best proof that Robert Dale Owen, on the eve of defeat, had achieved national prominence is to be found in the numerous and detailed newspaper notices of this single Congressional election in southwestern Indiana.

Little unanimity of opinion prevailed as to the cause of Owen's defeat. The victim both publicly and privately attributed it at first to his own overconfidence and carelessness. The victor, stretching the truth unjustifiably, claimed a clear-cut political triumph. The chief Democratic organ of the district blamed the result on religious hysteria; whereas the *Evansville Journal*, conveniently ignoring Embree's professed non-partisanship, interpreted the outcome as "a most glorious Whig triumph."[7] The pious *North American* expressed the widely accepted view that "Mr. Owen's religious, or irreligious, opinions have been the sole cause of his defeat"; and the Hoosier himself later concurred in order to gain the sympathy of freethinkers.[8] Other editors read their own individual opinions into the event. The conservative *New York Morning Express* thought Owen's alleged agrarian principles responsible, while the liberal *Boston Investigator* believed he had been rebuked by his more radical constituents. Quite naturally George Henry Evans declared that Owen's refusal to champion free

[6] *Indiana State Journal*, Aug. 31, 1847. The vote stood, Embree, 7,445; Owen, 7,054. Cf. Richard W. Thompson to Embree, Aug. 14, 1847, Caleb B. Smith to Embree, Aug. 26, 1847, Embree Papers; *Indiana State Sentinel*, Aug. 14, 1847; Brookville *Indiana American*, Aug. 13, 1847; *N. Y. Tribune*, Aug. 10, 1847; N. Y. *Sun*, Aug. 10, 1847; *Union*, Aug. 14, 1847.

[7] R. D. Owen to Robt. Owen, Aug. 20, 1847, Robert Owen Papers, no. 1508; *Democratic Clarion*, Aug. 7, 14, 1847.

[8] *North American*, Aug. 18, 1847. R. D. Owen to Robt. Owen, Nov. 9, 1847, Robert Owen Papers, no. 1533.

public lands was the primary factor; whereas Bryant, who a
year later was to place his paper behind the free soil movement,
and the abolitionists regarded the Indianan's vote against the
Wilmot Proviso as the real cause of his downfall. Horace
Greeley had still another explanation and, in a long editorial
résumé of the erstwhile reformer's course on Oregon, Texas,
slavery, and the war concluded,

In his whole career as a public man, Mr. Robert Dale Owen exhibited
himself as a simple, thorough-going average Party hack, and not
at all the Philosopher, the Philanthropist, the Reformer that he had
once professed to be and by many been considered — . . . . Had he
been truly the man of ideas, a devotee to his convictions — one who
attached himself to Party for the sake not of self but of Humanity —
had he been even so manlike as John C. Calhoun or O. A. Brownson,
who did not pretend to revolt at war nor believe in Universal Charity
and Human Equality — he could not have failed to make some open,
resolute effort to arrest the Country on the verge of the precipice down
which her rulers were recklessly spurring her to an unfathomed abyss
of blood. But Robert Dale Owen kept silent, or rather by voice and
vote cheered on the infernal work that was preparing. Shrinking from
aught that might endanger his popularity with his party, he missed
the opportunity to dissipate forever the prejudices harbored against
him because of his notorious infidelity. His fall affords a fresh illustration of the truth of the Divine saying that "He who would save his
life shall lose it." This is the true moral of his defeat. . . .[9]

No editor far removed from the scene could appreciate all
the causes responsible for Owen's downfall. The Indianan's
Congressional record was much more vulnerable in 1847 than
in 1845, and his foes not only took advantage of certain unwise
votes but also effectively misrepresented other proper ones.
Personal overconfidence, Democratic discord in the district,
and the decease of Burns all played a part in the debacle.
Some electors may have objected to Owen's stand on the Mexican War and the Wilmot Proviso, but the best evidence indicates

[9] N. Y. Tribune, Aug. 19, 1847. New Albany Democrat, Sept. 23, 1847;
Boston Investigator, Aug. 25, 1847; Young America, Aug. 14, 1847 quoted in
The Democratic Clarion, Sept. 11, 1847; Evening Post, Aug. 21, 1847. See also
The National Era, Aug. 19, 26, 1847; N. Y. National Anti-Slavery Standard,
Aug. 26, 1847.

that the Democrats, at least, saw eye to eye with their Representative on those matters. Then, too, political issues alone did not determine the outcome, for equally important was the feeling that the incumbent had served long enough. A desire for rotation in office and the distorted charge of nepotism were vital factors, and the sagacious Chapmans placed their finger on another fundamental cause when they blamed their followers in the "Pocket" for deserting their candidate at the polls instead of denying him renomination in the first place.[10]

Defeat brought to Owen keen disappointment and wounded pride. He realized that his future in national politics was seriously threatened. He honestly believed he had lost to a man of inferior ability, one whom he described to his father as "equally without talent & without principle." He knew only too well the hollowness of Embree's non-partisan pretensions; and he might have foreseen that the Chandler brothers, whose *Evansville Journal* had so violently assailed the numerous appointments of the Owen family, would themselves be among the most persistent applicants for office from the district under the new dispensation. The vanquished had to glean what satisfaction he could in the admission of Greeley's Indiana correspondent that the erstwhile reformer had been the state's "most talented and . . . gentlemanly Loco-Foco in Congress" and in the sorrow expressed by Ritchie in the national party organ that "We have lost one of the ablest representatives in Congress. . . . Those who know Mr. Owen the most intimately regret his defeat the most deeply." [11]

As in 1839, Owen was unable to accept the popular verdict in silence. Sensitive to all criticism, just or unjust, he again took up his pen to discuss in a series of letters in the Princeton *Democratic Clarion* those issues which he thought had been misrepresented or ignored in the recent canvass. "It is a

[10] *Indiana State Sentinel*, Aug. 17, 1847.
[11] R. D. Owen to Robt. Owen, Aug. 20, 1847, Robert Owen Papers, no. 1508. W. H. Chandler to Embree, Jan. 15, 22, Feb. 3, 18, Apr. 22, 1849; J. J. Chandler to Embree, Jan. 17, Feb. 7, 28, 1849, Embree Papers. *N. Y. Tribune*, Aug. 13, 1847; *Union*, Aug. 14, 1847.

small matter," he wrote, "and one which has happened to the best of men, to lose an election. But it is a serious matter . . . to lose public character and public confidence." With his customary felicity of expression and persuasiveness of argument Owen proceeded to justify, in his own mind at least, the acts of his second term and to expose the misleading statements his opponents had made regarding such questions as the soldiers' pay and the patronage. For the benefit of Eastern and British liberals the so-called "Betrayer of Freedom" addressed two of his articles to the slavery controversy, proclaming his hostility to the peculiar institution but defending his vote on the Wilmot Proviso.[12] Although he made no public reply to the land reformers, Evans' criticisms continued to rankle in his breast. "The wonder is," he told his father, "considering all I have said & written, (never retracting one word) not that I am defeated for Congress now, but that I was ever elected. No man ever was before, with a reputation half so heterodox." The Western Democrat denied that he had grown conservative with regard to humanitarian reforms and promised to deliver a lecture during the coming winter in which his hearers could "hardly complain that I am behind the spirit of the times." [13]

Owen's post-election letters served the purpose for which they were intended. They enabled him to vent his pent-up emotions and to place his case before the people. The Whigs, to be sure, except for Greeley, ignored the writings or dismissed them as the rantings of a repudiated demagogue; but the Democrats were more than kind. Future free soilers like Bryant were delighted with the Indianan's views on slavery. *The National Era* to its surprise found Owen and Wilmot in essential agreement on the subject and took pleasure in "withdrawing any imputations . . . made against the honesty" of the Hoosier Representative.[14] Most important of all, these essays were widely copied at home and freely commented upon in the East,

[12] *Democratic Clarion*, Aug. 21, 28, Sept. 4, 11, 18, 25, Oct. 2, 1847.

[13] R. D. Owen to Robt. Owen, Nov. 9, 1847, Robert Owen Papers, no. 1533.

[14] *Richmond Palladium*, Aug. 31, 1847; *N. Y. Tribune*, Sept. 13, 1847; *Evening Post*, Oct. 6, 1847; *National Era*, Oct. 21, 1847.

mute testimony that two terms in Congress had elevated Owen
to prominence on the national political scene.

Early in October 1847 Owen returned to Washington to
resume his work for the Smithsonian Institution. His term as
Congressional Regent did not expire until December, and there
was a possibility that the vacancy in the Board created by
Richard Rush's departure for Paris as our new minister might
be filled with his name. Undoubtedly such an appointment by
Congress would have been gratifying to the Hoosier, for the
prestige connected with the office was very desirable in his
hour of defeat. Outwardly, however, he remained unconcerned
and busied himself with the construction of the twelfth-century
Norman edifice that was already taking shape midst the leafy
foliage of the Mall. During the ensuing two months he also
helped to devise a four-year plan of finances by which $140,000
of the accrued interest could be saved from current expenses
and added to the principal.[15]

Meanwhile the progress of the young Institution was still
being hampered by the incessant criticism that had begun the
previous winter. If anything, these carpings had grown worse
as time went on. Some were political in origin; some reflected
the jealousy of other Eastern cities; but most resulted from
ignorance, malicious rumor, and downright hostility to any
national establishment. The Regents collectively were under
constant fire; but, as might have been expected, the vulnerable
Owen was singled out for the vilest attacks.[16] His very industry
exposed him to the shafts of those who wished him ill. Most
of the objections that were voiced against his actions were
unfair and hypocritical, too ridiculous or too trivial to notice
here; yet this campaign of detraction must have had something
to do with the abrupt and obscure severance of Owen's connection with the Institution.

[15] R. D. Owen to Robt. Owen, Aug. 20, Nov. 9, 1847, Robert Owen Papers,
nos. 1508, 1533; *Smithsonian Institution: Journals of the Board of Regents*,
447-451.
[16] See for example *The North American*, Apr. 24, 25, Dec. 7, 1846, Apr. 14, 17,
1847; *N. Y. Express*, Feb. 13, 1847.

On December 22, 1847, Owen's successor was appointed by the speaker of the House. The Indianan was not disappointed by this inevitable step, for only five days before the Regents had formally instructed one of their number to obtain the passage of a joint resolution electing him to the position lately held by Rush. For at least a week the chances of this move being made seemed good, and then something happened.[17] Whether the Board was afraid to follow up its resolution, whether the Congressional committees refused to sanction it, or whether the retention of the absent Rush's name for the sake of prestige seemed advisable is still a matter of conjecture. News of the proposal to reelect Owen did leak out and caused the Whigs to protest against the practice of making the Board of Regents "a hospital for destitute politicians." With several Congressmen already demanding that the Board's authority be curtailed, the governors had to be careful not even to appear to infringe upon the prerogatives of the legislature. Whatever the reasons, no law was ever enacted to carry out the Regents' resolution of December 17, and early in January 1848 Owen left Washington never again to influence the Institution he had done so much to found or to supervise the Norman edifice which he had "watched with a lover's eye." [18]

Owen's failure to figure in the later history of the Smithsonian Institution may be attributed chiefly to Joseph Henry. It was hardly likely that the Presbyterian professor should find the heterodox Western Democrat a congenial associate and, worse yet, the two men never did agree on the primary purpose of the establishment. The library feature, which Owen had been forced to tolerate, and the imposing building, which he actively championed, were both distasteful to Henry. Construction costs used up the lion's share of the income for several years, and during that time the Secretary was compelled to limit his care-

[17] House Journal, 30 Cong., 1 Sess., 153; Smithsonian Institution: Journals, 44–45, 460; Francis Markoe, Jr. to Samuel G. Morton, Dec. 30, 1847, Morton Papers.

[18] N. Y. Tribune, Dec. 27, 1847; Virginia J. Trist to Nicholas P. Trist, Jan. 5, 1848, Trist Papers, XXVIII.

fully integrated scheme of scholarly research, scientific experiment, and publications on the progress of knowledge. On the other hand, Owen's admiration for the physicist cooled as all vestiges were removed of the Institution's concern with the needs of the common man. Starting mildly in 1848, Henry became each year more and more insistent that no cheap tracts be disseminated, that the proposed *Contributions to Learning* be learned in character, and that the emphasis should be on the increase rather than the diffusion of knowledge. Finally, in 1852 he asked that the compromise on budgetary appropriations, reached by Owen, Choate and himself six years before, be abandoned.

The granting of Henry's request by the Board of Regents in May 1854 touched off an explosion that rocked the very foundations of the Smithsonian Institution. The details of this controversy, largely ignored in official histories, need not detain us; for Owen, then several thousand miles away, was not directly concerned. The real issue at stake was whether Henry, in his zeal to promote science, had not violated the enabling act of 1846, which act, it will be recalled, marked a definite triumph of the library scheme advocated by Choate and Marsh. Owen, whose desire for a democratic, educational establishment had received scant favor in Congress, was in 1854 fired upon by both sides. The disciples of Choate blamed him for minimizing in his plan of organization in December 1846 the role of the library, whereas the Secretary's followers criticized the Indianan by implication when they deplored at length the wastage of precious funds on an expensive and unnecessary building.[19]

Henry survived the upheaval of 1854–1855 and in the following years completely succeeded in making the Smithsonian Institution learned and scientific rather than popular and literary. His earlier colleagues, Owen, Choate, and Marsh,

---

[19] The last two paragraphs are based on Henry's annual reports, 1847–1855; the findings of the special Congressional committee raised in 1854; and a large amount of contemporary literature.

shut off from direct influence, seem gradually to have lost interest. Owen himself, apparently dissatisfied with the Henry regime, spoke little of the matter in later life.[20] No official notice was taken by the Regents of his death; and it was not until 1888, a decade after the scientist had also passed to the Great Beyond, that there began a ten-year struggle to erect on the Smithsonian grounds a statue to the Hoosier's memory. Five times in the House and thrice in the Senate a bill for that purpose was introduced. On four occasions it was favorably reported, and once it passed the upper chamber.[21] In the end, however, Congressional indifference or the secret opposition of Henry's admirers blocked the plan. Thus, today, on the Mall in Washington, before the many turreted, reddish-brown structure, stands appropriately, a statue of Joseph Henry, the man who directed the Institution into scientific channels. No monuments have yet been placed there for two other men who, holding ideas antagonistic to those of the great Secretary as well as to those of each other, were responsible above all others for enacting into law and starting on its distinguished career of service the bequest of James Smithson. Those men were Rufus Choate and Robert Dale Owen.

After leaving Washington in disappointment in January 1848 Owen did not remain idle. In the following month he delivered at Cincinnati a mildly liberal lecture on the evils of the Industrial Revolution. From April until July he was in the East at work on his architectural treatise for the Building Committee of the Smithsonian Institution. Politics, however, remained a constant preoccupation. The Democratic convention at Indianapolis in January had chosen him as one of the two state electors; and Owen grasped the opportunity, not unlike that

---

[20] Samuel G. Brown, *The Life of Rufus Choate* (2d edn., Boston, 1870), 149; Caroline C. Marsh, comp., *Life and Letters of George Perkins Marsh* (N. Y., 1888), I, 98–99. The evidence on Owen is not conclusive. See *Robert Owen's Millennial Gazette*, May 15, 1856; W. A. L. Taylor, *Katie Fox, Epoch Making Medium* (N. Y., 1933), 115; interview of the writer with the late Mrs. R. D. Templeton, Owen's daughter, Nov. 25, 1936.

[21] Rhees, *Smithsonian Institution: Documents*, II, 1136–1137, 1537–1538, 1688, 1710, 1805, 1538–1539, 1552–1553, 1688.

of 1840, to repair his own fortunes while ostensibly toiling only for the cause. Democratic victories in August and November could bring much to the Indianan, perhaps another Congressional nomination, perhaps a federal appointment, perhaps his elevation to the United States Senate.[22]

Owen's part in the Cass-Taylor contest is of interest mainly for his attitude on the slavery issue. In 1848 both major parties in Indiana, up to then conservative on the subject, manifested a momentary tendency toward free soilism.[23] Owen wished to combat the trend but found himself almost compelled to address his speeches to potential antislavery voters. The stand he took was essentially that outlined in his letters of the previous autumn. He continued to oppose the Wilmot Proviso as a needless irritant to the South. Slavery could not legally exist in the newly acquired territories, he reasserted, unless specifically created by an act of Congress. Since, however, not every one agreed with that assumption, he was prepared to acquiesce in a decision of the Supreme Court. With regard to the forthcoming presidential campaign, Owen flatly contradicted the Whig assertion that Taylor's election would be the best safeguard against the spread of the peculiar institution. In old Rough and Ready's pledge not to use the veto, the Indianan saw a danger that the South might enact positive legislation to encroach further on the area of freedom.[24]

In a manner not uncommon to the day the Hoosier Whigs blandly ignored Owen's arguments and fell back instead on irrelevant personal invective. The rapidly growing Free Soilers, on the other hand, behaved much more candidly. They gave an unusually full summary of the Democrat's speeches and praised him for his fairness. They doubted, however, the ex-

[22] *Labor: Its History and Prospects; an Address Delivered before the Young Men's Mercantile Association . . . on Tuesday, February 1, 1848* (Cincinnati, 1848). *Democratic Clarion,* May 6, 1848; *Indiana State Sentinel,* Jan. 11, 1848.

[23] William O. Lynch, "Anti-Slavery Tendencies of the Democratic Party in the Northwest, 1848–1850," *Mississippi Valley Historical Review,* XI, 319–331 (Dec. 1924).

[24] *Indiana State Sentinel,* Sept. 16, 1848, contains the fullest summary of Owen's campaign speech.

pediency of leaving the matter to the courts, territorial or
federal, and frankly expressed fear of a pro-slavery decision
from the nation's highest tribunal. Curiously enough, the Van
Buren editors considered Owen more "free soilish" than his
party and urged their own speakers to make special efforts to
refute his reasoning.[25]

Owen's canvass in 1848 was the most extended and difficult
he had ever undertaken. Before the local elections in August,
he confined his activity to the First District; but on September 2 he began a nine-week stumping tour that carried him
well over a thousand miles, through more than half the counties of the state, to meet some fifty scheduled appointments.
Starting at Madison on the Ohio, he made a complete circuit,
touching at Indianapolis, Fort Wayne, Wabash, Lafayette,
Terre Haute, Columbus, and Salem until he gained the Ohio
again at Rising Sun, northeast of the place he commenced.[26]
In most of the towns along the route Owen was making his first
public appearance, and the press notices were extraordinarily
full. Where his own party hailed him as "the pride of Indiana
Democracy, the ripest scholar in the State," the opposition
damned him as "the slanderer of Gen. Washington . . . the
reviler . . . of the Christian religion . . . [and the] defamer
of General Taylor." [27] Ostensibly pious county editors had a
field day with the writings in *The Free Enquirer* and solemnly
asserted that the very presence of their author on a public
platform insulted those who believed in God. They made great
sport of the homeliness of the "rather hard looking," red headed
Scotchman whose gestures consisted, wrote one commentator,
"of keeping his hands in his breeches pockets. As he warms
and rises in the importance of his subject, deeper does he
plunge his hands into his breeches." [28]

[25] Indianapolis *Free Soil Banner*, Sept. 22, 1848; Centreville *Free Territory
Sentinel*, Sept. 13, 27, Oct. 10, 1848.

[26] Itinerary printed in the *Indiana State Sentinel*, Sept. 2, 9, 16, 27, 1848.

[27] Richmond *Jeffersonian*, quoted in the *Evansville Journal*, Sept. 19, 1848;
New Albany Bulletin, Sept. 13, 1848.

[28] Richmond *Palladium*, Sept. 13, 1848; *Indiana American*, Sept. 8, 1848;
Logansport Telegraph, Oct. 7, 14, 1848; *Wabash Atlas*, Oct. 12, 1848.

November brought Owen another defeat. Although Cass received Indiana's twelve electoral votes, Taylor won handsomely in the nation. A federal appointment was thus out of the question for Owen for another four years. Cass, moreover, was only a minority victor in the Hoosier state as Van Buren more than quadrupled Birney's poll of 1844.[29] Thus did the free soil issue continue to loom ominously upon the horizon as the Western Democrat turned his thoughts to the election of another United States Senator.

When the legislature convened at Indianapolis in December 1848, Owen's party had a clear majority. The very size of that majority, however, encouraged the impotent Whigs and Free Soilers to fish in troubled waters, to throw their support to a moderate Democrat on the condition he would espouse the Wilmot Proviso.[30] Accordingly, on the eve of the caucus, each Senatorial candidate was publicly asked, first, whether he believed Congress possessed the power to prohibit slavery in the newly acquired territories and, second, whether he, if elected, would vote for such a proscriptive act. The replies exceeded the fondest hopes of the Free Soilers. Although but a few months before, all Cass men had dismissed the Proviso as humbug, most of the aspirants now answered both questions in the affirmative. Owen alone remained consistent. In a letter twice as long as any rival's, he acknowledged Congress's authority to keep slavery out of California and New Mexico, but his sole concession to free soil demands was a promise to introduce into the Senate a joint resolution declaring the existing free status of those territories. Such a resolution, he thought, would be as effective as Wilmot's and much more likely to pass.[31]

On December 7, 1848, the Democratic caucus nominated James Whitcomb. Lacking the governor's state-wide popularity

[29] *Indiana State Journal*, Dec. 4, 1848.

[30] Samuel W. Parker to Caleb B. Smith, Nov. 27, 1848; John D. Defrees to Smith, Dec. 13, 1848, Smith Papers, I; *Evansville Journal*, Dec. 12, 1848.

[31] *Indiana State Sentinel*, Dec. 14, 1848; *Indiana State Journal*, Dec. 18, 1848. John Law was consistent in his adherence to the Proviso, both before and during December 1848.

as well as his control of the patronage and unwilling to jump on the free soil bandwagon, Owen stood a poor second.[32] There was, to be sure, a distant possibility that one of the defeated candidates might rally enough Whigs, Free Soilers, and discontented Democrats to upset the caucus choice; but Owen was not the man for that job. By sacrificing expediency to consistency on the Wilmot Proviso, he had precluded support from the antislavery bloc; while the Whigs had no reason to regard him as other than a regular party man. In fact, in both 1842 and in 1845 Owen had been extremely loyal to the voice of the caucus. Now, once again, he refused to let his name go before the Assembly. As a result, Whitcomb was easily elected.[33]

By the close of 1848 Owen's political progress had come to a definite halt. Beaten twice in four Congressional contests, he could hardly expect the nomination in 1849. His third unsuccessful bid for Senator made it clear that the united support of the "Pocket" delegation was not enough to bring victory. Perhaps if his party returned to a more conservative position on the slavery issue, Owen's chances for promotion in the future would be better. But in December 1848 there was no indication of such a change. On the contrary, in the next few months the free soil tendencies among Hoosier Democrats continued to grow.[34] Thus the only consolation left to Owen was the realization that he had acted honorably, placing principle above opportunism. Even the Whigs were forced to admit that his course had been "entirely consistent," not exhibiting "that change of opinion (adopted to suit existing circumstances) which characterized the course of the other gentlemen." The Free Soilers likewise conceded that in a contest in which each

[32] *Indiana State Journal*, Dec. 25, 1848. The caucus vote stood, Whitcomb, 49; Owen, 12; Hannegan, 10; Chamberlain, 6.

[33] Samuel Judah to Caleb B. Smith, Dec. 7, 1848; D. P. Holloway to Smith, Dec. 13, 1848; Defrees to Smith, Dec. 13, 1848, Smith Papers, I; *Evansville Journal*, Dec. 21, 1848; *New Albany Democrat*, Dec. 21, 1848.

[34] Theodore C. Smith, *The Liberty and Free Soil Parties in the Northwest* (*Harvard Historical Studies*, VI, N. Y., 1897), 188–189; Lynch, "Anti-Slavery Tendencies of the Democratic Party in the Northwest, 1848–1850," *loc. cit.*

candidate had tried to prove himself the greatest Proviso advocate "without regard to principle or previous action," Owen was the only one to preserve his dignity and self-respect.[35]

But a defeat was a defeat, and this was the fourth suffered in less than eighteen months. Embree's surprising triumph had brought to an abrupt close Owen's promising career in the national legislature. The refusal of Congress to fill the vacancy in the Board of Regents with his name had terminated his connection with the Smithsonian Institution. The election of Taylor had postponed the possibility of an appointive office under the federal government. The much coveted seat in the Senate had again eluded his grasp. These four defeats, coming at the meridian of his life, go far to explain why today Robert Dale Owen is remembered more as an accomplished writer, a state legislator, and an exponent of social reform than as a prominent figure in national politics.

[35] *Indiana State Journal* [Dec. 18, 1848?]; Lafayette *Tippecanoe Journal* [Dec. 1848], mounted in "Political Memoranda."

CHAPTER XVI

INTELLECTUAL CURRENTS

For twelve years before 1849 national and state politics constituted the chief subject of Owen's actviity, thought, and aspirations. He devoted the very best part of his life to a public career, not for the spoils of office — though Owen was the first to admit a natural ambition for influence and prestige — but because it provided an arena in which he could most easily employ his varied accomplishments. Business he disliked; and journalism, for which he was admirably suited, seems to have lost its appeal. The professions were of course closed by his lack of adequate training. Both reformers and writers, roles which Owen filled at other periods, still found their trades unprofitable in mid-century Indiana. Public service, on the other hand, was better paid and more highly esteemed then than now. Especially in the West did the ablest men seek government positions, and in following that path Owen saw an opportunity both to benefit his neighbors and to dissipate among them the prejudices engendered by his youthful radicalism. The reverses of 1847 and 1848, therefore, did not destroy his political ambitions, though they tended to make him bolder and more independent. They did, however, initiate a brief interlude in which other interests came momentarily to the fore and during which we can best study the intellectual currents of his Indiana years.

While Owen was busy with public affairs at Indianapolis and Washington, changes were taking place in his village home. New faces were appearing, and those who had been young during the social experiment were now in middle age. Although it no longer boasted of many notable residents and its economic life was stagnant, New Harmony still retained distinctive features that set it apart from its neighbors. Its inhabitants were extremely congenial, and the hospitality with which they greeted visitors to their dramatic performances, balls, and Fourth of July festivities became a byword throughout the "Pocket." Three private libraries were freely patronized, a mutual instruction society stimulated adult education, while the laboratory and museum of David Dale Owen were virtually unrivalled west of the mountains. The influence of the Owenite community was reflected in the public celebration of Tom Paine's birthday, the lax observance of the Sabbath, and the absence, before 1850, of any church building. A residue of radicalism made possible an exotic and impotent Free Land Association and gave mild encouragement to Josiah Warren's "Time Store"; but by and large the exponents of socialism found New Harmony barren ground.[1]

The pressure of public affairs quite naturally compelled Owen to play a lesser part in village life during these years than he had in those immediately following his marriage. From December 1836 until June 1853 he was away from home fully half of the time. Thus nothing more was heard of his jockey clubs or acting before the Thespian Society. He did not join the New Harmony Sons of Temperance; he ignored the free land group, avoided the Paine anniversary dinners, and apparently manifested indifference to the "Time Store." This aloofness inevitably drew criticism from those who had an axe to grind, but little of it was justified.[2] Considering the extent of Owen's public activity and obligations, he did a great deal to benefit his village. If there was a patriotic oration to be delivered, a social gathering to be addressed, or a few appropriate words to be spoken to school children, he was always called upon. He lectured frequently and without pay to local organi-

[1] "Manuscripts and Collections of A. J. Macdonald"; Charles Lyell, *A Second Visit to the United States* (London, 1849), II, 270–272; Bailie, *Josiah Warren*, 40–49; *Vincennes Saturday Gazette*, July 10, 1841; *Indiana Statesman*, June 24, 1842; *Boston Investigator*, May 11, 1842, Mar. 15, 1843; *New Moral World*, Oct. 29, 1842, July 8, 1843; *Evansville Journal*, Sept. 11, 1851; *Western Odd Fellows' Magazine*, I, 167–168 (Nov. 1852).

[2] Bailie, *op. cit.*, 44; W. A. Twigg to Embree, May 17, 1847, Embree Papers; Indianapolis *Family Visitor*, Apr. 5, 1849.

zations and twice, in April 1842 and again in May 1849, wrote a vigorous public reply to pious detractors who sought to impugn the existing fair name of the village because of its notorious past.[3]

Despite his frequent absence from home during these years, Owen's charming family life remained unimpaired. Something has already been said of his filial loyalty as well as the political dangers he exposed himself to in seeking to promote the fortunes of his kin. In no way did the Owens more betray their Scottish birth than in the clannish relations of the numerous brothers and sisters. Time, of course, began to take its toll. In June 1842 William Owen passed away after a lingering illness, and in 1850 death struck again under tragic circumstances at the person of Robert Fauntleroy.[4] But the greatest sorrow experienced by Owen in these years was the loss in 1845 of his younger son, affectionately known in the village as "the little king." To his father the grief-stricken parent wrote,

Ernest was a child of very great promise; of much stronger natural powers than either of my remaining children. . . . I had felt assured that, if well trained, his character, both moral and intellectual, would be superior to my own. And I now find, that, in all my efforts & public successes I had unconsciously looked forward to the time when Ernest would understand & appreciate them. I feel, since his death, as if the edge of my ambition was destroyed. . . .

Lacking spiritual solace, the sceptic "resorted to the only efficient source of relief, *constant occupation*." Fortunately Mary bore up bravely in their great bereavement, her fortitude contrasting favorably with her weaker sister-in-law who was suffering under a similar affliction.[5] Never was the agnosticism

[3] Conclusions based on the records of local societies and local newspapers cited in the Bibliography. See also *The Town of New Harmony, and the Rev. Benjamin Halsted; Being a Report of the Proceedings of a Public Meeting of the Inhabitants, Held . . . the 13th April, 1842* (Evansville, 1842); *Family Visitor*, May 17, 1849.

[4] R. D. Owen to Robert Owen, June 3, 1842, *New Moral World*, Aug. 13, 1842; *New Albany Ledger*, Feb. 6, 1850.

[5] R. D. Owen to Robt. Owen, Oct. 12, 1845, Robert Owen Papers, no. 1394; *Indiana Statesman*, Aug. 30, 1845.

of the Owens put to a severer test than in the autumn of 1845. That they weathered the storm unshaken is proof palpable of the depth of their convictions.

Financially Owen did not prosper in these years. Mention has already been made of the difficulties that prompted the respite from politics in 1841. During the next two years Owen liquidated all the joint family mercantile enterprises that had come down from the "community days," and he bluntly assured his father that the brothers would never again engage in such business. Twelve months later he welcomed his sire to New Harmony with the warning that "you will find us all doing well here . . . except making money." [6] For the next few years, however, his eight-dollar-a-day salary as Congressman relieved Owen of pecuniary worry, and in 1848 he paid the last of the mortgage to D'Arusmont. After that date the source and extent of his income are less certain. He still owned a considerable amount of land about New Harmony from which he received rents, and in 1849 he and Dale realized about $10,000 from the sale of Cut-Off Island. During 1851 and 1852 he again received a stipend from public office, but that was transitory. His property itself brought less than $1,500 a year, and this continued shrinkage caused Owen to be concerned over his financial status until his death. [7]

As a literary figure in ante-bellum America Robert Dale Owen does not loom very large. In the Indiana backwoods, to be sure, his intellectual endeavors and his educational zeal were magnified so that there he appeared to many as an accomplished scholar. Realistic observers, however, regarded him as an enlightened legislator with a strong social conscience and undoubted cultural proclivities but one in whom the politician definitely took precedence over the reformer and the author. Just as the Western Democrat stood apart from the various

[6] R. D. Owen to Robt. Owen, Aug. 13, 1843, Sept. 18, 1844, *New Moral World*, Nov. 11, 1843, Robert Owen Papers, no. 1338.

[7] Posey County, "Deed Book," O, 526–527; memoranda and indentures in the Owen Papers; R. D. Owen to Joseph Lane, July 9, Nov. 1, 1852, Lane Papers.

national humanitarian crusades of the forties, antislavery, temperance, and world peace, so was he aloof from the notable literary coteries at Concord, Cambridge, and New York. It goes without saying that he made no significant contribution to the literature of the Golden Day and that his pioneer efforts in education were not so influential as those of Horace Mann or Henry Barnard.

Within these limitations Owen did pursue during his Indiana years certain intellectual endeavors. If none of these served to enhance his fame, they none the less illuminate the many facets of his character and clearly set him apart from the usual officeholder of the time. After the publication of *Pocahontas*, Owen did little creative writing. A few translations of Schiller printed in the *Democratic Review* and an occasional poem in an Eastern newspaper constituted the sum total of his efforts along that line, while in the field of fiction he did not utilize materials gathered in 1852 until eighteen years later. He did, to be sure, encourage local artists and poets and helped to make their works better known; but it was as educator, lyceum speaker, and author of useful treatises on various subjects that Owen won for himself among Hoosiers a reputation as a scholar in politics.[8]

Owen's educational interests were manifested during his Indiana years in three ways. As an individual he was always vitally concerned with the schools in New Harmony and also with opportunities for teachers, male and female, in the West.[9] As a legislator he twice, in 1836–1837 and in 1851–1852, made a definite contribution to the Hoosier school system, but was less successful in his attempt to graft a national normal college on the Smithsonian Institution. Finally, as a Trustee of Indiana University, he proved to be, over a long period of time, as

[8] Owen's poems and published addresses are listed in the Bibliography. Evidence of his other intellectual activities has been gleaned from Indiana newspapers, especially those of New Harmony, Evansville, New Albany, Madison, Terre Haute, and Indianapolis.

[9] See for example, Owen to J. D. Williams, Mar. 16, 1852, Indiana State Library, Miscellaneous.

useful and as conscientious as he had been as a Regent at Washington.

It was early in 1838, just after the state college was made a university, that the legislature chose Owen as one of twenty-one Trustees. Whether his selection was prompted by his success the previous year in adding to the Common School Fund or by his already widely accepted reputation as a scholar is not clear, but there is no doubt that the recipient welcomed the honor for the prestige it carried. His appointment, however, came at a critical moment; for the infant institution, rent by internal dissensions, weakened by malicious rumors, and subjected to the jealous competition of denominational colleges throughout the state, was in grave danger of being stillborn. All through 1838 and 1839 Indiana University was in dire peril as its enrollment declined and newspaper detraction continued. Finally in February 1840 the General Assembly felt compelled to raise a special committee to investigate the problem.[10]

Under these discouraging circumstances President Andrew Wylie called a special meeting of the Trustees in April. Feeling that drastic steps must be taken, that body appointed five of their number to convince the people of Indiana that the state university had been, and still was, worthy of their support. To Owen as one of the five fell the duty of wielding his facile pen, recently used in party convention, in a cause as important as any in which he had engaged while editing the *Daily Sentinel*. In a fifteen-page pamphlet, written on the eve of his canvass as a Van Buren elector, Owen discussed the history and purpose of the institution, related briefly the causes of its present difficulties, and painted a roseate view of the future. He admitted that the goal of free tuition had not been attained, but pointed out that the fees were far less than those charged for higher education elsewhere in Indiana. Indirectly Owen appealed for popular support on grounds close to his heart,

[10] Indiana General Assembly, *Local Laws, 1837–1838*, 294–298; *Documentary Journal*, 25th Session (1840–1841), 385–388; Theophilus Wylie, *Indiana University, Its History from 1820 . . . to 1890* (Indps., 1890), 52; *Bloomington Post*, Sept. 20, Oct. 18, Dec. 13, 1839.

namely, that Bloomington's was the only non-sectarian college in the state.[11]

Owen's address to the people marked the turn of the tide. Early in 1841 the legislative investigating committee placed its stamp of approval on both the policy of the Trustees and the opinions expressed in their manifesto. By autumn the university's attendance had begun to rise. Owen himself was rewarded by being one of the few Trustees who were reappointed when the Board was shaken up and abbreviated.[12] As a result, during the next decade the Western Democrat devoted considerable spare time to the welfare of the institution. In the fall of 1846, finding the burden of Congressman and Smithsonian Regent sufficient, he resigned as Trustee; but two years later, when again free, he was rechosen. In the subsequent movement to remedy Indiana's earlier neglect of her common schools by appropriating for their use the university's funds, Owen was found on the correct though less popular side of higher education. Although he resigned as Trustee again at the end of 1851, he continued to render valuable services at both Indianapolis and Washington; and it was not until his departure for distant climes in the summer of 1853 that the tie with Bloomington finally snapped.[13] That break, however, was complete, and today Owen's work as Trustee is largely forgotten. Yet the university owes a debt of gratitude to him and to his colleagues who guided its destinies and nourished its growth when the thoughts of men in a pioneer state were concerned with things other than collegiate instruction.

One of the most curious intellectual currents that coursed through Owen's Indiana years was his interest in architecture. Its origin was simple enough. In January 1847, after James

[11] Wylie to D. G. Mitchell, Apr. 7, 1840, English Collection; *Address by a Committee of the Trustees of Indiana University, to the People of Indiana* (Indps., 1840) ; Wylie, *op. cit.*, 52.

[12] *Documentary Journal*, 25 Sess., 385–402; *General Laws, 1840–1841*, 110–111; *Catalogue of the Officers and Students of Indiana University, 1840–1841* (Indps., 1841).

[13] "Excerpts from the Minutes of the Board of Trustees, Indiana University" (MS.).

Renwick had been chosen to build the Smithsonian Institution's future home, Owen proposed to the Regents that the Secretary and the Building Committee prepare a small volume that would satisfy public curiosity concerning the unfamiliar design and placate the dissatisfied competitors who thought that the rejected plans had not received sufficient publicity. Subsequent resolutions expanded the undertaking into "a treatise on architecture," but one that would be popular in character. The very fact that in March 1847 Owen himself was requested to be the author limited the profundity of the work and gave assurance that it would seek to diffuse rather than to increase knowledge. Why the Indianan was selected for the task is far from clear; the most probable reason is that no other Regent was willing to do it.[14]

Two years were to elapse before Owen's essay on architecture appeared. This delay arose in part from certain difficulties the printer encountered in preparing the expensive wood-cut illustrations and in part from the political activity of the Western Democrat. In fact, if it had not been for the unexpected winter of leisure between the disastrous Embree contest and the extended stumping tour for Lewis Cass, it is hard to see how the book would have been put before the public even in May 1849. But the loss of Owen the politician was the gain of Owen the intellectual, and during 1847 and 1848 he benefitted from frequent contacts with artists like Robert Mills, James Renwick, and Ashur B. Durand. In that same period he was compelled to read widely, if not deeply, and the result was another proof of his extraordinary versatility.[15]

The finished product, entitled *Hints on Public Architecture*, was a thin folio volume, profusely illustrated with attractive lithographs and containing among other things a complete de-

[14] *Smithsonian Institution: Journals of the Board of Regents*, 30, 32, 602. Owen later said that the book was written because the Building Committee had not been able to find the data therein contained elsewhere in condensed form and free from technicalities. *Hints on Public Architecture* (N. Y., 1849), v–vi.

[15] *Smithsonian Institution: Journals, passim*; "Third Annual Report of the Board of Regents . . . 1848," *House Miscellaneous Reports*, 39 Cong., 2 Sess., no. 48, 52; Owen to Trist, Mar. 20, 1849, Trist Papers, XXXIII.

scription of the Smithsonian Building, a critical discussion of earlier American edifices, and a useful appendix of information on construction materials. The text was devoted chiefly to a brief survey, borrowed from other writers, of the various styles of architecture with emphasis on their relative cost, accommodations provided, and their adaptability to modern conditions. The more original part of the work was the author's attempt to discover a national style of architecture suited to the needs and character of the young republic. In his review of the main schools of the past, Owen disagreed violently with those who had made a Greek temple the vogue of his day. "It is difficult to imagine," he wrote, "anything in the shape of a public edifice further removed, in purpose and adaptation, from modern wants in a climate like ours." [16] Owen's objections to these anomalous Doric and Ionic structures in agrarian America was based on utilitarian rather than aesthetic grounds. He criticized their inadequate facilities for lighting and heating, their failure to allow different interior arrangements, and, above all, their excessive cost. No form of post and lintel found favor in his eyes, and the Italian Romanesque fared little better. It was in the late Norman and early Gothic buildings of the twelfth century, especially as they appeared in England, with their excellent fenestration, their provisions for chimneys and staircases, and their ability to receive additional wings if needed that Owen saw "better promise of material out of which to erect for America a national style of architecture than among the monuments of any other style now extant." [17]

The Western Democrat felt too strongly the winds of nationalism then sweeping across the American scene to advise a slavish imitation of the art of another country and of another age. There were, however, in his opinion certain basic prerequisites for a national style. It must be flexible and avoid all inappropriate detail. It must not only depict the independent spirit of the people, but it must also serve their needs in a great variety of climates. It must be economical, for Americans would not

[16] *Hints on Public Architecture*, 35.　　　　　　[17] *Ibid.*, 31–46, 47–62, 76.

be taxed for lavish public buildings. It must be practical, allowing a maximum of covered space. It must be pure and faithfully represent the internal purpose of the external form. Finally, it must seek to employ as ornament the natural products of the land. Latrobe's "happy inspiration" in outlining stalks and ears of Indian corn on the shafts and capitals of the pillars in the vestibule of the Senate illustrated what Owen had in mind. The Hoosier believed that the commendable achievements in American painting and sculpture gave promise of an equally bright future in architecture.

Let us not, then lament [he wrote] the paucity in our land of memorials of the Past, but rather look on to our Future. If no school of Architecture . . . neither Egyptian . . . Grecian . . . Gothic, may, as a whole, serve as a suitable model for us, now in this nineteenth century and here on this North American continent, then the inquiry presents itself, may we not hope to see spring up in our midst, a school of our own; assimilated, more or less, to one or other of the old manners; yet asserting its privilege to originate as well as to adopt. . . ? [18]

This clarion call for a native style, suited to the needs of republican America and based on the late Norman and early Gothic, met with little response in subsequent architectural development. The Smithsonian Building did not inaugurate, as Owen had hoped, a series of similar edifices. From the beginning its critics were as numerous as its admirers, and since the disastrous fire of 1865 it has generally been considered one of the capital's least attractive edifices.[19] When a creative spirit was finally breathed into American architecture after the Civil War by Henry Hobson Richardson, the Romanesque of southern France, not the Norman or early Gothic, served as the model. Yet Owen's message, if unheeded, was none the less significant.

[18] *Hints on Public Architecture*, 6; 8–14.
[19] Critical opinions were expressed in J. J. Ampère, *Promenade en Amérique* (Paris, 1855), II, 80; C. R. Weld, *A Vacation Tour in the United States and Canada* (London, 1855), 271; William Ferguson, *America by River and Rail* (London, 1856), 161; Anthony Trollope, *North America* (Phila., 1862), II, 11, 19.

Except for beauty there was little justification for the Greek revival in the United States, and an appeal for a style adapted to and representative of our national needs and institutions was not improper. Owen's dream has been shared by many since his time; and even today there are those who readily admit that the magnificent monuments of Washington reflect little that is indigenous to America and who regard it as something of an anomaly that the Great Emancipator, a humble son of the frontier, should have as his memorial a Greek temple.

Owen's message not only went unheeded; it went largely unheard. The costly illustrations, one of the chief merits of the volume, as well as the over-large format tended to restrict its circulation. Then again, the Americans of the day were more interested in hints on private dwellings than those on public buildings. Thus, although the book was favorably commented upon by a special committee of notables to whom it was submitted before publication, it won disappointingly little attention in either general periodicals or professional circles.[20] Yet if Owen's treatise did not become a beacon light for American architects, it does illuminate for the biographer his character and his versatility. Whatever the result may have been, Owen did try to diffuse knowledge, to improve the taste of the common man. His essay reflected his desire for a Smithsonian Institution that would play a popular rather than a learned role. In his writing Owen revealed, too, his faith in the brilliant destiny of his adopted country. Only four years before Paulding had prophesied that the West would give American literature its distinctive character. Out of the West now came a demand for a national style of architecture.[21]

In one sense the essay was a complete failure. It gave Joseph

---

[20] *Hints on Public Architecture*, iii–iv; Edward Everett to J. G. Totten, Dec. 4, 1848; Everett to Owen, Dec. 4, 1848, Everett Papers, LXXXVII. *Democratic Review*, XXIV, 384 (Apr. 1849); *Southern Literary Messenger*, XV, 310–311 (May 1849); *Merchants' Magazine and Commercial Review*, XXI, 252 (Aug. 1849); *N. Y. Tribune*, May 12, 1849; *Evening Post*, June 2, 1849; *Evansville Journal*, Aug. 2, 1849. A scathing review appeared in the *Literary World*, IV, 510–511, V, 4–5 (June 16, July 7, 1849).

[21] Paulding to Owen, Jan. 6, 1845, Dreer Collection: American Prose, VI.

Henry no new reason to prolong Owen's connection with the Smithsonian Institution. On the contrary, it may have been a primary cause for the dislike that the scientist seems to have conceived for his former sponsor. For one thing the Secretary's pride was hurt by the Hoosier's neglect in not consulting him, as directed, in the preparation of the manuscript. The undue delay in its completion was naturally annoying; and with Congress continually talking of stricter supervision of the Institution, Henry was fearful lest he personally be placed in a false position. Nor did the book fit well into the physicist's plan of "active operations" of which he was inordinately proud, and it threatened to establish a precedent for the very thing he opposed — popular works that would diffuse rather than increase knowledge. Finally, Henry was distressed that, at a time when he was striving to devote every dollar of a meager income to what he considered the proper functions of the Institution, this bastard treatment should consume more than double its original appropriation. Inevitably *Hints on Public Architecture* must have become associated in Henry's mind with the expensive building it described, and that edifice together with Choate's library scheme were the two things which the Secretary criticized and combatted until he finally triumphed once and for all after the explosion of 1854–1855.[22]

Within four months of the appearance of *Hints on Public Architecture*, Owen was completely absorbed in another less profound but equally useful effort to aid and educate the common man. During late 1849 and early 1850 he became the West's outstanding advocate of plank roads. That cheap mode of transportation, designed both to precede and to supplement railways, were the subject in the decade from 1846 to 1856 of a veritable craze that stretched from New York to Alabama and from Virginia to Iowa. The country's first turnpike of wood

[22] "Third Annual Report . . . 1848," *loc. cit.*, 20, 52. On Dec. 11, 1848 Andrew Johnson asked that a Congressional committee investigate "the expediency of printing . . . a work . . . upon architecture — a kind of mongrel report prepared by some of the Regents." *Congressional Globe*, 30 Cong., 2 Sess., 23.

was constructed in central New York in 1846, and five years later there were more than 2,000 miles in the Empire State alone. The cheapness and alleged efficiency of plank roads made them especially attractive to rural districts and villages not visited by the iron horse. For a brief time editors throughout the West were solemnly asserting, "This has become the Plank Road age as well as the Railroad and Telegraph age. . . . Build up your towns by Plank Roads to that size which will permit you to erect Railroads."[23]

In Indiana poor facilities of communication and a plenitude of timber insured plank roads a full trial. Newspapers in the Hoosier capital began to discuss the topic as early as 1845, but it was not until four years later when a plank road was projected between New Harmony on the Wabash and Mt. Vernon on the Ohio that Owen's interest was aroused. Then, as in 1836 when he dreamed of uniting the two rivers by a canal from Chainville, he was carried away by his enthusiasm. In the fall of 1849 the Western Democrat hoped to make his village the center of a veritable network of plank roads, planning, in addition to the one to the county seat, others to Evansville, to Cynthiana, and, most ambitious of all, to St. Louis.[24] In behalf of these schemes he spent several weeks of October in western New York inspecting the construction details of the highways then in operation. He visited Cazenovia, Chittenago, Syracuse, and Utica; conversed with Thomas G. Alvord, an engineer of the first turnpike laid down; and met again several old Congressional colleagues who were sponsoring similar programs in their communities.[25] Upon his return to the West, Owen set out in the opposite direction to arouse interest and obtain subscriptions for the plank road through Carmi, McLeansboro, and Belleville to St. Louis. Poverty in southern

[23] *Evansville Journal*, Dec. 14, 1849. Joseph A. Durrenberger, *Turnpikes etc.* (Valdosta, Ga., 1931), ch. IX; Caroline E. MacGill, *History of Transportation in the United States before 1860* (Wash., 1917), ch. X.

[24] *Indiana State Sentinel*, Feb. 27, 1845; *Indiana State Journal*, May 14, 1845. *Evansville Journal*, Sept. 6, 20, Nov. 8, 1849.

[25] Robert Dale Owen, *A Brief Practical Treatise on the Construction and Management of Plank Roads* (New Albany, 1850), 1–2, 12, 73.

Illinois and indifference in Missouri caused the abandonment of that ambitious plan; but during the winter Owen continued to spread the new gospel in the "Pocket" and finally decided, characteristically enough, to diffuse through the printed page all that he knew about this improved method of travel.[26]

In origin and purpose Owen's new volume differed little from his recent effort in the field of architecture. Just as the Building Committee of the Smithsonian Institution had commissioned him to publish facts that the layman could not obtain in simple form, so now Owen presented the data he collected in New York and elsewhere because he could not refer his numerous Western correspondents to a non-technical work on plank roads. In form, the new treatise was less pretentious than *Hints on Public Architecture*, and in content it was even less original. The text was chiefly expository, with just enough appropriately illustrated argument that "any farmer or teamster" could understand, to break down the existing prejudice against toll highways. After briefly tracing the history of the new improvement, the author described with minute detail the methods of construction. Chapters were devoted to such topics as grading and excavation; pertinent facts were given on costs, durability, and, most important of all, on profits. Even a sample contract and a list of tools required by a road gang were included. The book, then, was essentially a manual with which intelligent men, lacking previous experience and the services of a trained engineer, would be able to lay down a plank road. As one reviewer said of it, "Indeed we don't know but plank roads will almost build themselves hereafter." [27]

Although Owen's essay was neither original nor definitive, it was both timely and useful. When it was first contemplated, not a single authoritative description of plank roads could be found except in fugitive newspaper articles. As is so often the case, however, the want was filled almost simultaneously

---

[26] *Evansville Journal*, Nov. 8, 23, 1849. *Ibid.*, Nov. 30, Dec. 14, 1849; *New Albany Ledger*, Mar. 27, Apr. 12, 13, 22, 1850.

[27] Quoted in the *Indiana State Sentinel*, June 26, 1850.

by several authors. In January 1850 appeared the third edition of Professor W. M. Gillespie's *Manual of the Principles
and Practice of Road-Making* containing twenty-three new
pages devoted to plank roads. Shortly thereafter George Geddes,
the real father of the movement, brought out a slight pamphlet
comprising thirteen pages of text and, like Owen's, an appendix
of state laws and judicial decisions. The Indianan's volume,
published in June 1850, was the third to be offered; and although
indebted to its predecessors, it was the longest, best written,
and most durably bound of all. In 1851 at least three more
accounts were printed, the most important being that by William Kingsford, a civil engineer.[28] Probably none of these
treatises achieved a very extensive national circulation. Each
was written, perhaps unconsciously, for a certain section or
class. Owen's proved to be the most useful and accessible for
the people of Indiana, Illinois, Kentucky, and Ohio. It was
greeted by the Western press without distinction of party, and
in the praise even George D. Prentice, an arch foe of the past,
joined. All saw in it, as the reader must, another proof of
Owen's extraordinary versatility.[29]

In the future success of plank roads Owen had never betrayed the slightest doubt. Yet while he was spreading the
gospel in speech and in print, their worth was being subjected
to a practical test along the fifteen-mile stretch between New
Harmony and Mt. Vernon. In December 1849 contracts for
timber had been let, and during part of the following year
Owen, as director of the joint-stock company financing the
project, was in the field supervising the construction. By January 1851 a part was in operation, and at the end of the summer
a ball was held at the county seat to celebrate the completion

---

[28] Kingsford, *History, Structure, and Statistics of Plank Roads, in the United
States and Canada* (Phila., 1851); William Gregg, *Essay on Plank Roads*
(Charleston, S. C., 1851); Joseph E. Ware, *Observations on Plank Roads:
Their Utility, Cost, and Expensive Character, Compared with Railroads* (St.
Louis, 1851).

[29] *New Albany Ledger*, June 25, 1850. Cf. *Indiana State Sentinel*, June 26,
1850; *Indiana State Journal*, July 22, 1850; *Evansville Journal*, Aug. 23, 1850,
Oct. 23, 1851.

of the whole work. For a time the Democratic leader seemed well pleased with the enterprise; but it quickly became apparent that there was not enough traffic between the two towns to make the undertaking profitable. The pike continued in use for some years but it was never replanked; and as failure was written across another of Owen's numerous schemes to help New Harmony, little more was heard in Posey of this new and great improvement of the West.[30]

The ultimate failure of the Mt. Vernon plank road foreshadowed a similar lack of success elsewhere. The decline of these farmers' railroads, as they were called, was almost as rapid as their spread. Competition from other forms of transportation was only partly responsible. In the West too many highways were opened in sparsely populated districts where the traffic was too light to bring profits to the stockholders. Even more disastrous was the inadequate nature of the materials used. Wood afforded a surface sufficiently smooth and, if properly laid down, perhaps sufficiently durable. Little attention, however, was paid to the effect of water; and as a result of improper drainage the planks decayed in five years. With building costs thus more than doubled and the efficiency lessened, enthusiasm for plank roads began to abate in the midfifties. In New York, where the movement had been the strongest, only five per cent of the highways constructed with that material were still in operation in 1860. Eight years later only seventeen of the 352 companies originally chartered remained in existence. But long before the movement had ended in failure, Owen had turned again to political life; and plank roads soon became a forgotten incident in the career of the Western Democrat.[31]

[30] *Evansville Journal*, Dec. 17, 1849; *New Albany Ledger*, Mar. 20, 1850; *Democratic Clarion*, Jan. 18, Feb. 15, Nov. 8, 1851; *History of Posey County* (Chicago, 1886), 373.

[31] Durrenberger, *op. cit.*, 150–152.

CHAPTER XVII

THE INDIANA CONSTITUTION

As HE SCANNED the election returns in August 1849, Robert Dale Owen found many grounds for satisfaction. In the First District Embree had gone down to an unexpected and painful defeat before an inexperienced rival. In the state the Democrats had won their greatest victory since the "revolution" six years before, thus dissipating once and for all the fear aroused in 1848 that the Free Soilers might come to hold a balance of power. The removal of that danger greatly enhanced the Indianan's prospects in the Senatorial election of 1850, for it enabled his party to return to its conservative position on slavery. Yet, in the end, it was the well-nigh unanimous demand of the voters for a new constitution that gave Owen the most pleasure. As early as 1840 he had vainly suggested that some change be made in the state's organic law. Not until the end of the decade, when a wave of constitutional reform was sweeping across the country, did the Hoosiers fall in line and seek to bring their fundamental charter closer to the people.[1]

Being widely regarded as one of Indiana's foremost citizens and legislators, Owen was naturally urged to serve in the forthcoming convention. Lacking for the moment more pressing duties and being keenly aware of the tremendous importance of such a body, he consented to run and in the summer of 1850 turned his attention from plank roads to constitutional principles. Besides speaking at public meetings throughout Posey and the "Pocket," he encouraged the editors of the *New Albany Ledger*, the Democratic daily in the state's largest city, to commence a weekly journal devoted exclusively to topics suitable for inclusion in the new charter. Owen himself contributed

---

[1] *Democratic Review*, XXIX, 3–18 (July 1851). Cf. *Indiana Democrat*, Feb. 25, 1840; *Wabash Enquirer*, June 10, 1840.

frequently to this *Constitution*, dealing for the most part with a reform little discussed up to then, the legal emancipation of married women. After an apparently uneventful canvass Owen was elected in the Democratic landslide in August to represent his own county.[2]

Shortly before ten o'clock on Monday morning, October 7, 1850, nearly one hundred and fifty delegates crowded into the specially arranged lower chamber in the State House. More than four months later, on February 10, they adjourned *sine die* in Masonic Hall, having completed the instrument that today remains the organic law of Indiana. During that time they discussed all matters of reform, resisted temptations to move to other cities, survived a cholera scare, indulged in extraneous political and personal debate, and, because of their extended sitting, were subjected to incessant criticism from the press, the General Assembly, and from their own number. While they were in session, the state legislature met, a United States Senator was elected, and a movement begun to elevate a native son to the presidency. In all of these matters Owen had a vital interest; and thanks to the telegraph, the increased number of newspapers, many of which were printed daily or tri-weekly, and to the official publication of the proceedings, as much is known about this phase of the Hoosier's career as almost any other.

From the moment he moved its first act, the election of a presiding officer, until he made the final report in the early hours of February 10, Owen was the most diligent, prominent, and influential delegate in the convention. To accord him that primacy is not to minimize the parts played by such colleagues as John Pettit and James Borden or such opponents as John Niles and Schuyler Colfax but merely to register what the contemporary documents reveal. It was not alone Owen's position as leader of the dominant party that secured his preëminence. Maturing years had brought balance to his thought,

[2] *Democratic Clarion*, Apr. 6, 1850; *New Albany Ledger*, Jan. 18, Feb. 26, Mar. 7, Apr. 20, 22, May 2, 9, 22, 28, 1850. *Evansville Journal*, Aug. 9, 1850.

and he now marshalled all of his previous training as a debater, legislator, and writer to make one of the most valuable contributions of a useful life. His tireless energy never showed to better advantage, and even the Whigs confessed that he was "an example of industry rarely to be found among our public men." [3]

He was made chairman of the standing Committee on Rights and Privileges, a valuable post for a humanitarian, and of the Committee on Revision, Arrangement, and Phraseology. To this second body, or rather to Owen and two others acting as a sub-committee, fell the task of placing the various sections of the new constitution in logical sequence and imbuing them with unity of style and expression. Thanks to Owen's command of English, the finished document stands high in readability. Still another important paper that came from his persuasive pen was an address to the people, recounting briefly the main differences between the old charter and the new. As one observer said, Owen "will certainly understand the new constitution, for he had something to do, by way of revision or otherwise, with almost every section of it." [4]

In adopting the reforms generally demanded throughout the state, the convention wasted little time and met little opposition. From the legislature was taken the power to enact special laws. Biennial sessions were decreed, and its freedom to borrow money was stringently curtailed. With both parties bidding for the alien vote, suffrage qualifications were reduced to an unwise minimum. All state officers, including supreme court justices, were made directly elective by the people. Provisions looking toward a simplification of court procedure and a codification of statute law were voted. A much discussed section on finances resulted in a compromise by which "free banking" was virtually allowed but the State Bank was not destroyed. The subject of education elicited remarkably little debate. County seminaries were abolished, a single school fund was established, and the Assembly required to provide for a uniform, public

[3] *Evansville Journal,* quoted in the *New Albany Ledger,* Jan. 8, 1851.
[4] *Madison Courier,* Feb. 10, 1851.

system.[5] On all of these topics Owen voted with his party; but, except on the bank issue where he strove earnestly for conciliation, he exerted his influence more in the Committee on Revision than on the floor itself.[6]

Aside from extraneous political debate, buncombe, and the bank question, most of the convention's time was consumed by matters neither urgently demanded nor universally desired by the electors in the preceding years. Three of these, homestead exemption, the treatment of Negroes, and the property rights of married women, came before Owen's standing committee and shed, thereby, some light on his claim to being a reformer. The first of these matters was eagerly sought among northern Hoosiers. Despite an ever increasing acceptance in other states, it was still considered a radical innovation in Indiana; and Owen, while approving homestead exemption laws in the abstract, doubted the wisdom of placing so bitterly disputed a measure in the new charter. Since most of his constituents, as well as his colleague from Posey, disliked the proposal, he was inclined to leave it for disposition by the next session of the legislature. Thus, although he fought valiantly for an unrestricted statement prohibiting imprisonment for debt and although he supported a general exemption clause, Owen twice voted against exempting homesteads as well.[7] Given the representative system of government, Owen's conservatism was not censurable, but it was unwise. The same argument used by him, that a radical reform should be decided upon by the legislature rather than by a constituent assembly, could be and was employed against his own favorite measure.

[5] Charles Kettelborough, *Constitution Making in Indiana: A Source Book of Constitutional Documents with Historical Introduction and Critical Notes* (*Indiana Historical Collections*, Indps., 1916), I, *passim*; Dunn, *Indiana and Indianans*, 435–497.

[6] Logansport *Democratic Pharos*, Jan. 29, 1851.

[7] *Journal of the Convention of the People of Indiana, to Amend the Constitution, Assembled at Indianapolis, October, 1850* (Indps., 1851), 148, 293, 702; *Report of the Debates and Proceedings of the Convention for the Revision of the Constitution of the State of Indiana, 1850* (Indps., 1850–1851), 767; Centreville *Indiana True Democrat*, Nov. 29, 1850.

The rights of colored persons came before the convention in two different forms. One was a referendum on the question of Negro suffrage. Owen supported the proposal on the grounds that it would give the minority a hearing and at the same time effectively reveal to the abolitionists the paucity of their numbers; but his ballot was cast in vain.[8] The other form comprised a series of resolutions, reported by Owen, prohibiting Negroes and mulattoes from settling in the state or purchasing real estate therein, and these passed by an average vote of two to one.[9] In thus writing into their new constitution a policy of exclusion, the Hoosier legislators did not act, as radicals often charged, through indifference or blind inhumanity. Men like Owen, whose lives brought them into daily contact with people residing on slave soil, could logically advocate exclusion and still regard themselves as true friends of the colored race. They argued that no body of people should live in a free country without possessing equal political and social rights. Since there already existed a deep-seated prejudice, proper or improper, against Negro equality and since some statutes already made partial discriminations, Owen saw no reason not to go the full length and separate the races completely. A liberal policy of colonization linked to the new prohibition seemed to him the best solution of a difficult problem. To be sure, this dream of colonization, the usual defence for exclusion, was a chimera as Owen himself later admitted. But it was a dream indulged in by some of the ablest statesmen of the day.[10]

In the months preceding the Constitutional Convention no reform had attracted less attention among the people of Indiana than civil equality for married women. Yet no subject played a more prominent role in its proceedings. For that fact Owen, and Owen alone, was responsible. During the spring

---

[8] *Convention: Journal*, 139, 141–142 (Oct. 26, 28); *Convention: Debates*, 231 (Oct. 26).

[9] *Convention: Journal*, 138, 164–165, 270–271, 652, 768, 769–770, 772 (Oct. 26, 31, Jan. 13, 24).

[10] *Convention: Debates*, 331, 1792–1793, 1816–1817 (Oct. 26, Jan. 23, 24). Cf. "Looking Back Across the War-Gulf," *Old and New*, I, 587 (May 1870).

and summer of 1850 his demand for the change was a veritable voice crying in the wilderness; but he plunged ahead doggedly, revealing for the first time in some years that on a social question he was leading public opinion, not following it.[11]

Although often obscured by legal verbiage, the evil Owen sought to eradicate is not difficult to understand. He wished a married woman to retain before the law the identity she possessed before marriage. Specifically, wives should control their own property, both that which they possessed when wed and that which they acquired thereafter. The subject was not, to be sure, a new one to Owen. As early as *The Free Enquirer* days he had inveighed against the legal enslavement of married women and, a few years later at Indianapolis, had made his first efforts to modify by statute the rigors of the English common law. In the ensuing decade he said little about the matter, partly, perhaps, for political reasons but mostly because he knew that his wishes could be carried into effect only by the state legislature. During these ten years the change he advocated, premature in 1837, was adopted in various forms in several states, though only the youngest commonwealths wrote the reform into their organic law. In 1847, without fanfare or opposition, Indiana had granted married women the right to devise property and to control their real estate, thereby placing the Hoosiers about midway between the most liberal and the most conservative states.[12] It was to supplement this legislation by extending it, for the benefit of less wealthy wives, to personal property and to safeguard it by incorporating it in the new constitution that Owen in the year 1850 reassumed the role of a reformer.

The vicissitudes that Owen's favorite measure experienced were dramatic in the extreme. First introduced on October 29, 1850, it was not seriously discussed for two weeks. Then, despite the sponsor's brilliant speech in which he eloquently

[11] *Convention: Debates*, 528 (Nov. 16); *New Albany Ledger*, May 2, 9, 22, 28, 1850.
[12] *General Laws, 1846–1847*, 45–46.

begged his colleagues to administer to ladies "a little less flattery and a little more justice," the proposal encountered enough opposition to suffer defeat by one vote on November 26.[13] Almost immediately, however, Owen and his followers threw their strength behind the less sweeping innovation of James E. Blythe, which merely extended the Act of 1847 to include personal property. Once again a lengthy debate ensued, featured by a clash between Owen and Oliver P. Badger, a "New Light" minister of Whig persuasion, on the theological implications of the question; but notwithstanding these pyrotechnics Blythe's amendment was on November 27 placed in the new constitution by a margin of seven votes.[14]

For a fortnight Owen rested in triumph and then there began a series of heartbreaking events. On December 10 the Indianapolis papers carried the following card. "On Behalf of the Women of Indiana."

Deprecating the efforts of those of our sex who desire to enter the political arena . . . and demanding only protection for the property that Providence may enable us to give our daughters . . . we tender our sincere acknowledgements to the high-minded gentlemen, delegates to the Constitutional Convention, who favored the adoption of the section securing to the married women of Indiana independent rights of property; and we have determined to present to the Hon. Robert Dale Owen, as the original mover, a testimonial in the form of a piece of plate, with suitable inscription, as a slight token of our lasting gratitude. That the women of Indiana, generally, may have an opportunity to contribute to this most laudable object, we have limited the contribution to one dollar each.[15]

The very next day James W. Borden, one of Owen's rivals in the impending Senatorial election, moved to reconsider the vote

---

[13] *Convention: Journal*, 148, 299; *Convention: Debates*, 462–469.

[14] *Convention: Debates*, 815–819, 821–826 (Nov. 27); *Convention: Journal*, 307. See also the note at the end of the chapter.

[15] *Indiana State Journal*, Dec. 10, 1850. The prime movers were Sarah T. Bolton, author of "Paddle Your Own Canoe," and then Indiana's leading poetess, and Priscilla H. Drake, wife of the state treasurer and a social leader of Indianapolis. Of the other twelve signatories at least six were wives of delegates to the convention, one of a United States District judge, one of a state supreme court justice, and one of a leading Hoosier educator.

by which Blythe's amendment was adopted. His motion was carried; and after another spell of personal insinuations and theological dialectics, the cherished reform failed to repass.[16] Nowise discouraged, Owen a month later, on January 16, reported a third version of his project; but this, after being, seemingly, on the verge of acceptance, was voted down on January 29. With the cup of victory again dashed from his lips, Owen might well have given up the fight, but he did not. Less than a week before the final adjournment, he won by a personal appeal the right to present his plan in a fourth and still weaker form. Amid general astonishment, it passed, and for the second time the civil equality of married women was written into the new Hoosier constitution.[17]

There it did not long remain. That very afternoon, while Owen was absent with the Committee on Revision, Milton Gregg, veteran Whig editor and previously a staunch supporter of the reform, moved a reconsideration of the morning's vote. When the convention assembled the following day to act upon the motion, rumors were current that Owen owed his last success to chicanery. These stories he immediately and completely refuted, but the tide had once more set against him. Whether the delegates were influenced by sheer boredom or by the fact that the measure, as Gregg later said, "had been frittered down to a mere shadow, and, as it then stood, was of decidedly more importance to the reputation of Mr. Owen, than of practical utility to the women of Indiana" is not certain.[18] But in another surprising reversal of sentiment the previous day's action was reconsidered, and by a vote of 68 to 63 the section conferring independent rights of property upon married women was again torn out of the new charter. That settlement was final.[19]

[16] Convention: Journal, 415, 453–454 (Dec. 11, 17).

[17] Convention: Journal, 692, 822, 894–897 (Jan. 16, 29, Feb. 4); Evansville Journal, Jan. 24, 1851; Madison Courier, Jan. 30, 1851.

[18] Madison Tribune, June 5, 1851.

[19] Convention: Journal, 903, 904–906 (Feb. 4, 5); Convention: Debates, 2011–2012.

Several factors help to explain the rejection of Owen's reform, though probably none was decisive in itself. There were in the convention many conservative lawyers who looked with horror at any inroads upon the English common law and many timid individuals who were content to leave disputed matters to the legislature. The fact that Owen's proposal had not been demanded by the people strengthened the hands of these two groups. Then, too, newspaper distortion linked the measure in the minds of many with the radical Woman's Rights movement in the East; and to the vast majority of Hoosiers the anti-slavery, female suffrage, and "Bloomer" excesses of that organization were anathema. The religious factor, of course, was present, but its influence may be exaggerated. The Scriptures furnished many of the arguments arrayed against the proposed change, and clergymen both within and without the convention were its bitterest opponents. But the former editor of *The Free Enquirer* had plenty of quotations with which to refute Biblical allusions; and when Reverend Mr. Badger tried to show that the reform was the logical outgrowth of its sponsor's earlier infidel writings, the agnostic welcomed the opportunity to set forth his religious creed, as many liberals have done before and since, in the words of Leigh Hunt's parable.

> Abou Ben Adhem (may his tribe increase!)
> Awoke one night from a deep dream of peace,
> And saw within the moonlight in his room,
> Making it rich, and like a lily in bloom,
> An angel writing in a book of gold: —
> Exceeding peace had made Ben Adhem bold
> And to the presence in the room he said,
> "What writest thou?" — The vision rais'd its head
> And with a look made of all sweet accord,
> Answer'd, "The names of those who love the Lord."
> "And is mine one?" said Abou. "Nay, not so,"
> Replied the angel. Abou spoke more low,
> But cheerily still; and said, "I pray thee then,
> "Write me as one that loves his fellow-men."
> The angel wrote, and vanish'd. The next night
> It came again with a great wakening light,

And show'd the names whom love of God had bless'd,
And lo! Ben Adhem's name led all the rest.[20]

Much more disastrous to Owen's reform than the opposition of the church was the hostility of the politicians. In an age of extreme partisanship there were, of course, many Whigs who voted against the measure merely because Owen introduced it, while there were even more Democrats eager to kill it lest success enhance the prestige of the sponsor in the forthcoming Senatorial contest. The tactics of Owen's friends did much to arouse jealousy among other members of the party. The appearance of the card announcing the Owen Testimonial was exceedingly ill-timed and a blunder of the first magnitude. It not only frightened other candidates for the Senate into reversing their votes but also alienated those delegates who were aiding Owen in his struggle but to whom the singling out of one man to receive the hero's laurels seemed unjust. On more than one occasion in the subsequent debates the power of the green-eyed monster was evident.[21] Although many forces were at work in effecting the final result, probably none was more potent than that expressed by the anonymous wit who wrote,

They vote the women all the rights
That have belonged to men,
And then because they got no plate,
They vote them back again.[22]

The refusal of the convention to write the legal equality of married women into the new Indiana constitution was to Owen a keen disappointment. He probably realized that his very advocacy of the measure was something of a handicap, for during the debates he deplored the attempts to arouse prejudice against the reform by personal abuse of its sponsor. When it was all over, however, he did his best to repress any bitter re-

[20] *Convention: Debates*, 825–826.
[21] *Convention: Debates*, 1162, 1177, 1191 (Bascom, Blythe, Pettit).
[22] "Address of the Carrier Boys," Indianapolis *Locomotive*, Jan. 4, 1851. See also the similar interpretation in two contemporary histories of the convention battle, Lawrenceburg *Independent Press*, Feb. 21, 1851; *Madison Tribune*, June 5, 1851.

marks, and only once did he record his own reason for the failure. That was in a letter to his father in which he placed the blame at the door of the clergy.[23]

While Owen was waging his losing battle on behalf of the married women of Indiana, another Senatorial election took place. As has been suggested, there was more than a temporal relation between the two events. In 1850 Owen held some hope that at last he would reach his goal. The free soil movement had collapsed. The August landslide insured the selection of a Democrat. Once again he was the choice of the "Pocket." [24] Finally he could expect the incumbent to be rotated out of office, for it had been almost twenty years since an Indiana Senator had succeeded himself.

Jesse D. Bright, however, was determined to retain the seat to which he had been so unexpectedly elevated in 1845. A consummate politician, he had scaled the heights of national fame rapidly and now left no stone unturned to secure reelection. He spent the fall mending his fences throughout the state; it was not until mid-December that he left belatedly to attend his duties in Congress. Soon after his departure Owen discovered what he thought to be a clear case of bribery among Bright's followers and on January 6 reluctantly published his findings.[25] Bright's stock dropped at once, but not for long. The very next day the Senator himself, having been warned before the story broke, arrived dramatically from Washington. With the incumbent upon the scene, his stock soared. For all the fuss over the alleged bribery, nothing incriminating the Senator directly had been revealed. Knowing ones continued to predict his renomination just as they had before the incident.[26]

[23] R. D. Owen to Robt. Owen, Feb. 25, 1851, *Robert Owen's Journal*, May 17, 1851.

[24] *Democratic Clarion*, Sept. 14, 1850; Indianapolis *Indiana Statesman*, Dec. 25, 1850; *New Albany Ledger*, Jan. 15, 1851.

[25] *Indiana American*, Nov. 15, 1850; *Madison Courier*, Dec. 13, 1850. The documents for the bribery incident involving George B. Graff are in the *Indiana State Journal*, Jan. 6, 1851; *Indiana State Sentinel*, Jan. 7, 9, 23, 1851; *Democratic Clarion*, Feb. 1, 1851.

[26] *Lafayette Courier*, Dec. 19, 1850; *Logansport Journal*, Jan. 11, 1851.

On the evening of January 10, 1851, the Democrats met in caucus. On the very first ballot Bright received eight votes more than was necessary for a choice. In this contest Owen made the best showing of his career, yet he mustered only nine supporters outside of his district.[27] Showing once again his party regularity, he accepted the caucus verdict in good faith, and on the next day Bright was reelected by a united Democracy. Publicly the loser took his defeat philosophically, but in private he betrayed intense disappointment. Writing to his father more than a month later, when momentary passions should have cooled, he attributed the result, unfairly, to Bright's unscrupulous use of his great wealth.[28]

Failure was not stamped on all of Owen's efforts at Indianapolis during the winter of 1850–1851. On the contrary, his most absorbing task, the framing of the new constitution, was eminently successful. Democrats and Whigs both lauded the finished product, and its adoption by an overwhelming vote seemed likely. The Committee on Revision came in for a fair share of the praise, and Owen himself was singled out for compliments. No delegate, it was said, had labored harder than he. "Though he has a hobby," wrote one commentator,

he is a working man, and as an enlightened Legislator, he stands at the head of the list of the great men of the Convention. I never knew a man of brains (and that's Bob Owen), who could perform more labor, or who worked more cheerfully.[29]

But in the end the source of Owen's greatest satisfaction during that arduous winter was the testimonial being planned for him by the "Women of Indiana." Undismayed by the

---

Charles B. Murphy, "The Political Career of Jesse D. Bright," Indiana Historical Society, *Publications*, X (Indps., 1931), 120–121.

[27] *Indiana State Sentinel*, Jan. 14, 1851. The poll stood, Bright, 56; Owen, 23; Pettit, 10; Chamberlain, 3; J. H. Lane, 1.

[28] *Independent Press*, Jan. 24, 1851; R. D. Owen to Robt. Owen, Feb. 25, 1851, *Robert Owen's Journal*, May 17, 1851.

[29] *Independent Press*, Feb. 21, 1851. Cf. *Indiana Statesman*, Apr. 2, 1851; *Madison Courier*, Feb. 10, 1851.

vicissitudes and ultimate rejection of Owen's reform, unabashed by the incessant newspaper ridicule, Sarah Bolton and the other sponsors matured their plans.[30] On the very hot evening of May 28, 1851, these bore fruit in what was one of the happiest moments of Owen's life. The Hall of Representatives, in which the Western Democrat had begun his political career, was tastefully decorated for the occasion. Green garlands hung from the massive columns that encircled the chamber, while within the bar stood crimson covered tables with gorgeous flowers. Only women were allowed on the floor of the assembly, the stronger sex being relegated to the galleries. The hall was filled as it had never been filled before, yet more than five hundred people were refused admittance.[31]

Promptly at eight o'clock, as the enlivening strains of Downie's Saxe Horn Band died away, Judge Thomas L. Smith of the state supreme court arose. After a few appropriate remarks, he yielded to William C. Larrabee, distinguished professor at Indiana Asbury University and later editor of the *Ladies' Repository*. That staunch Methodist had already called Owen "a true-hearted philanthropist, and . . . fearless reformer," and he now prophesied that civil equality would soon be granted to the married women of Indiana. He then handed to their champion a tall, classical silver pitcher, raised by subscriptions from Hoosier wives, on which were inscribed the words

Presented to the Hon. Robert Dale Owen, by the Women of Indiana, in acknowledgment of his true and noble advocacy of their independent rights to property in the Constitutional Convention of the State of Indiana, convened at Indianapolis, 1850.[32]

[30] *Locomotive*, Dec. 14, 21, 28, 1850, Jan. 11, 25, Feb. 15, Apr. 12, May 24, 31, 1851; *Lafayette Journal*, Dec. 26, 1850; South Bend *St. Joseph Valley Register*, Dec. 26, 1850.

[31] *Indiana State Journal*, Feb. 7, Mar. 17, May 30, 1851; *Indiana State Sentinel*, May 30, 1851; *Proceedings at the Presentation to the Hon. Robert Dale Owen of a Silver Pitcher, on Behalf of the Women of Indiana, on the 28th Day of May, 1851* (New Albany, 1851).

[32] *Proceedings at the Presentation . . . of a Silver Pitcher.* Cf. *Indiana State Journal*, Mar. 17, 1851.

Owen received the pitcher awkwardly, pressed it "affectionately to his stomach . . . in a high state of gratification," and then ascended the speaker's stand. In spite of the oppressive heat, he was listened to attentively for an hour; and even those hitherto most skeptical were forced to admit that, "however wild and erroneous some of his notions may be, he is unquestionably right in this." After a few gracious words of acceptance, Owen reviewed in detail the struggle in the convention, and without a trace of bitterness attributed his failure to those who had yielded to the forces of prejudice and jealousy. Rather ingeniously he compared the arguments used against his reform with those raised against the Declaration of Independence in 1775–1776. To the great glee of his audience he quoted some recent convention speeches and then translated them by substituting "loyalty" for "domestic obedience," "gracious king" for "generous husband," and "loving subject" for "devoted wife." In both instances, he pointed out, hoary abuse appealed for support to the religious sentiments of mankind. But the time was not far distant, the Indianan believed, when married women would receive more justice and less flattery. "The persecuted audacity of one day," he said,

becomes the common-place orthodoxy of the next. . . . In after days, it may need some such memorial as the rich and graceful gift that now stands before me, to remind a more enlightened generation, that time was, when the law took from the wives their property, and from parents the right to convey what they would to a child.[33]

The wide notice taken of the testimonial was not the least interesting aspect of the affair. The proceedings were printed in pamphlet form and occasioned much favorable comment. The correspondent of the New York *Home Journal*, for example, took the opportunity to call Owen "one of the brightest luminaries . . . of the nineteenth century" who stood "in bold relief above a vulgar crowd that have prostituted their lives to his defamation, and who are but beginning to reap their reward

[33] *Proceedings at the Presentation . . . of a Silver Pitcher*, 11–28; *Locomotive*, May 31, 1851.

which they so long ago deserved." [34] On the other hand, the barrage of vituperation and detraction that had preceded the ceremony continued, especially in Whig quarters. One temperance leader of that party violently objected to the presentation as calculated to increase the circulation among Hoosiers of the recipient's writings on agnosticism and birth control. Another editor declared with much more truth, that if, as Owen's admirers asserted, the reform had failed because of personal prejudice against the sponsor, then the women of Indiana owed very little to him. [35]

With the passage of time the gibes and carpings of contemporary scoffers were forgotten. "A more enlightened generation" did come to appreciate Owen's pioneer strivings to make husbands and wives equal before the law. By the time of his death they were already recognized as one of his strongest claims to fame. [36] Even then, however, the exact nature of his services to the women of his adopted state was becoming blurred in the public mind, and subsequent events only tended to create further confusion. Early in the present century, when the feminist cause was nearing its goal, a second and more permanent memorial was bestowed upon Owen in the form of a bronze bust, at the south entrance of the Hoosier capitol. [37] As a result of the propaganda and publicity attendant upon this new testimonial, the Owen legend was distorted still more until today his achievements in 1850 and 1851 are misunderstood by layman and historian alike. To Owen and the small, talented group of ladies who supported him must go some, but not all, of the credit for the reform's eventual triumph in 1853. As is so often the case, however, other men who should be remembered have been forgotten. For Owen there is glory enough in

[34] *Home Journal*, June 21, 1851; *New Albany Ledger*, June 25, 1851.

[35] *Evansville Journal*, June 5, 1851; *Madison Tribune*, June 10, 21, 23, 1851.

[36] *Indianapolis News*, June 27, 1877; *Indianapolis Journal*, June 27, 1877; *Springfield Republican*, June 26, 1877; *Nation*, July 5, 1877; Boston *Woman's Journal*, June 30, 1877.

[37] *Proceedings at the Unveiling of the Portrait Bust of Robert Dale Owen at the State House, Indianapolis, Indiana, March 2nd, 1911* (n. p., n. d.).

the true facts. Beyond any other individual he was responsible for the form and content of the constitution under which Indiana has lived for almost a century. But in the convention that framed that charter he accomplished nothing materially for the cause of women. He but broke the ground. His real contribution, as well as many other reforms for which he deserves a prominent niche in the Hoosier state's monument to her famous sons, was not made until he returned to Indianapolis the following winter to complete the work.

NOTE

Owen's attempt to give married women independent control of their own property, real and personal, was presented to the Constitution Convention in the following four forms.

(1) October 29, 1850. *Convention: Journal*, 148

Women hereafter married . . . shall have the right to acquire and possess property to their sole use and disposal: and laws shall be passed securing to them, under equitable conditions, all property, real and personal, whether owned by them before marriage, or acquired afterwards, by purchase, gift, devise, descent, or in any other way. . . . Laws shall be passed securing to women now married, the right to all property hereafter to be acquired.

(2) November 27, 1850. *Convention: Journal*, 300

The real and personal property of women, whether owned before marriage or afterwards acquired by purchase or gift, other than from the husband in fraud of his creditors, devise or descent, shall be and remain secured to them under equitable conditions by law.

(3) January 16, 1851. *Convention: Journal*, 692

The real and personal property of married women, and a liberal provision for widows, shall be and remain secured to them respectively under equitable conditions by law.

(4) February 4, 1851. *Convention: Journal*, 894

Laws shall be passed for the security of the property of married women, of widows, and of orphans.

CHAPTER XVIII

COMPLETING THE WORK

ON AUGUST 4, 1851, the people of Indiana gave an overwhelming approval to the work of the late convention. On that same day Owen was elected as one of Posey's two delegates to the lower house of the state legislature. In thus returning to the scene of his first political efforts, Owen was governed as much by a sense of duty as he was by personal desire or ambition. Already he was probably making plans that were to bring the Indiana years to a close. In the previous February he had announced, for reasons not given, that he would not be a candidate for Congress, and it was only in July that he was prevailed upon to run for the legislature.[1]

It was not an ordinary session of the Assembly in which Owen consented to serve. To it fell the task of giving substance and meaning to the new constitutional provisions for public schools, banking, and Negro exclusion. Upon it lay the requirement of replacing the innumerable local and special laws, now prohibited, by general legislation. In it would be renewed the struggle over such disputed reforms as homestead exemption, prohibition, and the civil equality of married women. The length of the session was extraordinary in itself. Instead of the usual two-or-three-month sitting, it lasted, except for a six-week adjournment, from December until late June. The caliber of its members was exceedingly high. John W. Davis, former speaker in Congress, presided over the lower house. Owen himself had refused to be a candidate for that office in order that he might be on the important committees. He was made chairman of those on Education and on the Rights

[1] *Indiana Statesman*, Aug. 20, 1851. The vote stood, Owen, 1,435; Marrs (W), 1,031; Mills (D), 963. See also, *ibid.*, Apr. 2, July 9, 1851; *Indiana State Sentinel*, Feb. 26, 1851; *Madison Courier*, July 5, 1851; *New Albany Ledger*, July 9, 1851.

and Privileges of Citizens; he sat on those specially raised to report on "free banking" and homestead exemption; and in March he was elected head of the group from both houses to which was entrusted the revision of the statute law.[2]

Many of the contested matters left unsettled by the convention were promptly liquidated. A "free banking" system, based upon a report written by Owen, was enacted. The Maine liquor law, then attracting much attention, was rejected, and the moderate policy urged by Owen was followed. Homestead exemption still failed to find favor, but Owen's compromise measure exempting $300 worth of real and personal property from seizure proved successful. In view of the decisive popular mandate in August, Negro exclusion was easily effected. More difficulty was experienced with a colonization fund, regarded by Owen and others as a necessary complement to exclusion; but by dint of great efforts, public and private, a bill appropriating $5,000, half the figure desired by Owen, was passed.[3]

The legislation most anticipated by the people was the new school law. Although the principle for which enlightened men were then striving, compulsory taxation for the support of free primary instruction, is universally accepted today, in 1851 few states had traveled that far. Indiana had never imposed a levy upon all her citizens for such a purpose; but a growing agitation in the forties, led by Caleb Mills and Henry F. West, and climaxed by the peremptory wording of the new constitution, placed the issue squarely before the General Assembly. Despite his earlier interest in the subject, Owen did not participate in the Hoosier educational campaign of the last decade, nor were his efforts in the convention along that line especially notable. It was only when he returned to the legislature, the most stra-

[2] Indiana General Assembly, *House Journal*, 36th Session (1851–1852), 32, 33, 71, 100, 243, 340, 797, 1214. Cf. *Indiana State Sentinel*, Nov. 29, 1851.

[3] *House Journal*, 36 Sess., 803–808, 1712–1714; 1343–1344, 1656–1657; 643, 649, 691–692; 1584–1585; 1346–1347. See also Owen's speeches on the subjects in the *Indiana State Journal*, Jan. 28, Feb. 7, 10, Apr. 27, 28, 1852; *Indiana Statesman*, Feb. 4, 11, 1852.

tegic place in which to do good, did he reappear as a champion of the public school system.[4]

In the legislature that met in December 1851 Owen made two contributions to the cause of education. The first and less popular was his dogged defense of Indiana University. Just as in the previous year, the institution at Bloomington was being threatened by those who wished to use its endowment for the common schools. Parsimonious lawmakers who once neglected the elementary grades for grandiose schemes of internal improvements now proposed to make belated amends by destroying the single non-sectarian college in the state. Owen boldly opposed this demagogic move. The only concession that he would make was one he had offered in the Constitutional Convention, to wit, the creation of a normal school as an integral part of the establishment at Bloomington.[5] Such a compromise, however, failed to win acceptance; and on February 2, 1852, Owen's valiant maneuvers notwithstanding, the lower house went on record as favoring the diversion of the entire income and property of Indiana University to the common school system of the state.[6] Fortunately for the cause of higher learning that vote was merely an expression of opinion. Fortunately, too, Owen as chairman of the Committee on Education, was in a position to block any bill seeking to make that opinion effective. This he did, and it was not until mid-June, when he was absent attending the Democratic National Convention, that the enemies of the university were able to report a measure depriving it of its funds. By then the strength of the movement had been sapped, and the proposal was rejected.[7] Thus did Owen add still another service to the long list he had already rendered collegiate instruction in his adopted state.

[4] Dunn, *Indiana and Indianans*, I, 473–480, II, 890–895, gives the best account of educational trends in Indiana from 1836 to 1851.

[5] *House Journal*, 36 Sess., 105–108 (Dec. 10). Cf. *Convention: Debates*, 1863 (Jan. 27, 1851).

[6] *House Journal*, 36 Sess., 312–313, 718–721 (Dec. 31, Feb. 2); *Indiana State Journal*, Jan. 31, 1852; *Indiana State Sentinel*, Feb. 3, 1852.

[7] *House Journal*, 36 Sess., 2130, 2154 (June 11, 12).

Owen's second contribution to Hoosier education during the winter of 1851–1852 came in connection with the new school law. He was not, as is sometimes asserted, its author; for its general outline was the product of many minds and its specific details the work of James R. M. Bryant, a Whig Representative from Warren county.[8] As with the Smithsonian Bill, however, Owen was eminently useful both as a persuasive speaker in its behalf and as a legislative steersman who secured a full and fair hearing and a prompt settlement. Early in the session Owen committed himself to a scheme of compulsory taxation; and after his committee's bill was reported, he took special pains to defend that feature. Without such a general levy, he showed, the schools could be kept open only a month and a half each year, certainly not the period the constitution contemplated. A tax of five cents on each $100 worth of property netted the expenses of an additional month. In an eloquent appeal against the easy and popular course of light taxation, Owen dramatically held aloft a shining five-cent piece, the sum, he said, daily expended by each Hoosier on liquor and tobacco. To collect five times that amount from every taxpayer for the purpose of instructing the young was the goal at which the Western Democrat was aiming.[9]

In the middle of May Owen reported back from the Committee on Revision the new school bill. During the next ten days it was again debated and amended, but finally on May 20 it passed by a vote of 57 to 31. Despite important modifications of Owen's wishes, the law formed a landmark in the history of Hoosier education. For the first time the whole state was to be taxed for the benefit of its children and at a rate equal to the optional levy of 1849. For thirty-five years the requirements of the old constitution had gone unfulfilled; within a single year those of the new were met. For this result Robert Dale Owen was in no small way responsible. Under his leadership the entire elementary system was centralized, a single Com-

---

[8] Owen's statement, *Indiana State Journal*, Feb. 11, 1852.
[9] *Indiana State Journal*, Jan. 1, Mar. 19, 1852.

mon School Fund was established, uniform textbooks were introduced, a Superintendent of Public Instruction was created, and, most important of all, an *ad valorem* impost of ten cents on every $100 worth of property decreed. One valuable section for which Owen especially strove required the formation of a free library in every township. No provision was more bitterly fought than this, but by a humorous analogy Owen saved the day, and the township libraries remained to become one of the most useful features of the epochal law of 1852.[10]

Less spectacular and less well known than his contribution to the public school system was Owen's equally important part in revising the Indiana statute law. Legal reform had been a prominent demand among the people in 1849 and 1850, and the new constitution not only required a simplification of procedure in the courts of justice but also looked toward the reduction of all earlier legislation into a systematic code. Once before, during 1837–1838, Owen had served on a Committee of Revision; and now on March 8, after an unpleasant but insignificant controversy, he was named chairman of a group comprising members of both houses which was to sit during the six-week mid-session adjournment of the Assembly.[11] This appointment was deemed important enough to precipitate a blast from the Whig press which regretted that Owen was now in a position to "fix up 'woman's rights' or any other of his cherished reforms." One correspondent called him "a theorist, a speculatist, a visionary . . . [who] in all probability would load the laws with his extreme radical notions. . . ."[12]

But the man whose hand was most prominent in the revision of 1852 was not a radical theorist. With the relish for propagandism long since dead, Owen had become a practical, industrious legislator, occasionally mistaken in his tactics, but never

---

[10] *House Journal*, 36 Sess., 1602–1621, 1687–1691, 1697–1699, 1747–1750 (May 12, 17, 18, 20); *Revised Statutes of the State of Indiana, Passed at the Thirty-Sixth Session*, I, 439–457; *Indiana State Journal*, May 19, 1852.

[11] *House Journal*, 36 Sess., 1212; *Indiana State Journal*, Mar. 8, 10, 1852.

[12] *Delphi Journal*, Mar. 25, 1852; *Madison Banner*, Mar. 10, 1852.

pressing unduly a reform far in advance of its day. One predilection alone he had retained from *The Free Enquirer* days, and that was a desire to extirpate excessive verbiage and meaningless forms from the law. His advanced ideas on the treatment of debts, his statute of descent in 1838, and his struggle for the civil equality of married women had given evidence of this. A very practical bill that he championed at this time reducing the terms employed to acknowledge deeds and mortgages, eliminating the use of seals, and instituting a less expensive recording fee afforded further proof.[13] The conviction that the law should be comprehensible to the common man was, then, the spirit in which Owen directed the revision. Over five hundred pages of the old code were eliminated. The distinction between law and equity was abolished. Recent acts legalizing the short form of deeds, prohibiting distress for rent, and exempting $300 worth of real and personal property from seizure were approved. The resulting code embodied Owen's conception of justice, intelligible because of its simplicity, available because of its cheapness, and democratic because of its equal treatment of all.[14]

The one item in the revised statutes in which Owen took the most pride was the new law of descent. The inequitable provisions of the common law governing the estate of a husband dying without a will were an old story to him. He had long known that, whether in such a case a wife had children or not, she was entitled to but one third of the property, real and personal, and that even the former, the so-called widow's dower, was held in tenancy, not outright ownership. He had long known that few estates in the West exceeded $3,000, the annual income from a third of which was obviously insufficient to maintain the widow. He knew, too, that the problem was a

---

[13] *House Journal*, 36 Sess., 503–505, 537–540, 609 (Jan. 16, 19, 24); *Indiana State Sentinel*, Jan. 29, 1852.

[14] *Indiana State Sentinel*, May 20, 1852; Owen to Trist, July 7, 1852, Trist Papers, XXXIV; "Memoranda of the Important Changes, as Compared with the Old Law, Made in the Bills Reported from the Committee on Revision." (MS.)

very real one, for in Indiana five people in six died intestate.[15]
A notable triumph early in his legislative career had been the
law of 1838 which gave the surviving wife two thirds of the
personal property and the third of the real in fee absolute. This
change had been bitterly assailed by able Hoosier lawyers and
had been omitted in the revision of 1843. In the Constitutional
Convention Owen had injudiciously subordinated a juster treatment for widows to the more radical civil equality of married
women, with the result that he failed to achieve either reform.
Thus, when he returned to Indianapolis in 1851 to complete the
work, he kept silent on the property rights of wives and concentrated on the law of descent. Even this moderate policy
drew snarls from the opposition editors who declared that "the
champion of woman's rights" had again mounted his hobby and
that his "nonsensical efforts" and "fanatical vagaries" would
be the bore of the session.[16]

The progress of Owen's proposed changes was almost as
tortuous and dramatic as the struggle of the previous winter.
Nearly five months elapsed between their introduction and
passage. Four different versions of the measure were presented
and twice it was actually defeated. Yet in the end, the bill
became law in almost the exact form in which Owen had drawn
it up. It abolished all tenancies either in dower or in curtesy.
Every widow, even those whose husbands left a will, was entitled to $300 worth of personal property and one third of the
real estate in fee absolute. Widows of intestates with more
than one child now received their third of real property in
outright ownership. Those with one child divided equally with
it the entire real estate. Those without any offspring received
three quarters of the property, the remainder going to the
deceased's parents. If no parents survived, the widow obtained

---

[15] Owen's speech, Dec. 15, 1851, *Indiana State Journal*, Dec. 19, 1851;
R. D. Owen to Robt. Owen, Apr. 11, 1852, *Robert Owen's Journal*, May 29,
1852.

[16] *Lafayette Journal*, Dec. 25, 1851; *Logansport Journal*, Dec. 13, 1851. Cf.
R. D. Owen to Robt. Owen, Apr. 11, 1852, *Robert Owen's Journal*, May 29,
1852.

the whole to the exclusion of brothers, nephews, and other male kin who had formerly been provided for. Where grandchildren were the sole heirs, the property was divided among them equally as individuals rather than equally as families, a change Owen had first made in 1838.[17]

The new law of descent was Owen's most important single achievement during his second winter at Indianapolis. It was a fitting culmination for a protracted session which saw him obtain more positive legislation, reform or otherwise, than at any other period of his career. In six months life had been breathed into the new constitution, and the statutes had been so well codified that another revision was not authorized until 1881.[18] Owen's hand had been felt not only there but also in the banking system, the school law, the simplification of legal processes, and the salutary reforms enacted for debtors and widows. The Representative from Posey thought he and his colleagues had done "pretty well for one session," and the people agreed. In attempting to recapture the state in 1852, the Whigs made an issue of the time and money spent by the Democrats in the convention and in the legislature on both necessary and unnecessary changes. As a leader in those bodies and a champion of many novel measures, Owen was subjected to false and insulting accusations of graft, corruption, and wilfulness. Despite these desperate efforts, the opposition was unable to stem the tide. The October election clearly revealed that in Indiana the party was on the eve of dissolution.[19]

Owen's work in the legislature supplemented that of the convention, and for it he is entitled to rank high in the Hoosier scroll of honor. For his law of descent he deserved, it was

[17] House Journal, 36 Sess., 83, 188, 1264, 1327, 1371–1372, 1388–1389, 1394–1395, 1415–1419 (Dec. 8, 16, Apr. 21, 24, 27, 28, 29, 30). Revised Statutes, I, 248–255. A summary comparison with the old law appeared in the Indiana State Sentinel, May 21, 1852.

[18] J. G. Rauch and Nellie C. Armstrong, A Bibliography of the Laws of Indiana, 1788–1927 (Indiana Historical Collections, XVI, Indps., 1928), 76.

[19] Owen to Trist, July 7, 1852, Trist Papers, XXXIV. New Albany Tribune, Apr. 7, 1852 et seq.; Indiana State Journal, July 28, 29, 1852; Indiana State Sentinel, Oct. 25, 27, 29, Nov. 13, 1852.

said, another pitcher, this time a gold one. "There is no man," wrote a Pittsburgh editor, "to whom that State [Indiana] owes so much in her attempts to break the shackles of old and almost heathen prejudices, as she owes to Robert Dale Owen." Even the Whigs admitted that "there is far less of a demagogue and far more of a statesman in his composition than he gets credit for." [20] But these contemporary encomiums must not lead us, as they have led others, to exaggeration. Owen was not "truly the legislative father of the Indiana common-school system," for Bryant and his other colleagues deserve equal credit. Owen did not "put Indiana ahead of all other states in enlightened laws for women," nor was it "years before other states came abreast." Writers at the time admitted that with respect to the property rights of married women, the Hoosiers still lagged behind many of their neighbors.[21] Owen did not bestow, as has often been asserted, civil equality upon married women. The Revised Code of 1852 gave wives control of only their real estate, and the addition of personal property was not effected until the following year when the Western Democrat was no longer in the legislature.[22]

The three years after 1850 are significant in Owen's life as the first since 1836 in which the reformer eclipsed the politician. The former editor of *The Free Enquirer* never did merit the epithet of "party hack"; but his hostility toward the abolitionists, his silence in freethought circles, and his coldness concerning Fourierism and homesteads had led some to believe that he had forsaken the cause of humanity for the emoluments of political warfare. But in these years he exhibited

[20] *Democratic Clarion*, June 5, 1852; quotations in the *New Albany Ledger*, July 21, 1852; *Indiana Statesman*, June 2, 1852.

[21] Lockwood, *New Harmony Movement*, 290; Caroline D. Snedeker, *The Town of the Fearless* (Garden City, 1931), 284–285. Cf. *contra*, *Indiana State Journal*, Feb. 11, 1852; *Indiana State Sentinel*, June 25, 1852.

[22] On Mar. 2, 1853, virtually unnoticed in the excitement attendant upon Pierce's inauguration, the state senate passed with only three dissenting votes a bill practically identical to Blythe's amendment accepted and then rejected in the Constitutional Convention. Owen was in Washington. *Senate Journal*, 37th Session (1852–1853), 554–555.

moral courage in advocating not only novel legal reforms and advanced concepts of property rights but also unpopular measures like the Salaries Bill and the School Law that required higher taxes in an election year. Yet it should be noticed that this reemergence of the reformer did not mean a return to the ultraism of the New York period. When in October 1851 Eastern feminists joined with Wayne county abolitionists to organize a woman's rights society at Dublin, Indiana, neither Owen nor the ladies who had sponsored his testimonial took part.[23] The Western Democrat had a very definite picture of himself as a liberal, for he told the legislature at this time,

I hope I am entitled to the character of a reformer. And by that word I mean nothing more than a man, who, when he firmly believes that a thing is wrong, employs earnest endeavor — gives thought and labor — to aid in setting it right. . . . But I do not think that now, however it may have been in earlier years, I am an ultra radical reformer.[24]

Compared to Henry C. Wright who addressed that Dublin gathering, Owen, to be sure, was no radical. He was, rather, still a Western Democrat, but one with some very liberal ideas. Thus on the one hand, Alexander Campbell, visiting Indianapolis in November 1850, found the Hoosier "still in quest of a new order of society." [25] On the other hand, at the very time his reform zeal was reappearing, Owen was engaged in a game of president-making that ultimately changed the course of his entire life.

The move to make Joseph Lane president of the United States in 1852 was born when the disappointed Hoosier Democracy learned of Zachary Taylor's election. To the politically sagacious Chapmans, editors of the *Indiana State Sentinel*, belonged the credit for the first important, public suggestion of the candidate who was to combine the appeal of martial fame

---

[23] "Preamble and Constitution of the Woman's Suffrage [Rights from 1851–1869] Association of Indiana with Names of Charter Members. Minutes of Annual Meetings etc." (MS.) ; *Indiana State Sentinel*, Sept. 24, Nov. 11, 1851.

[24] *Indiana State Sentinel*, Jan. 29, 1852.

[25] *Millennial Harbinger*, 4th ser., I, 17 (Jan. 1852).

with that of local pride.[26] The beneficiary of this boom was hardly great. Compared even to Owen his talents and ability were slight. But he was descended of plain American stock, born in humble circumstances in North Carolina's famous Buncombe county; and having risen without the aid of much schooling through the ranks of office-boy, farmer, lawyer, and legislator, he conformed to the American ideal of the self-made man. The Mexican War had elevated him from an obscure local personage to a figure of national prominence, and his excellent administration as the first governor of the new Oregon Territory confirmed that rise. Meanwhile Owen had watched with unalloyed pleasure the rapid progress of his neighbor and undoubtedly felt, in a small way, responsible for it. It was he who in June 1846 recommended Lane rather than his own brother Richard to Polk as a brigadier general from his district. It was he who as early as mid-summer 1849 wrote to Lane that his chances for the nomination in 1852 were excellent.[27]

For over a year after the Chapmans' original suggestion little was done openly to promote Lane's candidacy. It was not until Owen's visit to Indianapolis in January 1850, in the midst of his plank road enthusiasm, that the ball was officially put in motion. In an address before the Democratic members of the legislature Owen declared that the party's next presidential nominee ought to come from the West and should combine military fame with parliamentary experience. Almost spontaneously his audience responded with three cheers for Joe Lane. At another meeting later in the month Owen presented a formal letter to be signed by leading Hoosiers requesting Lane to return home from Oregon. After twelve months of quiet percolation the next step was taken on January 18, 1851, when a crowded gathering at the State House nominated for president

---

[26] *Indiana State Sentinel*, Nov. 18, 1848.

[27] Owen's letter in the *Indiana State Journal*, Jan. 7, 1851; Owen to Lane, Feb. 1, 1852, Lane Papers. According to tradition, Owen visited Polk after the battle of Buena Vista and asked him what he thought of the Hoosier general. " 'Ah,' said the president, with a quiet smile, 'Mr. Owen, you are safe out of that scrape.' " Quoted in *The Democratic Clarion*, May 6, 1848.

Joseph Lane, "the Marion of the Mexican War, and the Andrew Jackson of Indiana." At least four other Lane meetings were held at the Hoosier capital that winter and in all Owen's pen and voice played a leading role. During the summer and autumn these propagandist efforts continued, and in November Lane himself was received at Indianapolis as a conquering hero. Three months later the Democratic State Convention chose his followers to attend the national gathering at Baltimore. Once again Owen proved useful in drawing up the resolutions for his friend's candidacy, furnishing a platform which he believed to be "at once just, safe & popular." [28]

One more step remained to complete the Lane boom. That was to make "Andrew Jackson of Indiana" better known outside of the state. The Hoosier Democrats had long been aware that their man lacked the national reputation of Cass, Buchanan, and Douglas and that, except for their state, he was the first choice of no other commonwealth. As early as the fall of 1849 Nathaniel Bolton, husband of the poetess and then correspondent of the *New Albany Ledger*, asked Owen to write a short biography of Lane, sufficient to keep his war fame from being forgotten. Owen agreed, and in December Bolton mentioned the fact in his column without directly naming Owen. The political meeting that Owen attended a month later formally resolved that he should prepare a campaign sketch, and those present understood him to have consented.[29] During 1850 and 1851 little more was heard of the forthcoming publication except by way of ridicule in the Whig press, and the correspondence in the Lane Papers has surprisingly few references to the matter.[30] Early in May 1852, however, there appeared in Washington a forty-page anonymous *Biography*

[28] Owen to Lane, Apr. 20, 1852, Lane Papers. *Indiana State Sentinel*, Jan. 17, Nov. 16, 1850, Jan. 14, 25, Feb. 6, Mar. 25, May 29, Nov. 8, 12, 13, 1851, Feb. 25, 1852; *New Albany Ledger*, Jan. 15, 17, 1850; *Indiana Statesman*, Nov. 13, 1850.

[29] *New Albany Ledger*, Dec. 6, 1849, Jan. 17, 1850; Bolton's letter in the *Indiana State Sentinel*, Jan. 23, 1851.

[30] Nellie B. Pipes to the author, Mar. 30, 1936. Cf. *Indiana State Journal*, Jan. 16, 1850, Nov. 18, 21, Dec. 9, 10, 22, 1851; *Evansville Journal*, Oct. 23, 1851.

of Joseph Lane "Not Inappropriately Styled by His Brother Officers and Soldiers, the Marion of the War." It was designed to give, without offence to any other candidate, an account of the man who was the first choice of the Hoosiers, in the hope that if the convention was unable to decide upon another, it might unite behind this new Cincinnatus fresh from the people. Lane's early life was compressed into two pages, and even the glorious exploits of his Mexican campaigns were subordinated to the constructive achievements of Oregon's first territorial governor. Both from its clear, terse style and its wealth of anecdote this slight volume ranks among the most readable of campaign biographies. Although the name of the author, who called himself "Western," was carefully concealed at the time and although it has not been discovered by the leading libraries of the country today, there can be little doubt that it was Robert Dale Owen. It is something of a coincidence that his facile pen should be turned to the service of an old friend in the same year that Nathaniel Hawthorne was making his contribution to the election of Franklin Pierce. Both men were to have their reward.[31]

As a final favor to Lane, Owen attended the Baltimore Convention, thereby violating the maxim laid down by himself ten years before that no legislator should forsake public business for partisan activity. He might have spared himself the trouble, for his role was neither conspicuous nor decisive. He was placed on the Committee of Resolutions, but there is no evidence that he was in any way responsible for the conservative platform that emanated from that body. He made no speech from the floor, and the real voice of the Indiana delegation was not Owen's but that of Jesse D. Bright.[32]

For thirty ballots that voice was heard in support of Joe Lane, but the Hoosier favorite never obtained more than one vote in addition to Indiana's thirteen. When after a day and

[31] The evidence for Owen is not conclusive. See the note appended to the title in the Bibliography.

[32] Owen to Lane, Feb. 1, 1852, Lane Papers; *Proceedings of the Democratic National Convention, Held at Baltimore, June 1–5, 1852* (Wash., 1852).

a half of casting Douglas finally swept into the lead, Bright decided to abandon the "Marion of the War" and throw his strength behind the state's second choice, Lewis Cass. The net result of the shift was the total collapse of the Lane boom and the eventual nomination of a man who was under no obligation to the Hoosier delegates for his success. As it turned out, however, neither Owen nor Lane manifested any bitterness over the denouement. Both agreed that the convention's choice had been judicious and both believed that Franklin Pierce would be elected. Owen felt, perhaps, that his colleagues had not worked hard enough, but he had no reproaches to make nor reward to claim for his own services. "It was," he wrote, "but my bounden duty; it was but carrying out the undoubted will of our State." Yet for his part in this nationally insignificant presidential maneuver, the Western Democrat received an appointment that brought the Indiana years to a close.[33]

During the winter of 1851–1852 Owen virtually decided to cross the ocean once more. As early as January 1849 he had mentioned to Trist the possibility of visiting Europe that summer, but no particulars were given and the project was soon abandoned. Now, however, he seemed convinced that his family could not obtain in New Harmony the type of education he wanted it to have; and he contemplated taking his wife, his sister, and their children to Germany and then returning alone to Indiana in search of remunerative employment, preferably public office.[34] Evidence of this intention was to be found in part in his resignation in December 1851 as Trustee of Indiana University, and in part in his stubborn refusal that same month, despite widespread demand, to stand as the Democratic candidate for the newly created position of State Superintendent of Public Instruction.[35]

---

[33] Owen to Lane, June 29, 1852, Lane Papers; Lane to Owen, June 18, 1852, cited in *ibid.*

[34] Owen to Trist, Jan. 29, Mar. 20, 1849, Trist Papers, XXXIII; Owen to Lane, June 29, 1852, Lane Papers.

[35] *House Journal*, 36 Sess., 487–493; *Indiana State Journal*, Dec. 24, 1851. Cf. *ibid.*, Sept. 17, 1851; *Madison Tribune*, Oct. 7, 1851; *Democratic Clarion*,

Upon his return to New Harmony late in June 1852 a new factor entered Owen's plans. There he found a letter from Joe Lane containing an unprompted offer to unite, in event of Pierce's election, with the Indiana members of Congress in recommending Owen for any diplomatic post he might wish. If he had not considered such a mission before in connection with his family plans, Owen must have then realized that a minor sinecure at Rome or Naples would enable him not only to escort his wife and children across the Atlantic but also to remain near them while holding public office. The same letter, however, mentioned the possible resignation of Senator Whitcomb whose term had a couple of years still to run. Of the two openings Owen first leaned to the seat in the upper house. He felt that, if an interim appointment had to be made, his own chances were good and that, once in office, he would be confirmed by the next Democratic legislature. Optimistic as ever, he wrote at once to his Indianapolis friends to discover Governor Wright's intentions and to Lane to stress the importance of having Whitcomb resign before Congress adjourned.[36]

As the summer of 1852 wore on, a diplomatic position, especially that at Naples, became more attractive. Owen, of course, could not afford, even if he could obtain, a mission to a major power; and he did not wish, as he said, to bury himself in South America. Early in July he was quizzing Trist on the duties of a chargé d'affaires and writing to a former incumbent at the Neapolitan court for further details. Yet it must be admitted that this growing preference for a foreign post resulted from the increasing difficulty of attaining the Senatorship. Whitcomb gave no more indications of resigning; and even when he died suddenly in the autumn, Wright announced that the selection of a successor would be left to the Assembly.[37]

Dec. 6, 1851, Jan. 3, 1852; *Indiana Statesman*, Dec. 17, 1851; *New Albany Ledger*, Dec. 9, 17, 1851.

[36] Owen to Lane, June 29, 1852, Lane Papers, citing Lane to Owen, June 18, 1852.

[37] Owen to Trist, July 7, 1852, Trist Papers, XXXIV; Owen to Lane, July 9, 1852, Lane Papers; *Indiana State Sentinel*, Oct. 8, 20, 1852.

From that body Owen could expect nothing. He had taken no part in the campaign of 1852, and already his reforms of the previous year were being criticized, especially in the south where his strength had always been the greatest. Thus even as early as November Owen was willing, more from necessity than from choice, to withdraw from the Senatorial contest, provided the president gave some sign of encouragement. If no word of hope, however, was received by December, he told Lane, he would be compelled to let his name go before the caucus. While in Indianapolis in January Owen finally received two letters from Lane which, although not affording assurance of the Neapolitan appointment, were sufficient to make him stand aloof for the first time since 1838 from an election to the United States Senate.[38]

As the final decision on his future was delayed during the autumn, winter, and spring, Owen's patience was sorely tried. For the most part he had to leave the matter to Lane, but what little he could do for himself, he did. As soon as he learned that Pierce would be guided by the advice of governors in Democratic states, Owen obtained a strong letter from Wright in which the latter shut himself off from supporting any other applicant. He secured, too, recommendations from high state officers, justices of the Indiana supreme court, and members of the faculty at Bloomington. Professor Larrabee, an alumnus of Pierce's college, wrote on his own initiative,

Among all the men whom I have ever known, I have found no one deserving a higher or more honorable place among gentlemen, scholars and philanthropists than Robert Dale Owen. . . . Were I at liberty to select among us a single individual to make a Constitution and Laws for the Government of a people such as we are . . . there is no one whom I would so soon . . . select. . . . I do assure the President, Mr. Owen is not a visionary theorist, but a plain, practical, sincere and judicious man, ardently devoted to human improvement. . . .

[38] Owen to Lane, Nov. 1, 7, 8, Dec. 11, 23, 1852, Jan. 11, 1853, Lane Papers. See also *Indiana State Sentinel*, Oct. 2, 18, Dec. 22, 1852; *Democratic Clarion*, Nov. 6, 1852.

At Washington, Owen sought the aid of such old friends as
Buchanan, Rush, Dallas, and Hunter, while at home he tried
to enlist the press in his cause. For some time papers in and
out of the state had mentioned him as a cabinet possibility,
but after his visit to Madison in February, the Democratic
journal in that city changed its tone and stated that a chargé-
ship would be most fitting for him.[39]

Upon the advice of friends Owen left for Washington early
in February. A convenient opportunity was afforded by his
selection as chairman of a committee to obtain plans for a new
Odd Fellows' Hall at Indianapolis. In the East Owen discharged that duty and performed a final service for Indiana
University, but his main concern was the diplomatic post. By
March he was confident of success, but it was not until two
months later that the long suspense ended. Then, out of sixty-
six applicants Owen was chosen as chargé d'affaires to the
Kingdom of the Two Sicilies, the sinecure he had desired above
all others.[40] The appointment was well received by the press.
Even Greeley, who six years before had spoken uncomplimen-
tary things about Embree's victim, now said of the selection,
"We are heartily glad of it. He [Owen] is not so good nor so
thoroughly honest as his father . . . but he is amiable, intelligent, kindhearted, and unlike the general run of party hacks,
has ideas in his head." [41] To Joe Lane, Owen could pay no
higher tribute than one he had rendered before victory had
been achieved. "It will always be," he had written, "a true
pleasure to me to remember, that, in the heartless world of
politics, I met so true a friend as you." More than a score

[39] Owen to Lane, Jan. 20, 1853, Lane Papers; W. C. Larrabee to Franklin
Pierce, Jan. 18, 1853 (copy), Robert Owen Papers, no. 2102. *Madison Courier*,
Feb. 12, 1853. Cf. *ibid.*, Dec. 8, 1852; *Indiana State Sentinel*, Feb. 8, 1853;
New Albany Ledger, Feb. 11, 1853.

[40] Owen to Lane, Jan. 11, 20, Mar. 11, 1853, Lane Papers; Dunn, *Greater
Indianapolis*, I, 377-380; "Excerpts from the Minutes of the Board of Trustees,
Indiana University" (Aug. 1, 1853). *N. Y. Herald*, May 26, 1853.

[41] *N. Y. Tribune*, May 25, 1853. Cf. *N. Y. Herald*, May 26, 1853; *Indiana
State Sentinel*, May 28, 1853; *New Albany Ledger*, May 30, 1853; *Evansville
Journal*, May 31, 1853.

of years later Owen still recalled with gratitude that token of friendship.[42]

No man appears to advantage while soliciting an appointive office, yet some light may be thrown on his character by his words and deeds at such a time. Thus Owen was too conscientious not to tell Lane after listing his capacities for the post,

I am exceedingly anxious not to appear . . . one of that countless army of office-seekers, who besiege the doors of every newly elected President. . . . But somebody must fill these offices. And all that is really reprehensible is to apply, without the requisite qualifications.

Perseverance was also one of Owen's strong points, and his actions during 1852–1853 reveal his tenacity. Optimism and outward equanimity were likewise characteristic. When Lane feared that, despite the Hoosier's withdrawal from the Senatorial contest, Bright and his henchmen might yet block Owen's recommendation, the latter replied, "Don't trouble yourself, for a moment, even if the chance for Naples should fail. We have acted for the best. And it is only children who sit down & complain, if after all proper exertion, the cards turn up against them." [43]

After a five-month absence Owen returned to New Harmony on June 8 in triumph. Two weeks later several carriages and wagons containing Mary and himself; their four children, ranging from Florence aged seventeen to the second Ernest aged three; Jane and her family; Dale's son Alfred; and numerous trunks and cases that foretold a long journey rolled over the new plank road to Mt. Vernon. Low water on the Ohio detained the party somewhat, and further delay was occasioned by Owen's illness after he had gone to Washington for final instructions. It was not until August 4, 1853, that the numerous and happy group set sail from New York aboard the packet-ship *Devonshire*.[44]

[42] Owen to Lane, Mar. 11, 1853, Dec. 10, 1876, Lane Papers.
[43] Owen to Lane, Nov. 1, 1852, Jan. 11, 1853, Lane Papers.
[44] Owen to W. L. Marcy, June 30, 1853; Oct. 22, 1853, no. 1, Department of State, "Despatches: Naples," II.

As Owen watched the dim American coastline fade away in the hot August evening, his thoughts must have returned to that bright May day twenty-one years before when he and Mary, literally and figuratively, embarked upon their voyage through life together. Just as it was not apparent then, so was it not clear to him now that this departure, like the last, was bringing to a close a definite period of his life. For more than ten years prior to his marriage he had lived, both in England and in America, in an atmosphere of reform where the ideal had been to aid humanity by attacking without reserve every evil in the world and every foible of mankind. After 1833 a new environment, together with maturing years and family responsibilities, changed that ideal. During the next two decades Owen had sought political advancement, not for the spoils of office but as a legitimate and customary way of developing his own powers, winning the esteem of his neighbors, and influencing the lives of his fellow men. Some of his older friends suspected in these years that he was sacrificing his humanitarian principles for the loaves and fishes of party politics; but, on the whole, he managed to resist that temptation. In the years 1850 to 1852, in the proper sphere of state legislation, Owen achieved in a conservative way many of his cherished reforms that he had first broached as editor of a freethought paper more than twenty years before.

While standing on the ship's deck, Owen perhaps thought, too, of those old friends. Maclure and his corps of scientists were dead. Except for his octogenarian father and the oldest inhabitants of New Harmony, Owen had lost touch with all the participants in the abortive experiment on the banks of the Wabash. Only the friendship with Trist remained from the New York years. Death had claimed Frances Wright, Kneeland, and Baxter. Brownson was already an important figure in Catholic circles. Evans had lapsed into silence, and Gilbert was alienated by Owen's course on slavery.

During the remaining years of his life Owen was to live in still another environment and among friends who differed from the associates of his middle years. After three winters of invaluable service to its progress, he was leaving his adopted state. Never again was he to play so prominent a role in the life of the commonwealth. He left it when he was at the height of his physical and mental powers. He left it when the principles of government in which he believed and for which, during almost a score of years, he had striven were at last firmly implanted in its organic and statute law. He left it when the party that had espoused them stood practically unopposed. It was more than six years before he came back again to the Hoosier state, and by that time its political problems and complexion, as well as those of the nation, had changed. Nor was it the same Owen who returned, for his outlook and purpose in life were altered. In a very real sense, Owen's departure for Naples marked the close of the Indiana years.

PART THREE

THE INTELLECTUAL

CHAPTER XIX

NAPLES

FAR from the American West, with its physical crudities, party warfare, and sectarian bickering, Owen began the third period of an eventful life. In his opinion Naples embodied all that was outwardly splendid and beautiful in this world. More than a score of years after he had first gazed upon it, he thus described the scene that never faded from his mind:

London is unmatched in its way; Paris is a dazzling wonder; Switzerland is a marvel of majestic beauty; but — save the rose-hued fairyland of my infancy, Rosebank . . . Naples stands alone, unrivalled in memory. . . . If he who has seen what is fairest in this world may be satisfied to depart in peace, then one can appreciate the force of the adage: "See Naples and die!" [1]

The setting of Owen's new home was unequalled in loveliness. From his windows he commanded a magnificent view of the glorious bay with the enchanting islands that dotted its languid waters. At his door lay the city's most fashionable parks and avenues. A favorite ride in the balmy air over the broad Strada Nuova along the rock-bound, vine-clad shore brought him to Baiae, beloved of the Augustan Age. Near by were Pompeii and Herculaneum, mute symbols of a rich and ancient civilization, while over all loomed Vesuvius the destroyer.

It is easy to understand why Owen the intellectual, the dabbler in literature, art, and religion, should prefer romantic Naples as a place of foreign residence. It is not so easy to comprehend why Owen the Western Democrat, accustomed for twenty years to the equalitarian spirit of a pioneer state, should desire a diplomatic post in that country where, above all others, absolutism reigned supreme. During the early fifties the King-

[1] Robert Dale Owen, "Naples under the Old Regime. A Chapter of Autobiography," *Atlantic Monthly*, XXXIII, 136 (Feb. 1874).

dom of the Two Sicilies was a virtual pariah among the nations of the world. After the revolutionary movements of the previous decade, it had fallen prey to a government dedicated to repression, honeycombed by corruption, and sustained by espionage and terror. The diabolical persecutions of political opponents by its ruler Ferdinand II, widely known as "Bomba," made his name stink in the nostrils of liberals everywhere and in no place more so than republican America. To a people who had recently applauded Webster's insulting reply to Hülsemann and idolized the exiled Kossuth, "Bomba" represented "murder enthroned and crowned" and his country the victim of "the foulest and fiercest misrule that ever trampled a nation to the dust." It was openly asserted that the mission to which the Western Democrat had so ardently aspired would have long since been abolished in the name of decency if it had not been a useful sinecure for deserving party workers.[2]

Owen reached Naples in the early autumn, just as the blistering summer heat was waning. Seven weeks before he had landed in England for a joyous reunion with his aged sire. After a six-year separation Owen found his father well, as sanguine as ever, and engrossed in the study of a new force with which he hoped to ameliorate the lot of suffering humanity. To please his insistent forebear the son attended one or two spiritualist séances and then, unconvinced, hurried on with his family to Rotterdam. From that Dutch city he ascended the Rhine to Mannheim, passing places he had not seen since his return from Hofwyl thirty-two years before, and then crossed by way of Heidelberg to Stuttgart. There he left Mary, Jane, and the children for twelve months of German life and retraced his steps to London. Late in September he recrossed the Channel to meet in Paris his predecessor, E. Joy Morris, and discuss with him Naples and the Neapolitans. From there Owen went

[2] N. Y. Times, Apr. 3, 13, 1852. Cf. William R. Thayer, The Life and Times of Cavour (Boston, 1911), I, 188–202; W. E. Gladstone, Two Letters to the Earl of Aberdeen on the State Prosecutions of the Neapolitan Government (2d edn., London, 1851); Howard R. Marraro, American Opinion of the Unification of Italy, 1846–1861 (N. Y., 1932), 102–105.

to Marseilles whence he took a steamer which, after calls at Genoa, Leghorn, and the Civita Vecchia, brought him at last to his destination on October 17, 1853.[3]

At the outset, Owen's mission to this discredited kingdom seemed to offer little difficulty. As the new chargé read through the archives of the legation, established in 1831, he learned that important diplomatic problems seldom arose, that only two treaties had been negotiated in the past, and that the chief business consisted of the prevention of commercial and maritime discriminations and the settlement of petty claims. Fortunately Morris had liquidated all of the latter, and his own instructions were limited to securing a removal of some vexatious quarantine regulations in Neapolitan ports. Thus the new representative could be cordially received by Luigi Carafa, the Sicilian Minister of Foreign Affairs; and on October 28 he journeyed northward to Caserta for a pleasant audience with the notorious Ferdinand. Owen soon discovered, however, that all was not to be clear sailing, for minor officials were constantly and deliberately violating the trade treaty of 1846. With "Bomba" and his government heartily detested at home, the Indianan had to take a strong stand on these trivial annoyances, yet the men with whom he had to deal were so dilatory, so evasive, and so mendacious that for more than a year his tenure was filled with complaints and quarrels that seriously jeopardized amicable relations with the country to which he was accredited.[4]

The details of these recurrent, petty conflicts need not concern us long. It is sufficient to indicate their nature. James Carbone, a naturalized American arrested at Messina while visiting his parents, was detained, despite the objections of our

[3] Owen to Trist, Oct. 28, 1853, Trist Papers, XXXVII; Owen to Marcy, Oct. 22, 1853, no. 1, Department of State, "Despatches: Naples," II; *Robert Owen's Rational Quarterly Review and Journal*, I, 222–238 (Nov. 1853).

[4] Marcy to Owen, July 2, 1853, no. 1, "Instructions: Naples;" Morris to Marcy, Apr. 26, 1853, no. 29; Owen to Marcy, Oct. 26, Nov. 21, 1853, nos. 1, 2, "Despatches: Naples," II. See also Louis M. Sears, "Robert Dale Owen's Mission to Naples," *Indiana History Bulletin*, VI, extra no. 2, 43–51 (May 1929).

consul, for several weeks on the ground that once a citizen, always a citizen. In the same autumn of 1853 an allegedly unlawful search of the *Governor Brown* led Owen to protest against this typical infraction by Messina authorities of the pact of 1846. Both these cases took an unnecessarily long time to settle and tried Owen's patience sorely, but in both he had nothing to do but quietly affirm his country's rights. Much more difficult was his defense of Emanuel Sartorio, another naturalized American, who was clearly guilty of forbidden Masonic agitation.[5] Other less important but equally troublesome matters plagued the chargé's first year. He won a relaxation of the stringent quarantine laws, secured reparation for an insult upon our flag, and probed some fraudulent insurance claims of American mariners. How well he succeeded in eliminating these sources of friction was evidenced on January 1, 1855, when at a royal reception "Bomba" informed Owen that, as a special favor, the proceedings against the guilty Sartorio were being quashed. It was something of a tribute to the Hoosier's tact and tolerance that he could write home at that time,

I have the satisfaction, on this first day of the new year, of finding myself, for the first time since my arrival in Naples, with the calendar of the Legation entirely clear, and with not a case on hand involving cause of complaint or reclamation; all those which have arisen during my residence here, having been settled in an amicable and satisfactory manner.[6]

The year 1855 saw Owen draft two treaties, unquestionably the most important work of his mission. The first concerned the rights of neutrals at sea, an old question revived by the outbreak of the Crimean War in March 1854. In September Secretary of State Marcy addressed a general letter to American diplomatic representatives abroad, requesting them to negotiate

[5] Owen to Marcy, Dec. 29, 1853, Feb. 4, 8, Apr. 11, May 15, Aug. 17, Nov. 14, 20, Dec. 6, 1854, nos. 4, 5, 6, 10, 12, 18, 24, 25, 26, "Despatches: Naples," II.
[6] Owen to Marcy, Jan. 1, 1855, no. 29. See also nos. 10, 14, 20, Apr. 11, June 6, Sept. 26, 1854, "Despatches: Naples," II.

conventions embracing the principles that, except for contraband, free ships make free goods and that neutral property aboard belligerent vessels is not confiscable. A pact just signed by Russia and the United States was to serve as a model. Owen received these instructions in mid-October and by the 25th had won Sicilian consent to the project. After waiting for his powers as negotiator, he went to work again; and within another twelve days the treaty was on its way to Washington for approval by the Senate before adjournment.[7] Owen was not wholly satisfied with the completed protocol since Carafa had not given him a free hand, but he did think that it contained everything desired by the secretary of state. By his prompt action, moreover, he became the first of Marcy's envoys to execute the instructions of September 8, 1854.[8]

The more important treaty drafted by Owen dealt with amity, trade, and navigation. In December 1854 the Indianan informed the State Department that certain privileges, recently granted by Naples to the Papal States, could be obtained for American commerce under a reciprocal agreement. Marcy's reply went beyond this suggestion and empowered his minister to draw up an entirely new pact to replace that of 1846, which would soon expire. In the ensuing negotiations the main point in dispute was the right of alien Protestants to private worship and sepulcher. At his chief's urgent request Owen had, without much hope, included such a provision in his draft, but it had been eliminated at once by the Sicilians. They bluntly stated they had no authority to grant the right and that they were prepared to abandon the treaty altogether if the United States made it a *sine qua non*. Having disposed of other matters in

[7] Marcy to Owen, Sept. 8, 1854, no. 8, "Instructions: Naples"; Owen to Marcy, Oct. 21, 25, 1854, Jan. 1, 13, 1855, nos. 21, 22, 29, 30, "Despatches: Naples," II.

[8] Owen to Francis Markoe, Jr., Jan. 13, 1855, Ford Collection; W. M. Malloy, ed., *Treaties, Conventions, International Acts, Protocols, and Agreements between the United States of America and Other Powers, 1776–1909* (Wash., 1910), II, 1812–1813; *Journal of the Executive Proceedings of the Senate of the United States of America* (Wash., 1887), IX, 418, 422, 430 (Feb. 20, 28, Mar. 3, 1855).

disagreement, Owen reluctantly gave way, thus making possible the signing of the covenant on October 1, 1855. Owen considered the finished product as not only more liberal than its predecessor but also as containing the most sweeping concessions which a foreign country had yet obtained from the Kingdom of the Two Sicilies. He was especially pleased with the abolition of differential duties, with the greater protection given rights of person and property, and with the equality that Americans enjoyed with the Neapolitans in indirect trade. The failure to obtain religious freedom was, he felt, less serious in practice than in principle.[9]

Although acceptable to the State Department, Owen's treaty encountered opposition in the Senate. Certain members of that body thought that the extradition clauses, ones on which Owen had deferred to Carafa, might be abused with regard to political offenders. The protocol was first rejected, but after reconsideration it passed with but slight amendments. These changes were agreed to in Naples, and on December 10, 1856, the pact was formally proclaimed.[10] Already twelve months before, however, Owen had begun to reap the reward for his successful dealings with Ferdinand's government: 1855 had been singularly free from the irksome wrangling of 1854; and as tension grew between "Bomba" and the Western powers, the stock of the American representative rose. Concessions began to be granted almost unasked; and the king openly signified his wish that Owen's rank, already advanced to that of minister resident, be raised again to that of minister plenipotentiary.[11]

The third and fourth years of Owen's mission were marked by the increasing embarrassments of Naples in foreign affairs

[9] Marcy to Owen, Feb. 6, 1855, no. 12, "Instructions: Naples." Owen to Marcy, Dec. 9, 20, 1854, June 20, July 12, Sept. 7, Oct. 2, 5, 1855, nos. 27, 28, 41, 42, 47, 48, 49, "Despatches: Naples," II.

[10] *Senate Executive Journal*, X, 12–13, 122, 139, 142–144 (Jan. 3, July 15, Aug. 9, 13, 1856) ; *N. Y. Times*, Aug. 14, 1856; Malloy, *op. cit.*, II, 1814–1824. Owen to Marcy, Oct. 20, Nov. 8, 1856, nos. 68, 69, "Despatches: Naples," II.

[11] Owen to Marcy, Sept. 7, 1855, no. 47, "Despatches: Naples," II.

and a mounting unrest among her people. In the autumn of 1856 England and France, fearful lest Ferdinand's policy of repression endanger the peace of Europe and encouraged by popular sentiment, despatched several warships to frighten the stubborn despot into mending his ways. The American public was delighted by that move, but Owen discreetly refused to express an opinion on the justice of intervention. When the allied fleet anchored outside the harbor, he requested that an American naval vessel be placed at his disposal. Though on October 25 the Anglo-French ministers were withdrawn, the crisis already was passing. Neither of the powers was prepared to initiate hostilities, and the obstinate Neapolitan monarch refused to be bluffed into reform.[12]

Foreign difficulties, however, stirred domestic turbulence. In December 1856 at a military review Owen witnessed a singlehanded but unsuccessful attempt to assassinate the king. Winter brought a revolt in Sicily, and the mysterious destruction of the navy's largest warship. Fear swept the court. All state balls were cancelled. Owen doubted the imminency of a popular uprising but to reassure American travelers he again obtained a frigate from the Mediterranean squadron. By February the panic was over. Owen, however, saw no hope for a long period of quiet unless the king altered his policies. This Ferdinand did not do, and the country continued to seethe with unrest. But in these stirring days Owen was more a spectator than an actor. His despatches reveal an entire absence of the disputes and complaints that had marred the first part of his tenure.[13]

---

[12] Owen to James Buchanan, Oct. 2, 1856, Buchanan Papers; Owen to Marcy, Oct. 20, Nov. 8, 1856, nos. 68, 69, "Despatches: Naples," II; R. D. Owen to Robt. Owen, Oct. 26, 1856, Robert Owen Papers, no. 2530. Thayer, *op. cit.*, I, 431–433; Herbert Maxwell, *The Life and Letters of George William Frederick, Fourth Earl of Clarendon* (London, 1913), II, 123–124; Marraro, *op. cit.*, 112–113.

[13] Robert Dale Owen, "Naples: Her Volcano, Her People, and Her King. A Chapter of Autobiography," *Atlantic Monthly*, XXXIII, 651–652 (June 1874); Owen to Marcy, Dec. 10, 1856, Jan. 30, Mar. 1, 4, 1857, nos. 71, 73, 75, 76, "Despatches: Naples," II; Thayer, *op. cit.*, I, 445.

In September 1858 Owen's five-year residence at Naples came to an end. His term had been unmarked by any incident significant in American diplomatic history, and it closed before Garibaldi's epochal march. Yet if Owen's work was unimportant, it was none the less well done. The first duty of a minister is to maintain friendly relations with the nation to which he is accredited. That Owen did despite American prejudices against Neapolitan despotism. He succeeded where a Soulé would have failed because he showed respect even for that which he disliked and because, unlike his British colleague, he refused to intrigue with Italian exiles and revolutionists. From September 1855, when Ferdinand suggested that his rank be raised, until the final audience three years later, Owen remained one of the most popular representatives at the court of the Two Sicilies.[14]

Owen discharged equally well the second fundamental duty of a diplomat, scrupulous care of his country's interests. While striving to please the despot with whom he had to deal, he never forgot that he was an American. With the State Department, moreover, he remained on the best of terms. None of his actions were disapproved; some were specially commended. His suggestions on Neapolitan affairs were usually followed. To be sure, the Indianan was not particularly fitted either by previous experience or by training in international law for the post he held, but such defects were not exceptional in the chargés of the day. His linguistic accomplishments, on the other hand, were extremely good. Finally, Owen was not a troublesome envoy. Although he had to threaten at times to gain his ends and on four occasions summoned warships to Naples, he never went so far as to break off relations. "I exceedingly dislike," he had written during the exasperating Carbone case, "the éclat and annoyance attendant upon even a temporary rupture and am of opinion, that in nine cases out of ten . . . a

[14] "Naples under the Old Regime," loc. cit., XXXIII, 135–136; Constance Brooks, Antonio Panizzi, Scholar and Patriot (Manchester, 1931), 103–105; N. Y. Times, July 18, 1855; London Times, Oct. 5, 1858.

minister may, by prudent management, avoid such a contingency." [15]

During his first year at Naples Owen's title was changed to minister resident. This promotion was not a reward for any meritorious deed but rather part of a general reorganization of the diplomatic service. The new grade, however, did not carry with it a larger stipend, and the Indianan quickly discovered that $4,500 was insufficient to make ends meet. In March 1855 Congress sought to replace all ministers resident by ministers plenipotentiary with a corresponding increase in salary; but Pierce, to the great chagrin of Owen, who had already purchased a carriage and horses in anticipation, refused to sanction the step. Owen's private correspondence that fall clearly reveals his displeasure at the executive's course. In August 1856 the confusion was finally straightened out by a supplemental law, effective from the previous July, authorizing a remuneration of $7,500. Consequently the Hoosier soon ceased to draw on his personal income.[16]

With the presidential election of 1856 came the question of continuance in office. More than a month before that event Owen wrote directly to Buchanan to learn the policy of what he expected to be the next administration. The incumbent did not suppose that he would be allowed another full term abroad; but he would like, he said, to remain at least one year longer both because of the probable advancement in his rank and because his older son had not yet completed his studies in Germany. The Pennsylvanian's reply was brief and to the point. As a result of the recent canvass the number of deserving party workers was so large that the president-elect would be pleased

---

[15] Owen to Marcy, Nov. 14, 1854, no. 24, "Despatches: Naples," II.

[16] Marcy to Owen, July 17, 1854, no. 6, "Instructions: Naples"; Owen to Marcy, Mar. 8, July 6, 1854, July 25, 1855, Oct. 20, 1856, nos. 11, 16, Private, 68, "Despatches: Naples," II. Mary J. Owen to Richard Owen, Aug. 21, 1855, Neal Letters; Owen to John Cooper, July 31, 1855, Library of the Workingmen's Institute, Miscellaneous; Owen to Buchanan, Aug. 7, 1855, Buchanan Papers; R. D. Owen to Mary Owen, Aug. 11, 1855, Stone Letters; S. F. Bemis, ed., *The American Secretaries of State and Their Diplomacy* (N. Y., 1928), VI, 170–174.

to have every Democratic diplomat who had served four years or more ask to be recalled. Once again Owen bowed to rotation in office and on March 4, 1857, submitted his resignation, effective whenever the executive desired it.[17] Buchanan, however, delayed his nominations unduly, and as late as April 1858 the Indianan felt he might remain at Naples for another year. But three months later he learned of his successor's appointment and rather sadly, yet philosophically, began to make plans for his departure.[18]

Owen's reluctance to terminate his foreign mission suggests that the Western Democrat had found life enjoyable at the court of absolutism. In his later autobiographical writings he did not depict Naples as a den of iniquity or corruption; even the notorious "Bomba" was portrayed as the victim of an outmoded system.[19] It is not altogether surprising that, after a stormy career in politics, the intellectually inclined Owen should relish the calm of his romantic retreat. There were no reelections to worry about and no attacks on past heresies to answer. Except in winter the work was not arduous, and the society in which he moved was more cultured than that of his Hoosier home. A steady income was assured, one which by 1856 had become ample for his needs. Finally, the position conferred personal prestige, a concomitant of public service on which Owen always set much store.

As minister of a great power Owen lived well. He rented part of the Palazzo Valli, a large house centrally located on the Chiaia, kept several servants, and gave occasional balls to which even the Sicilian nobility came. During part of his tenure the Indianan led a bachelor's existence. Up to June 1855 Mary and the children remained at Stuttgart, and then all but Julian moved to a little cottage near Nice, delightfully situated amid

[17] Owen to Buchanan, Oct. 2, 1856; Buchanan to Owen, Dec. 8, 1856 (copy), Buchanan Papers. Owen to Marcy, Mar. 4, 1857, no. 76, "Despatches: Naples," II.

[18] Owen to Markoe, Apr. 22, 1858, Ford Collection; Owen to William C. Bryant, July 17, 1858, Duyckinck Collection; R. D. Owen to Robt. Owen, July 17, 1858, Robert Owen Papers, no. 2792.

[19] "Naples: Her Volcano, Her People, and Her King," loc. cit., XXXIII, 651.

flower gardens on an eminence overlooking the Mediterranean. It was not until 1856, when Florence married James Cooper of New Harmony and returned to America, that Mrs. Owen with the two youngsters joined her husband at Naples.[20]

Memorable phenomena of nature and an endless stream of tourists helped to break the ordinary routine of Owen's diplomatic life. Early in June 1854 a cholera plague swept the Neapolitan capital. A month later the daily death toll was estimated in the thousands. Over a ninth of the population, including the aged American consul, fled in horror from the pestilential city; but Owen remained at his post even though three persons in his own building were stricken. Less disagreeable and less disastrous was the eruption of Vesuvius the next May. For twenty-eight consecutive days the ancient volcano belched forth a stream of lava that covered field, orchard and vineyard, rolling almost to Naples itself. Owen went several times to the newly opened craters and later wrote detailed descriptions of the scene to his scientific brother.[21]

Entertaining the numerous distinguished travelers, American and otherwise, was one of the more pleasant tasks Owen had to perform. Among those who may have partaken of his hospitality during the years from 1853 to 1858 were Charles Dickens, Sara Clarke Lippincott, and Fredrika Bremer, the Swedish writer and commentator. Those with whom the minister definitely had contact included Martin Van Buren and his son "Prince John," Dorothea Dix, who inspected with Owen the Neapolitan hospital for the insane, Daniel Dunglas Home, the celebrated spiritualist medium, and John Pendleton Kennedy, author of *Swallow Barn* and a former colleague in Con-

---

[20] "Naples: Her Volcano, Her People, and Her King," *loc. cit.*, XXXIII, 648; Octavia W. Le Vert, *Souvenirs of Travel* (Mobile, 1857), II, 181. R. D. Owen to Richard Owen, July 6, 1855; Mary J. Owen to Richard Owen, Aug. 21, 1855, Neal Letters.

[21] Owen to Marcy, Aug. 11, 18, Sept. 20, 1854, nos. 17, 18, 20, "Despatches: Naples," II; R. D. Owen to D. D. Owen, May 20, 1855, Chamberlain Collection; R. D. Owen to Julian D. Owen, May 8, 1855, Stone Letters; "Naples under the Old Regime," *loc. cit.*, XXXIII, 137–139; "Naples: Her Volcano, Her People, and Her King," *loc. cit.*, XXXIII, 642–645.

gress. It was in this period also that Owen formed valuable friendships with William Cullen Bryant and Harriet Beecher Stowe.[22] It remained for Andrew D. White, then in his twenties, however, to record the fullest picture of the host. The American minister must have made a deep impression upon his youthful mind, for many years later the celebrated president of Cornell wrote,

An episode of much importance to me at this time was my meeting . . . Robert Dale Owen. His talks on the political state of Italy, and his pictures of the monstrous despotism of "King Bomba" took strong hold upon me. Not even the pages of Colletta or of Settembrini have done so much to arouse in me a sense of the moral virtue of political history.[23]

From the lips of these frequent visitors Owen heard of the turbulent scenes then convulsing his adopted country. The reemergence of the slavery quarrel, occasioned by the Kansas-Nebraska Act, probably brought sorrow to the Western Democrat, but unfortunately no important observation of his on that all engrossing topic has survived. He may have been in Paris along with many other diplomats before the issuance of the Ostend Manifesto, but he was not in favor of annexing Cuba by force. He seems to have been friendly with Buchanan, though that may have been a matter of expediency. At any rate he hoped the Pennsylvanian's administration would be a moderate one so as to encourage "those who had begun almost to despair of the Republic, and to fear that sectional heart-

[22] *Giornale del Regno delle Due Sicilie*, Nov. 8, 1853; Grace Greenwood, *Haps and Mishaps of a Tour in Europe* (Boston, 1854), 314–353; Fredrika Bremer, *Two Years in Switzerland and Italy* (Mary Howitt, tr., London, 1861); "The Autobiography of Martin Van Buren," American Historical Association, *Report for 1919*, II, 7–8; *N. Y. Times*, Aug. 18, 1854; Francis Tiffany, *Life of Dorothea Lynde Dix* (Boston, 1891), 283–286; D. D. Home, *Incidents in My Life* (N. Y., 1863), 136–137; John P. Kennedy, "Journal of European Visit, 1857–58" (MS.), 134–138 (Jan. 19–27, 1858); Parke Godwin, *A Biography of William Cullen Bryant* (N. Y., 1883), II, 103–106; Charles E. Stowe, *Life of Harriet Beecher Stowe* (Boston, 1889), 464.

[23] *Autobiography of Andrew Dickson White* (N. Y., 1905), I, 41. Cf. *ibid.*, I, 72, II, 552. Anne H. M. Brewster, *St. Martin's Summer* (Boston, 1866), contains a pleasing picture of the Owens under the fictitious name of the Rochesters.

burnings might at last prove hot and violent enough . . . to sever those federal bonds, the integrity of which alone secures to us prosperity, peace, greatness, even a separate independent existence." [24]

Except to deplore the prohibitionist tendency of the temperance movement, Owen recorded his opinion fully on only one political issue of the hour. That was Know-Nothingism. Since he had excoriated the earlier nativist tendencies of the forties in both Congress and on the stump, it was not likely that its more powerful successor of the fifties would find favor in his eyes, especially when its journals blamed Pierce for appointing foreigners to diplomatic posts. To Marcy Owen wrote anent the Sartorio case,

One cannot daily witness, as I do, the insecurity to property, liberty & life . . . without an emotion of pride and pleasure in reflecting that our country, ever since she first asserted her independence, has freely offered to political sufferers in this Eastern hemisphere, an assured refuge. . . . I cannot but feel, that if . . . our naturalization laws had been so changed, that during his life time, or for the twenty best years of it, the privilege of republican citizenship was now denied to the emigrant, the effect would be, not perhaps greatly to check emigration to the United States, but, very surely, to degrade its motives & lower its character. He whose only object was, to find lucrative employment . . . would still emigrate as before. But he, the man of cultivation, the thinker, the republican at heart . . . would be disheartened & deterred. . . . The Chinese policy of exclusion is better than the modern doctrine of disfranchisement. The one arrests the obnoxious stream; the other poisons its sources. . . .[25]

The sudden ebbing of this new tide of Americanism delighted Owen. He never doubted, he told Buchanan, its ephemeral character. "Our politicians," he said, "ought to have learned . . . that no party can stand, based on one idea. And history

[24] Owen to Cass, Apr. 2, 1857, no. 77, "Despatches: Naples," II; Amos A. Ettinger, *The Mission to Spain of Pierre Soulé, 1853–1855* (*Yale Historical Publications, Miscellany*, XXII, New Haven, 1932), 349; R. D. Owen to Mary Owen, Aug. 11, 1855, Stone Letters.

[25] Owen to Marcy, Apr. 12, 1855, no. 36, "Despatches: Naples," II. On his views on prohibition see the *Western Democratic Review*, II, 167–171 (Sept. 1854). See also the Concord *State Capitol Register*, Feb. 2, 1855, quoted in Ettinger, *op. cit.*, 495–496.

might have taught them . . . that in matters of religious toleration, the world advances, not recedes." [26]

Historically, Owen's five years in Naples were insignificant, but upon the man's life they left lasting results. Politically, they isolated him from the heresies and factionalism then convulsing the Democracy. During his subsequent public career Owen sought to stand aloof from and above parties. Culturally, they broadened his interests and deepened his knowledge. Many of his later writings reflect this foreign residence. Spiritually, the years were of greatest moment. Without the leisure afforded by a minor diplomatic post and the contacts made at the Sicilian court he would have had neither the time nor the inclination to pursue the study that was to color the remainder of his life.

Early in September 1858 Owen presented his successor to Carafa and on the twentieth had a final audience with King Ferdinand. As he took the steamer the next day for Marseilles, his feelings were obviously mixed. He was leaving behind a large circle of friends and admirers. He had been kindly treated by the Neapolitans and saw in their extreme courtesy, imperturbable good nature, and universal charity virtues that compensated for "a multitude of sins." But he had learned all that Naples had to teach. It had been "an interesting page in life," but one which by constant repetition might become flat and profitless. After five years he did "feel the want of a freer moral atmosphere" and did wish "to be doing something of more importance than the observance of diplomatic etiquette." [27] In his final despatch to Cass he wrote, "No one who has resided for years in this, one of the most beautiful regions of the civilized world, can leave it without regret, a regret tempered in my case, by the prospect of returning, once more, to a country of liberty & of progress." [28]

[26] Owen to Buchanan, Aug. 7, 1855, Buchanan Papers.

[27] R. D. Owen to Robt. Owen, July 17, 1858, Robert Owen Papers, no. 2792. See also *Giornale del Regno delle Due Sicilie*, Sept. 24, 1858; London *Times*, Oct. 5, 1858.

[28] Owen to Cass, Sept. 20, 1858, no. 94, "Despatches: Naples," II.

CHAPTER XX

SPIRITUALISM

WHEN Owen left Naples in the autumn of 1858, he believed that his public career was at an end. There was no office save that of United States Senator to which he aspired, and his prolonged absence from Indiana hardly improved his chances for that. Even before his departure, moreover, he had found a new interest, "something more serious & important than any party struggle." Logically and fearlessly pursued, it would block for the moment, perhaps for all time, his election to any governmental position. Owen was not blind to the consequences. Late in 1856 he told Buchanan, "I hope ever to take an active interest in the politics of our country; but, for the rest of my life, in a private station only." [1]

The fact is, Owen had become absorbed in the study of spiritualism. It was on the 25th of March, 1856, that he had called informally in the evening at the home of Kakoschkine, the Russian plenipotentiary. There the conversation turned to automatic spirit writing, and in a moment of levity the gathering decided to make a test of the mysterious force. Each person present was seated before a table and given a lead pencil to rest upon a blank piece of paper. After a time the hand of an American lady, one of Owen's friends, began to make lines but no words. Not satisfied, Madame Frescobaldi, the wife of the Tuscan minister, asked aloud who had given her the gold pins she was then wearing in her dress. Once again the same person's pencil moved, this time completing the illegible and apparently irrelevant sentence, "the one that gives you a maid and cook." While the amused company roared with laughter, the questioner turned pale and excitedly explained that the pins

---

[1] R. D. Owen to Robt. Owen, Jan. 13, 1857, Stone Letters; Owen to Buchanan, Oct. 2, 1856, Buchanan Papers.

were the gift of a cousin in Florence, the very one who in the last fortnight had recommended to her both a new cook and a new personal servant.[2]

Why Owen should have sought an ultramundane explanation for this coincidence is a question for a psychologist rather than a biographer. The latter must be content merely to point out what had gone before. Unlike many converts to spiritualism, Owen had experienced no recent bereavement among family or among friends. In 1842 he had shown a momentary interest in Joseph Rhodes Buchanan's experiments in mesmerism, but these certainly did not shake his conviction that this world is the be all and the end all. A decade later in the Indiana legislature he had said while eulogizing a deceased colleague,

> Well has it been said: whatsoever thy hand findeth to do, do it with all thy might; for there is no work, nor device, no knowledge nor wisdom in the grave. . . . The little good a man may do in this world, he must do quickly. The years pass, even while we are taking thought how they should be spent. . . . Let us be up and doing while it is yet day; the night cometh, when no man shall work.

At that time the Western Democrat took no notice of American spiritualism either when he traveled near its birthplace in New York while investigating plank roads or when the first rappings invaded Indianapolis and the "Pocket." In 1853, on hearing of Robert Owen's conversion, he regretted "as every judicious friend must, the strange infatuation which has overtaken my good father."[3] Only after he had been at Naples for a time and had witnessed with D. D. Home some startling manifestations was his curiosity whetted; and even then it was not until that momentous March evening when, according to his later account, he sat up late, pensive and alone, puzzled by what

[2] Robert Dale Owen, *Footfalls on the Boundary of Another World. With Narrative Illustrations* (Phila., 1860), 3; *The Debatable Land between This World and the Next, With Illustrative Narrations* (N. Y., 1872), 281–286.

[3] Owen to Trist, June 10, 1853, Trist Papers, XXXVI. Cf. N. Y. *Evening Post*, July 13, 1842; Indiana General Assembly, *House Journal*, 36th Session, 1350 (Apr. 26, 1852); *Locomotive*, Jan. 24, 1852; *Democratic Clarion*, July 3, 1852.

he had just seen, that after almost a half century of indifference, the agnostic began to ponder once more the eternal question, "If a man die, shall he live again?" That very night he
made a silent vow to probe the matter to its depths, to see
whether the phenomenon was evidence of a future existence or
simply a delusion. Out of the slight incident of three gold pins
grew a study which, Owen later confessed, "eventually changed
the whole feelings and tenor of my life." [4]

The subject which Owen proposed to investigate was a vast
one, for since the beginning of time man has tried to solve the
riddle of the next world. Interest in the supernatural and the
preternatural has not been alien to America; and in the nineteenth century the foundations of the movement with which we
are concerned was laid by the Swedenborgians, the Shakers,
the mesmerists of the forties, and finally by the clairvoyant
deeds of Andrew Jackson Davis. To Kate Fox, nine-year-old
daughter of an obscure farmer in western New York, however,
goes the credit for recognizing on March 31, 1848, the first
manifestations of "modern spiritualism." From the tiny hamlet
of Hydesville in Wayne county spread the word that certain
noises or rappings exhibited intelligence when spoken to and
that, by means of a simple alphabet, conversation could be had
with the shades of the departed. The consequences were in-
calculable. Ultramundane communications which formerly had
been sought only by trained scientists, a special priestcraft,
or by secluded mystics became in democratic America the
solace and the plaything of the common man. Untutored persons of both sexes, whose thoughts had seldom before strayed
from the workaday world, attained fame overnight as mediums
through which deceased scholars and statesmen spoke. Thanks
to favorable conditions and, perhaps, competitive pressure, the
phenomena in the United States grew more and more spectacular. The mental excitability of the people and the wide dissemination of the printed page insured the spread of the movement

[4] Home, *Incidents in My Life*, 136–137; *Footfalls*, 3, 110 n.; *Debatable Land*,
283–286.

until it became, at last, a new religion and a new reform. But in the early fifties it was, as yet, neither but rather, to use Owen's definition, an "American epidemic." [5]

Owen's conversion to spiritualism was a very gradual one. After three months of frequent séances and extensive reading he was still puzzled and inclined to attribute the phenomena to animal magnetism. After more than one hundred sittings he had yet to find any conclusive evidence and thought it might be some time before he could speak with certainty. In January 1857 he remained unconvinced but was ready to spend his next years in an attempt to solve the problem. "If," he told his father, "it be a delusion, it is a very dangerous one, & ought to be thoroughly exposed. But if it be a reality, then I deem it a more powerful lever for the gradual amelioration of mankind than any other with which I am acquainted." [6]

When he left Naples, Owen apparently had not fully accepted the theory of ultramundane intervention. At the end of the manuscript volume of "Personal Observations," which he was then keeping, he listed his conclusions up to that date. He believed that there was a phase of life after death in which individual identity and character were retained. He believed that under certain conditions, one of which was the presence of a medium, the dead could communicate with the living. Their spirits might, on occasion, move considerable weights, produce sounds, and read minds. All these manifestations took place in accordance with natural laws. To substantiate such an hypothesis Owen admitted that he had, as yet, insufficient data. Yet he knew of no non-spiritual explanation that accounted so well for certain undeniable facts. "It remains to be seen," he concluded, "whether further experiments will confirm or disprove

---

[5] *Footfalls*, 25. On early American spiritualism see Emma Hardinge, *Modern American Spiritualism* (N. Y., 1870); Cole, *The Irrepressible Conflict, 1850–1865*, 251; E. Douglas Branch, *The Sentimental Years, 1836–1860* (N. Y., 1934), 361–378; and the works listed in the Bibliography.

[6] "How I Came to Study Spiritual Phenomena. A Chapter of Autobiography," *Atlantic Monthly*, XXXIV, 581 (Nov. 1874); R. D. Owen to Robt. Owen, Nov. 30, 1856, Jan. 18, 1857, Robert Owen Papers, no. 2487, Stone Letters. See also Kennedy, "Diary," 138 (Jan. 24, 1858).

this theory; or whether any other theory can be suggested, involving less of marvel than the above yet adequate to the explanation of the phenomena in question." [7]

Upon leaving Naples Owen went alone directly to Paris. There he visited with his son Julian (Mary and the other two children having sailed for home in July), but the main purpose was to consult Baron de Guldenstubbé, author of a recent treatise on spirit writing. While engrossed in studies of the ultramundane, Owen received word that his father was dying. At once he crossed the Channel and reached the Park Farm at Sevenoaks, Kent, on October 7. He found his aged sire out of danger but suffering painfully from an enlarged prostate gland. The reunion was cordial but brief. Seeing no cause for immediate worry if due caution were observed, the son proceeded to London and then on to Edinburgh where, as newly appointed trustee of the David Dale estate, his presence was required. It was probably on this occasion that he returned to Glasgow after an absence of three decades to be shocked by the industrialization of the section about Charlotte Street; and it may have been then that he saw for the first time in as many years Margaret, the sweetheart of his youth. She, too, was happily married; and after exchanging fond recollections, the old lovers parted, never to meet or hear of each other again.[8]

Meanwhile, the ailing Robert Owen, having collapsed while making an unnecessary speech at Liverpool, had gone to Newtown to lay, as he said, "my bones whence I derived them." Thither the son was called from London by an urgent message on November 15. A rail journey took him to Shrewsbury, and then through the bleakest night he had ever known he sat for thirty-two miles on the outside of a mail stage. Morning brought him to the picturesque Welsh market town, beautifully situated

---

[7] Quoted in "How I Came to Study Spiritual Phenomena," *loc. cit.*, XXXIV, 589–590.

[8] Guldenstubbé to Owen, Aug. 30, 1858, Dreer Collection: Psychologists; *Debatable Land*, 370; Owen to Bryant, July 17, 1858, Duyckinck Collection; *New Harmony Advertiser*, Sept. 25, 1858; R. D. Owen to Mary Owen, Dec. 4, 1858 (copy), Stone Letters; Podmore, *Robert Owen*, II, 625; J. A. Campbell to Robt. Owen, Nov. 14, 1858, Owen Papers; *Threading My Way*, 21, 230–232.

between grassy green hills. Owen found his father at death's door but unwilling to recognize the fact. All that day the garrulous octogenarian talked of his plans for the future, but when night fell, he sank steadily. As the first pale glimmer of light crept into the room the next morning, a feeble voice murmured, "Very easy and comfortable." Then, without the contraction of a muscle or the least expression of pain, as gently and as quietly as if he had been falling asleep, the aged socialist's breathing gradually became slower and slower until at last it stopped. Twenty minutes before the end, the life-long agitator said softly but distinctly, "Relief has come." [9]

In taking leave of this last tie that bound Owen to his youth, a final comparison cannot be avoided of two men, so alike and yet so unlike, and so unequally esteemed by posterity. Both were optimists in their social thought; both believed in the steady progress of mankind toward universal knowledge, universal happiness, and universal peace. Neither would have accepted the Marxian doctrine of class struggle or the Spenglerian theory of Western decay. Each led a life of incessant activity; and each, after many disappointments, wrote in his last years an autobiography breathing a fervent faith in the bright destiny of the human race. Both received an undue share of publicity during their careers. Each was a religionist in youth, an agnostic in middle age, and a spiritualist at death. In looks, manner, and speech there was also a striking resemblance between the two men. But there the similarity ends. The son was never a practical man of business; the father was never elected to political office. The latter's mind roamed freely and influenced thousands by ethereal ideals. The former was less original and limited his objectives, for the most part, to things attainable in a lifetime. After the New Harmony fiasco there was no essential agreement between the two on reform, especially on the speed with which the world could be made over. "I know &

[9] R. D. Owen to Mary Owen, Dec. 4, 1858, Stone Letters; J. G. Holyoake, *Life and Last Days of Robert Owen* (London, 1871), 7; Podmore, *op. cit.*, II. 624–626; Cole, *Robert Owen*, 234.

respect your sanguine faith," wrote the American minister, but "I do not share it."

I have so often told you that I cannot be so sanguine as you, that I need not repeat it here. My experience has induced me to believe, that great changes in human society take place gradually; as the apple ripens slowly, & will not drop, (or drops useless & immature) until it be fully ripe.[10]

On November 21, 1858, Robert Owen was laid to rest beside his parents in the Newtown churchyard. His freethinking disciples were highly disgusted by the religious services accompanying the burial, but a more tolerant son acquiesced in order to avoid a needless scene and an offence to the Christian villagers. After the ceremony Owen returned to London to settle, among other things, his father's estate. Except for the annual income derived from the trust created by his sons in 1844 out of lands in New Harmony, the aged philanthropist had died penniless; and his debts and funeral expenses amounted to $2,500. Thus it was extraordinarily convenient that the American diplomat recovered at this time from Queen Victoria by a tactful letter a loan of $6,000 made by his father to the Duke of Kent a quarter of a century before.[11]

For some months longer Owen tarried in Europe. Most of the time he spent collecting materials for a book which he hoped to publish before the end of 1859. Originally entitled "Researches Bearing on the Future Destiny of the Soul & an Explanation of the Phenomena Connected Therewith," this work, as belief grew, came to be called "Probabilities of Ultramundane Communication." More than a hundred pages had been written before his departure from Naples. Some of these were perused there by Bryant and Kennedy; others were read to a select but enthusiastic gathering at Great Marylebone Street on the tenth of March. During these months Owen became ac-

[10] R. D. Owen to Robt. Owen, Nov. 30, 1856, Jan. 13, 1857, Robert Owen Papers, no. 2487, Stone Letters.

[11] London *Reasoner*, Dec. 5, 1858; R. D. Owen to Mary Owen, Dec. 4, 1858, Mar. 12, 1859 (copies), Stone Letters. Cf. Posey County, "Deed Book," M, 394–400; Robert Owen Papers, no. 1338.

quainted with the leading British adherents of the new faith, Dr. John Ashburner, William and Mary Howitt, and Mr. and Mrs. Samuel Carter Hall. Early in April he went to Paris for further experiments with Guldenstubbé, and then on May 25, 1859, sailed for home from Liverpool aboard the *City of Washington* in the company of Dr. Henry F. Gardner, a noted Boston spiritualist.[12]

Early in June Owen set foot on American soil for the first time in almost six years. Despite this prolonged absence he did not return at once to Indiana but passed the summer in the East winding up business with the Department of State and procuring more data for his forthcoming volume. In New York he was introduced to John Worth Edmonds, eminent jurist and perhaps the most distinguished advocate of spiritualism in America. Edmonds had read some of Owen's chapters in manuscript while the latter was still in England and had written the *Banner of Light* that it would be the best book on the subject yet to appear. Another prominent convert, met at this time, was James J. Mapes, able New Jersey agriculturist and father of Mary Mapes Dodge. At Roslyn he visited Bryant and it was on the poet's advice that he contracted with J. B. Lippincott for the publication of his work. The Indianan had preferred at first a New York firm but changed his mind when he learned from Susan Warner, author of *The Wide, Wide World*, that the Philadelphian did twice the business of Harper's or Appleton's. Highly elated by the favorable terms obtained and by Lippincott's roseate predictions of a 50,000 volume circulation, he finally reached New Harmony at the end of August. Six weeks later he again turned his back on the "Pocket" and hurried to the Quaker City to see his book through the press.[13]

---

[12] R. D. Owen to Robt. Owen, Oct. 26, 1856, Jan. 9, July 17, 1858, Robert Owen Papers, nos. 2530, 2732, 2792; Jan. 13, 1857, Stone Letters; Godwin, *op. cit.*, II, 106; Kennedy, "Diary," 138 (Jan. 24, 1858). *British Spiritual Telegraph*, Apr. 1, June 15, 1859; *Reasoner*, Mar. 6, 1859; *Footfalls*, 369, 373, 447; Boston *Banner of Light*, May 28, 1859.

[13] *Footfalls*, 180 n., 290 n., 324 n., 327 n., 340 n., 458; *Banner of Light*,

On the first day of the eventful year 1860 appeared Owen's *Footfalls on the Boundary of Another World*. Its purpose was succinctly stated in an advertisement in the *Tribune* of January 7.

This work [it said] is devoted to an inquiry whether occasional interference from another world in this be reality or delusion. It treats of the phenomena of Sleep, Dreams, Somnambulism. It examines the alleged evidence for presentiments, second-sight, house-hauntings, and apparitions; referring to the most approved modern works on hallucinations, insanity, and the nervous system. It inquires whether, when we set down the narratives of all ages (including our own) that touch on the marvels referred to, as mere vulgar superstitions, we are overlooking any actual phenomena.

The book was not the ordinary spiritualist outpouring that Owen himself had so often criticized as harmful to the cause. It did not discuss mediumship, rappings, table turnings, or any of the sensational manifestations that had been developed since 1848. It was restricted to spontaneous as contrasted with evoked phenomena. Even the reality of the former the author was careful to qualify by the use of such adjectives as "so-called" or "alleged." The bulk of the work comprised narratives containing instances, past and present, of hauntings, clairvoyance, and somnambulism. Each topic was prefaced by the best explanation that the latest scientific writings afforded. Thus the discussion of dreams was preceded by observations on sleep in general; and the treatment of apparitions, by a consideration of hallucinations. Each narrative was taken from a well-known source or was obtained at first hand, sometimes at second, from witnesses of the marvelous incident. Wherever possible the author had submitted his notes for corroboration to the person quoted.

Only in the last thirty pages of a 500-page book did Owen suggest an ultramundane hypothesis for facts which his reason and his senses told him were true. In that part, which he con-

---

Apr. 16, 1859; R. D. Owen to Mary Owen, Aug. 1, 1859, Stone Letters; *New Harmony Advertiser*, Aug. 27, Nov. 5, 1859.

sidered the essence of the work, he refused to dismiss all dreams as meaningless or testimony of hauntings that would be accepted in a court of law. There he boldly sketched the next phase of existence. The spirit, he wrote,

must retain, for a longer or shorter period, not only its general habits of thought and motives of action, but even its petty peculiarities and favorite predilections. There must be no sudden change . . . at the moment of death. . . . Men will awake in another life, the body left behind, and, with it, its corporeal instincts, its physical infirmities; yet each will awake the same individual, morally, socially, intellectually. . . .

Such a phantom might by sound, touch, or sight make itself perceptible to the living. But that was not its purpose. In this second stage of life there were tasks to be performed, obligations to be fulfilled, pleasures to be enjoyed. The spirit had still to prepare itself for the Day of Judgment. Realizing that he had traveled far from the beaten path, the author said curtly, with a flash of *The Free Enquirer* style, "All this may sound heterodox. The more important inquiry is, whether it is irrational." [14]

Although primarily concerned with the reality, not the advantages of ultramundane intervention, Owen did not shirk the question so often hurled at spiritualists, *"Cui bono?"* The manifestations, he thought, gave assurance of immortality to those unable to believe in it. They tended to keep men's thoughts from purely material objects and "to correct that absorbing worldliness, the besetting sin of the present age." Their investigation gave comfort to those of advanced years. Most important of all, these epiphanies might prove a powerful lever of reform by encouraging self-improvement and coöperation with one's neighbors. The author came curiously close to the doctrine of natural rewards and punishments, embraced in his first book written almost forty years before, when he said,

What motive to exertion in self-culture can be proposed to man more powerful than the assurance, that not an effort to train our hearts or

14 *Footfalls*, 480. Cf. *ibid.*, 478–512.

store our minds made here, in time, but has its results and its rewards, hereafter, in eternity? We are the architects of our own
destiny: we inflict our own punishments; we select our own rewards. . . . We choose: and our Choice assumes place as inexorable
judge. . . . When death calls, he neither deprives us of the virtues,
nor relieves us of the vices, of which he finds us possessed. Both
must go. Those qualities, moral, social, intellectual, which may have
distinguished us in this world will be ours also in another. . . . And
as the good, so the evil. That dark vestment of sin with which, in
man's progress through life, he may have become gradually endued
will cling to him. . . . He retains his evil identity and decides his
degraded rank. . . . Is there in the anticipation of a material Hell,
begirt with flames, stronger influence to deter from vice, than in the
terrible looming up of an inevitable fate like that? [15]

In attempting to reconcile spiritualism with religion, Owen
revealed a curious confusion of ideas. Most of his positions
were still unorthodox. He relied on reason rather than faith
and insisted upon a material proof of immortality. His interpretation of miracles was also unacceptable to zealous
churchmen. On the other hand, his book was hardly calculated
to arouse the enthusiasm of freethinkers. Eager to win additional converts and to make the new faith respectable, the
author refrained from saying aught against the clerical profession he had once scourged. A similar reversal of sentiment
was evident when he who thirty years earlier had written, "I
have often said that I thought it a waste of time and talent to
anticipate our destiny beyond the grave," now urged rational
men to concern themselves with their future existence. Owen
in 1860 spoke of the Scriptures as if they were a superior authority, of God's omnipotence as if there were a God, and of the
Creator's intentions as if those could be known. Nature no
longer loomed as the ultimate criterion of right and wrong;
its place was taken by a personal deity, a fact which clearly
distinguished the younger Owen as a spiritualist from the
elder.[16]

[15] *Footfalls*, 510–511. See also *ibid.*, 54–59, 86.
[16] *Footfalls*, 28, 31, 40, 58, 70, 88–89, 91, 432, 484, 485, 596. Cf. *Free Enquirer*, July 1, 1829.

The publication of *Footfalls* created something of a literary sensation. A first edition of two thousand copies was exhausted in a week; a second, in a month; and a third, by the end of March. Financially the book became the most successful of the new season.[17] The notices in both newspapers and periodicals were extremely full and, in many respects, surprisingly kind. None of the reviewers, to be sure, accepted the manifestations recounted as evidence for anything significant, but most agreed that the author had handled his material with judgment and restraint and had fashioned it into an eminently readable essay. The Indianan's fairness, calm, and caution were particularly commended. Very pleasing to Owen was the fact that this praise appeared not only in the journals of friends like Bryant and Tilton but also in those of such old political enemies as the *New York Tribune* and the *Boston Transcript*.[18] Orestes A. Brownson, a former editorial colleague but now a rabid anti-spiritualist, was especially requested by Owen to write a critical review; but although he promised a full discussion, the Catholic did no more than call attention to the large number of non-Christians adhering to the new faith.[19]

The most virulent attacks on *Footfalls* came not from the daily press or the conservative magazines but from the freethinkers. Already eighteen months before, they had been aroused by a false report of Owen's conversion to Catholicism. At first it was indignantly denied that so doughty a champion could ever renounce his scepticism; but when it became evident that some change was taking place in Owen's thought, a different

---

[17] *New Harmony Advertiser*, Jan. 14, Apr. 28, 1860; N. Y. *Evening Post*, Feb. 1, 1860; *Boston Transcript*, Feb. 15, 1860.

[18] Various types of reviews may be sampled in the Philadelphia *Press*, Jan. 6, 1860; N. Y. *Tribune*, Jan. 7, 1860; *National Intelligencer*, Jan. 11, 1860; *Evening Post*, Jan. 13, 1860; *Indianapolis Journal*, Jan. 18, 1860; *Indiana State Sentinel*, Jan. 23, 1860; *Boston Transcript*, Feb. 9, 1860; N. Y. *Independent*, Feb. 9, 1860; *Harper's New Monthly Magazine*, XX, 549 (Feb. 1860); *North American Review*, XC, 549–550 (Apr. 1860); *Christian Examiner*, 5th ser., VI, 306–309 (Mar. 1860); *New Englander*, XVIII, 381–411 (May 1860).

[19] Owen to Brownson, Jan. 10, 1860, Brownson Papers; *Brownson's Quarterly Review*, 3d ser., I, 265 (Apr. 1860).

position was assumed.[20] John Chappelsmith, an atheistical scientist living at New Harmony, uncovered a lecture given by Owen in January 1853 in which Christianity had received unexpected praise; and he suggested that the Western Democrat had come to believe in God as early as then. Other agnostics remarked upon Owen's long silence on freethought topics and hinted that this apparent step toward orthodoxy was being taken solely for political purposes.[21] But it was not until early 1860 that the correspondents of the nation's leading heterodox journal rose in all their fury. One writer deplored that such a man, "or rather what was a MAN," should so basely and foully prostitute his fine talents to bolster up blighting superstition. He complained that the Indianan spoke "as fluently of God . . . as if he had but recently been favored with a personal interview." "An Observer" branded the former editor of *The Free Enquirer* as a pharisee who had agreed "to shirk his Infidel principles for the sake of obtaining political office." Chappelsmith presented an interesting comparison of the type of evidence demanded by Owen in his debate with Origen Bacheler with that accepted in his new book. He vehemently denied that his fellow townsman deserved encomiums for honesty and impartiality, asserting without proof that Owen had been deluded by Buchanan's neurological experiments in 1842 but had never admitted the fact.[22] By May 1860 detraction and vilification had become so incessant that Horace Seaver had to close his columns to further discussion of *Footfalls*.[23]

This obloquy heaped upon him by old associates could not fail to stir the sensitive Owen. He felt especially aggrieved that, after a long public career in which he never recanted his heterodoxy for political advantage, he should now be accused, when he no longer sought office, of truckling to orthodoxy. To the editor of the *Boston Investigator* he wrote a bristling letter

[20] On this incident see *The New Harmony Advertiser*, Sept. 4, 1858; *Boston Investigator*, June 30, July 7, 14, 28, Aug. 11, 25, Sept. 8, 29, Nov. 7, 14, 1858.
[21] *Boston Investigator*, Sept. 8, 1859; Sept. 1, Nov. 17, 1858, Apr. 20, 1859.
[22] *Boston Investigator*, Feb. 22; Mar. 21; Feb. 29, Apr. 11, May 9, 1860.
[23] *Ibid.*, May 16, 1860.

which clearly showed that his controversialist pen had not rusted with the years. "It is not," he declared,

worth any one's while to take much trouble about my consistency. . . . It is much more important to test the truth or falsehood of a man's opinions than to inquire whether he has always held them. . . . Bigotry consists, not in believing too much or too little, but in believing in its own infallibility. . . . He who would clip or stretch the creed of his neighbor on the Procrustean bed of his own belief or disbelief, is an invader of good will upon earth, and an enemy of free inquiry. . . . Some of your correspondents have yet to learn that abuse proves nothing except the lack of good sense and good feeling in the abuser.

Owen then cited his earlier writings as not wanting in moral courage nor a "desire to abandon truth let her lead whither she will." These, he said, showed that he had studied the infidel attitude toward immortality and that his present conclusions could not be attributed to ignorance. He begged freethinkers everywhere to give his book a fair hearing; and he hoped, at least, that, if it "should fail to convince them that ultramundane agencies sometimes operate here, it may persuade them that no former work of the author bears evidence of . . . more conscientious research than this." [24]

In the history of American spiritualism *Footfalls on the Boundary of Another World* deserves a prominent place. It was exceptional in that it was the first book of its kind to be brought out by a nationally known, non-spiritualist publisher. The volume, moreover, possessed an air of scholarship, an attribute unheard of in the literature of the movement. It contained an index which, for the time, was excellent, and a bibliography listing more than 130 titles dealing with psychology, mental diseases, and the nervous system. Extensive footnotes gave accurate citations and brief summaries of allied topics. Finally, caution, restraint, and an absence of dogmatism were distinctive features of the work. The author knew that he was pioneering in a debatable land and acted accordingly.[25]

[24] *Boston Investigator*, Mar. 14, 1860.   [25] *Footfalls*, 6.

Owen's book was important because it was timely. After more than a decade of ridicule and denunciation spiritualism not only had survived but was becoming more formidable. A new wave of interest in the subject about 1860 was evident in the extended reviews accorded *Footfalls*. It was apparent in the elaborate article, prepared by a spiritualist, in the new encyclopedia that George Ripley and Charles A. Dana were editing for Appleton's. It was seen in the additional definitions offered in the latest Webster and Worcester dictionaries. It was revealed in the tendency of believers to form a national organization. The earlier disappointments occasioned by Congress' inaction on the mammoth memorial and by the American Association for the Advancement of Science's unnecessary humiliation of Robert Hare were being forgotten. Spiritualist registers were now boasting of more than 1,500,000 adherents, a thousand meeting places, and thirty periodicals at home and abroad.[26] Although untrustworthy, these compilations, by their very existence were significant; and it is true that by the summer of 1860 such magazines as the *Spiritual Telegraph* and the *Banner of Light* had lived eight and three years respectively. On the eve of secession the prospects of this new religion were brightening. Small wonder that sincere advocates should be carried away by the grandeur of their mission. In asking Owen to write another volume, former United States Senator Nathaniel P. Tallmadge said,

Nothing will do so much to benefit mankind. . . . If you have the least ambition to be remembered on earth . . . such a work will do more for you than all you have ever done during the whole course of your public life. . . . I have served the public for nearly a quarter of a century. . . . And yet, if I am to be remembered hereafter for any thing I have done, let it be for my *moral courage* in avowing my belief in Spiritualism.[27]

[26] [William Fishbough], "Spiritualism," *The New American Cyclopaedia: A Popular Dictionary of General Knowledge* (George Ripley and C. A. Dana, eds., 16 v., N. Y., 1859–1863), XV, 1–4; *New Englander*, XVIII, 381–382; Hardinge, *op. cit.*, 128–133; *N. Y. Tribune*, Aug. 28, 29, 30, 1856; Mr. & Mrs. Uriah Clark, eds., *Fourth Annual Spiritual Register* (Auburn, 1860), 36.
[27] Tallmadge to Owen, Mar. 28, 1860, Dreer Collection: Psychologists.

The undoubted success of his first literary venture in pneumatology confirmed Owen's intention to remain clear of politics. Urged on by his friends, he began to gather materials for a second book; and except for his widely noticed debate on divorce with Horace Greeley in the columns of the *Tribune*, he dropped from public view for most of the momentous year 1860. On the evening of February 28, twenty-four hours after his friend Bryant had introduced Abraham Lincoln to a cheering multitude at Cooper Institute, Owen was being feted by the leading spiritualists of New York City. On May 5, two days after his old party had adjourned from Charleston, hopelessly split along sectional lines, he sailed aboard the *Vanderbilt* for Southampton.[28]

The primary purpose of this new ocean crossing was to collect an old claim, apparently a personal debt, at Naples. At the same time, however, a request by his brothers that he visit Scotland and effect, if possible, a final sale of the family's portion of the Dale estate, enabled Owen to perform a task much closer to his heart, the supervision of an English edition of his recent work. Just as thirty years before he had eagerly disseminated his tract on contraception, so now was he anxious to spread the results of his latest efforts to aid mankind, all the more so since spiritualism in Great Britain was but a pale shadow of the movement in the United States. Thus in mid-August 1860, just six weeks after the author had reached London, *Footfalls* was published by Trübner, one of the leading firms of the British capital.[29]

As in the United States, Owen's volume was eagerly awaited by freethinkers. The arrival of the American edition in the spring of 1860 had dispelled the doubts over the Indianan's position existing since his rumored conversion to Catholicism in

[28] *Banner of Light*, Mar. 3, 1860; *Debatable Land*, 348; *N. Y. Times*, Mar. 2, 1860; *N. Y. Tribune*, May 7, 1860.
[29] Richard Owen to R. D. Owen, Mar. 4, 1860; J. A. Campbell to Owen, May 5, 1860, Owen Papers; R. D. Owen, "Report of Proceedings as Trustee of the David Dale Estate" (MS. copy), Stone Papers. *A New Series of Yorkshire Spiritual Tracts* (Keighley, 1860), no. 10.

1858.[30] At once the secular platform and press resounded with denunciation of a new apostate. Men who had revered Owen for the militancy of his agnosticism and for the name he bore were astonished, dismayed, and finally enraged to find him quoting the Scriptures he had once rejected. They blamed him, not for repudiating his scepticism, but for failing to do it openly, for not explaining wherein he considered his old doctrines at fault. To some his book seemed timid and apologetic; to others, the vagaries of a deranged mind. By all it was regarded as an insult to free enquiry. In a two-page editorial George Jacob Holyoake, a leading English secularist, lashed out against his former idol thus:

To use Yankee language, Mr. Owen takes his place on the orthodox "stump." He has left the free platform . . . like a deserter. . . . No clang of arms announces his change of sides. He does not look his old colleagues in the face. He passes from them with his head averted, if not hanging down. One who bears so bold a name owed . . . some courageous words in justification of his conduct when he bade farewell to the glory of his house. It appears that when we laid down the noble father in the churchyard of Newtown, we buried there all that made the name of Owen an inspiration of fearlessness among men. Robert Dale was the only hope of his race. The heroism of that race is now suspended, if not extinct.[31]

If criticism from the left was harsher in England than in America, that from the right was even more so. Several of the great quarterlies were moved by Owen's book to reexamine spiritualism; but all agreed that the facts adduced led nowhere and their compiler was set down as incompetent, overcredulous, and blasphemous. Even Dickens' weekly entered a strong dissent, although the novelist privately expressed a genuine regard for the author.[32]

[30] *Reasoner*, Aug. 4, 1858, Jan. 30, 1859; *Boston Investigator*, Sept. 15, 1859.

[31] *Reasoner*, June 20, 1860. Cf. *ibid.*, June 22, July 8, 29, Sept. 9, 23, 30, Oct. 7, 14, 21, 28, Nov. 18, 1860; *National Reformer*, May 12, June 30, July 28, 1860.

[32] *Blackwood's Edinburgh Magazine*, LXXXVIII, 381–395 (Oct. 1860); *Westminster Review*, XIX, 244–245 (Jan. 1861); *North British Review*, XXXIV, 110–141 (Feb. 1861); *London Review*, XVI, 167–189 (Apr. 1861); *All the Year*

Undismayed by these strictures, Owen remained abroad well into September, continuing his research in the ultramundane. At Edinburgh he despatched the business of the Dale estate and visited with Robert Chambers, the publisher, who manifested great interest in spiritualism. It was in the company of the Scot that Owen sailed by the *Europa* from Liverpool and reached Boston on September 21, 1860.[33]

Although the American people were then on the eve of the most crucial presidential election in their history, the Western Democrat, upon his return, continued to devote his time to intellectual pursuits. While fervid orators addressed vast throngs on Black Republicanism and slavery, Owen sat in a small group listening to strange rappings. While great torchlight parades wound their way through New York's noisy streets to win more votes for Lincoln, Douglas, or Breckinridge, Owen sought in the quiet of a semi-darkened room the truth concerning materialized spirits. While the best minds of the nation were already puzzling over the tripartite riddle of secession, coercion, and compromise, Owen was trying to explain how a heavy dining room table could remain suspended, untouched, in mid-air.[34] Convictions on the impending contest the Indianan undoubtedly had, but he did not place them on record. Nor did he return, as his followers had hoped more than a year before, to lead the Democracy of the "Pocket" again to victory.[35]

Owen, however, did not feel he was misusing his time. Encouraged by the extensive circulation of *Footfalls*, he plunged ahead on its sequel. In order to witness mediumship at its best, he actually lived for several weeks in the autumn with the Fox sisters at the Underhill home in New York.[36] At that time a

---

Round, Sept. 15, 1860. Dickens to Owen, Aug. 31, 1860, Dreer Collection: English Prose, II.

[33] *Spiritual Magazine*, I, 444–445 (Oct. 1860); "Report of My Proceedings as Trustee etc.," Stone Papers; *Boston Courier*, Sept. 22, 1860.

[34] For evidence of these séances in Oct. 1860, see *The Debatable Land*, 354, 357, 360, 363, 364, 386, 394, 460, 464.

[35] Quoted in *The New Harmony Advertiser*, July 3, 1859.

[36] *N. Y. Tribune*, Sept. 22, 1860; *Debatable Land*, 343; Leah F. Underhill, *The Missing Link in Modern Spiritualism* (N. Y., 1885), 338.

critical letter from Cornelius C. Felton, president of Harvard University and a bitter foe of spiritualism, forced Owen to justify for himself the utility of his research. In a long reply he said,

Desiring after twenty years of public life, some more tranquil and philosophical field of labor, I discovered none which appear to promise more useful results than this. If, as you allege, "all phenomena are due to . . . delusion or imposture," then these should be detected. . . . If, as I believe, there is a foundation of truth underlying them, still there is an imperative demand for the exercise of prudence. . . . A source of good may eventuate in evil. . . . Time the great teacher will decide between us. Ten years — probably less — will see the question determined. . . . I am content to bide the event. Meanwhile, following my convictions of the useful, I propose next year . . . to follow up my first work by another . . . to examine what I have not yet touched upon. . . .[37]

This second volume appeared not one year later but twelve. Less than a week before Owen had written to Felton, Abraham Lincoln had been elected president of the United States, and in the fiery ordeal of the War of Secession disappeared the versatile Hoosier's desire for a "more tranquil and philosophical field of labor."

[37] Owen to Felton, Nov. 12, 1860, Underhill, *op. cit.*, 328–337.

CHAPTER XXI

WAR DEMOCRAT

SCARCELY had the ink dried on Owen's letter outlining his plans for further research in spiritualism than Death tore it to shreds. On November 13 David Dale Owen passed away in New Harmony, a victim of constant exposure in the field and incessant overwork in the laboratory.[1] Called home by this tragic event, Owen reached Indianapolis late in the month. There at the scene of his first political strivings he turned at last from intellectual theories to the practical problems of the hour. There in the Hoosier capital he found men of all parties discussing the primary issue raised by the recent election, the policy to be pursued toward the Southern states about to secede from the Union.

Owen always had great confidence in the power of his pen. Believing now that a seven-years' absence from the political arena allowed him to write dispassionately, he published in the leading Indianapolis papers a thoughtful, non-partisan letter on "The Question of Coercion." In this he steered a middle course, blaming radicals on both sides for the present crisis. His old views on slavery had not changed. He did not go out of his way to brand it an intolerable evil, but he certainly did not accept the Dred Scott decision. He simply reasserted the stand first taken in 1847, that human bondage could not legally exist in the territories unless established there by a positive act of Congress. As to secession, Owen denied its constitutionality and upheld the right of the government to coerce recalcitrant states into obedience. But what was right, he pointed out, was not always expedient. The sword never convinced, whereas a conciliatory attitude would prevent further

---

[1] *New Harmony Advertiser*, Nov. 17, 1860; Merrill, *The First One Hundred Years of American Geology*, 199 n. 41.

defections and facilitate the return of South Carolina to her former allegiance. Owen warned that a baptism of blood would but confer perpetuity upon the present quarrel.[2]

This policy of permitting the erring sisters to go in peace, so incomprehensible to a later generation, was widely held during the confused and uncertain winter of 1860–1861. It was endorsed by those who believed that a sovereign commonwealth could not be coerced by a federal government of limited powers. It was advocated by compromisers of all shades. It was the last refuge of pacifists who shrank from the horror of war. No less a Republican than Horace Greeley preferred it under certain conditions, and the Lincoln state organ in Indiana expressed similar views. But even before Owen's letter appeared, many leaders of the victorious party had set their faces resolutely against temporizing. In the East Bryant editorially declared "Peaceable Secession an Absurdity"; while in the West Oliver P. Morton, soon to be governor of the Hoosier state, was ready to keep South Carolina loyal "at the point of the bayonet." In time even Democrats came to oppose peaceful secession as a bar to compromise.[3]

Since 1853 political parties in Indiana had undergone a tremendous transformation, and in the new alignment, which found the Republicans dominant, Owen felt confused and ill at ease. As a life-long Democrat he must have been pained to see the well-oiled machine that had stood unchallenged upon his departure for Naples now discordant, defeated, and well-nigh disgraced. For the Breckinridge faction, to which Jesse Bright and Joe Lane still clung, Owen could have little sympathy as long as it demanded that human property be given protection in the territories. Although treated very courteously by Berry Sulgrove's Republican *Journal*, the foreign born free

---

[2] *Indianapolis Journal*, Nov. 28, 1860; *Indiana State Sentinel*, Nov. 28, 1860.

[3] Ralph R. Fahrney, *Horace Greeley and the Tribune in the Civil War* (Cedar Rapids, 1936), 43–53; Charles Kettleborough, "Indiana on the Eve of the Civil War," Indiana Historical Society, *Publications*, VI (Indps., n. d.), 185; *Indianapolis Journal*, Nov. 19, 27, 1860; *Evening Post*, Nov. 12, 1860; *Indiana State Sentinel*, Dec. 17, 1860.

trader could hardly feel at home among the strange conglomera-
tion of abolitionists, nativists, protectionists, and old-line Whigs.
On slavery Owen probably stood closest to the Douglas Democrats, but a new generation of politicians and editors had
replaced his former associates, and his hold upon the electorate,
even in Posey, had disappeared with time. In the end, the
intellectual failed to ally himself with any one party, and in
that failure lay both the strength and the weakness of his
political position during the Civil War and Reconstruction.

Upon reaching New Harmony early in December, Owen did
not slip back into private life. At the request of the local publisher he prepared a commentary on Buchanan's last annual
message in which he contradicted almost every argument of
the executive and concluded with a flash of realism, not again
evident for some time, that no compromise was possible if the
South were unwilling to remain in the Union as a minority
section.[4] Two weeks later he took a leading part at Mt. Vernon
in the largest political gathering in the county's history. All
groups were represented, and Owen was classified as a Douglas
Democrat. At a similar meeting in New Harmony on January 5 the ex-diplomat was again prominent, being chiefly
responsible for the resolutions that endorsed a scheme not
unlike the Crittenden proposals. In a carefully prepared speech,
"The Question of Compromise," he pointed out the necessity of
settling in the Constitution the legal status of slavery in the
territories lest the question continue to be the football of a
changing court and a changing legislature.[5]

During the next month the drums of war sounded more distinctly. On January 9 the *Star of the West* was driven off by
the hostile guns of Fort Moultrie. Four weeks later seven
cotton states had withdrawn from the Union, while the Border
commonwealths were meeting in a futile Peace Convention at
Washington. In New York every Republican paper now op-

---

[4] *New Harmony Advertiser*, Dec. 15, 1860.
[5] *New Harmony Advertiser*, Jan. 5, 12, 1861; *State Sentinel*, Jan. 5, 1861;
Indianapolis Journal, Jan. 14, 1861.

posed compromise, and the Hoosier journals followed suit.[6]
It was under these disheartening circumstances that Owen
went to Indianapolis on business connected with Dale's geological collection. While there he consented to speak with
Caleb B. Smith and Richard W. Thompson, Whig rivals of
by-gone days, at a mass meeting to be held the night before
Lincoln's arrival. Unfortunately a last minute change in the
plans of the president-elect deprived Owen of utilizing that
strategic moment, and the speech had to be postponed until
after the future Emancipator had passed to the eastward.[7]

On the evening of February 13, 1861, Owen stood once again,
and for the last time, in the Hall of Representatives, the scene
of his earlier struggles and triumphs. Knowing that Lincoln's
words had puzzled Republicans and dissatisfied Democrats, he
made before an overflowing audience a supreme appeal for
peace. More in sorrow than in anger, he reviewed "as one no
longer engaged in public life" the causes of the existing crisis.
In his opinion there was only one issue in dispute. Every Southern demand regarding personal liberty acts, the fugitive slave
law, and involuntary servitude in the states he considered justified; only the insistence that the territories be opened to slavery
was unwarranted. Yet even there Owen was ready to make
some compromise in order to retain the allegiance of the Border
States. Any concession, he concluded, was, in the long run,
trifling. As a practical matter the North could and should
yield.

A failure to compromise [he warned] produces a united South. . . .
Coercion . . . let it assume what shape it will, is, first *Disunion*, then
War. . . . Fellow citizens of Indiana! You were told two days since,
by one who will soon be the chief magistrate of our country, that the
preservation of the Union was your business. . . . Never was re-
minder more in place. . . . On you and your children, on your de-
scendants for ages to come, will fall the suffering, if, by the action of

---

[6] Allan Nevins, *The Evening Post, A Century of Journalism* (N. Y., 1922),
272-273; *Indianapolis Journal*, Feb. 8, 1861.

[7] *New Harmony Advertiser*, Feb. 2, 1861; *State Sentinel*, Feb. 5, 1861;
Indianapolis Journal, Feb. 11, 12, 1861.

Presidents and politicians and office seekers, you are hurried so far on the road of violence, that there is no return save only over fields of civil warfare, dyed with brothers' blood. . . . Up and be doing, ere it be too late! . . . If you believe that by compromise only can this Confederacy be held together, declare it. . . . For myself, while the sword remains undrawn, while kindred blood remains unshed, never shall I despair of the Republic. While there is PEACE there is hope, for PEACE is the life of the Union.[8]

Historians, made wise by a knowledge of what was to be, may call Owen's effort a "maundering tirade" or "a pathetic appeal"; but the fact remains that no speech delivered by an Indianan after November received greater publicity or more generally favorable notice in the local press. It filled five columns in the state paper of each major party, obtained full summaries in the Indianapolis correspondence of Cincinnati journals, and was reprinted in pamphlet form. Breckinridge old-line guard, Douglas Democrat, and moderate Republican all had some kind remark to make. Only the radicals were censorious.[9] To be sure, Owen's words were not those of a War Democrat, one who would support any measure designed to bring the rebellious states to book. They were those of a man eager for peace, above party, and willing to sacrifice, in the best sense of the word, principle to expediency. They did reflect the sentiments of a large number, perhaps a majority, of the Hoosiers.

Until the very end, Owen did not cease to hope that an appeal to arms would be averted. On February 22 he spoke again at an Indianapolis gathering assembled "to adopt such measures as may be calculated to prevent civil war and preserve the Union," and there he drafted resolutions endorsing the Crittenden or a similar compromise. Since the Republicans dis-

[8] Robert Dale Owen, *Perils and Exigencies of the Present Crisis; An Address Delivered Feb. 13, 1861, in the Hall of Representatives, Indianapolis* (Indps., 1861), 15–16.

[9] *Indiana State Guard*, Feb. 16, 1861; *State Sentinel*, Feb. 14, 1861; *Indianapolis Journal*, Feb. 14, 15, 1861; Madison *Courier*, Feb. 5, 1861; *Cincinnati Gazette*, Feb. 15, 1861. Cf. Logan Esarey, *A History of Indiana* (2 v. Indps., 1915–1918), II, 668; Lockwood, *New Harmony Movement*, 364.

missed this supposedly non-partisan meeting as but another Democratic maneuver, Owen's second public appearance required some courage and exposed him, at the very time he was most eager to avoid all semblance of political affiliations, to such characterizations as a leader of the faction responsible for the crime of Kansas and the Lecompton swindle.[10] Nowise discouraged, Owen returned to New Harmony and redelivered his talk on the "Perils and Exigencies of the Present Crisis." Midst thickening clouds of war he wrote for the local paper a long review of Lincoln's inaugural in which he persuasively argued for compromise and for peace.[11]

The attack on Fort Sumter dashed all hopes of a pacific settlement. As soon as blood had been shed, Owen abandoned his policy of conciliation and demanded that the war be prosecuted at once "with vigor and humanity." "The time for action," he wrote, "has come." To discuss the causes of the conflict or to speculate on how it might have been avoided was no longer profitable. Every one, even those who, like himself, had been willing to make extreme concessions to prevent hostilities, must now put his shoulder to the wheel. Yet, while blaming Ruffinian hotheads for precipitating the fratricidal struggle, Owen was not swept off his feet by momentary hysteria. He manifested no desire to emancipate the slaves or to overrun the cotton kingdom with soldiery. The sole aim of the war, as he saw it, was to bring the seceders into the conference hall where, as equals, they would negotiate for reunion.[12] With this idea in mind he rebuked the now radical Greeley for his talk of plowing Maryland's rebellious soil with cannon balls and annihilating the "pestilent city" of Baltimore. Such blind, futile inhumanity, worthy of a "Bomba," said Owen, would delay reconciliation and even make it impossible. These strictures, however just, cost the writer an unpleasant con-

---

[10] *State Sentinel*, Feb. 17, 18, 21, 22, 23, 1861. Cf. *Indianapolis Journal*, Feb. 23, 25, Mar. 7, 1861.

[11] *New Harmony Advertiser*, Mar. 2, 9, 1861.

[12] *Ibid.*, Apr. 20, 27, May 4, 18, 1861.

troversy in which he was presented in an unfavorable light in the *Tribune's* columns.[13]

During the crisis of 1860–1861 Owen's course was consistent, sincere, and honorable. He pleaded for peace until it no longer existed and then strongly supported the war as the surest way to attain his original goal. By most contemporaries, however, his post-Sumter New Harmony editorials passed unnoticed; and in the ensuing months he was thought of as one who had scored abolitionists, favored peaceable secession, and proposed to admit slavery into some of the territories. With Bryant he had been in complete disagreement, and with Greeley he had openly clashed. In his desire for peace he had on February 22 publicly associated himself with the Copperheads of the future. Given these facts and his past conservatism on the slavery issue, it was evident that in May 1861 Owen was nowhere regarded as a War Democrat.

On the thirtieth of May Owen was commissioned by Governor Morton to be Indiana's agent for the purchase of all ordnance required by her troops. To appreciate the importance of that position one must understand the state rights principle upon which the war was administered in its early months. During his first weeks in office Lincoln did nothing to place the country in a state of preparedness. When the storm broke, the War Department was utterly unable to arm and equip even the inadequate number of volunteers called for. Upon the individual states fell the task not only of recruiting soldiers but also of providing them with guns, food, and clothing. Each governor was frankly told to obtain for himself those materials as best he could and then present the bill at Washington. This policy compelled the commonwealths to undertake tremendous business operations and incur great financial indebtedness. They were forced to contest with each other at home and abroad for the scanty war stocks then available, and they became the

[13] *New Harmony Advertiser*, May 11, June 8, 29, 1861; *N. Y. Tribune*, Apr. 27, May 1, 27, June 5, 11, 1861.

victims of much profiteering, much shoddy, and much graft.[14] Owen's selection as Indiana's purchasing agent came as something of a surprise. It was made by one whose policy he had but recently opposed. It was made without any apparent solicitation on his part and at the governor's urgent request. The choice of a man "whose integrity has never been questioned in thirty years of partisan strife" was pronounced eminently fitting by most Hoosier journals. The radical Republicans, to be sure, were disgruntled; and one timorous editorial seemed to think a belief in spiritualism made the recipient unsuited for the job. "He may," it said,

be familiar with Kant but what does he know of Colt? . . . Is not Mr. Owen polished down to too fine a point, too keen an edge, for this plain, practical common-sense business? Is there not some danger that when about concluding some important contract for arms in Germany, he may suddenly break off negotiations to chase some ghosts through the ancient castles and chateaus of the Rhine? [15]

These gloomy forebodings of a local scribe proved to be wholly unjustified. During the next twenty months Owen bid in the most competitive of markets, inspected ordnance and quartermaster's stores on which he was, admittedly, not an expert, and made instant decisions involving vast sums of money. Before his commission expired on February 6, 1863, he had bought $891,836.25 worth of rifles, revolvers, carbines, blankets, overcoats, and cavalry appurtenances.[16] Yet no irregularities and no indiscretions were ever found in his work. In addition, Owen was more than a purchasing agent. On innumerable occasions he acted as Morton's personal representa-

[14] Morton to Owen, May 30, 1861, "State of Indiana: Governor (O. P. Morton, 1861–1867), Telegrams and Despatches" (MS.), I, Part 2, Private; Fred A. Shannon, *The Organization and the Administration of the Union Army, 1861–1865* (Cleveland, 1928), I, 15, 22–48, 53–55, 88.

[15] *Lafayette Journal*, quoted in *The New Harmony Advertiser*, July 20, 1861. R. D. Owen to Mary Owen, May 28, 1861, *New Harmony Advertiser*, June 1, 1861. *Ibid.*, June 1, 1861; *Evansville Journal*, quoted in *ibid.*, June 8, 1861; *Indianapolis Journal*, May 30, 1861; *New Albany Ledger*, May 30, 1861.

[16] Manuscript report by R. D. Owen, Feb. 6, 1863, Indiana State Library, Archives Division, Department of the Adjutant General.

tive in the East. It was through Owen that the Hoosier war governor during 1861 transacted much of his business with the president and the heads of the departments. Owen spent a good part of June and most of September in the capital arranging for the government's acceptance of Indiana's volunteers and then reporting on the condition of the food, equipment, and morale of those encamped in and about Washington. At the end of the year he returned again to supervise the War Department's assumption of the contracts made in its behalf and to win final approval for the construction of an arsenal at Indianapolis.[17]

The complete success of Owen's agency is indicated by all available evidence. The Republican organ at home quite naturally carried glowing accounts of his efficiency; less biased was the favorable testimony given before a Congressional Committee by the United States Ordnance Officer stationed at Governor's Island. Owen himself boasted of having paid in many cases a "very considerably lower" price for guns than had the federal government. In 1863 a Democratic legislative attempt to discover abuses in the establishment of the arsenal ended in a complete vindication of Owen and others. A year later an auditing committee of the General Assembly reported that "Mr. Owen exhibited much foresight in making the various purchases at the time he did. His duties were discharged with commendable fidelity and energy, and certainly the trust could not have been confided to an abler or more faithful agent." [18]

---

[17] *The War of the Rebellion: A Compilation of the Official Records of the Union and Confederate Armies* (70 v., Wash., 1880–1901), 3d ser., I, 275, 291, 339–340; Owen to Morton, June 22, Sept. 18, 1861, Jan. 8, 1862; Morton to Owen, Sept. 3, 1861, Jan. 6, 1862, "Indiana: Governor, Telegrams," I, II; Owen to Morton, July 20, Sept. 11, 17, 18, 19, 24, 25, Oct. 3, Dec. 28, 1861, Jan. 2, 5, 13, 1862, Indiana Archives; *New Harmony Advertiser*, July 20, 1861.

[18] *Indianapolis Journal*, July 22, Aug. 17, 30, Oct. 28, 1861; *ibid.*, Feb. 26, 1862; *Report of Robert Dale Owen, Agent to Purchase Arms, &c., for the State of Indiana, Made to His Excellency, O. P. Morton, Governor of the State, September 4, 1862* (Indps., 1863), 7; W. R. Holloway to Morton, May 19, 1863, W. H. H. Terrell to — ? —, May 18, 1863, "Indiana: Govenor, Telegrams," XI; *State Sentinel*, Apr. 18, May 29, 1863; *Report of the Adjutant General of the State of Indiana* (Indps., 1869), I, 435.

Owen had good reason to be pleased with the results of his work. He had done his bit for the Union cause. He had proved that a spiritualist could also be a man of business. He had again held a remunerative public office. He had won the good will and respect of the governor.[19] Most important of all, he had obtained a contact with the president and the cabinet that was to make possible a higher and more significant appointment.

On March 13, 1862, Joseph Holt, Unionist member of Buchanan's cabinet and a War Democrat, and Owen were chosen by Stanton as a special committee "to audit and adjust all contracts, orders, and claims on the War Department, in respect to ordnance, arms, and ammunition." Aided by the testimony of interested parties, they were to investigate the validity, execution, and reasonableness of these obligations and to report those worthy of payment. It was by this means that the administration hoped to check, in part, the profiteering and graft that had marked the first year of the struggle.[20]

Owen's labors as Ordnance Commissioner were useful rather than interesting and need not detain us long. In their final report, dated July 1, 1862, Holt and Owen declared that they had audited, mostly by public hearings at the War Department Building, one hundred and four contracts, amounting to $50,000,000. By rejecting some of these and curtailing others they had reduced the government's indebtedness by $17,000,000. Yet in no case had they deprived a claimant of a reasonable profit. The report scored the Cameron regime for its lax system of issuing contracts, its violation of the law requiring public advertisements, and its toleration of the senseless competitive bidding between federal and state agents. Many inexplicable discrepancies and cases of peculation were disclosed. It was learned that although the Colt Company was asked to supply 31,000 pistols at $25, the Remington firm, charging $15 for the identical weapon, could obtain an order for only five

---

[19] Morton's inscription on Owen to Morton, July 10, 1862, Indiana Archives.
[20] *War of the Rebellion: Official Records*, 3d ser., I, 927.

thousand. Or again, it was discovered that an honest manufacturer, despairing of success through his own efforts, paid a
middleman $10,000 to procure a contract for five thousand
guns. Nine days later he himself applied for an order of twice
that number, but it was refused on the grounds that the revolver
was not a desirable one for the service. A month afterward he
again resorted to the middleman and was given a commission
for another 5,000 pistols of the very kind just called undesir-
able.[21]

From the beginning the Ordnance Commission was a popular one. The necessity for it was recognized by men of both
parties, and the progress of its work was given favorable notice.
Even before the final report was submitted, the amount that
it would save the government was being estimated by the hundreds of thousands of dollars.[22] For the diminished number
of frauds committed against the United States in the later years
of the war, the findings of Holt and Owen were in a small way
responsible. Thanks to their efforts, to the more exhaustive
investigation of the Van Wyck Committee, and to the decision
of the War Department to abandon the state rights principles
of administration, the booty available to profiteering vultures
was greatly restricted.[23] For their assistance in bringing about
this desirable result both men deserve credit, though Holt's
claim, as chairman of the commission and author of its report,
is the greater.

For more than a year after the outbreak of the war Owen
was busy in the East as state agent and Ordnance Commissioner. From May 1861 until August 1862 he was absent from
conservative Indiana where both parties viewed with distaste
the liberation of the bondmen. During that time he enlarged

---

[21] "Report of the Commission on Ordnance and Ordnance Stores, Made to
the War Department," *Senate Executive Documents*, 37th Congress, 2nd
Session, VI, no. 72, 13–17.

[22] *N. Y. Tribune*, Mar. 14, 17, 19, 24, Apr. 21, June 2, 1862; *Philadelphia
Inquirer*, Mar. 15, 1862; *Indianapolis Journal*, Mar. 18, 1862; *N. Y. Herald*,
Mar. 18, 19, 1862; *N. Y. Times*, July 1, 11, 1862; *Evening Post*, July 14, 1862.

[23] Shannon, *op. cit.*, I, 73–75.

his acquaintances among abolitionists, kept in close touch with Morton, champion of an aggressive war policy, and had frequent contacts with Chase and other radical members of the cabinet. In such an environment the Hoosier gradually modified his attitude toward slavery as a practical problem. Not possessed of a strikingly original mind, Owen had ever been able to seize the ideas of others and by persistent study or by facility of expression disseminate them more effectively than their authors. Thus when, in the summer of 1862, he became a pamphleteer for emancipation, he was merely spreading the doctrines of men like Stanton and Chase but in a style and with a tenacity that they, or few others, could command.

Owen's coöperation with the future Peace Democrats in Indianapolis on February 22, 1861, was followed, except for his unnoticed New Harmony editorials, by eighteen months of silence. During that time his conversion to the War Democracy was undoubtedly under way, but unfortunately for the attainment of a life-long ambition that silence was still unbroken on February 5, 1862. For on that day, after a sensational three-week debate, his ancient foe, Jesse D. Bright, was expelled from the United States Senate, ostensibly for treasonous correspondence with Jefferson Davis but actually for his uncompromising Copperhead convictions. Owen and Morton were working together in Washington at the time, and several correspondents immediately mentioned the former as a likely successor to the vacant place. The governor, however, refused to make his choice before sampling opinion at home.[24] That decision blasted Owen's hopes, if any he had, for he possessed no reputation among Hoosier Republicans as a Union man. Thus, later in the month, the coveted seat was awarded to Joseph A. Wright, whose advancement, like Owen's, had previously been balked by the imperious Bright. Unlike Owen, the

[24] Murphy, "Political Career of Jesse D. Bright," Indiana Historical Society, *Publications*, X, 138–144; Holloway to Owen, Feb. 7, 1862, Owen to Holloway, Feb. 7, 1862, "Indiana: Governor, Telegrams," III. *N. Y. Tribune*, Jan. 22, Feb. 7, 1862; *Cincinnati Gazette*, Jan. 22, Feb. 12, 1862; *Cincinnati Commercial*, Feb. 5, 6, 1862.

ex-governor was not handicapped by the taint of spiritualism or by speeches against forcible resistance to secesssion. Nor had he hesitated to advocate from the stump the measures of the Republican administration.[25]

While Owen awaited a favorable opportunity for a public endorsement of the Lincoln regime, the slavery issue again came to the fore. The war, it will be remembered, had not been begun to free the Negro. The Crittenden Resolution of July 1861 disavowed any intention to interfere with the established institutions of the South. Later in the year both Frémont and Cameron were reprimanded for departing from that policy. In 1862, however, the pressure of the struggle caused a modification of this tolerance; and in June, after preliminary steps, the Republican goal was achieved when the territories were declared forever free. A month later the second Confiscation Act provided for the liberation, when in Federal hands, of all slaves of rebellious masters. Finally on July 22 the president discussed with his cabinet a proclamation for the general manumission of all bondmen still under Confederate control. On advice, he agreed to delay its issuance until the military situation improved.[26]

On the day following that momentous cabinet meeting, Owen sent to Stanton from New York a lengthy letter entitled "The Way Out." In this the author spoke briefly of his Democratic antecedents and his life-long hatred of slavery. Formerly he had believed that non-interference was the wisest course for such a Northerner to pursue, but the necessity for terminating the suicidal struggle had forced him to alter his opinion. The Indianan did not say that emancipation was the only means of ending the war; he did consider it the sole guarantee against its resumption. In the government's acknowledged power to take private property for public use while making just compensation Owen saw "the way out." Manumission, he warned,

---

[25] *Indianapolis Journal*, Feb. 25, 1862. Cf. *ibid.*, Sept. 9, 1861, Jan. 7, 1862; *N. Y. Tribune*, Aug. 8, 1861.

[26] J. G. Randall, *The Civil War and Reconstruction* (Boston, 1937), 477–489.

must come quickly. Each week saw the national treasure further depleted and the wherewithal to compensate loyal slaveholders wasted. Promptness was necessary, also, in order to forestall foreign intervention and to win world-wide sympathy as the champion of human liberty. The whole trend of the administration's policy on slavery made further action inescapable. "Stand where we are," he concluded,

we cannot; and to go on is less dangerous than to retrace our steps. . . . It is time that men were taking sides. . . . I think the people are ready. . . . I feel assured that final success awaits us in pursuing such a path, and I see no other road out of the darkness.[27]

This carefully prepared argument for general emancipation, however intended, could not be kept private for long. At the request of several New York Republicans it was printed in *The Evening Post* and thus became the first public exposition of Owen's War Democracy. Its reception was gratifying. In an editorial headed "A Strong Word in Season," Bryant's paper declared, "We have not published since the beginning of the war a more significant or persuasive document." Confidentially the poet said it was a "capital thing, and is making much impression." Greeley termed it the "Words of a True Democrat"; while an abolitionist commentator, in noticing the remarkable change in Owen's views, confessed, "We can't help thinking that the day of jubilee is at hand."[28] Stanton thought so highly of the letter that he sent it to Lincoln who "read it with a high appreciation of the breadth and justness of the views" therein. Chase was "delighted." He, too, reported that "the President has read your letter attentively & that it has impressed him profoundly." "God grant," the secretary added, "that his action be not long delayed."[29]

At home Owen's arguments were less favorably received.

[27] Owen to Stanton, July 23, 1862, *Evening Post*, Aug. 8, 1862.

[28] *Evening Post*, Aug. 8, 1862; Bryant to Owen, Aug. 12, 1862, Dreer Collection: American Poets, I; *N. Y. Tribune*, Aug. 11, 1862; *National Anti-Slavery Standard*, Aug. 11, 1862.

[29] P. H. Watson to Owen, July 31, 1862; Chase to Owen, Aug. 11, 1862, Dreer Collection: American Statesmen, VI; Presidents, III.

The Republicans called his ideas radical, while the Democrats were even more outspoken in their condemnation. In January they had formally resolved that any proposal to liberate and arm the Negro slave was "unconstitutional, insulting . . . a disgrace to the age, and . . . calculated to retard the suppression of the rebellion." Six months later they went on record against all forms of compensated emancipation. Thus it came to pass that Owen's epistle was not reprinted by the organ of his old party; and he whose praises had long been sung in its columns was now set down as a "theorist . . . not a statesman . . . not a practical man, so far as public policy is concerned." [30] Still harsher words were to be spoken in the next years.

Once committed to emancipation, Owen allowed nothing to dampen his ardor. A flying visit to Indiana in August revealed anew the conservatism of the Hoosiers, but the pamphleteer continued to urge his course upon the administration, always adding that the loyal masters in the Border States should be adequately recompensed. On the twenty-third of September, he declared to Chase, the sixty days of grace provided in the Confiscation Act would expire. "God grant our Chief magistrate the wisdom to see and the courage to act! . . . The people are athirst for decisive action. . . . The 23d of September is *the day*, — nay the eleventh hour." [31] But the inauspicious progress of the war stayed the president's hand. Early in September the Federals suffered their third defeat at Bull Run, and the audacious Lee swung his gray-clad columns into Maryland. Owen returned to the dejected capital on the sixth and hastily concluded his business for Morton before all egress was cut off. "I wish," he wrote to a friend, "I could send something encouraging. . . . But it is all as dark as can be." [32]

In the gloomy days before Antietam Owen was confined to his

---

[30] *Indianapolis Journal*, Aug. 11, 1862; *State Sentinel*, Jan. 9, July 31, Aug. 12, 1862.

[31] Owen to Chase, Aug. 20, 1862, Chase Papers. Cf. Owen to Morton, Aug. 11, 1862, Indiana Archives.

[32] Owen to Terrell, Sept. 7, 1862, Indiana Archives.

bed in New York. His mind and pen, however, remained active; and on the 12th he composed a second formal letter on the national situation, this time to Chase. Once again he called for emancipation in order to paralyze Southern man power. Once again he insisted that the exigencies of the struggle made the step necessary and constitutional. In an accompanying note Owen requested the secretary to place these arguments before the president, saying of the latter, "I think his heart is in the right place, but it needs awakening." [33]

On the seventeenth Lee's invasion was halted at Sharpsburg. That evening Bryant editorially besought the chief executive to act "While the Iron Is Hot." Under the same date Owen completed "The Twenty-third of September," the last in his trilogy on emancipation. Writing directly to Lincoln, he repeated as persuasively as he could all that he had said before on the subject. Now, however, he vaguely hinted that further delay would encourage a military cabal to reorganize the cabinet to suit its own wishes. "The twenty-third of September," Owen declared, "approaches." "It is within your power . . . not only to consummate an act of enlighted statesmanship, but as the instrument of the Almighty, to restore to freedom a race of men." "Extirpate," he implored, "the blighting curse . . . that has smitten at last with desolation a land to whom God has granted everything but wisdom." On September 19 Secretary Chase handed this missive to Lincoln. Three days later the Emancipation Proclamation was read to the cabinet.[34]

The opportune arrival of Owen's letter has caused some writers to exaggerate its importance. The Indianan was not the only one during those trying days who urged emancipation upon the president. As early as July 22, moreover, the chief executive had determined to liberate the slaves in rebel hands and awaited only a favorable opportunity to speak. That came

[33] Owen to Chase, Sept. 12, 15, 1862, Chase Papers. Cf. Owen to [Terrell?], Sept. 13, 1862, Indiana Archives.
[34] Owen to Lincoln, Sept. 17, 1862, N. Y. Tribune, Oct. 23, 1862; "Diary and Correspondence of Salmon P. Chase," American Historical Association, Report for 1902, II, 86.

after Antietam. Yet Owen's message is historically significant, if only because men at the time believed it had "a potent influence in producing the proclamation." One Negrophile went so far as to call it the origin of that act.[35] What Lincoln thought of Owen's words was not divulged, but Chase was certain that they could not fail to impress him. "You will hardly ever," he wrote, "accomplish a greater work than this letter. . . . [It] thrilled me like a bugle call; and when published . . . I hope it may be a trumpet of resurrection. . . ." Modestly Owen responded saying, if it had influence, "I shall think of it with as much pleasure as of any act of my life; and if it had not, I am glad it was not needed." [36]

Believing that Lincoln's proclamation must eventuate in general manumission, Owen continued to agitate for compensated emancipation in the Border States. First he revised his second formal letter, the one to Chase, and had it published as the "Conditions of a Lasting Peace." Then he issued through Lippincott's a forty-eight-page pamphlet containing all three epistles and entitled *The Policy of Emancipation*. In still another tract the following year he pointed out the importance of supplementing the president's action by Congressional legislation. The details of such a law he sketched in an elaborate article in *The Atlantic Monthly* for July 1863.[37]

With his work as pamphleteer for emancipation ends the first phase of Owen's Civil War activity. Through his writings he had earned the title of War Democrat. Once again Bryant could call him, as he had in the mid-forties, "one of our most distinguished statesmen"; and for the first time Greeley was

[35] *N. Y. Commercial Advertiser*, Sept. 27, 1862; *National Anti-Slavery Standard*, Oct. 4, 1862. See also *N. Y. Tribune*, Sept. 24, Oct. 23, 1862.
[36] Chase to Owen, Sept. 20, 1862, Dreer Collection: Presidents, III; Owen to Chase, Sept. 23, 1862, Chase Papers.
[37] Owen to Chase, Sept. 23, Oct. 22, 1862, Chase Papers; *Evening Post*, Nov. 22, 1862; *The Policy of Emancipation: In Three Letters to the Secretary of War, the President of the United States, and the Secretary of the Treasury* (Phila., 1863); *Emancipation Is Peace* (Loyal Publication Society, *Pamphlets*, no. 22 [N. Y., 1863]); "The Claims to Service or Labor," *Atlantic Monthly*, XII, 116–125.

really cordial. During the winter of 1862–1863, before entering upon the second and more radical phase, Owen was something of a political jack-of-all-trades. He lobbied in Congress for legislation favorable to Indiana. He served temporarily as assistant secretary of war and seemed slated for a permanent post. Chase used him as a mouthpiece.[38] All the while he continued to act as Morton's unofficial agent at large, and it was at the prompting of the Hoosier executive that he turned his attention and his pen to the bogey of a Northwestern conspiracy.

Owen's attitude toward the alleged plot to reconstruct the nation without the New England states was the supreme test of his War Democracy. That any large number of responsible Indiana Democrats in February 1863 advocated reunion with the Secessionists at the expense of their Northeastern allies is difficult to believe. Undoubtedly Davis and his command would have liked to detach the Hoosier state and its neighbors from the seaboard regions, and it cannot be denied that secret societies had already begun to flourish in the Old Northwest.[39] But the strong peace without victory sentiment that existed there hardly spelled treason, at this time at least; and Owen all too readily accepted the idea of a plot from those who had a political axe to grind. It was not until after he visited Indianapolis in December 1862, at which time Morton was battling unsuccessfully with an obstinate Democratic legislature, that Owen began to talk of traitorous intrigues. From then on his suspicions seemed to grow by leaps and bounds until finally he placed his pen at the governor's disposal and in March 1863 published a sixteen-page address to the citizens

---

[38] *Evening Post*, Nov. 22, 1862; *N. Y. Tribune*, Aug. 11, 1862; Owen to Morton, Oct. 22, 1862, Feb. 13, 1863, Indiana Archives; Owen to Holloway, Jan. 30, 1863, "Indiana: Governor, Telegrams," X; *N. Y. Times*, Feb. 2, 1863; Owen to Chase, Dec. 20, 1862, Chase Papers.

[39] James A. Woodburn, "Party Politics in Indiana during the Civil War," American Historical Association, *Report for 1902*, I, 223–251; Mayo Fesler, "Secret Political Societies in the North during the Civil War," *Indiana Magazine of History*, XIV, 183–286 (Sept. 1917); Henry C. Hubbart, *The Older Middle West, 1840–1880* (N. Y., 1936), 208–210.

of Indiana entitled, *The Future of the North-West: in Connection with the Scheme of Reconstruction without New England.*[40] This tract gave no evidence of treason in Indiana. In many ways it was more of a plea than an accusation. The author was too wise to glorify New England or defend emancipation before a Hoosier audience. Instead he concentrated his attack upon the South, painting a dark picture of its way of life and placing the war guilt at its door. An alliance with the Secessionists, he said, would be not a compromise but a confession of failure. It would give the rebels political control of the new Union. It would permit them to strike down the Negro exclusion clause in the Indiana constitution. It would ultimately lead to civil war in the Hoosier state.

Let there be no deception [he warned]. If we are to do this thing, let us look it honestly in the face. . . . Let Indiana . . . resolve to purchase Southern favor by Northern dismemberment . . . but let her know . . . that her road will lie over the bodies of her murdered sons, past prostrate cabins, past ruined farms. . . . Let her know that before she can link her fate to a system . . . doomed to ultimate extinction, there will be war within her own borders, to which all we have yet endured, will be but as the summer's gale . . . compared to the hurricane.[41]

Thanks to Parke Godwin and other influential Union leaders, Owen's essay was printed as the first pamphlet of the newly established Loyal Publication Society. Although pitched at a higher intellectual level than most of the succeeding numbers, it enjoyed an extensive circulation in the East, where its patriotic note won the author new friends among old foes.[42] But in

---

[40] Owen to Morton, Feb. 13, Mar. 3, 10, 1863, Indiana Archives; *Cincinnati Commercial*, Dec. 18, 1862; William D. Foulke, *Life of Oliver P. Morton* (Indps., 1899), I, 208–216. Cf. Owen to Chase, Oct. 22, 1862, Chase Papers.

[41] *The Future of the North-West: In Connection with the Scheme of Reconstruction without New England. Addressed to the People of Indiana* (Loyal Publication Society, *Pamphlets*, no. 1, N. Y., 1863), 14–15.

[42] Owen to Morton, Feb. 13, Mar. 3, 10, 1863, Indiana Archives; *N. Y. Tribune*, June 26, 1877; Frank Freidel, "The Loyal Publication Society: a Pro-Union Propaganda Agency," *Mississippi Valley Historical Review*, XXVI, 365 (Dec. 1939).

Indiana it attracted slight attention.[43] A few Republican papers reprinted it without comment; the Democrats ignored it. The latter had violently disagreed with Owen on emancipation; but since that was a matter of policy, they were willing to discuss its wisdom. Now, however, they saw the pen, so long devoted to their interests, placed at the service of one who had branded the whole party as disloyal. They felt, therefore, no obligation to answer the unsubstantiated outpourings of the man who, as they later said, was "everything by turns and nothing long — a mere parasite of power." [44] Thus it happened that just as freethinkers on both sides of the Atlantic considered Owen the Christian spiritualist as a traitor to liberalism so did his old political associates in Indiana regard as an apostate Owen the War Democrat.

[43] For a different interpretation, see Lockwood, *op. cit.*, 375.
[44] *State Sentinel*, July 3, 1865.

CHAPTER XXII

RADICAL REPUBLICAN

EMANCIPATION, as the moderates had warned, created as many problems as it removed. One of the most important of these during the remainder of the war was the treatment of freedmen under Federal control. On March 16, 1863, therefore, Stanton named Owen and two other strong Unionists

to investigate the condition of the colored population emancipated by acts of Congress and the President's proclamation . . . to report what measures will best contribute to their protection and improvement, so that they may defend and support themselves; and also how they can be most usefully employed in the service of the government for the suppression of the Rebellion.[1]

The appointment of this American Freedmen's Inquiry Commission, long demanded by the Negrophiles, comprising Owen, James McKaye, an original sponsor of the Loyal Publication Society, and Samuel Gridley Howe, humanitarian friend of the Boston abolitionists, to deal with a subject distasteful to most Indiana Republicans and all Hoosier Democrats, properly marked the beginning of the second and more radical phase of Owen's Civil War activity.

Highly pleased to hold again a remunerative public office, Owen entered upon his new duties with characteristic enthusiasm. Since Stanton had left the details to the commissioners, the chairman grandly planned to study the status of the liberated blacks not only in Virginia and the lower Mississippi Valley but also in the British West Indies. In April headquarters were set up in New York on Second Avenue and Ninth Street, a mile or so from the old Hall of Science. Much of the time, however, was spent elsewhere. In order to confer with Governor Andrew on the use of Negroes as soldiers Owen and

[1] *War of the Rebellion: Official Records*, 3d ser., III, 73.

Howe journeyed to Boston; afterwards they visited Fortress Monroe and northern Virginia to see for themselves the condition of the bondmen flocking into the Federal lines. In June McKaye traveled alone to Port Royal. Most of the summer, despite the Draft Riots which thoroughly alarmed Owen, was passed in New York, doing research on Negro history and sending out long questionnaires. The end of the year found the trio again on the road. Owen and Howe made a month's tour through Kentucky, Tennessee, and Missouri, taking testimony and consulting generals who were already caring for refugee blacks. In February McKaye inspected the situation in New Orleans and other near-by districts in Unionist hands. Shortage of funds troubled the last months of the commission; but although the West Indian tour had to be abandoned, the members managed to make ends meet until their labors were completed.[2]

The American Freedmen's Inquiry Commission submitted four reports that eventually found their way into print. Two by Howe and McKaye dealt with special topics and were not, to the chagrin of the authors, published by the government.[3] The other two, from the pen of Chairman Owen, were more general in nature. The first, dated June 30, 1863, depicted the character of the freedmen in the District of Columbia, eastern Virginia, the Carolinas, and Florida. It recommended that Negroes be employed as soldiers and military laborers and that Union generals systematically encourage slaves in adjacent

---

[2] American Freedmen's Inquiry Commission, Miscellaneous Papers, I, II. Owen and McKaye to Howe, Mar. 19, 1863, *ibid.* Boston *Commonwealth*, May 1, 1863; *N. Y. Tribune*, May 14, 1863; *N. Y. Times*, June 19, 1863; St. Louis *Missouri Democrat*, Dec. 3, 1863; *Indianapolis Journal*, Dec. 5, 1863; Owen to Howe, July 17, 1864, A. F. I. C. Papers, I; R. D. Owen to Richard Owen, July 14, 1863, Purdue Collection; Owen to B. F. Butler, Dec. 10, 1863 (copy), Ford Collection; Owen to Sumner, May 22, June 19, 1863, Jan. 16, 1864; McKaye to Sumner, Dec. 31, 1863, Jan. 20, Feb. 5, 1864, Sumner Papers, LXIV, LXVI, LXVII; R. D. Owen to Mary Owen, June 6, 1864, Stone Letters.

[3] S. G. Howe, *The Refugees from Slavery in Canada West* (Boston, 1864); James McKaye, *The Mastership and Its Fruits: The Emancipated Slave Face to Face with His Old Master* (N. Y., 1864).

regions to flee to Federal territory. Most important of all, there was set forth "a plan of provisional organization for the improvement, protection, and employment of refugee freedmen." This scheme envisaged the creation in the Southern seaboard states of three departments, each controlled by a superintendent of colonel's rank and each subdivided into smaller units containing about 5,000 liberated slaves. The entire system was to be governed by a Superintendent-General, chosen by the president from officers of brigadier grade. The purpose of this form of guardianship, admittedly temporary, was to enable the former bondmen to learn by working abandoned farms and plantations how to support themselves. They were, however, to have no connection with the regular army except when requisitioned for military service. The officers in charge, it was urged, should be selected for their philanthropic views as well as for their administrative ability, and at all times the coöperation of private charity workers was to be encouraged.[4]

Owen's final report of May 15, 1864, was broader and more philosophical in nature. It discussed at length the history of slavery in the Western Hemisphere, the wisdom of emancipation, and the future of the colored race in the United States. Involuntary servitude was portrayed as a political, social, and moral evil, responsible above any other single factor for the Civil War. Manumission was considered in its humanitarian and legal aspects. With regard to the future position of the freedmen in American society the author was optimistic. He did not say that the blacks would be accepted as social equals, but he did believe that the war had dissipated the popular notion that a Negro was by nature intellectually and morally inferior to the white. He hoped and he expected that the geniality, humility, and innate kindness of the African would temper the harshness of the American national character.

[4] "Preliminary Report Touching the Condition and Management of Emancipated Refugees, Made to the Secretary of War by the American Freedmen's Inquiry Commission," *Senate Executive Documents*, 38th Congress, 1st Session, no. 53, 2–24.

Finally, and most important, he felt that, once the freedman was armed with equal civil and political rights, he could stand on his own feet without being a burden to the government.[5]

The question of printing a document so glowing in its delineation of the ex-slave precipitated a stormy debate in the Senate. Already the preliminary report had appeared in the daily press, being greeted with approbation by the radicals and virulent denunciation by the Democrats.[6] In the upper house Charles Sumner, vociferously seconded by Ben Wade, championed a motion to publish 3,000 extra copies of the survey. "I have no hesitation in saying," he declared, "that it is one of the most able contributions to this question that has ever appeared in this country or in any other country." Thomas A. Hendricks, who thirteen years before had helped Owen write the Negro exclusion clause into the Indiana constitution, led the opposition. The chief arguments used were that the motion was unwarranted, the commission illegal, and the findings unauthoritative. One Senator took the position that nothing worthy of public attention could be written by the author of *Footfalls on the Boundary of Another World*. The Republicans eventually carried the day, but their rivals saw in the vote an intention to turn Owen's essay into a campaign document.[7]

Even before Sumner had triumphed in the Senate, Owen had decided to publish the report in book form under his own name. He was impelled to do this less from fear that his brain child would molder in the War Department archives than from a desire to present in a condensed volume, "which busy men may read in a few hours," the facts and law bearing upon a momentous national question.[8] As with *Hints on Public Archi-*

[5] "Final Report of the American Freedmen's Inquiry Commission to the Secretary of War," *Senate Executive Documents*, 38 Cong., 1 Sess., no. 53, 25–110.

[6] *Evening Post*, Aug. 5, 1863; *N. Y. Tribune*, Aug. 6, 1863; *National Anti-Slavery Standard*, Aug. 8, 1863; *Liberator*, Aug. 14, 1863. *N. Y. Herald*, Aug. 8, 15, 1863; *State Sentinel*, Aug. 13, 14, 1863.

[7] *Senate Journal*, 35 Cong., 1 Sess., 649–650; *Congressional Globe*, 35 Cong., 1 Sess., 3285–3287 (June 27, 1864). *Missouri Republican*, quoted in the *New Albany Ledger*, July 6, 1864.

[8] Robert Dale Owen, *The Wrong of Slavery* (Phila., 1864), 5.

tecture and his treatise on plank roads, Owen sought to diffuse in a popular work the fruits of his own investigations which, if not learned, possessed utilitarian value. The result, *The Wrong of Slavery, the Right of Emancipation, and the Future of the African Race in the United States*, was an attractive, well-indexed, two-hundred-page book, almost identical in content and wording with the final report. By Owen's new radical friends this publication was lavishly praised for its temperate tone, its comprehensiveness, and its timeliness. The extremists disliked the author's criticism of amalgamation, but some Republican editors believed that its dissemination would be "the cheapest as well as the most effectual mode of electioneering for the Union cause." [9] In what company the former Western Democrat now moved was evident in the commendatory letters he received from Lewis Tappan, pious antislavery target for Owen's agnostic shafts of years gone by, and Wendell Phillips. The latter enthusiastically thanked the ex-betrayer of freedom, saying, "Surely you may feel you have done knightly service in this whole war. Would your hand were nearer the helm of state." [10]

Interesting as Owen's report is as a guide to his changing thought, its historical significance is associated with the establishment of the Freedmen's Bureau. The idea of guardianship was not original with Owen, but the semi-official recommendations of his committee must have aided Representative Thomas D. Eliot and the various Freedmen's Aid Societies to achieve their goal of a formal superintendency. [11] In the ultimate estab-

[9] *National Anti-Slavery Standard*, Dec. 17, 1864. Cf. *Liberator*, Sept. 2, 1864; *N. Y. Tribune*, Sept. 3, 1864; *Independent*, Sept. 29, 1864; *Atlantic Monthly*, XIV, 518 (Oct. 1864).

[10] Phillips to Owen, Aug. 14, 1864; Tappan to Owen, Aug. 22, 1864, Dreer Collection: Philanthropists.

[11] Paul S. Peirce, *The Freedmen's Bureau: A Chapter in the History of Reconstruction* (University of Iowa, *Studies in Sociology, Economics, Politics and History*, III, no. 1, Iowa City, 1904), 3–74; *Autobiography of Oliver Otis Howard* (N. Y., 1907), II, 168–205; Bell I. Wiley, *Southern Negroes, 1861–1865* (*Yale Historical Publications, Miscellany*, XXXI, New Haven, 1938). See also Owen's suggestions concerning the Bureau in Owen to Sumner, Jan. 15, Mar. 24, 1864, Sumner Papers, LXVII.

lishment of the Bureau Owen had no direct part, but his name was mentioned among the candidates from whom the first head would be chosen. Thanks to John Wilkes Booth, the final selection was entrusted not to Lincoln but to an old Congressional foe, and early in May 1865 Andrew Johnson named General Oliver O. Howard, commander of the army in Tennessee. A few days before this news reached him, Owen learned at second hand that Lincoln had once informed Sumner of his intention to appoint the Hoosier to that position. There is a little evidence to substantiate that rumor, but it probably signifies nothing more than the Emancipator's high opinion of Owen. It had long been forecast that a military man would head the new Bureau, and the failure of certain appropriations made that step a necessity.[12]

During the final months of the war Owen dropped momentarily into the background. Although he performed occasional services for Morton, he ceased to hold office, national or state. Much of the time he spent in the West on private business. In September 1864 he did make one political speech, later circulated as a campaign tract by the Union State Central Committee of Indiana, in which he urged a vigorous prosecution of the war and frankly confessed the error of his own pacific policy of 1861.[13] The use made of that address suggests that for all intents and purposes Owen had become a Republican, a change that was no less real because it was made in silence. It remained, however, for his views on Reconstruction to reveal the true extent to which the War Democrat had given way to the Radical Republican.

In his numerous pamphlets Owen had asserted that universal emancipation was the only guarantee against a second civil war. He had written that opinion into his government

---

[9] *National Anti-Slavery Standard*, Dec. 17, 1864. Cf. *Liberator*, Sept. 2, 1865, Sumner Papers, LXXII; Owen to F. J. Dreer, May 24, 1865, Dreer Collection: Psychologists. *N. Y. Times*, Mar. 14, 1865; *N. Y. Tribune*, May 27, 1865.

[13] "Domestic Tranquility or Civil War," *Indianapolis Journal*, Sept. 13, 1864; *Evansville Journal*, Sept. 5, 7, 8, 1864.

reports and on three occasions had sketched the legislation that would carry the Manifesto of January 1 to its logical conclusion. He early took the stand that the Confederate states should not be readmitted to the Union until they had agreed never to reestablish slavery. To justify that position, he elaborated a "forfeited rights" doctrine, not unlike Sumner's "state suicide" theory, which during the autumn of 1863 he urged upon Lincoln in print and in person.[14] His ideas on Negro suffrage were particularly advanced, for there was a strong implication in both the final report on the refugee freedmen and in *The Wrong of Slavery* that the blacks should receive the franchise immediately. In an often overlooked public letter to Johnson on June 21, 1865, the Indianan went even farther. In a rather demagogic manner he protested against the increased representation that the South would enjoy in Congress as soon as the three-fifths ratio was abolished. He was unwilling that each voter in the late rebellious states possess thrice the political power of each elector among his recent conquerors and demanded that the organic law of North Carolina and her sisters be rejected if the ballot was withheld from the ex-slave. The following November, in a second public letter, Owen handled the same problem in a more balanced fashion. He proposed a constitutional amendment giving the federal government the power to determine the qualifications of all voters participating in presidential and Congressional elections, specifically requiring a literacy test and definitely prohibiting discrimination because of color. He would make its ratification a prerequisite to the readmission

[14] "The Claims to Service or Labor," *Atlantic Monthly*, XII, 123–124; *Wrong of Slavery*, 234–236; "A Bill to Emancipate Persons of African Descent, Held to Service or Labor in Certain of the United States" (MS.). *The Condition of Reconstruction; In a Letter from Robert Dale Owen to the Secretary of State* (Loyal Publication Society, *Pamphlets*, no. 25, N. Y., 1863); "The Legal Condition of the Insurgent States," *Evening Post*, Oct. 21, 1863; "The Pardoning Power: Historical Precedents," *N. Y. Tribune*, Dec. 18, 1863; "The Pardoning Power in Relation to Reconstruction" (MS.), Dreer Collection. See also F. B. Carpenter, *Six Months at the White House with Abraham Lincoln: The Story of a Picture* (N. Y., 1867), 98–101.

to Congress of delegates from the late Confederate states.[15] This second solution was not, as Owen insisted to both Johnson and the abolitionists, a compromise.[16] On the contrary it afforded additional evidence of the radical tenor of its author's thought. To be sure, the Hoosier was not one who would place the prostrate cotton kingdom under military rule. He had no particular desire to maintain any group of men in power, though he did sincerely believe that the unreconciled, unadjusted Southern Democrat could not be as intensely loyal as the Northern Republican. But on Negro suffrage he was ahead of his time. He insisted that the ballot be conferred upon the freedmen even if it had to be done under federal authority. Yet relatively few influential men in either party were willing to entrust the ex-slave with the franchise in any form, and therein lies the explanation for the vicissitudes of Owen's subsequent draft of the Fourteenth Amendment.

During the winter of 1865–1866 a bitter struggle, almost unparalled in our history, was waged between the president and Congress for control of Reconstruction policies. In this contest Owen took no part, but he did watch with increasing interest and anxiety the futile attempts of the legislature to devise some formula for restoring the rebellious states to the Union. When by mid-April at least three different proposals had failed to find favor and both Democrats and Republicans had begun to grow restive at Congressional inaction, the Indianan decided to try to formulate a constitutional amendment of his own.[17] The result, which he first showed to Morton

[15] "Final Report of the American Freedmen's Inquiry Commission," *loc. cit.*, 99, 110; *Wrong of Slavery*, 198–202; "Negro Suffrage and Representative Population," *N. Y. Tribune*, June 24, 1865; "The Constitutional Guaranty of a Republican Form of Government," *Evening Post*, Nov. 25, 1865.

[16] Owen to Johnson, Nov. 25, 1865, Johnson Papers, LXXXI; Owen to Garrison, Nov. 25, 1865, Garrison Papers; Owen to Sumner, Nov. 26, 1865, Sumner Papers, LXXV.

[17] Howard K. Beale, *The Critical Year. A Study of Andrew Johnson and Reconstruction* (N. Y., 1931), 51–112; Benjamin B. Kendrick, *The Journal of the Joint Committee of Fifteen on Reconstruction* (Columbia University, Studies in History, Economics, and Public Law, LXII, N. Y., 1914), 56–65,

about the middle of the month, repudiated the Confederate debt; gave the freedmen equal civil and, after July 4, 1876, equal political rights; and provided for omitting from the basis of representation all colored persons barred from the polls before that date by state action. An accompanying bill promised the repeal of all confiscatory laws, all disabilities, and the immediate restoration of the insurrectionary states to full power in Congress as soon as the amendment became part of the federal Constitution. The only men to be disqualified from the national legislature were those who had left positions of trust under the United States in 1860 and 1861 to join the rebellion. Thus did the versatile Hoosier, acting as a free lance, use his facile pen to gather into one clear formula most of the schemes previously advanced for liquidating the problems left by the Civil War.[18]

Encouraged by Morton's warm approval, Owen took his

198–201, 252–253, 292–295; Randall, *Civil War and Reconstruction*, 731–740; Owen to John A. Andrew, Apr. 5, 1866, Andrew Papers, XXXV.

[18] As entered upon the committee's journal (see Kendrick, *op. cit.*, 83–84), Owen's amendment read:

"Section 1. No discrimination shall be made by any state, nor by the United States, as to the civil rights of persons because of race, color, or previous condition of servitude.

"Section 2. From and after the fourth day of July, in the year one thousand eight hundred and seventy-six, no discrimination shall be made by any state, nor by the United States, as to the enjoyment by classes of persons of the right of suffrage, because of race, color, or previous condition of servitude.

"Section 3. Until the fourth day of July, one thousand eight hundred and seventy-six, no class of persons, as to the right of any of whom to suffrage discrimination shall be made by any state, because of race, color, or previous condition of servitude, shall be included in the basis of representation.

"Section 4. Debts incurred in aid of insurrection or of war against the Union, and claims of compensation for loss of involuntary service or labor, shall not be paid by any state nor by the United States.

"Section 5. Congress shall have power to enforce by appropriate legislation, the provisions of this article."

The accompanying bill, printed in Kendrick, should be supplemented by that given in Owen's account of the incident, "The Political Results of the Varioloid. A Leaf from History," *Atlantic Monthly*, XXXV, 660–670 (June 1875). Stevens failed to present the clause repealing the confiscatory laws. See also Horace E. Flack, *The Adoption of the Fourteenth Amendment* (Johns Hopkins University, *Studies in Historical and Political Science*, extra vol., XXVI, Balt., 1908), 70.

plan to Thaddeus Stevens, who promptly pronounced it the best he had yet seen. The Pennsylvanian was reluctant to postpone giving the ballot to the freedmen, but he admitted that neither house would accept immediate Negro suffrage. Personally he thought the accompanying bill too lenient but promised to submit both it and the amendment to the Joint Committee of Fifteen. Owen found the chairman of that body, William Pitt Fessenden, less enthusiastic but equally of the opinion that no better proposal had yet been presented. Most of his Republican colleagues also gave a more or less qualified approval, but the Democrats held back. Charles Sumner, not a member of the Fifteen, was strongly opposed to his friend's project, refusing to compromise with immediate suffrage even though he had no hope of success then or in the very near future. One conversation on the subject Owen, curiously enough, failed to recall. That was his interview with the president on the evening of April 17. It is not difficult to surmise that the two men found themselves in as complete a disagreement on the matter as they had on the Smithsonian Institution twenty years before.[19]

This private discussion of Owen's plan coincided with the growing public demand that Congress take some positive action. On Monday April 16, the day before the Indianan's conference at the White House, the Joint Committee assembled for the first time in six weeks. Nothing was accomplished; but at its next meeting, on Saturday the twenty-first, Stevens submitted a plan of Reconstruction, not of his own framing, but one which he would support. It was Owen's. No final decision was reached at that time; but except for the addition of a clause similar to the present one on "privileges and immunities," fathered by Representative Bingham, the original draft was approved without material change. Owen's accompanying bill met with little favor; but on April 25 the committee, after eliminating Bingham's provision, formally decided by a vote

[19] "Political Results from the Varioloid," *loc. cit.*, XXXV, 663–665; Owen to Johnson, Apr. 16, 1866, Johnson Papers, XCIII.

of seven to six to report the Hoosier's amendment to Congress.
As the members were about to disperse, a motion to reconsider
that vote was offered and finally agreed to, apparently so as
not to offend Chairman Fessenden, then confined to his room
with the varioloid. In the two-day interval before the next
session something happened, for on Saturday the 28th Owen's
draft was amended beyond all recognition. Bingham's broad
clause giving the federal government jurisdiction over civil
rights was restored, a new section on representation was introduced, and Owen's specific provision for Negro suffrage
after 1876 was omitted. This more conservative version was
presented to the legislature on the last day of April and after
further modification was sent to the states for ratification as
the Fourteenth Amendment.[20]

The reason for this sudden reversal was that Owen's scheme
was too radical. Such was the explanation given to its author
by Stevens, and his statement was amply confirmed in the
contemporary press. Even before its introduction in the committee, Owen's proposal, in all its essential details, was published in the Chicago Tribune. On April 23 the New York
World gave an equally complete description, terming it the
most radical project yet suggested. This notoriety made possible partisan criticism before the committee reached its final
decision. On April 25 the Democratic World editorially proclaimed "Robert Dale Owen's Plan of Reconstruction" as the
leading issue in the fall elections. The supposedly impartial
Herald indulged during four consecutive days in a campaign
of mockery and vituperation, in which Owen's career was
reviewed at length from his first fling as an ultra-reformer in
New York until the time he entered the war a spiritualist and
emerged "a radical with all the modern improvements and
more too." Bennett's writers did not hesitate to associate the
quondam opponent of the Wilmot Proviso with such men as

---

[20] Kendrick, op. cit., 78–83, 85–88, 90–92, 98–117, 304–319; "Political Results from the Varioloid," loc. cit., XXXV, 665–666; "A Bit of History,"
N. Y. Tribune, May 4, 1866.

Wendell Phillips, Frederick Douglass, and Ben Butler, nor to offer the following "Advertisement Extraordinary."

WANTED IMMEDIATELY — A *plan* for the reconstruction of the Union. The Congressional Reconstruction Committee have been in labor on the subject for many months and brought forward no fruits. Many old political midwives have been applied to without success. Some *plan* of reconstruction is now positively required, and a reward of *one hundred thousand dollars* . . . will be given for a suitable *plan*. Applications may be addressed to Charles Sumner, United States Senate Chamber; Ben Wade, anywhere in Radicaldom; Thad Stevens, House of Representatives; or Robert Dale Owen, of New Harmony.[21]

Publicity also gave conservative Republicans a chance to oppose Owen's scheme. On April 27 Bryant editorially deplored that Sumner and Stevens were in control, and even before that date Representatives from Indiana and Illinois were demanding a less radical program with which to go before the voters in 1866. The decisive blow, however, was struck by the New York caucus, meeting on the very night that the decision to report Owen's amendment was reconsidered. That influential body resolved that Congress should leave the suffrage question to the states and restrict its own plan of Reconstruction to an equitable basis of representation, a guarantee of the national debt, and the disqualification of Confederate leaders. These resolutions, published before the Fifteen met on April 28, practically forced the committee's hand. They sealed the fate of Owen's amendment.[22]

In 1875 Owen intimated that Fessenden's illness had changed the entire political development of the nation. The critical historian can hardly accept such a verdict but will discover the cause of the Indianan's disappointment in the advanced character of his views on Negro suffrage, a fact he seemed to

[21] *N. Y. Herald*, Apr. 25, 26, 27, 28, 1866; "Political Results from the Varioloid," *loc. cit.*, XXXV, 666; *Chicago Tribune*, Apr. 16, 17, 18, 1866; *World*, Apr. 23, 25, 1866.
[22] *Evening Post*, Apr. 26, 1866; *N. Y. Times*, Apr. 26, 27, 1866; Washington *Star*, Apr. 26, 1866; *N. Y. Tribune*, Apr. 28, 1866; *New Albany Ledger*, May 3, 1866 (Washington correspondent).

forget in later years. It is not true, as several authorities have asserted, that after the war Owen opposed giving the blacks the ballot at once. On the contrary, he clearly preferred to let the freedmen vote immediately but felt compelled to propose a prospective franchise as a compromise. Even then he sought to penalize those states which kept the ex-slaves from the polls before 1876.[23] All contemporary evidence points to the conclusion that the Hoosier's amendment was rejected because it was too radical for the hour. It was only a decade afterward that a different perspective made Owen's plan, advanced when first offered, seem conservative in comparison with the subsequent excesses of the Vindictives.[24]

Yet for more than one reason it is regrettable that Owen's version did not prevail. Prospective Negro suffrage was an essentially sound policy. Owen's phraseology avoided a recognition in our organic law of the past existence of slavery. It would have been more charitable to disfranchise the Confederate leaders, as he wished, in a separate bill rather than in the Constitution. It would have been wiser to avoid the ambiguous "due process" clause that has done so much to protect vested interests and to prevent, in the words of Justice Holmes, "the making of social experiments that an important part of the community desires in the insulated chambers afforded by the several States." [25]

The same winter that saw Owen drafting plans for a Fourteenth Amendment found him even more deeply engrossed in another post-war problem, the reestablishment of republican rule in Mexico. Ever since 1862 American public opinion had been outraged, first by Louis Napoleon's armed intervention to collect debts from the hapless Juarez regime and then by

[23] N. Y. Tribune, June 24, 1865; Evening Post, Nov. 25, 1865. Cf. Lockwood, New Harmony Movement, 376; Dictionary of American Biography, XIV, 120.

[24] N. Y. Herald, Apr. 29, 30, 1866; N. Y. World, Apr. 30, 1866; Indianapolis Journal, May 2, 1866; Indianapolis Herald, May 3, 1866; New Albany Ledger, May 3, 1866; N. Y. Tribune, May 4, 1866.

[25] Truax v. Corrigan, 257 U. S., 344.

his creation of an empire under Maximilian of Hapsburg. Some protest had been made both in Congress and in the press; but until secession was conquered the Lincoln administration felt powerless to act. In 1865, however, men of many types turned their eyes to the land of the Montezumas. Some hoped to reunite the Blue and the Gray by a joint invasion against the imperial pretender. Nationalists wished to vindicate the Monroe Doctrine; militarists, to win more glory. Alarmists warned that the last stand of the Confederacy would be made south of the Rio Grande. Less disinterested persons were ready to help Juarez regain power in return for valuable land, mining, and railroad concessions. Bryant, Chase, McKaye, Henry Winter Davis, to mention but a few of Owen's friends, were then concerned with Mexico's future; and it was not strange that he should become so too. What was surprising was the form that interest took.

In the autumn of 1865 Owen entered the employ of J. W. Tifft, a member of the New York banking house of John W. Corlies and Company. A few weeks before, that firm had contracted with General José M. J. Carvajal, representing Juarez, to sell $30,000,000 worth of bonds, the proceeds from which were to be used to purchase arms and ammunition for the republican armies. Carvajal had come to the United States with General Lew Wallace, and it was at the latter's suggestion that he hired another Indianan, Herman Sturm, to supervise the transfer of supplies to Mexico. Sturm, who had worked with Owen in establishing the arsenal at Indianapolis during the war, quickly perceived the necessity of obtaining the aid of influential men to sell the idea of a Mexican loan to the public. It was through Sturm that Owen first met Tifft. Owen's industry, integrity, active pen, and political connections seemed to make him an ideal man for the job Sturm had in mind.[26] His

---

[26] *Lew Wallace, An Autobiography* (N. Y., 1905), II, 843–846; Herman Sturm, *The Republic of Mexico and Its American Creditors* (Indps., 1869), 17–21; *Correspondencia de la Legacion Mexicana en Washington durante la Intervencion Extranjera, 1860–1868* (10 t., Mexico City, 1870–1879), X, 282, 312–313.

own reasons for accepting were chiefly financial; as early as 1864 the Hoosier was greatly concerned over pecuniary matters.[27]

In his new capacity Owen's efforts were directed along three main lines. First in point of time, he helped to publicize the bond issue that Corlies & Co. were trying to float. On November 2, 1865, he attended the gala opening of Tifft's Mexican Financial Agency at 57 Broadway, New York; and there, surrounded by swarthy diplomats and comic opera generals, he spoke briefly on the danger inherent in an empire to the south.[28] A few days later, in order to encourage hesitant investors, he went to Washington to secure in person from the president some assurance that Maximilian would never be recognized.[29] When all these stratagems failed to sell the bonds, Owen tried, among other things, to interest Jay Cooke in disposing of the loan. In January 1866, for a time, the Philadelphia banker seemed to look with favor upon the project; but as he hesitated, he received friendly advice from the secretary of the treasury to steer clear of the enterprise. As a result, the banker decided not to commit himself but to keep Tifft and Owen, those "Mexicans" as he called them, in "tow" for a while longer.[30]

The most important and the most onerous phase of Owen's activity was his attempt to wring from Congress a formal guarantee to repay bondholders of the $40,000,000 loan should the Mexican government fail to do so. In his efforts to lobby such a bill through the legislature the Hoosier had two more interviews with the president, wrote appealing letters to Charles Sumner, testified in person before the House Committee on Foreign Affairs, and sought to persuade ex-Governor Andrew of Massachusetts to act as counsel for Mexico. The Indianan's

[27] R. D. Owen to Mary Owen, Mar. 12, 1864, Stone Letters.

[28] *Correspondencia*, V, 749; *N. Y. Herald*, Nov. 3, 1865.

[29] *Correspondencia*, V, 811–812.

[30] Tifft to Cooke, Dec. 20, 23, 28, 1865, Jan. 6, 12, 1866; Jay Cooke to H. D. Cooke, Dec. 26, 1865, Feb. 2, 13, 1866; H. D. Cooke to Jay Cooke, Dec. 26, 1865, Feb. 9, 1866, Cooke Papers. See also Ellis P. Oberholtzer, *Jay Cooke, Financier of the Civil War* (Phila., 1907), II, 88–89.

ever ready pen sketched the legislation necessary to carry out the guarantee and composed a long memorandum, which he read to Johnson, in support of it.[31] During 1866 Owen wrote at least six anonymous pamphlets, published at Tifft's expense and designed to manufacture Congressional support for his proposal. In July under his own name he repeated in a long letter to the Washington *Chronicle* much of the material contained in these tracts, suggesting in addition that the United States should take, in return for the guarantee, a mortgage on Lower California and all Mexican territory north of a line drawn from Guaymas due east to the Rio Grande. Later in the month he answered, as "A Friend to Republican Mexico," Bryant's recent strictures on the loan scheme; in November, using the same pseudonym, he tried to refute the *Tribune's* statements on the unreliability of Mexican credit.[32]

In spite of many modifications to make the guarantee more palatable, Congress would have none of it. Even if Reconstruction had not been the all engrossing issue, there were other obstacles to success. Mexican credit in the United States had reached its nadir, and there was a genuine fear that this loan would benefit "a parcel of brokers and jobbers" rather than Juarez and his troops. The press was almost unanimous in its hostility; and even Bryant, who favored a bold assertion of

[31] *Correspondencia*, VII, 48–51, 218 (Jan. 17, Feb. 28, 1866); Owen to Sumner, Dec. 18, 1865, Dec. 20, 1866, Sumner Papers, LXXV, LXXX; *Correspondencia*, VII, 308; Owen to John A. Andrew, Mar. 9, 13, 16, 19, Apr. 5, 1866; Andrew to Owen, Mar. 26, 1866, Andrew Papers, XXXV, XXXVI, XLVI; *World*, Mar. 16, 1866; *Indianapolis Journal*, Mar. 17, 1866; *New Albany Ledger*, Mar. 17, 1866.

[32] [Robert Dale Owen], *Mexico. No. 1. Shall Our Government Act, or Refrain from Acting, in Mexican Affairs?* (n. p., n. d.); *Mexico. No. 2. Historical and Financial Items* (n. p., n. d.); *Mexico. No. 3. Biographical Sketch of the Constitutional President of the Republic of Mexico. Juarez: Who and What Is He?* (n. p., n. d.); *Mexico. No. 4. Oppressions and Cruelties Resulting from French Intervention in Mexico* (n. p., n. d.); *Mexico. No. 5. General Gonzalez Ortega and His Nine Endorsers versus the Mexican Republic and the Constitutional President of Its Unanimous Choice. With an Appendix Containing Accompanying Documents* (Wash., 1866); *Mexico. What Shall Our Policy Be?* (n. p., n. d.). *Morning Chronicle*, July 3, 1866; *Evening Post*, Aug. 7, 1866; *N. Y. Tribune*, Nov. 21, 1866. On Owen's authorship see *Correspondencia*, VII, 316–317, 730; VIII, 31, 166, 737; X, 313.

the Monroe Doctrine, rejoiced at the eventual defeat of the measure.[33] But the chief stumbling block, both during the spring of 1866 and at the end of the year when the scheme was broached again, was the opposition of such influential statesmen as Sumner, McCulloch, and above all, Seward. From the first, the secretary of state believed that Napoleon intended to withdraw his troops from below the Rio Grande, and he wanted no excuse to be given that would cause him to change his mind. Matias Romero, the shrewd Mexican minister, realized that fact and as early as March 1866 advised Tifft to abandon the idea of a guarantee. When Owen began to talk of the United States acquiring more Mexican soil, Romero was certain that the wrong approach was being used.[34] Thus the expiring contract with Corlies & Co. was not renewed at the end of 1866 and by the next spring Owen's connection with Tifft appears to have ceased. After the execution of Maximilian had placed Juarez and his cause under a cloud, little more was heard of Owen's interest in Mexican affairs; and this curious episode, perhaps the least commendable in a long career, was conveniently forgotten when the Indianan came to write his reminiscences.[35]

As a footnote to the Mexican bonds incident may be added Owen's tenuous connection with Jay Cooke's activities in the spring of 1866. At that time the Philadelphian was using every weapon of propaganda from his well-stocked armory to pass a refunding law with five per cent bonds tax exempt. On the same day Joseph Medill telegraphed his "scoop" of Owen's draft amendment to the *Chicago Tribune*, Henry Cooke suggested to his brother that they enlist the Hoosier's services in the fight for the exemption clause, saying, "He could, I think, work *effectively*. He is indefatigable, is known to be sincere

[33] Sturm, *op. cit.*, 21–22; *Evening Post*, July 30, 1866; James M. Callahan, *American Foreign Policy in Mexican Relations* (N. Y., 1932), 308–309.

[34] *Correspondencia*, V, 890, 894; VII, 40, 305; VIII, 132, 745–746; IX, 171–172.

[35] *Correspondencia*, VI, 885; IX, 171–172. See, however, Owen to Hiram Barney et al, Sept. 20, 1867, *Banquet to Señor Matias Romero . . . by the Citizens of New York, October 2nd, 1867* (N. Y., 1867), 18–20.

and disinterested in such matters, and has much influence with a certain class of politicians in Congress." This suggestion met with a qualified approval, but whatever help Owen may have given was insufficient to carry through the unpopular loan bill.[36] In these months Cooke aroused Owen's momentary interest also in an obscure "Industrial Credit," designed to reconstruct the South on a solid economic basis and to pave the road to reunion with silver and gold. That, too, eventuated in nothing.[37]

One cannot read deeply in the sources of the Civil War period without being struck, not by Owen's importance, but by his prominence. In an official capacity he served on two federal commissions, and for his state he acted as the governor's itinerant assistant. As a publicist he penned a half-dozen war pamphlets each of which enjoyed a circulation estimated at from one to two million copies, "almost unexampled in the case of a private individual." [38] During Reconstruction he wrote several provocative open letters which, together with his plan for the Fourteenth Amendment, attracted considerable attention. As a littérateur he finished one book and contributed six articles to The Atlantic Monthly on Hofwyl, spiritualism, and the war. When it was announced in May 1865 that he would write an intimate biography of Lincoln, he was called the man best fitted for the task.[39] Minor matters also claimed his time, such as assisting the Port Royal mission or organizing the Woman's National Loyal League.[40] Some of this work was useful, some of it may have been influential; all of it was well

---

[36] H. D. Cooke to Jay Cooke, Apr. 14, 1866, Jay Cooke to H. D. Cooke, Apr. 16, 19, 1866, Cooke Papers; Henrietta M. Larson, Jay Cooke, Private Banker (Harvard Studies in Business History, II, Cambridge, 1936), 213.

[37] Jay Cooke to H. D. Cooke, Apr. 23, 1866; H. D. Cooke to Jay Cooke, Apr. 28, 30, 1866; S. P. Andrews to Jay Cooke, May 5, 1866, Cooke Papers. See also Oberholtzer, op. cit., II, 23–24.

[38] E. A. and G. L. Duyckinck, The Cyclopaedia of American Literature from the Earliest Period to the Present Day (Edited to date by M. L. Simons, Phila., 1875), II, 847.

[39] Boston Transcript, May 27, 1865.

[40] Liberator, Nov. 21, 1862. N. Y. Tribune, June 29, 1863; Owen to Sumner, Sept. 28, 1863, Sumner Papers, CXXV; History of Woman Suffrage, II, 50, 81.

known. In many ways Owen had become as prominent on the national political scene as when he represented the First District of Indiana. If he now accomplished less, it was because he stood alone, a free lance as it were. It was because when he spoke or wrote, he was speaking or writing for Robert Dale Owen and not for any party, section, or electorate.[41]

But the Owen of the sixties was not the Owen of the forties. He had passed the meridian of his life. Agnosticism had yielded to faith. The "betrayer of freedom" had become the champion of the Negro. The fiery ordeal of secession had tempered a state rights philosophy with a stronger nationalism. Most complete of all was the break with former associates in Indiana. To a six-year absence abroad was now added an extended residence in the East. No longer did Owen visit the state university. No longer did he initiate improvements in New Harmony. No longer did he assemble with party conventions at Indianapolis. He ceased to find friends among the Lanes, Chapmans, or Pettits. Those who had once called him the purest man in the state now made sport of his alleged free love principles and dared him to preach Negro suffrage in the commonwealth from which he had helped exclude the colored race. The same editor who had described him a decade before as laborious and practical now dismissed him as an incurable visionary and constant failure.[42] To such strictures Owen paid scant heed; he had found new friends and a new purpose in living. He now mingled with a Chase, a Sumner, a Bryant, or an Edmonds. By them he was esteemed for his sterling patriotism, his able pen, his charming company, and his unquestioning belief in a future existence. If Owen the Western Democrat had lost repute among Hoosier politicians, Owen the intellectual had gained it among Eastern literary people and Christian spiritualists. With each of these last two classes he was to spend the remaining decade of his life.

[41] Cf. *N. Y. Times*, May 22, 1866.
[42] Cf. *New Albany Democrat*, Oct. 5, 1848, *New Albany Ledger*, May 30, 1853, with *New Albany Ledger*, Dec. 24, 1863, June 29, 1864, July 5, 1865.

CHAPTER XXIII

THE DEBATABLE LAND

RENEWED participation in national affairs had not destroyed Owen's deep faith in a future life. Even during the stirring days of civil strife he continued to pioneer in the debatable land. Interspersed with his writings on secession, emancipation, and Negro suffrage were articles on the ultramundane. Political opponents ridiculed this new belief as they had once scored his unbelief; but the white-haired, genial, and garrulous sexagenarian was more immune to personal criticism than the Western Democrat of the thirties. After the final termination of his public career early in 1867 Owen found an outlet for his boundless energy in the study and propagation of his new religion. Humanitarian crusades might attract his attention for a time and economic needs might force him into literary ventures, but the predominant interest of his last decade was spiritualism.

Spiritualism had not enjoyed an uninterrupted growth during the war. Like other reform movements it had been dealt a body blow by the internecine struggle. The efforts of its leaders were diverted to other channels, regular meetings were sparsely attended, and the rising cost of paper discouraged new publications.[1] Yet the arbitrament of the sword was not an unmitigated evil. By making death a stark reality to this generation, it sowed the seeds of a vigorous spiritualistic renascence. Scarcely a home in the land failed to suffer some bereavement, and thousands sought solace in communication with the departed loved ones.

This post-bellum revival was abundantly attested. A mass meeting at Chicago in August 1864 initiated an unbroken series of annual conventions and led four years later to the formation

---

[1] Emma Hardinge, *Modern American Spiritualism* (3d edn., N. Y., 1870), 490–507; *Banner of Light*, Jan. 3, 1863.

of the American Association of Spiritualists. Paralleling this national organization were state societies, found by 1871 in twenty-two commonwealths. By that date fourteen new periodicals devoted solely to ultramundane phenomena had been begun since Appomattox, while seven others included spiritualism among their major interests. The widespread establishment of Children's Progressive Lyceums revealed a growing concern for the proper training of the young.[2] So impressive had the movement become by the late sixties that both foreign travelers and such distinguished spiritualists as Judge Edmonds were estimating the number of adherents in the tens of millions. As a matter of fact, there were probably not over 600,000 Americans, if that many, who attributed certain physical manifestations to the agency of the spirits of the deceased.[3]

Despite the enthusiasm of its followers, spiritualism in 1867 had not yet become respectable. It was still an object of ridicule for the average man and anathema to the sectarian. It was still largely associated in the public mind with socialism, atheism, and free love. None were more critical than the scientists; and the same spirit that had humiliated the venerable Hare in 1856 reappeared in Huxley's statement that "the only good that I can see in . . . 'Spiritualism,' is to furnish an additional argument against suicide. Better live a crossing-sweeper than die and be made to talk twaddle by a 'medium' hired at a guinea a *séance*." [4]

In the advance of this movement Owen played an important

[2] *Banner of Light*, 1865–1871, *Religio-Philosophical Journal*, 1865, 1867–1871, *passim*; *The Year-Book of Spiritualism for 1871* (H. Tuttle and J. M. Peebles, eds., Boston, 1871); Epes Sargent, "Spiritualism," *American Cyclopaedia* (N. Y., 1873–1876), XV, 275–278.

[3] *Spiritual Magazine*, 2d ser., IV (1869), 126–127; Edmonds to the editor, May 4, 1867, *ibid.*, II (1867), 327–333; *Year-Book of Spiritualism for 1871*, 94–97; *Banner of Light*, Mar. 7, 1874. Cf. contra, *Spiritual Scientist*, Mar. 4, 1875; *Spiritual Magazine*, 2d ser., II (1867), 158–160; *ibid.*, VII (1871), 565–566; *Index*, Feb. 10, 1872; *Eleventh Census, 1890. XVI. Report of Statistics of the Churches*, 767–777; George Lawton, *The Drama of Life after Death* (*American Religion Series*, VI, N. Y., 1932), 156. Following Lawton's method, I have multiplied the number of spiritualist church-goers by fifteen.

[4] *Report on Spiritualism of the Committee of the London Dialectical Society* (London, 1871), 229–230.

yet circumscribed role. A comparatively late convert, he was not known widely among spiritualists until the publication of *Footfalls*. That volume immediately placed him among the outstanding spokesmen of the cause. Secession interrupted his study of the unseen, and late in 1861 he publicly admitted that his mind was more occupied with mundane than ultramundane matters. To the regret of his English followers, Owen's second volume was indefinitely postponed. In 1864 he published in *The Atlantic Monthly* several narratives too long for inclusion in *Footfalls*; but it was not until some time afterwards that there appeared in print his investigations of rappings, spirit writing, materializations, and other evoked phenomena to which public interest was turning.[5]

Owen remained aloof from organized spiritualism. He never attended national conventions and was present but once, and then for a specific purpose, at a state gathering. He seldom contributed to the spiritualist press and declined to use his unquestioned journalistic talent to improve its tone. Although after 1867 he spoke frequently on his favorite topic to private groups and lyceum audiences, he did not rival Warren Chase, Andrew J. Davis, or other frequenters of the spiritualist rostrum. Yet this reserve stemmed only in part from his life-long hostility to associational activity. There was much in the movement that he found distasteful. Its literature wanted culture and exactness, and the lax check made of the morality of mediums encouraged cheats and charlatans to hover like vultures on the fringes of the new faith. Professional believers he especially disliked. "Money changers," he declared, "are out of place in the spiritual temple. Man's destiny is to earn his bread by industry, not by divination."[6]

---

[5] *Philadelphia Inquirer*, Dec. 12, 1861; *Herald of Progress*, July 13, 1861; *Spiritual Magazine*, III (1862), 74. "The Convulsionists of St. Medard," *Atlantic Monthly*, XIII, 209-222, 339-352 (Feb., Mar. 1864); "The Electric Girl of La Perrière," *ibid.*, XIV, 284-292 (Sept. 1864); "Why the Putkammer Castle Was Destroyed," *ibid.*, XVI, 513-519 (Nov. 1865).

[6] *The Debatable Land*, 239. See also "Samples of Evidence for Spiritual Phenomena," *Spiritual Magazine*, 2d ser., V, 77 (Feb. 1870).

The key to Owen's attitude is to be found in the tendency of spiritualists to mix in other radical causes. No true believer, it was often asserted, could ignore other humanitarian movements; for it was the mission of the spirits to pulverize all creeds and to synthesize all reforms.[7] Thus between 1864 and 1871 national conventions endorsed such matters as Negro and woman suffrage, Indian, prison and dress reform, world peace, temperance, and industrial education. In their denunciation of Sabbatarianism, the use of the Bible in state institutions, and the agitation to put God in the Constitution the spiritualists rivalled extreme freethinkers. To one who was striving to make the belief a respectable, bourgeois Christian religion such resolutions seemed both extraneous and unwise. The election in 1871 to the presidency of the American Association of Spiritualists of Victoria Claflin Woodhull, the most ignorant, notorious, and radical feminist of the day, one who had until then manifested no interest in spiritualism and who did not even know the correct name of the organization that thus honored her, seemed to Owen the logical result of the trend he was combatting. To the new executive's declaration that what slavery had been to the abolitionist, the woman question would henceforth be to the spiritualist, the Indianan entered a vigorous public dissent.[8] In a carefully prepared address, delivered at Terre Haute on the twenty-fourth anniversary of the Hydesville rappings, he drew a sharp distinction between spiritualism as a religion and spiritualism as a reform. He upheld in unmistakable terms the Christian aspect of his new faith and denied the right of self-constituted conventions to speak for all believers. He specifically warned them against meddling in other humanitarian movements.[9] At least two

---

[7] *Religio-Philosophical Journal*, July 14, 1866; *Herald of Progress*, Feb. 4, 1860; *Progressive Annual for 1862* (N. Y., 1862), 31.

[8] *Woodhull and Claflin's Weekly*, Nov. 4, 1871. On Miss Woodhull's "New Departure" see her magazine; *The American Spiritualist; Banner of Light; Religio-Philosophical Journal*, 1871–1873, *passim*; Frank L. Mott, *History of American Magazines, 1865–1885* (Cambridge, 1938), 443–453.

[9] *Religio-Philosophical Journal*, Apr. 20, 1872.

atheistic spiritualists criticized Owen's blast, but its general tenor was approved by the outstanding editors and leaders of the cause.[10]

Owen's emphasis on the religious significance of the ultra-mundane did not blind him to the manifold evils of the Gilded Age. He was quite willing, in fact he strongly urged, that spiritualists in their individual capacity take part in reform movements.[11] By his speeches as vice-president of the Free Religious Association and his coöperation with the National Liberal League he struck a timely blow at the forces of sectarianism and intolerance. He frequently deplored the decline in civic morals, and he advised a literary test for every governmental office. He expressed a willingness to aid Greeley in his fight for more enlightened penological methods and later wrote a description of the Irish prison system, a topic he also touched upon in his novel *Beyond the Breakers*. From the lyceum platform he preached the virtues of universal peace, and in the temperance crusade he manifested an increasing interest.[12]

The inaccurate legend of Owen's legislative achievements in Indiana assured him a place in the woman's rights movement. In February 1860 he was invited to speak with Henry Ward Beecher and Lucy Stone in Cooper Institute at a meeting designed to forward a memorial praying for increased feminine rights of franchise and citizenship in the Empire State.[13] A month later Horace Greeley's careless allegation that Owen and John Pettit were responsible for the lax divorce law that

---

[10] *Medium and Daybreak*, May 10, 1872; *Present Age*, May 11, 1872. *Banner of Light*, Apr. 27, 1872; J. W. Edmonds to S. S. Jones, *ibid.*, May 18, 1872; A. J. Davis to Owen, Apr. 14, 1872; J. M. Peebles, to Owen, May 9, 1872, Dreer Collection: Psychologists. Cf. *Religio-Philosophical Journal*, Apr. 13, 20, 1872.

[11] *Religio-Philosophical Journal*, Apr. 20, 1872.

[12] *Report of Addresses at a Meeting Held in Boston, May 30, 1867, to Consider the Condition, Wants, and Prospects of Free Religion in America* (Boston, [1867]), 16–28; Free Religious Association, *Proceedings at the Sixth Annual Meeting . . . 1873* (Boston, 1873), 51–57; *Index*, July 13, 1876. *Boston Daily Advertiser*, Feb. 11, 1869. Owen to Greeley, Aug. 7, 1867, Ford Collection; *Indianapolis News*, June 26, 1877. Owen to Dreer, Dec. 20, 1867, Gratz Collection; *Debatable Land*, 110 n.

[13] *N. Y. Tribune*, Jan. 30, 31, 1860; *Evening Post*, Feb. 1, 1860; *N. Y. Herald*, Feb. 4, 1860.

was making Indiana "the paradise of free lovers" precipitated a long and, on the whole, a good-tempered journalistic debate between the Hoosier and the *Tribune* editor in which the former reiterated opinions first voiced thirty years before.[14] During the war Owen helped Susan B. Anthony and others form the Woman's National Loyal League and at its close was chosen an officer of the new Equal Rights Association. For a year he served as vice-president of the Indiana Woman's Suffrage Association; and in 1871 he was presented to the annual meeting of one of the national organizations as the first man to introduce legislation conferring civil equality upon wives, a title, of course, wholly unmerited.[15] But in feminism, as with other postwar reforms, Owen's interest was transitory. His attitude was that of a liberal intellectual rather than that of a determined reformer. Spiritualism alone was an all engrossing subject.

That spiritualism should pervade Owen's family life was not surprising. Richard the scientist politely ignored his brother's theories on the ultramundane; but his nephews and niece, who had resided abroad in their impressionable years, believed in communications from the dead as long as their father lived.[16] Mrs. Owen also shared her husband's views. What that faith meant to the couple was evidenced in 1871 when Mary's sudden death obliged her more aged spouse to perform a service he had expected her to fulfill for him. In accordance with their joint wishes no mournful bell tolled as the funeral procession wended its way under the warm August sun from the village to the Maple Hill Cemetery. Cheerful music was sung at the grave to dispel sadness. Then, without a tremor in his voice, the widower stepped forward to speak informally of his wife's religion.

[14] *N. Y. Tribune*, Mar. 1, 5, 6, 12, 17, 28, Apr. 7, 21, May 1, 1860; Horace Greeley, *Recollections of a Busy Life* (N. Y., 1868), xi, 571–617; "An Earnest Sowing of Wild Oats," *Atlantic Monthly*, XXXIV, 76 (July 1874).

[15] *N. Y. Tribune*, May 15, June 29, 1863, May 17, 1864; *History of Woman Suffrage*, II, 50, 81. "Preamble and Constitution of the Woman's Suffrage [Rights from 1851–1869] Association of Indiana" (MS.); *Press*, Nov. 22, 23, 1871.

[16] Information from Miss Eleanor R. Cooper of New Harmony.

I do not believe [he said] and here I speak also for her whose departure from among us we mourn to-day — I do not believe more firmly in these trees that spread their shade over us, in this hill on which we stand, in those sepulchral monuments which we see around us here — than I do that human life, once granted, perishes never more. A death-change there is, often terrible to witness, leaving us behind desolate and forsaken for a few years on earth, but no death. . . . She believed, as I believe, that one life succeeds the other without interval. . . . Neither of us could believe in the old idea

> That man when laid in the lonesome grave
> Shall sleep in death's dark gloom,
> Till th' eternal morning wake
> The slumbers of the tomb.

Such is not Christ's doctrine. "To-day," he said to the repentant thief on the cross, "to-day shalt thou be with me in paradise." Again I believe, as she did, in the meeting and recognition of friends in Heaven. . . . I agreed with her also in the belief that there are in Heaven duties, avocations, enjoyments even, as various as are those of Earth; but far higher and nobler, in scope and purpose. Finally I believe, as she believed . . . in guardian care by the inhabitants of Heaven, exercised towards those of earth. As to the virtues and the good deeds of her who has left us, if nearly forty years' life and conversation in our village suffice not in witness, any word from me would be worse than worthless. Better to imitate her example than to speak her praise. Well has a great poet and thinker reminded us:

"He mourns the dead who lives as they desire." [17]

Mary's decease caused no profound change in Owen's life. Perhaps he tended to spend more time in the East than before, but such had been his growing custom since his return from Naples. Adequate expression of his feelings has not been preserved, but he appears to have busied himself in work already planned, quietly confident that he would soon meet all those dear to him in a higher sphere of existence. The year after August 1871 was, in fact, one of the most active since his retirement from public affairs. In October he completed the manuscript of his second volume on pneumatology. The winter was spent in New York correcting proof and doing other literary

[17] *New Harmony Register*, Aug. 19, 1871.

jobs. In March he uttered his warning at Terre Haute against the radical tendencies of spiritualism. In May he presided at the Indiana state society's convention and interested himself in defending the will of Robert Barnes against the challenge of the Evansville orthodox churches. During Commencement Week he was awarded *in absentia* the honorary degree of doctor of laws by an object of his former affection, Indiana University. Mid-June found him in Moravia, New York, investigating the remarkable spirit forms obtained through the mediumship of Mrs. Mary Andrews. He summered at Lake George, where he met the lady who was to become his second wife, and by autumn he had settled down in Boston to write his autobiography for *The Atlantic Monthly*.[18]

Early in December 1871 there appeared simultaneously in New York and London the long delayed sequel to *Footfalls*. *The Debatable Land between This World and the Next* represented ten years of more or less constant psychical research and should properly be regarded as the outstanding writing of Owen's late years. It can be argued, to be sure, that age had dulled the author's critical faculties and that approaching death made him eager to trust the manifestations he had witnessed. It is true that the New York reformer would have scoffed at the work and that the Indiana Democrat would have avoided so controversial a subject. But Owen the intellectual frankly acknowledged his past ignorance and offered to guide those who were still threading their way through the bog of materialism. To contemporary religion, then experiencing the threefold assault of Darwinism, Biblical criticism, and the comparative study of all faiths, he devoted much attention.[19] That fact alone made the new book more significant than the collection of inexplicable narratives on hauntings, hallucinations, and clairvoyance published in 1860.

[18] *Religio-Philosophical Journal*, Apr. 20, June 22, 29, 1872; *Annual Report of Indiana University . . . 1872–1873*, 71; Owen to Mrs. [Anna H.] Leonowens, Aug. 9, Sept. 7, 1872, Ford Collection.

[19] Arthur M. Schlesinger, *The Rise of the City, 1878–1898* (*A History of American Life*, A. M. Schlesinger and D. R. Fox, eds., X, N. Y., 1933), 322–326.

Like its predecessor, *The Debatable Land* was a stout volume of more than five hundred pages, well indexed and documented, and issued on both sides of the Atlantic by reputable publishing houses. Almost a third of its contents consisted of a prefatory address to the Protestant clergy, discussing the ecclesiastical attitude toward miracles, infallibility, and the discoveries of modern science. Professing great alarm at the relative decline of Protestantism before the onrush of a revived Catholicism and a militant secularism, the former editor of *The Free Enquirer* offered spiritualsim as a necessary adjunct to orthodox faiths. Its epiphanies he regarded as identical in kind with the marvels that had astonished the disciples and biographers of Jesus. They afforded palpable proof of immortality, the greatest religious need of the nineteenth century. Undoubtedly the author believed that he was spiritualizing Christianity, but the tendency of his argument was to Christianize spiritualism. Quite bluntly he declared,

Spiritualism is the complement of Christianity. Spiritual phenomena are the witnesses of Christianity. All thoughtful believers will be Christians as soon as they learn to distinguish between the simple grandeur of Christ's teachings, . . . and the Augustinian version of St. Paul's theology.[20]

An ally of Christianity, not a substitute, was Owen's faith. The Indianan wanted no formal spiritualist creed, no separate spiritualist church. He hoped that its doctrines would soften the asperities of existing sects and afford consolation to the aged. As always, Owen rejected the idea of innate depravity, the divine inspiration of the Bible, and the orthodox explanation of miracles. The world, he now thought, was ruled by a loving God; and Christ was elevated by him above Socrates as the greatest teacher known to man. The basic propositions which all spiritualists accepted he listed under fourteen heads. One existence, these declared, followed immediately upon the other, and the life stage was essentially one of preparation.

[20] *Debatable Land*, 235. *Ibid.*, 154–181.

Man's initial state in each sphere was determined not by predestination but by his record in the preceding one. The individual retained his original personality during this progress and found himself under the same natural laws that governed mundane affairs. Some communication between the living and the deceased, these propositions continued, undoubtedly existed. At worst it might provide idle gossip and even falsehoods. At best it supplied valuable guides for conduct in this world and tangible evidence of a life to come.[21]

The larger part of Owen's book was devoted to physical manifestations. He approached the question of table-tipping and materialization with the feeling of Sir John Herschel, who had once written, "Occurrences which, according to received opinions, ought not to happen, are the facts which serve as clues to new discoveries." [22] In thus discussing phenomena evoked by mediums, paid and unpaid, rather than those taking place spontaneously, the author went far beyond his earlier work. His findings were more sensational and controversial and, being based partly upon his own experience, more personal. Throughout, however, the writer sought to maintain the scientific attitude, even going so far as to criticize the evolutionary hypothesis.[23] But although in this new volume, as in the old, Owen insisted that witnesses place their testimony in writing, many accounts were recorded at second or third hand in a manner unacceptable to modern students of psychical research. The author's own crude method of investigation is revealed in the following excerpt which, however, profoundly impressed English spiritualists:

It was on the evening of Sunday, the twenty-first of October, 1860. The sitting was held in Mr. Underhill's dining-room, lasting from ten till eleven o'clock P. M.

The room was lighted by gas. There were two windows fronting the street; three doors. . . . Before we had any demonstrations the raps requested us to wait until the domestics had retired. There

---

[21] *Debatable Land*, 171–176.
[22] *Ibid.*, iii.   [23] *Ibid.*, 260–263.

were two servant girls in the kitchen, whom Mrs. Underhill sent upstairs to bed. . . .

Before commencing the session, at Mr. Underhill's request, I shut and locked the three doors above referred to, leaving the keys in the doors; so that no one, even if furnished with keys, could open them from without. I satisfied myself, by careful personal inspection . . . that there was no one in the pantry, nor any one in the dining-room except the three persons who, along with myself, assisted at the sitting.

These persons were Mr. Daniel Underhill, Mrs. Underhill (Leah Fox), and her nephew, Charles, twelve years old. We sat down to a centre-table. . . . (I had previously looked under it; nothing to be seen there.) . . .

The rappings commenced, gradually increasing in number and force. After a short interval they spelled: "Put out the gas." It was accordingly extinguished and the room remained in total darkness. Then, "Join hands." Shortly after doing so I felt several times, a cool breeze blowing on my cheek. Then was spelled: "Do not break the circle." We obeyed; and, except for a second or two at a time, it remained, on my part unbroken throughout the rest of the sitting.

After a few minutes I perceived a light, apparently of a phos-phorescent character, on my left, near the floor. . . . For a time it moved about . . . then it rose into the air and floated . . . over our heads.

After a time it changed its appearance. . . . It then resembled an opaque oval substance, about the size of a child's head, muffled up in the folds of some very white and shining material. . . . As it moved about, I began to hear . . . the rustling as of a silk dress, or of other light article of female apparel. . . . Then the light passed behind Mrs. Underhill; then I saw it close to Mr. Underhill and just oppo-site me. Mr. Underhill said: "Can you not go to Mr. Owen; do try." Thereupon it moved slowly around to my left side. This time the folds appeared to have dropped; and what seemed a face . . . came bending down within five or six inches of my own. . . . As it ap-proached, I plainly distinguished the semi-luminous outline of an entire figure of the usual female stature. . . . I could distinguish no features: nor were the outlines of the body . . . sharply defined.

While this was taking place I held Mrs. Underhill's hand and Charles's. As the various phases of the phenomena succeeded each other, I remarked on what I saw; and Mr. Underhill, from the opposite side of the table, responded to my remarks; so that I am quite certain he was seated there.

I expressed a wish that the figure would touch me; and Mr. Underhill said, from his place: "We are very anxious that the spirit should touch Mr. Owen, if it can."

Thereupon I felt what seemed a human hand laid on my head. And, as I looked steadily at the figure, which stood on my left side, I saw its head. . . . A moment afterward I *felt*, and simultaneously *heard*, just behind the point of that shoulder, a kiss imprinted.

I could not, for any physical fact, obtain the evidence of three senses — sight, touch, and hearing — more distinctly than in this case I did.

*   *   *   *

Suddenly we heard a noise as of the door opposite to me being unlocked; then of its being hastily opened and shut; then the rustling sound approached me on the left, and a key was laid on my left hand. Then a second door was heard to be unlocked in the same way, and I heard another key laid on the table just before me. Then a third door. . . .

While we were conversing, there was a rattling of the crockery in the cupboard. Mrs. Underhill expressed her apprehensions as to some favorite china, but Mr. Underhill replied: "I will trust the spirits;" and then added: "Cannot the spirit bring something to Mr. Owen?" Almost immediately there was set down on the table, close to my left hand, some object which I touched, and it proved to be a cut-glass goblet.

*   *   *   *

When, soon after, we were bidden, by the raps, to relight the gas, I found the three door-keys on the table, the goblet also. . . . Both the room-doors were closed, but on trying them, I found that neither was locked. Two of the keys on the table fitted them. . . .

These are the facts, all briefly noted down the same evening on which they happened, and written out in full the next morning.[24]

However inadequate such evidence may seem today, it excited widespread interest among Owen's contemporaries. Like *Footfalls, The Debatable Land* became at once a best-seller. The first American edition was exhausted in ten days, and a month later four thousand copies had been sold.[25] Like its predecessor,

---

[24] *Debatable Land*, 460–465. Cf. *The Spiritualist*, Feb. 15, 1872; Podmore, *Modern Spiritualism*, II, 96.

[25] *Religio-Philosophical Journal*, Dec. 16, 1871; *American Spiritualist*, Jan. 20, 1872.

the volume was one of the few books on spiritualism to receive a detailed and respectful notice from non-believers. To be sure, critics reached no agreement on its merits. That a large number accepted the reality of the phenomena described and asked for further study was in itself a triumph for spiritualists. Most reviewers thought the author was addicted to credulity and woefully lacked a scientific technique, but none doubted his honesty. Even the most friendly refused to ascribe a spiritual origin to the manifestations or see in them a means of revitalizing Christianity. Some rejoiced that the former infidel acknowledged Jesus' primacy as a teacher of men, but others doubted that orthodoxy had benefitted from the conversion of one who ignored the divinity of the Nazarene and compared His miracles to the cheap tricks of mountebanks and mediums. The Hoosier, it is true, had a strange group of writers to please. The elder Henry James declared that men should discover immortality through their intellect not their senses. John Weiss flatly denied the necessity of discovering its existence in any way. Warren Chase regretted Owen's pro-Christian tendencies, whereas Orestes Brownson thought his former colleague's faith as little worthy of being called Christianity as the Unitarianism of Channing, the Deism of Paine, and the Free Religion of Emerson.[26]

As might be expected, the harshest words were spoken by freethinkers. Although forty years had passed since Owen had stepped down as the champion of agnosticism, his successors never ceased to bemoan what they called his apostasy. Dis-

[26] Henry James, "Spiritism New and Old," *Atlantic Monthly*, XXIX, 358–362 (Mar. 1872); O. A. Brownson, "Owen on Spiritism," *Catholic World*, XIV, 803–812 (Mar. 1872); John Weiss in *The Radical*, X, 387–389 (Apr. 1872); Warren Chase in the *Banner of Light*, Feb. 10, 1872; Harriet B. Stowe in *The Christian Union*, Jan. 24, 1872; unsigned notices in *ibid.*, Dec. 13, 1871; *Scribner's Monthly*, III, 635–636 (Mar. 1872); *Galaxy*, XIII, 566–567 (Apr. 1872); *Nation*, Oct. 24, 1872; *Independent*, Jan. 4, 1872; *Golden Age*, Dec. 30, 1871; *Home Journal*, Mar. 13, 1872; *Boston Investigator*, Dec. 6, 13, 1871, Jan. 31, 1872; *Index*, Feb. 10, 1872; *N. Y. Tribune*, Dec. 26, 1871; *Evening Post*, Jan. 11, 1872; *N. Y. Times*, Jan. 27, 1872; *Press*, Nov. 29, 1871; *Westminster Review*, XCVIII, 217–218 (July 1872); *Saturday Review*, Jan. 20, 1872; *National Reformer*, Feb. 4, 1872.

mayed by the resemblance to orthodoxy of his former idol's arguments, Horace Seaver admitted that a once brilliant mind had "wandered from the path of reason." Two members of the Free Religious Association, John Weiss and Edward Towne, joined the irascible John Chappelsmith in combatting the flood of bouquets showered upon the former editor of *The Free Enquirer*.[27] As in 1860, Owen replied to Seaver's strictures through the columns of the *Boston Investigator*. He insisted that he now possessed evidence of a future life that he had lacked in his younger days and that his pioneering in the outer fringes of the human intellect entitled him to the name of a free enquirer. In direct contrast to his older view he now deemed belief in immortality a necessary prerequisite for reformers.[28] The non-Christian spiritualists, whose existence he had gently deplored in *The Debatable Land*, Owen ignored; but he must have been cheered by the letters of approbation his work received from Edmonds, Davis, Emma Britten, William Howitt, and other leaders.[29]

The reception accorded Owen's second volume enables one to mark the progress of spiritualism. In 1860 Orestes Brownson devoted less than a half page to remarks on the demoniacal character of the belief. More than nine pages of *The Catholic World* were required to reiterate that opinion in 1872. The *Methodist Quarterly Review* had waited eleven years to notice *Footfalls*; its sequel was the subject of comment within a month of publication. *The Atlantic Monthly* allotted four pages to a review of *The Debatable Land*, while it had ignored its predecessor.[30] Even more striking were three articles that

---

[27] *Boston Investigator*, Dec. 6, 1871. *Ibid.*, Feb. 12, Mar. 5, 19, 26, 1873; *Radical*, X, 387–389 (May 1872); *Index*, Feb. 10, June 8, 1872.

[28] *Boston Investigator*, Jan. 31, 1872.

[29] Edmonds to John Gray, Oct. 12, 1871; Gray to Owen, Oct. 13, 1871; Mary F. Davis to Owen, Dec. 30, 1871; Emma H. Britten to Owen, Dec. 29, 1871; Howitt to Owen, Feb. 18, 1872, Dreer Collection: Psychologists.

[30] *Brownson's Quarterly Review*, 3d ser., I, 265 (Apr. 1860); *Catholic World*, XIV, 803–813 (Mar. 1872); *Methodist Quarterly Review*, LIII, 346–347, LIV, 162–163 (Apr. 1871, Jan. 1872); *Atlantic Monthly*, XXIX, 358–362 (Mar. 1872).

revealed gains made among different but important elements of public opinion. Godkin's *Nation*, critical journal of intelligent men of affairs, warmly welcomed Owen's work and chided scientists for neglecting so significant a field of inquiry. Harriet Beecher Stowe, writing in her brother's organ for orthodox, bourgeois reformers, compared *The Debatable Land* to Darwin's *Voyage of a Naturalist* in its purpose, spirit, and study of the obscure facts of nature.[31] The review, however, that was called the greatest single victory in a quarter century of spiritualism appeared in the "Notices of Scientific Works" in the London *Quarterly Journal of Science*. The author, Alfred Russel Wallace, co-discoverer of the evolutionary hypothesis, declared that Owen was thoroughly imbued with the spirit and teachings of modern science. Cutting the ground from beneath the feet of those who refused to do more than admit the reality of psychical phenomena, the great biologist concluded,

It is now becoming almost a common thing to acknowledge that there is a certain amount of truth in the facts; with a proviso, always, of the writer's repudiation of the spiritual theory. For my own part the only thing that makes the facts credible on evidence *is* the spiritual theory. . . .[32]

Like *Footfalls, The Debatable Land* had the good fortune to be published near the peak of one of the regular cycles that have characterized the history of spiritualism. More than its predecessor, however, it contributed to the upswing that made the few years prior to December 1874 one of the flood tides of the cause in America. Ever since the end of the rebellion a revival had been under way, and at the beginning of the eighth decade it received a powerful impetus from the now full grown British movement. Eighteen seventy-one was an *annus mirabilis* for English spiritualists. It saw the establishment of its fifth periodical, the appearance of the long awaited

---

[31] *Nation*, Oct. 24, 1872; *Christian Union*, Jan. 24, 1872.
[32] *Quarterly Journal of Science*, IX, 237–247 (Apr. 1872). Cf. *Banner of Light*, May 18, 1872.

Dialectical Society report, another attack by Wallace upon the negligence of his scientific colleagues, and the endorsement by a famous chemist, William Crookes, of the idea of a psychic force.[33] Led on by the revelations in Owen's work, Crookes continued his experiments until in 1874, he too, like Wallace, publicly accepted the spiritual theory.[34]

Across the Atlantic similar milestones were being passed. In 1870 and 1871 came the first full length history of spiritualism and the first large-scale annual devoted to the cause. Both publications sadly lacked impartiality and accuracy, but they sold well and impressed their readers with the longevity of the movement.[35] Early in 1872 Owen wrote the thesis of his *Debatable Land* into an article for Johnson's forthcoming encyclopedia, and a few years later Epes Sargent was selected to contribute the account on spiritualism in the new edition of Ripley and Dana.[36] Notable attempts to improve the quality of spiritual periodicals were made in 1872 by Emma Britten's short-lived *Western Star*, a monthly, and in 1873 by S. B. Brittan's more ambitious *Journal of Spiritual Science*, a quarterly. Sensational physical manifestations, rivalling the more scientific experiments of Crookes with Katie King, the spirit of John Morgan's daughter, were obtained at this time by Mrs. Mary Andrews at Moravia, the Eddy brothers at Chittenden, Vermont, and Mr. and Mrs. Nelson Holmes in Philadelphia.

Widespread discussion in popular magazines and newspapers marked this flood tide of spiritualism. A New York daily

[33] *Report on Spiritualism of the Committee of the London Dialectical Society*; Wallace, "On the Attitude of Men of Science towards the Investigators of Spiritualism," *Year-Book of Spiritualism for 1871*, 28–31; Crookes, "Experimental Investigations of a New Force," "Some Further Experiments on Psychic Force," *Quarterly Journal of Science*, VIII, 339–349, 471–493 (July, Oct. 1871); *Psychic Force and Modern Spiritualism* (London, 1871).

[34] Crookes, "Notes of an Inquiry into the Phenomena Called Spiritualism during the Years 1870–1873," *Quarterly Journal of Science*, XI, 77–97 (Jan. 1874); Wallace, "A Defence of Modern Spiritualism," *Fortnightly Review*, XXI, 630–657, 785–807 (May 1, June 1, 1874).

[35] Emma Hardinge, *Modern American Spiritualism; The Year-Book of Spiritualism for 1871* (H. Tuttle and J. M. Peebles, eds.).

[36] *Johnson's New Universal Cyclopaedia*, IV (N. Y., 1878), 435–437; *The American Cyclopaedia*, XV, 275–278.

supposedly trebled its circulation by its special semi-weekly correspondence on the Chittenden phenomena.[37] Accounts of séances in *Lippincott's*, *The Galaxy*, and the *Atlantic* in 1874 caused Bryant's paper to express astonishment at the prominence thus given the subject. Yet the *Tribune* allotted a third of a page to Crookes' latest article, and *The World* carried a column and a half editorial on the one by Wallace. Late in 1873 *The Catholic World* was forced to admit that

It can hardly be denied that . . . spiritualism is forcing itself every year more and more upon the public attention; and that a belief in the reality of the phenomena, and . . . their at least partially preternatural character is on the increase amongst honest and intelligent persons.[38]

Referring to this rapid progress, Epes Sargent, one of the sanest adherents of the cause, wrote, "There has been nothing like it since the breaking out of the phenomena at Hydesville." [39] And at Philadelphia, a cheerful, white-haired gentleman, just seventy-three, declared, as if hoping to crown in triumph the last chapter in a life of many struggles and many disappointments, "The battle which Spiritualism has been waging with popular opinion may be said to have been virtually won." [40]

[37] *Daily Graphic*, Oct.-Nov. 1874; R. D. Owen, "Spiritual Progress in America," *Spiritual Magazine*, 3d ser., I, 35–41 (Jan. 1875).

[38] *Catholic World*, XVIII, 145 (Nov. 1873). *Evening Post*, Nov. 18, 1874; *N. Y. Tribune*, Jan. 17, 1874; *World*, June 15, 1874.

[39] Sargent to Benjamin Coleman, n. d., *Spiritualist Newspaper*, Jan. 1, 1875.

[40] Owen, "Spiritual Progress in America," *loc. cit.*, 3d ser., I, 41 (Jan. 1875).

CHAPTER XXIV

LAST YEARS

THE study of pneumatology was for the aging Owen a congenial task. "It is good," he repeatedly said, "to take with us through life a great and encouraging subject. We feel this the more as we advance in years." Spiritualism gave the Indianan a buoyant confidence in facing the Unknown. In 1873 he bluntly confessed that he would feel less cheerful if he had not discovered unmistakable proof of a future existence.[1]

Owen, however, was no solitary mystic, insensible to the pleasures and problems of this world. Gregarious by nature, he owned a wide circle of friends among non-spiritualists. Contemporaries pictured him as a genial, courteous, and exceedingly well-informed gentleman, free from the slightest trace of dogmatism and possessed of "that rare social gift, the ability to make his companions interesting to themselves and to him." [2] Financial insecurity, moreover, forced upon him the mundane task of earning a living. Psychical research was an unremunerative employment, and Owen was not rich. An ill-advised investment about 1866 cost him his entire savings and plunged him deeply into debt. Too old to enter business, excluded from elective office by his religious beliefs, he had but one weapon with which to fight adversity, his pen.[3]

Forced by pecuniary need into literary ventures, Owen proposed first to write a biography of Abraham Lincoln. Late in May 1865 he contracted with a leading Cincinnati publisher

[1] *Report of Addresses at a Meeting . . . May 30, 1867, to Consider the Conditions, Wants, and Prospects of Free Religion*, 27; Free Religious Association, *Proceedings at the Sixth Annual Meeting . . . 1873*, 53.

[2] *Evening Post*, June 26, 1877. Cf. Taylor, *Katie Fox*, 114; *N. Y. Tribune*, July 15, 1875.

[3] R. D. Owen to Julian D. Owen, Nov. 7, 1869, Owen Papers; *Banner of Light*, July 7, 1877; Rosamond D. Owen's sketch in the English Collection.

to complete the project in two years, and he told a friend enthusiastically that it would be *"the* life . . . a standard work that will endure when I am gone." Despite encouragement from the press and from such men as Chief Justice Chase, the book was never finished; in 1869 the author was released from his obligation.[4] Whether the enterprise was abandoned because Owen was busy elsewhere or because other studies were printed first is not clear, but the only tangible result was a sketch of the Emancipator that the Hoosier drew for the *Old and New* in four articles on the Civil War.[5]

In 1868 Owen made one contribution to the *Northern Monthly* and several to the *Chicagoan,* a new high grade weekly. The spring of that year he spent lecturing in the Middle West. This last was a new role, for his appearances on the ante-bellum lyceum were neither frequent nor inspired by remunerative considerations. His lectures comprised "Labor, Its History and Prospects," first delivered in Cincinnati in 1848; "The Law of Progress Deduced from History," originally given at Terre Haute in 1853; "Spiritualism as a Phase of the Religious Sentiment of the Day," the same paper read to the Free Religious Association in 1867; and "Abraham Lincoln and the Crisis which Called Him Forth."[6] The exact itinerary that the lecturer followed cannot be traced, but he did visit Chicago, Springfield, and New Harmony. Some profits may have been realized, for less than two years later he had paid off half of his $12,000 debt.[7]

[4] Duplicate contract and release with Moore, Wilstach and Baldwin, Owen Papers. Owen to Dreer, May 24, 1865; Chase to Owen, Aug. 7, 1867, Dreer Collection: Psychologists, Presidents, III; Chase to Isaac B. Arnold, Mar. 2, 1867, R. B. Warden, *An Account of the Private Life and Public Services of Salmon Portland Chase* (Cinn., 1874), 652; *Evening Post,* May 19, 1865; *Boston Transcript,* May 27, 1865; *Religio-Philosophical Journal,* Oct. 21, 1865.

[5] "Looking Back across the War Gulf," *Old and New,* I, 577–589, III, 28–43, 273–284, IV, 333–346 (May 1870, Jan., Mar., Sept. 1871).

[6] "Naples and Vesuvius," *Northern Monthly Magazine,* II, 393–401 (Feb. 1868); Mott, *History of American Magazines, 1865–1885,* 52; *Banner of Light,* July 27, 1867; *New Harmony Register,* Aug. 10, 1867.

[7] *Religio-Philosophical Journal,* Apr. 11, 1868; *Illinois State Journal,* Apr. 14, 15, 17, 1868; *New Harmony Register,* May 2, 16, 23, 1868. R. D. Owen to J. D. Owen, Nov. 7, 1869, Owen Papers.

In his efforts to relieve financial pressure Owen turned next to fiction. During the summer of 1868 he remained in the West writing a portion of *Beyond the Breakers,* which was published as a serial in *Lippincott's Magazine* the next year.[8] In this first novel the inexperienced hand was only too evident, and the result did little to increase Owen's fame as a man of letters. The plot was weak, the tone didactic, and an almost sickening sentimentality pervaded its pages. Yet the tale is of interest both because of its autobiographical touches and because the pioneer Indiana delineated by Owen was less crude and less brutal than that drawn by Edward Eggleston two years later. The passage of time had given a roseate hue to Owen's early life in a frontier village, and fictitious Chicksauga represented an idealized New Harmony. Similarly, the hero, Franklin Sydenham, cosmopolitan intellectual, lover of Schiller and of Norman architecture, benefactor of his little town, was the man Owen wished he might have been or perhaps thought that he had been. Old persons and incidents were resurrected. Mt. Vernon became Mt. Sharon; Amos Clark, Amos Cranstoun, the dishonest lawyer; Elisha Embree, Judge Emberly, the Methodist politician. The Chicksauga Institute, the village Thespian Society, and even a Congressional canvass, reminiscent of the tumultuous election of 1839 were sketched. Occasionally the story lapsed into a mere vehicle for the writer's views on prison reform, spiritualism, and the property rights of married women; but such faults were to be expected of a novice.

The most successful of Owen's literary enterprises was his autobiography, undertaken late in 1872 at the suggestion of William Dean Howells. The opportunity to spread his life story in sixteen numbers of the then preëminent *Atlantic Monthly* caused the Indianan to begin the task diligently and cautiously, fully aware of the poet's warning, which he used as his motto

[8] "Beyond the Breakers: an American Novel," *Lippincott's Magazine,* I–II (Jan. 1869–Feb. 1870); *Beyond the Breakers, a Story of the Present Day* [*Village Life in the West*] (Phila., 1870).

"Que faites-vous là, seul et rêveur?"
"Je m'entretiens avec moi-même."
"Ah! prenez garde du péril extrême
De causer avec un flatteur." [9]

The result was an eminently readable volume, valuable alike for its charming story as for its source material on David Dale, Robert Owen, and other British reformers, on the New Harmony experiment, radical journalism in New York, and the vicissitudes of a proposed Fourteenth Amendment. The author had no axe to grind. He had made his peace with God and the world. A golden glow of nostalgia bathed his pages, which recalled scenes long past, gave tolerant judgments of foes long dead, and frankly acknowledged errors long since atoned for. When Alfred Russel Wallace sat down many years later to record the events of his life, he despaired of matching Owen's artistry.[10]

The memoirs, to be sure, were not without their defects. The author's sources were not always complete, and his wish was sometimes father to his thought. The sketch of Frances Wright was not the one he would have drawn in 1832. The feeling of uneasiness and uncertainty, attributed to his days of scepticism, and the reason alleged for his entrance into politics were both contradicted by contemporary evidence. Admittedly unfinished, the autobiography had made no mention in its eighteen chapters of the Oregon boundary dispute, the Smithsonian Institution, the Indiana constitution, the Mexican loan incident, or his interest in architecture and plank roads. Several essays were filled solely with anecdotes of famous persons, and one was wasted on the youthful romance with Margaret. The turbulent New York years, on the other hand, were compressed into a few pages; and the accounts of

[9] *Threading My Way. Twenty-Seven Years of Autobiography* (N. Y., 1874), 3, 7. The first eleven chapters were published in book form on both sides of the Atlantic under this title. See also Owen to Mrs. Leonowens, Sept. 7, 1872, Ford Collection.

[10] James Marchant, *Alfred Russel Wallace, Letters and Reminiscences* (N. Y., 1916), II, 225.

the New Harmony experiment, Western politics, and the Mexican War were either inaccurate or inadequate. It must be remembered, however, that the author wrote after his philosophy of life had undergone a profound change. It was almost impossible for Owen the intellectual, living midst literary friends in élite Boston, at a time when honesty in public office had reached its nadir, to appreciate the political aspirations of the Western Democrat of the thirties. Nor could the mild, tolerant, Christian spiritualist do justice to the bold, militant agnostic who had edited *The Free Enquirer*.

While engaged upon his autobiography, Owen did not interrupt his psychical research. In fact it was the investigation and ill-advised inclusion of the Katie King manifestations that terminated his lucrative connection with the *Atlantic* and cast a cloud over his last years. Early in June 1874, as the spiritualist tide was nearing its flood, Owen arrived in Philadelphia to witness at the request of his close friend Dr. Henry T. Child the latest ultramundane phenomena that were setting the Quaker City agog and which were soon to rival as topics of conversation the Beecher-Tilton scandal and the abduction of Charlie Ross. What the Hoosier saw at the North Ninth Street residence of Mr. and Mrs. Nelson Holmes was truly amazing. In a semi-darkened parlor, light enough to distinguish forms and faces, one, two, and sometimes three figures, fully shaped and clothed, emerged from a wooden cabinet set against a flat wall. Apparently possessed of every human attribute, these phantoms touched, conversed, and even joked with those present. They were freely questioned; and their answers, sometimes trite, sometimes consoling, sometimes revealing, were, for some, sufficient evidence of their spiritual origin. The most astonishing part of the whole performance was that both mediums generally sat, unentranced, outside of the cabinet.[11]

The very completeness of these manifestations should have

[11] R. D. Owen, "Touching Visitants from a Higher Life," *Atlantic Monthly*, XXXV, 57–69 (Jan. 1875); F. J. Lippitt, "Was It Katie King?" *Galaxy*, XVIII, 754–766 (Dec. 1874); *N. Y. Times*, July 21, 1874; *Frank Leslie's Illustrated Newspaper*, Aug. 22, 1874.

placed Owen on guard. Even the diligent, scientific experiments of Crookes had never achieved such marvels. Yet the Holmeses were professional exhibitors of the lowest sort, crude to the point of vulgarity. They had just returned from England where their honesty had been questioned; and although spiritualists often asserted that the moral character of mediums did not affect their psychical power, impartial and cautious observers could not ignore such considerations.[12] The Holmes séances, moreover, resembled a three-ring circus rather than a sober study of pneumatology or a reverent act of religious devotion. Many undesirables, attracted by advertisements, found their way into the circle merely because they possessed the price of admission. Plausible charges of duplicity soon became rife. The story told by the American Katie King was shown to contradict that of her British sister. Photographs of the Philadelphia spirit failed to tally with those taken by Crookes. Worst of all, during a summer vacation at Blissfield, Michigan, the Holmeses were accused of having been caught using an accomplice in their materializations.[13]

Despite these danger signals, Owen gave, after the most critical examination of which he was capable, a complete endorsement to the Holmeses' materializations.[14] Such a certification from one known to be hostile to professional mediums and averse to printing any evidence for psychical phenomena until a year or two after witnessing them made a profound impression upon believers and non-believers on both sides of the Atlantic. From Lake George, where he spent the summer, the Indianan reiterated his opinion for English spiritualists. While there he discounted the reported exposé in the West, for the account in the Detroit journals was obviously too prejudiced and con-

---

[12] *Medium and Daybreak*, Aug. 9, 16, 23, 1872; Mar. 14, July 18, 1873; June 14, Nov. 23, 1874; *Spiritualist Newspaper*, June 5, 1874; *N. Y. Tribune*, Dec. 21, 1874; *Religio-Philosophical Journal*, May 30, June 6, 20, 1874.

[13] *Religio-Philosophical Journal*, Aug. 8, 1874; Detroit *News*, Sept. 14, 19, Oct. 7, 1874.

[14] Owen to Child, July 1, 1874, *Banner of Light*, July 11, 1874. Owen's tests were described in "Touching Visitants from a Higher Life," *loc. cit.*

tradictory to win general credence. In October Owen told a Worcester paper that minor discrepancies in the case could not shake his belief; and later in the month he complained to an important spiritualist editor who had refused to be convinced, "I stake whatever of reputation I may have acquired after eighteen years' study . . . upon the genuine character of the phenomena." [15] Four days later he sent a similar letter to the *Banner of Light*. In spite of a warning from Crookes, he repeated twice the next month that opinion for the benefit of British readers.[16] He prepared a detailed account of the entire proceedings as an autobiographical chapter in *The Atlantic Monthly*. In that article he said,

The proof lies in a nutshell. . . . Human beings cannot pass at will, through the substance of a brick wall, or of a stout wood partition. . . . Either Katie was, what she professed to be . . . or else she was a confederate. . . . But under conditions as they were arranged, entrance to . . . the cabinet except by . . . the parlor . . . was a physical impossibility. Therefore Katie, not being an inhabitant of this world, was a denizen of another, made visible to us, for the time, by some process which has been called materialization.[17]

Six days after his final emphatic endorsement of the Katie King phenomena Owen despatched under his own name identical cards to the two leading spiritualist newspapers, saying, "Circumstantial evidence which I have just obtained, induces me to withdraw the assurances I have heretofore given of my confidence in the genuine character of certain manifestations presented last summer, in my presence, through Mr. and Mrs. Nelson Holmes." [18]

In the forty years separating the Hydesville rappings and the Fox sisters' public confession of deceit, no event had so

---

[15] *Spiritualist Newspaper*, July 10, Aug. 28, 1874; *Worcester Spy*, Oct. 20, 1874; *Religio-Philosophical Journal*, Nov. 14, 1874.

[16] *Banner of Light*, Nov. 7, 1874. Crookes to Owen, Oct. 22, 1874, Dreer Collection: Psychologists; *Spiritual Newspaper*, Dec. 18, 1874; "Spiritual Progress in America," *Spiritual Magazine*, 3d ser., I, 35-41 (Jan. 1875).

[17] "Touching Visitants from a Higher Life," *loc. cit.*, XXXV, 66.

[18] Owen to the editor, Dec. 6, 1874, *Banner of Light*, Dec. 12, 1874.

shaken the spiritualist world as Owen's dramatic repudiation of the Philadelphia materializations. Coming on the heels of his repeated approbations, it stunned believers everywhere into momentary silence. The terse but damning card unleashed the ridicule of the secular press, which had of late been cowed by the movement's significant advance. Yet upon Owen's aged head the severest blows fell. A long standing and dearly cherished reputation among people of all classes as one of the most careful and competent students of pneumatology was shattered by a single misstep. The retraction, ironically enough, preceded the most elaborate testimony supporting the phenomena, and opponents gleefully placed Owen's contradictory statements side by side. On December 4, a fortnight before the story "broke," the Hoosier frantically telegraphed Boston in order to hold up his forthcoming article in the *Atlantic*.[19] The message, however, arrived too late; and the January number appeared as planned, except for the insertion of a thin sheet on which was printed the brief but eloquent announcement, "The Editors of The Atlantic desire to advertise their friends of the Press and Public that with Mr. Robert Dale Owen rests all responsibility for the statements of his articles on Spiritual Phenomena."

Owen knew that the public would never be satisfied with his first short statement. Even before it appeared, therefore, he forwarded a fuller explanation to the *Banner of Light*; but that paper, obviously hoping to gloss over the unfortunate affair, delayed its publication for more than a week. In the interim the Philadelphia press, shamelessly mingling fact and fiction, built up so plausible a story that Owen, despite Howells' wishes, felt constrained to write an open letter to the nation's leading daily.[20] In these communications he described what he considered "a direct attempt to deceive." Since their return from

[19] Owen to W. D. Howells, Dec. 4, 1874, Howells Papers.

[20] Owen to the editor, Dec. 10, 1874, *Banner of Light*, Dec. 19, 1874; Owen to the editor, Dec. 20, 1874, *N. Y. Tribune*, Dec. 21, 1874. See also Owen to Howells, Dec. 7, 12, 1874, Howells Papers; *Philadelphia Inquirer*, Dec. 18, 1874; *Press*, Dec. 19, 1874.

the West, the Holmeses had so arranged their parlor that a confederate could easily be employed. They had resorted with increasing frequency to dark séances and had refused both to move their cabinet or permit Owen to approach it during the sittings as he had been accustomed to do. On several occasions Katie failed to materialize; and even when she did appear, her face was noticeably altered. On December 4 a member of the circle, W. O. Leslie, revealed to Owen the confession of one Mrs. White, a seamstress and former resident in the Holmes home, who substantiated her assertion that she had impersonated the spirit of the pirate's daughter by producing many of the presents given Katie the previous summer. The next evening that lady, heavily veiled, gave a mock séance to show how the duplicity was effected. About the same time Owen received proof from England that Mr. Holmes had forged two cheques while there; and these facts caused him to send his disavowal to the leading spiritualist periodicals, omitting, because of a pledge to Leslie, all details. The Indianan did not say that all he had previously witnessed was fraudulent, nor did he deny the ability of the Holmeses to produce materialization without trickery. He merely declared that such doubt had been cast on the facts he had collected in June and July that he would not use them in any subsequent book he might write.

By the time Owen's letters were printed, the country was already being regaled by the most preposterous and derisive versions of the exposure. The comely Katie, for weeks a national mystery, had become a national joke. In the light of latest developments, the sober, detailed, and previously sought after accounts by Lippitt and Owen seemed monstrous absurdities. Non-believers were amazed at the apparent credulity of these men experienced in public affairs; and they chuckled over the song allegedly used to invoke the flesh and blood seamstress:

> Oh gather 'round and let us sing
> The praises of sweet Katie King,

Who, from her bright and happy sphere,
Comes smiling to us mortals here.
Then with glad voices, let all sing
The praises of sweet Katie King.[21]

Most of these later disclosures were, to be sure, untrue in whole or in part. The two widely quoted accounts of how the deceit was perpetrated differed in many important details. An autobiography, supposedly written by Mrs. White, contained so many errors along with its germ of truth that it is unusable as a source.[22] Yet the specious fabrications were made easy by the publicity previously given the original descriptions of the séances as well as by the willingness of the people at large to believe the worst.

A frank admission that he had been fooled did not impair Owen's belief in spiritualism. To a distinguished critic he replied,

We who have made so palpable a mistake in the Katie King affair must be content for the time to be laughed at. . . . [But] I have during a long life engaged, sometimes successfully, in a good many of what were pronounced "hopeless tasks," and very certainly I shall prosecute this to the end. . . . Our failures teach better lessons than our successes.[23]

Nor was this sturdy profession of faith merely for public consumption. Contrary to newspaper assertions Owen did not feel humiliated or downcast. "I was deeply annoyed at first," he wrote in private, "but I have got over it." More than thirty years of public life, he declared elsewhere, had case-hardened him to ridicule and abuse; within a month he expected the incident to be forgotten. His sole regret was his failure to discover the fraud in time to prevent the publication of his last article in the *Atlantic*.[24]

[21] *Philadelphia Inquirer*, Dec. 18, 1874.

[22] *Press*, Dec. 19, 1874; *Philadelphia Inquirer*, Dec. 18, 1874. *Ibid.*, Jan. 9, 11, 1875.

[23] Owen to the editor, Dec. 24, 1874, *Springfield Republican*, Dec. 29, 1874.

[24] Owen to Mrs. Louisa Andrews, Dec. 22, 26, 1874, quoted *ibid.*, Aug. 1, 1877; Owen to Howells, Dec. 29, 1874, Howells Papers.

The sequel to the Katie King affair placed neither spiritualists nor their opponents in a good light. Reckless statements and questionable tactics bordering on perjury destroyed much of the latter's case. The former, on the other hand, after revealing through the detective-like methods of Henry S. Olcott and Francis J. Lippitt, two of Owen's friends, the worthlessness of Mrs. White's testimony, seemed more intent on proving that the Holmeses possessed psychic power than on explaining or censuring the trickery that had been resorted to.[25] Thus, as one editor declared, believers preferred to repudiate Owen's leadership to admitting that two professionals of doubtful character had been guilty of fraud.[26] For a corollary to the Lippitt-Olcott reports, not expressed to be sure, was that Robert Dale Owen, by his undue haste in denouncing genuine mediums on the evidence of interested parties had inflicted an irreparable injury upon the movement. That Owen had been guilty of extreme carelessness as an investigator, of rare indiscretion in rushing his findings into print, and of inexplicable persistency in endorsing the phenomena even after his suspicions had been aroused cannot be denied. But in the furore that succeeded his initial error no one, believer or sceptic, acted with greater dignity, moderation, or more sincere desire to do justice to all parties concerned than the venerable Hoosier.

For more than four months after December 26 Owen kept silent on the Holmes fiasco. Then on April 15 he presented his mature opinion in an address to American spiritualists. He refused to accept the conclusion, fast becoming held by the latter, that the exposure had been simply a plot of the Young Men's Christian Association. He believed that the mediums possessed undoubted psychic powers but that they had in the past deceitfully supplemented them. Whether or not he had witnessed real or spurious phenomena the previous June he felt unable to decide, but he was determined to exclude the

---

[25] "Gen. F. J. Lippitt's Report," *Banner of Light*, Feb. 6, 13, 1875; Olcott, *People from the Other World* (Hartford, 1875), 425–478.

[26] *Religio-Philosophical Journal*, Mar. 27, July 17, 1875.

Philadelphia *cause célèbre* from his next book on pneumatology. In conclusion he rejoiced that the incident "taken as
a whole, instead of justifying suspicion touching the possibility
of the phenomena known as spirit-materialization, *furnishes
satisfactory proof of its reality.*" [27]

A dissent may well be entered to the last statement. The
average man in the street probably never read the spiritualist
counter-attack against the exposure but remained satisfied
that the demoniacal religion had been crushed once and for
all. And, in truth, American spiritualism fell on evil days, the
gloom of which was heightened by the embarrassing news that
on July 10, 1875, Robert Dale Owen had been admitted to the
Indiana Hospital for the Insane.

Owen's insanity, though of short duration, is of more than
passing interest. Following close upon the heels of the Philadelphia fiasco, it was widely attributed to a loss of religious
faith.[28] Yet neither the cause nor the effect was what the
secular press thought. Mental and bodily exhaustion was
chiefly to blame for the Hoosier's infirmity. Until his seventy-
second year Owen's health was generally good. While in Boston writing his autobiography, he first overtaxed his strength
and in the fall of 1873 felt unable to pen some reviews for *The
Atlantic Monthly.* By November his condition had become
serious. A medical friend, a spiritualist himself, found the Indianan in a highly excitable state, suffering from an inflamed
membrane in the transverse colon. Warned that excessive
mental labor would result in softening of the brain, Owen
apparently promised to rest.[29] The next year, however, saw
five more chapters of his life story published, the dramatic
events in Philadelphia, and the nervous strain and chagrin

[27] "The Mystery of Katie King," *Banner of Light*, May 1, 1875.
[28] *Chicago Daily Tribune*, July 2, 1875; *Philadelphia Inquirer*, July 15, 1875;
World, July 16, 1875.
[29] R. D. Owen to Richard Owen, Apr. 1, 1871; Apr. 26, 1873, Neal Letters;
Purdue Collection. Owen to Howells, Sept. 14, 18, 1873, Howells Papers.
Statements of Rosamond Dale Owen, Dr. F. L. H. Willis, and Mrs. R. T. Hallock,
a sister-in-law, in *The Evening Post*, July 20, 1875; *Banner of Light*, July 17,
1875; *Medium and Daybreak*, Aug. 13, 1875.

that accompanied the denouement. In February 1875 he was confined to his bed for several days by influenza. He chafed at this interruption of his psychical research, and then he began to worry about placating Howells. That editor seemed indifferent about printing a paper, long since planned, on Owen's married life; while at the same time Houghton and Company withheld, temporarily at least, the payment for the ill-advised January contribution. Worst of all, the creator of Silas Lapham, apparently annoyed by the mishap, refused to accept an article condoning Owen's method of investigating spiritual phenomena. As a matter of fact, only one more piece from the Hoosier's pen ever appeared in the *Atlantic*.[30]

In the middle of March Owen left Philadelphia to visit his daughter at the Home on the Hillside, a water cure in Dansville, New York. Outwardly he was in perfect health; but a thorough examination shortly after his arrival disclosed congestion in his digestive organs, an irritated kidney, poor circulation, and a debilitated nervous system. Already an intellectual restlessness and impatience at restraints were apparent.[31] After some hesitation he agreed to take a complete rest, a decision he found himself unable to carry out. At this time he worked over his article on "The Mystery of Katie King," published by the *Banner of Light*. His presence in the small community attracted an endless stream of visitors; and then late in April he went to Rochester, forty-five miles distant, to lecture on spiritualism. A severe cold caught on that rainy night developed into a genuinely critical asthmatic fever.

After losing twenty pounds he began to recover. While still convalescent and so weak that he could barely hold a pen, he despatched several business letters, worried about the Dale

[30] R. D. Owen to Rosamond D. Owen, Feb. 6, 1875, Owen Papers; H. T. Child in the *Cincinnati Commercial*, July 25, 1875; Owen to Howells, Nov. 24, Dec. 29, 1874, Howells Papers; Howells' inscription on Owen to Howells, Dec. 7, 1874, *ibid.*; "Political Results from the Varioloid," *Atlantic Monthly*, XXXV, 660–670 (June 1875).

[31] Dr. James C. Jackson, superintendent of the Home on the Hillside, quoted in the *Philadelphia Inquirer*, Aug. 5, 1875.

estate that was about to be liquidated in Scotland, and laid
plans for his next book. Unless watched, he would try to work
several hours at a stretch.[32] Then the *Banner of Light*, still
pursuing a course inimical to the best interests of spiritualism,
reprinted the fateful article from the January *Atlantic*, adding
by way of comment that it was *"true to the letter."* Visibly
annoyed, the sick man rejoined with a logical and forceful
dissent. Exactly a week later his actions at the Dansville
Fair Grounds clearly betrayed his insanity.[33]

The symptoms of his derangement curiously recalled incidents of his early life. He referred constantly to the title of
earl held by his great-great-great-grandfather. He spoke too
of his own inestimable services to Queen Victoria. One moment his mind would revert to the fine horses he had raised
at New Harmony in the thirties; the next, to *Pocahontas*,
which he considered the greatest drama ever written. He revealed a strong desire to buy and sell land, and he had made
several purchases in Dansville before he was stopped.[34] On
June 29 the difficult journey back to Indiana was begun, Owen
then being in the opinion of the Home's superintendent "decidedly insane." Once established on the Wabash, he so opposed every reasonable restriction of his liberty that his
children saw no other course but to confine him, after a formal
examination, in the state institution. This was done, and on
July 9 the former Democratic champion of the "Pocket" returned in a distracted state to the scene of his first political
triumphs.[35]

Although unnoticed on a visit to the Railroad City three

[32] *Banner of Light,* Apr. 24, May 1, 1875; *Philadelphia Inquirer,* Aug. 5,
1875; R. D. Owen to James Lamond, May 19, 1875 (copy), Neal Letters; Owen
to the editor, *Spiritualist Newspaper,* July 23, 1875; Rosamond D. Owen in
The Evening Post, July 20, 1875; E. D. Owen in the *Philadelphia Inquirer,*
July 20, 1875.

[33] *Banner of Light,* June 12, 1875; Owen to the editor, June 15, 1875, *ibid.,*
July 10, 1875; Rochester *Express,* July 2, 1875.

[34] *Indianapolis Journal,* July 15, 1875; *World,* July 15, 1875; *Evening Post,*
July 20, 1875.

[35] *New Harmony Register,* July 10, 1875; *Indianapolis Sentinel,* July 10,
1875; Dr. J. C. Jackson in the *Spiritual Scientist,* July 15, 1875.

years before, Owen was now the cynosure of all eyes. His malady had become a news item of international interest. Reporters flocked to New Harmony, to his Indianapolis hotel, and even to the asylum. Eastern dailies described his aberration at length, and even the British press gave it attention. Spiritualists heatedly denied that the misfortune was in any way due to the Katie King affair.[36] Non-believers, seeing little hope for his recovery, laid aside their animosities and lauded him, in some cases, far beyond his deserts. For all intents and purposes his obituary was being written.[37]

Meanwhile the object of these eulogies was slowly but steadily recovering his reason. Early reports that death was imminent proved unfounded, and by September complete normalcy was but a question of time.[38] After the first weeks of confinement Owen had many lucid periods, and it must have been a harrowing experience for him at those times to live with idiots. At a later date he quite naturally questioned the wisdom of his children's treatment of his case but admitted with his customary kindness that he was not a capable judge. Just before his release he summed up the incident in genial fashion when he wrote to the superintendent of the asylum thus:

I seem, also, to have made gain by my seclusion here, in the way of reputation. If a man wishes to be well spoken of by those who had hitherto slighted or reproved him, he had better either die or suffer a temporary civic death by confinement in a lunatic asylum. *De mortuis nil nisi bonum.* . . . This has been amply illustrated by the many newspaper notices of myself which have fallen under my observation since an inmate of this institution. I trust that on entering the world again, I shall give no cause for retraction of those good opinions. . . .[39]

---

[36] *Banner of Light*, June 22, 1872. London *News*, July 20, 1875; *Spiritualist Newspaper*, July 13, 20, 1875; *Medium and Daybreak*, Aug. 6, 13, 1875. See letters of denial in *The Evening Post*, July 13, 20, 1875; *Philadelphia Inquirer*, July 20, 1875; *Cincinnati Commercial*, July 25, 1875; *Banner of Light*, July 31, 1875.

[37] *Chicago Tribune*, July 2, 1875; *N. Y. Tribune*, July 15, 1875; *Philadelphia Inquirer*, July 15, 1875.

[38] *New Harmony Register*, July 24, 31, Aug. 21, Sept. 4, 1875.

[39] *Indianapolis Journal*, Oct. 5, 1875.

Old Fauntleroy Home

Historical Society of Pennsylvania

ROBERT DALE OWEN IN HIS LAST YEARS

Owen's rapid recovery was not paralleled by the religion he so dearly loved. The spiritualist tide was clearly ebbing from the flood of 1871 to 1874. Whatever the justice of the Katie King exposure, its paralyzing effects cannot be denied. Quite probably it did not cause a single believer to renounce his faith, but it certainly deterred hundreds from investigating the subject. It drove a discussion of psychical science from the pages of many popular periodicals, split the ranks of the faithful, and made future organization difficult. Owen's insanity was an added blow. The same paper that in June hailed Olcott's report on the Holmeses as initiating a "New Epoch," lamented two months later the "Eclipse of Spiritualism." [40] Signs of retrogression multiplied. Like Owen, Crookes was soon criticized for refusing to endorse every new marvel. Spiritualist papers bickered among themselves, and the breach between the Christian and radical wings widened. The depression of 1873 delayed the appearance of several important publications and forced authors to print their works at their own expense. Exposures of famous mediums were repeatedly alleged; a prominent American psychic was prosecuted in London for fraud; and new legislation against spiritualist charlatans was threatened.[41] Spiritualism, to be sure, was not dead; but realistic observers noticed a lessened interest and predicted that the late period of sensation would "be followed by a season of quietude and apparent public indifference." [42] The movement did not emerge from this downward cycle until Owen had passed to a higher sphere.

On his seventy-fourth birthday Owen was again in New Harmony midst family and friends. Although fully restored in

[40] *Spiritual Scientist*, June 24, Aug. 9, 1875.

[41] *Ibid.*, Nov. 4, 1875; *Medium and Daybreak*, June 30, Aug. 4, Sept. 15, 1876; *Banner of Light*, July 29, 1876; *Religio-Philosophical Journal*, Aug. 19, Oct. 21, Dec. 23, 30, 1876; *American Spiritual Magazine*, II, 294–296 (Oct. 1876) ; *Spiritualist Newspaper*, Aug. 18, 1876; *World*, July 16, 1875; and, in general, the files of spiritualist periodicals, 1875–1877.

[42] Epes Sargent to the editor, *Spiritualist Newspaper*, Aug. 6, 1875; Eugene Crowell to the editor, *Medium and Daybreak*, June 16, 1876; letters of Robert Cooper, *ibid.*, Feb. 18, June 30, 1876.

mind, he could not engage in any strenuous activity. The winter of 1875–1876 he spent at St. Joseph, Marquette, and at home, idling, visiting relatives, and fussing over business matters. Looking perfectly fit, he left in March for New York whence he intended to sail with a few companions for a final glimpse of the scenes of his childhood. In the East he was showered with kindnesses, but at the last minute was forced to forgo his European tour because of finances.[43] Then on June 23, 1876, the telegraph wires flashed the astonishing news that on that day at Caldwell, New York, Robert Dale Owen had wed Lottie Walton Kellogg.

This marriage, surprising even to the bridegroom's family, could have come only in the last third of the Indianan's life. It is difficult to place Lottie Kellogg in the environment of Owen the reformer or Owen the Western Democrat. But to the aging intellectual who, after 1853, spent most of his time away from New Harmony she made a definite appeal. Born in Hartford about 1840 of strict Congregationalist parents, she had traveled widely and through study abroad had become "an artist of very fair powers and great promise." [44] Her refined tastes and broad culture, together with certain motherly qualities suggestive of Mary, attracted the spiritualist who, after several solitary winters in the East, had been made more lonely by his wife's death. The couple first met, apparently, when Owen visited her brother-in-law at Lake George in the summer of 1872. By autumn a betrothal was rumored.[45] Late the next year *Threading My Way* was dedicated to this new friend. Owen revisited Miss Kellogg's home during the next summers, and even his illness did not seem to check the romance. And thus it came to pass that a little known figure, who enters our story almost at its close, did much to brighten and cheer the Hoosier's last years.

    [43] *New Harmony Register*, Nov. 27, 1875, Jan. 22, Mar. 4, 1876; *N. Y. Tribune*, Apr. 25, 1876; R. D. Owen to Richard Owen, July 11, 1876, Neal Letters.
    [44] R. D. Owen to Mrs. Leonowens, Aug. 9, 1872, Ford Collection; R. D. Owen to Richard Owen, Aug. 1, 1876, Neal Letters; *N. Y. Tribune*, June 26, 1876.   [45] *New Harmony Register*, Nov. 11, 1872.

After the ceremony Owen remained at his wife's beautiful cottage on the eastern shore of Lake George until late autumn. He continued to write copiously to liberal religionists, to spiritualists, to feminists, and even to "My dear old Friend," Joe Lane, whom he had not seen for nearly two decades.[46] He worked, too, on the last chapters of his autobiography; but they were inferior to their predecessors and it was well for the *Atlantic* that Howells' reluctance to publish anything by Owen caused two of the six to appear instead in *Scribner's Monthly*.[47] He wintered in New Harmony, disposing of business details and playing the venerable patriarch at children's parties. In April 1877 he left again, promising to return at the earliest opportunity to the village he had loved and honored for upwards of half a century. Only a few weeks before his departure he had added two bedrooms to the drawings for his new house, planned ever since his return from Naples.[48]

But Owen had bade farewell to the Wabash for the last time. Chronic inflammation of the mucous membrane threatened to cut his life at any moment. The first fortnight in June he spent in Brooklyn with his close friend Dr. Eugene Crowell. The latter saw that the case was hopeless. Séances were held frequently, and the spirits gave unmistakable evidence that the end was at hand. Owen faced death calmly. His religion taught that it but ushered in a higher existence, and that faith sustained him to the last. Having outlived by five years the Biblical span, he was content to go, hopeful only that he would be spared prolonged physical pain.[49] At a sitting one warm June afternoon the spirit of Silas Stringham, an old acquaintance

---

[46] *Index*, July 6, 13, 1876; *American Spiritual Magazine*, II, 294–296 (Oct. 1876); *History of Woman Suffrage*, I, 292–293; Owen to Lane, Dec. 10, 1876, Lane Papers.

[47] Owen to Howells, Nov. 4, 1876, Howells Papers. On the unpublished chapters see *Banner of Light*, July 21, 1877.

[48] Owen Papers, *passim*; *New Harmony Register*, Dec. 29, 1876, Jan. 19, Mar. 2, 23, June 29, 1877; plan in the Owen Papers.

[49] Dr. Crowell in the *Spiritualist Newspaper*, June 22, 1877, in the *Banner of Light*, July 7, 21, 1877. Owen to Mrs. Louisa Andrews [Dec. 1876?], quoted in the *Springfield Republican*, Aug. 1, 1877.

from Naples, appeared, saying, "You can't row your boat much longer; it is time for you to go into the cabin." At first the dying man thought this meant his sloop at Lake George; but when the commander added, "You have sailed a good ship, you have kept a straight course . . . you will soon come to anchor," he understood. Silently he left the room, and the circle then learned that his soul would flee ere the autumn leaves fell.[50]

On the fifteenth of June Owen started for his summer residence. Upon his arrival he added a last codicil to his will. A few days later the final attack came. Although his body was racked with pain, he manifested a "patient, sweet submission . . . not one murmur of complaint, only a deep longing to be released from such *intense* suffering, which he termed his 'forty days in the wilderness.' " On the evening of the twenty-third his wife and sisters-in-law sat around his bed singing softly his favorite tunes. These he acknowledged by a firm pressure of the hand.[51] By ten o'clock the next morning his free enquiring spirit had learned the answer to the enigma of the ages.

They buried him in the quiet Caldwell cemetery across the lake from his final home. Simple private services were conducted by the same Presbyterian minister who, curiously enough, had performed the wedding ceremony a year before, mute testimony that a once outstanding infidel had learned to live in peace with orthodoxy. Upon his grave was carved the brief epitaph, "Author of Footfalls on the Boundary of Another World, and The Debatable Land between This World and the Next. 'Love Is the Fulfilling of the Law.' " There he rested for sixty years until, with the consent of his aged daughter, the remains were taken to New Harmony and placed with those of his first wife and children on Maple Hill.[52]

[50] *Boston Herald*, July 1, 1877.

[51] Lottie D. Owen to Richard Owen, Sept. 19, 1877, Neal Letters; Posey County, "Will Record," II, 229 (June 17, 1877).

[52] Lottie D. Owen to Richard Owen, Sept. 19, 1877, Neal Letters; *Banner of Light*, Aug. 25, 1877; *New Harmony Times*, Oct. 4, 1929; *N. Y. Times*, Oct. 10, 1937.

At his death the name of Robert Dale Owen was well known throughout the land. The obituaries in the public press were extraordinarily full. Bryant himself, or some other close friend on the *Post*, declared that the memory of the spiritualist would be revered "because of his long and varied public service, his rare sincerity and courage, and his uprightness of . . . character." *The Nation* prophesied that posterity would judge him a greater man than his father.[53] The finest eulogy, however, was penned by an editor of his adopted state.

In scholarship, general attainments, varied achievements [said John H. Halliday], as author, statesman, politician, and leader of a new religious faith, he was unquestionably the most prominent man Indiana ever owned. . . . No other Hoosier was ever so widely known, or so likely to do the state credit by being known, and no other has ever before held so prominent a place so long with a history so unspotted with selfishness, duplicity, or injustice.[54]

Such was the verdict of 1877. Time, however, has dimmed the luster of his fame; and today, outside of Indiana, Owen is largely forgotten. For this unexpected eclipse Owen himself was partly to blame. He was a religious liberal and radical reformer before the Transcendentalists, Greeley, and Ingersoll had made such trades respectable. He devoted his best years to politics, the issues of which were by their very nature transitory. The last third of his life was largely dedicated to the study and propagation of an unpopular faith, and he himself was content to be remembered for his books on that subject. His strongest and most significant trait, an extraordinary versatility, proved to be a liability; for, in general, it kept him from that single-minded devotion to one cause which brought honor and glory to a Weld, a Burritt, and an Anthony.

Owen deserves a better treatment than he has heretofore received. His career is of interest and value to students of our political, social, economic, and religious history. His life's story is an instructive one, and his worth-while achievements

[53] *Evening Post*, June 26, 1877; *Nation*, July 5, 1877.
[54] *Indianapolis News*, June 26, 1877.

many. A strong liberal and a consistent democrat, he possessed a deep faith in human progress. By his many lovable qualities and personal example he made this a better world to live in.

Owen wished no oration spoken over his bier but rather a simple statement of his spiritualist belief. That service Dr. Crowell performed when he wrote of him, "His presence was truly a benediction. . . . He is not dead, neither is his mission to humanity ended. The crystal gates are ever open. Death to him is immortal life." [55]

[55] *Banner of Light*, July 21, 1877.

APPENDICES

In the following Appendices an asterisk means that the edition of the work is known to have been published but has not been located.

The various libraries in which manuscripts, newspapers, periodicals, and rare imprints have been examined are denoted by the following key:

AAS	American Antiquarian Society
BA	Boston Athenaeum
BM	British Museum
BPL	Boston Public Library
CUL	Chicago University Library
HCL	Harvard College Library
HHM	Holyoake House, Manchester, England
HSP	Historical Society of Pennsylvania
IHS	Indiana Historical Society
IPL	Indianapolis Public Library
ISL	Indiana State Library
LC	Library of Congress
LWI	Workingmen's Institute, New Harmony
MHS	Massachusetts Historical Society
NL	Newberry Library, Chicago
NDUL	Notre Dame University Library
NYHS	New York Historical Society
NYPL	New York Public Library
NYSL	New York Society Library
OHS	Oregon Historical Society
PI	Peabody Institute, Baltimore
PLC	Library Company, Philadelphia
PPL	Princeton (Ind.) Public Library
PUL	Purdue University Library
ROMM	Robert Owen Memorial Museum, Newtown, Wales
WHS	State Historical Society of Wisconsin
WL	Willard Library, Evansville
YUL	Yale University Library

APPENDIX I

A LIST OF THE WRITINGS OF ROBERT DALE OWEN

A NOTE ON THE OWEN MANUSCRIPTS

THERE is no single collection of Robert Dale Owen's papers. Some letters received by him are still in the hands of his family; a large number are preserved in the manuscript collection of his friend Ferdinand J. Dreer. Many letters written by Owen are scattered among the papers of his contemporaries (listed in Appendix II), and there may be collections of these that the author has not seen. Other letters written by Owen are to be found in the papers of Robert Owen and Richard Owen. The author has not seen all of the manuscripts of David Dale Owen and of Richard Owen, but he has been assured by their present owners that they contain little or nothing that is relevant to this biography. Under these circumstances a distinction between those family papers consulted and the manuscripts of Owen's contemporaries is somewhat arbitrary. The former, nevertheless, are described in more detail because they are less well known.

Owen Papers (LWI). Business letters, originals and copies, together with some deeds, lists of property, plans for a house. Kept by Owen and bequeathed to his eldest son. Now on loan through the courtesy of Miss Eleanor R. Cooper.

Stone Papers (Private). A selection of the most valuable items from the above collection. Contains some documents dealing with the purchase of the New Harmony property. In the possession of Mrs. Grace Zaring Stone, a great-granddaughter of Owen.

Stone Letters (Private). Correspondence between Owen and his wife. Most of the letters were written by Owen in 1832 and 1833. There are no items between 1834 and 1855. There are a few pieces addressed to other members of the family. In the possession of Mrs. Grace Zaring Stone.

Robert Owen Papers (HHM). Approximately 3,000 pieces beginning around 1823 and continuing until 1858. Probably collected for the second volume, never written, of the elder Owen's autobiography. There are about twenty valuable letters by Robert Dale Owen. Other correspondents include Mary J., William, and Richard Owen, Frances Wright, and Marie D. Fretageot.

Neal Letters (Private). A few important letters written mostly to Richard Owen. Some are by Robert Dale Owen; some by other members of the family. In the possession of Mrs. Aline Owen Neal. The author understands that these letters do not comprise the whole of Richard Owen's manuscripts.

Purdue Collection (PUL). Contains five pieces: "Journal . . . No. 1," a diary kept from March 6 to April 22, 1824; "Aufsatze," a bound notebook of exercises written in several languages while at Hofwyl; "Notes on the Subject of Civil Engineering," compiled in June 1835; and two other notebooks, one describing mechanical contrivances observed from 1824 to 1827, one containing notes on travel and data for a biography of Galileo.

"Political Memoranda" (ISL). Valuable notes by Owen on the legislative elections of 1836, 1837, and 1838, together with a description of his tactics in diverting a portion of the federal surplus revenue to the Indiana Common School Fund. Contains also mounted letters, handbills, and newspaper clippings relative to his political career, mostly for the years 1836 to 1839.

Miscellaneous:

"A Bill to Emancipate Persons of African Descent, Held to Service or Labor in Certain of the United States" (HCL).

"Memoranda of the Important Changes, as Compared with the Old Law, Made in Bills, Reported from the Committee of Revision" (IHS). Contains notes for *Beyond the Breakers*.

"The Pardoning Power in Relation to Reconstruction" (HSP). Inscription reveals this was written in New York, Sept. 30, 1863, read to Pres. Lincoln on Oct. 11, and withheld from publication at his request.

1. BOOKS

Beyond the Breakers. A Story of the Present Day. [*Village Life in the West*]. Phila., 1870.

A Brief Practical Treatise on the Construction and Management of Plank Roads. New Albany, 1850.

The Debatable Land between This World and the Next. N.Y., 1872. Other editions, London, 1871, and several after 1877.

Discussion on the Existence of God and the Authenticity of the Bible between Origen Bacheler and Robert Dale Owen. N.Y., 1831.* Other editions, London, 1832 (BM); N.Y., 1833*; London, 1840; London, 1842; London, 1853.

Footfalls on the Boundary of Another World. Phila., 1860. Other editions, Phila., 1860; London, 1860; London, 1861; Phila., 1863; Phila., 1865; and several after 1877.

Hints on Public Architecture. N.Y., 1849.

Moral Physiology; or, a Brief and Plain Treatise on the Population Question. N.Y., 1830*. Other editions, N.Y., 1831 (LWI, YUL); N.Y., 1831 (BM); N.Y., 1831*; N.Y., 1831*; N.Y., 1832*; London, 1832*; London, 1832 (BM); London, 1833*; London, 1833 (BM); N.Y., 1835 (YUL); N.Y., 1836; N.Y., 1839*; London, [1833–1841?]*; London, 1840; N.Y., 1842*; London, 1844; London, 1846; N.Y., 1846; N.Y., 1858; London, [1870?]; Boston, 1875; and several after 1877.

An Outline of the System of Education at New Lanark. Glasgow, 1824. Other editions, London, 1824; Cincinnati, 1825.

Pocahontas: a Historical Drama in Five Acts; with an Introductory Essay and Notes by a "Citizen of the West." N.Y., 1837.

Popular Tracts by Robert Dale Owen, Frances Wright and Others. 14 v. in one, N.Y., 1830. Other editions, 11 v. in one, London, 1851; London, 1851; N.Y., 1854. Contents of later editions vary.

Threading My Way. Twenty-seven Years of Autobiography. N.Y., 1874. Another edition, London, 1874.

The Wrong of Slavery, the Right of Emancipation, and the Future of the African Race in the United States. Phila., 1864.

2. Magazine Articles (Arranged Chronologically)

"One of the Problems of the Age," *United States Magazine and Democratic Review*, xiv, 156–167 (Feb. 1844). Unsigned.

"The Province of Legislation," *Democratic Monthly Magazine and Western Review*, i, 31–37, 112–120, 219–228 (May, June, July, 1844). Signed "O."

"The Too Much and the Too Little," *Western Odd Fellows' Magazine*, i, 95–96, 121–122 (Sept., Oct., 1852).

"The Claims to Service or Labor," *Atlantic Monthly*, xii, 116–125 (July 1863).

"The Convulsionists of St. Medard," *Atlantic Monthly*, xiii, 209–222, 339–352 (Feb., Mar. 1864).

"The Electric Girl of La Perrière," *Atlantic Monthly*, xiv, 284–292 (Sept. 1864).

"My Student Life at Hofwyl," *Atlantic Monthly*, xv, 550–560 (May 1865).

"Why the Putkammer Castle Was Destroyed," *Atlantic Monthly*, xvi, 513–519 (Nov. 1865).

"Naples and Vesuvius," *Northern Monthly Magazine*, ii, 393–401 (Feb. 1868).

"Beyond the Breakers: an American Novel," *Lippincott's Magazine*, i, 9–32, 129–147, 241–261, 353–373, 465–485, 577–595; ii, 61–78, 187–201, 292–310, 409–432, 515–533, 633–651; iii, 74–85, 198–212 (Jan.-Dec. 1869; Jan., Feb. 1870).

"Samples of Evidence for Spiritual Phenomena," *Spiritual Magazine*, 2d ser., v, 77–87, 124–130 (Feb., Mar. 1870).

"Looking Back across the War Gulf," *Old and New*, i, 577–589 (May 1870); iii, 28–43, 273–284; iv, 333–346 (Jan., Mar., Sept. 1871).

"A Chapter of Autobiography," *Atlantic Monthly*, xxxi, 1–16 (Jan. 1873).

"Boy-Life in a Scottish Country-Seat. A Chapter of Autobiography," *Atlantic Monthly*, xxxi, 146–158 (Feb. 1873).

"Robert Owen at New Lanark. A Chapter etc.," *Atlantic Monthly*, XXXI, 31–321 (Mar. 1873).

"Thomas Clarkson and Nicholas of Russia," *Atlantic Monthly*, XXXI, 449–461 (Apr. 1873).

"Emanuel von Fellenberg and His Self-Governing College," *Atlantic Monthly*, XXXI, 585–597 (May 1873).

"A German Baron and English Reformers," *Atlantic Monthly*, XXXI, 730–743 (June 1873).

"Educating a Wife," *Atlantic Monthly*, XXXII, 52–63 (July 1873).

"The Social Experiment at New Harmony," *Atlantic Monthly*, XXXII, 224–236 (Aug. 1873).

"My Experience of Community Life," *Atlantic Monthly*, XXXII, 224–236 (Sept. 1873).

"Frances Wright, General Lafayette, and Mary Wollstonecraft Shelley," *Atlantic Monthly*, XXXII, 448–459 (Oct. 1873).

"Interesting People Whom I Met in London," *Atlantic Monthly*, XXXII, 560–572 (Nov. 1873).

"Naples under the Old Regime. A Chapter of Autobiography," *Atlantic Monthly*, XXXIII, 129–140 (Feb. 1874).

"Naples: Her Volcano, Her People, and Her King. A Chapter etc.," *Atlantic Monthly*, XXXIII, 641–653 (June 1874).

"An Earnest Sowing of Wild Oats," *Atlantic Monthly*, XXXIV, 67–78 (July 1874).

"How I Came to Study Spiritual Phenomena," *Atlantic Monthly*, XXXIV, 578–590 (Nov. 1874).

"Some Results from My Spiritual Studies," *Atlantic Monthly*, XXXIV, 719–731 (Dec. 1874).

"Touching Visitants from a Higher Life," *Atlantic Monthly*, XXXV, 57–69 (Jan. 1875).

"Spiritual Progress in America," *Spiritual Magazine*, 3d ser., I, 35–41 (Jan. 1875).

"Political Results from the Varioloid. A Leaf of History," *Atlantic Monthly*, XXXV, 660–670 (June 1875).

"Recallings from a Public Life. Western People and Politicians Forty Years Ago," *Scribner's Monthly*, XVI, 255–263 (Dec. 1877).

"Recallings from a Public Life — II. Texas and the Peace of Guadalupe Hidalgo," *Scribner's Monthly*, XVI, 868–878 (Oct. 1878).

3. PAMPHLETS AND TRACTS

Address by a Committee of Trustees of Indiana University, to the People of Indiana. Indianapolis, 1840. R. D. Owen, author.

Address on Free Enquiry; On Fear as a Motive of Action. London, 1840. Another edition, London, 1853.

Address on the Hopes and Destinies of the Human Species. London, 1832. (LC). Other editions, London, [1840?]; London, 1853.

Address on the Influence of the Clerical Profession. N.Y., 1831. Other editions, N.Y., 1832*; London, 1832*; Mannheim, 1861 (a German translation).

Address on the Influence of the Clerical Profession, to Which Is Added, a Tract and a Warning; Truth and Error; On the Fear of God. London, 1840. Other editions, London, [1845?]; London, 1853.

Address to the Conductors of the New York Periodical Press (Popular Tracts, no. 3). N.Y., 1830.

Address to the People of Indiana at an Adjourned Meeting of the Democratic Party . . . 10th Feb. 1838. Indianapolis, 1838.

Address Touching an Error of General Prevalence in Society; Delivered . . . before the Monroe County Lyceum . . . September [28], 1841. n.p., n.d.

Address Touching the Influence and Progress of Literature and the Sciences: Delivered before the Philomathean Society of the Indiana University . . . September, 1838. Richmond, 1838.

The Anatomy of Taxation by One of the Council of the National Political Union [Robert Dale Owen]. London, 1833*.

Annexation of Texas. Speech of Mr. Owen . . . May 21, 1844, on the Right and Duty of the United States now to Accept the Offer Made by Texas on Annexation. [Wash., 1844].

Biography of Joseph Lane by "Western" [Robert Dale Owen?]. Wash., 1852. The author of this tract is still in doubt. The Lane Papers throw no light on the question. John Savage, *Our Living Representative Men* (Phila., 1860), 368 n. attributed it to David Levy Yulee of Florida and his view was accepted by the *Portraits and Sketches of John C. Breckinridge and Joseph Lane* (N.Y., 1860), 8. There is no reason to acquiesce in that conclusion. Yulee was not the type of man we would expect to write such a pamphlet; he was not an Indianan acquainted with local politics; he was not a "Westerner." William W. Woollen, editor of the *Madison Banner* in 1852 and a keen observer of Hoosier politics, attributes it to Owen. *Biographical and Historical Sketches of Early Indiana* (Indianapolis, 1883), 417. Other evidence in Owen's favor is the course of the Lane boom, Owen's two verbal agreements to undertake the work, his intimate acquaintance with Lane, and the similarity of the pseudonym assumed for *Pocahontas.* See also such internal evidence as the synoptic chapter headings and the concluding paragraph of chapter III.

Cause of the People. (Popular Tracts, no. 5). N.Y., 1830.

Circular Addressed to the Friends of Liberal Education. n.p., n.d.

The Conditions of Reconstruction; in a Letter from Robert Dale Owen to the Secretary of State (Loyal Publication Society, *Pamphlets,* no. 25). N.Y., 1863.

The Cost of Peace; Letter from Robert Dale Owen to the Hon. Salmon P. Chase. [N.Y., 1862].

Darby and Susan. A Tale of Old England. London, [1840?]. Another edition, London, 1852.

Divorce: Being a Correspondence between Horace Greeley and Robert Dale Owen. N.Y., 1860.

Effects of Missionary Labours (Popular Tracts, no. 7). N.Y., 1830.

Emancipation Is Peace (Loyal Publication Society, *Pamphlets,* no. 22). [N.Y., 1863].

The French Revolution (Popular Tracts, no. 9). N.Y., 1830.

The Future of the North-West; In Connection with the Scheme of Reconstruction without New England (Loyal Publication Society, *Pamphlets,* no. 1). N.Y., 1863. Another edition, Phila., 1863.

Galileo and the Inquisition (Popular Tracts, no. 12). N.Y., 1830.

Galileo and the Inquisition; Effects of Missionary Labours. London, 1854.

Labor: Its History and Prospects; an Address Delivered before the Young Men's Mercantile Association of Cincinnati . . . February 1, 1848. Cincinnati, 1848. Another edition, N.Y., 1851.

Lecture on Consistency. London, 1841. Another edition, London, 1853.

Letters to William Gibbons. Phila., 1830*.

Mexico. No. 1. Shall Our Government Act, or Refrain from Acting, in Mexican Affairs? [by Robert Dale Owen]. n.p., n.d.

Mexico. No. 2. Historical and Financial Items. n.p., n.d.

Mexico. No. 3. Biographical Sketch of . . . Juarez. n.p., n.d.

Mexico. No. 4. Oppression and Cruelties Resulting from French Intervention in Mexico. n.p., n.d.

Mexico. No. 5. General Gonzalez Ortega and His Nine Endorsers. Wash., 1866.

Mexico. What Shall Our Policy Be? n.p., n.d. The Library of Congress Catalogue does not attribute these six anonymous pamphlets to Owen, but for conclusive proof of his authorship see *ante,* 375 n. 32.

"Native Americanism." Extracts from an Address Delivered at Madison, Indiana, July 26, 1844. [Louisville, 1844].

Neurology; an Account of Some Experiments in Cerebral Physiology, by Dr. [Joseph Rodes] *Buchanan.* London, 1842. Another edition, London, 1852.

Occupation of Oregon. Speech of Mr. Owen . . . Jan. 23 and 24, 1844, on the Question of Joint Occupancy. [Wash., 1844].

Oration in Memory of Andrew Jackson . . . Delivered at Terre Haute, Ind., 20th Sep. 1845. n.p., n.d.

Oregon and the Nootka Convention. Speech of Mr. Robert Dale Owen . . . Jan. 28, 1844 [1846]. [Wash., 1846].

Perils and Exigencies of the Present Crisis: an Address Delivered Feb. 13, 1861. Indianapolis, 1861.

The Policy of Emancipation: In Three Letters to the Secretary of War, the President of the United States, and the Secretary of the Treasury. Phila., 1863.

Prossimo's Experience (Popular Tracts, no. 4). N.Y., 1830.

Prossimo's Experience; On the Study of Theology; "Safest to Believe," or the Balance Struck. London, [1841?] Other editions, London, 1845; London, 1852.

Reply to a Report of the New York Typographical Society. [N.Y., 1830].

A Sermon on Loyalty . . . and a Sermon on Free Enquiry (Popular Tracts, no. 6). N.Y., 1830.

A Sermon on Loyalty; and a Sermon on Free Enquiry. Observations on Public Worship. London, [1840]. Another edition, London, 1853.

Situations: Lawyers, Clergy, Physicians, Men and Women (Popular Tracts, no. 10). N.Y., 1830. Other editions, London, 1839; London, 1851.

Six Essays on Public Education [by Robert Dale Owen]. N.Y., 1830. Another edition, London, 1833*.

The System of Commercial Restriction. [Speech of Mr. Owen . . . June 19, 1846]. [Wash., 1846].

A Tale of Old England (Popular Tracts, no. 1). N.Y., 1830.

Texas and Her Relations with Mexico. Speech of Mr. Owen . . . Jan. 8, 1845. [Wash., 1845].

Theory of Tariff Protection. Speech of Mr. Owen . . . April 22, 1844. [Wash., 1844].

To the Electors of the First Congressional District of Indiana. n.p., n.d. [1843].

A Tract and a Warning (Popular Tracts, no. 13). N.Y., 1830.

Tracts on Republican Government and National Education by R. D. Owen and Frances Wright. London, 1851.

Truth and Error (Popular Tracts, no. 2). N.Y., 1830.

The War with Mexico. Speech of Robert Dale Owen . . . Jan. 4, 1847. [Wash., 1847].

Wealth and Misery (Popular Tracts, no. 11). N.Y., 1830. Other editions, London [1840?]; London, 1852.

4. Reports

"Final Report of the American Freedmen's Inquiry Commission to the Secretary of War," 38 Cong., 1 Sess., *Senate Executive Documents,* no. 53 (May 15, 1864), 25–110.

"Preliminary Report Touching the Condition and Management of Emancipated Refugees, Made to the Secretary of War by the American Freedmen's Inquiry Commission, June 30, 1863, 38 Cong., 1 Sess., *Senate Executive Documents*, no. 53, 2–24. Another edition, N.Y., 1863.

"Railroad to Oregon," 28 Cong., 2 Sess., *Reports of the Committees*, no. 199 (Mar. 3, 1845).

"Report of Robert Dale Owen, Agent to Purchase Arms, &c., . . . September 4, 1862," Indiana General Assembly, *Documentary Journal*, 42 Sess., Part 2, II, no. 14, 909–929. Another edition, Indianapolis, 1862. A revision of this report, dated Feb. 6, 1863 and never printed, is in the Indiana State Library, Archives Division, Department of the Adjutant General.

"Report of the Commission on Ordnance and Ordnance Stores Made to the War Department, 37 Cong., 2 Sess., *Senate Executive Documents*, VI, no. 72 (July 1, 1862). Written by Holt and signed by Owen.

Report of the Organization Committee of the Smithsonian Institution. Wash., 1847.

"Wabash and Erie Canal," 28 Cong., 1 Sess., *Reports of the Committees*, III, no. 545 (June 7, 1844).

5. POETRY

"The Vessel of Freedom," *Free Enquirer*, Aug. 28, 1830.

"The Marseillaise Hymn" (translation), *Free Enquirer*, Oct. 2, 1830.

"Simile," *Free Enquirer*, May 7, 1831.

" 'Tis Home Where'er the Heart Is," *Pocahontas* (N.Y., 1837), 74.

"The Diver," Translated from the German of Schiller by the Author of "Pocahontas," *Democratic Review*, V, 29–32 (Jan. 1839).

"The Ideal," Translated from the German of Schiller by the Author of "Pocahontas," *Democratic Review*, VI, 43–45 (July 1839).

"A Song," *New York Tribune*, Aug. 26, 1845.

"A Song," Washington *Metropolitan*, July 12, 1851.

6. SELECTED SPEECHES AND LETTERS TO NEWSPAPERS (ARRANGED BY DATE)

"To the editor of the *Glasgow Chronicle*," *Globe*, Oct. 1, 1823.

"Indiana's Great Work," by "Tullius" [Robert Dale Owen], *Indiana Journal*, June 8, 29, July 23, 1836.

"To the Citizens of the First Congressional District of Indiana," *Beacon*, Oct. 19, 1839.

"To the People of Indiana," *Wabash Enquirer*, Jan. 22, 1840. Address at the Democratic State Convention, Jan. 8, 1840.

"Letters to the *South-Western Sentinel*," *Western Sun*, June 27, July 4, 11, 18, 25, Aug. 1, 8, 15, 22, 1840; *Wabash Enquirer*, Aug. 26, Sept. 16, Oct. 14, 21, 1840; *Indiana Democrat*, Oct. 2, 1840.

"The Slavery Extension Question," *Democratic Clarion*, Sept. 18, Oct. 2, 1847.

"Property of Married Women," *New Albany Ledger*, May 2, 9, 22, 28, 1850. Copied from *The Constitution*.

"The Law of Progress Deduced from History," *Western Odd Fellows' Magazine*, I, 297–301 (Apr. 1853). See also summaries in *The Locomotive*, Jan. 29, 1853; *Indiana State Sentinel*, Jan. 24, 1853; *Indiana State Journal*, Jan. 27, 1853.

"The Question of Coercion," *Indianapolis Journal*, Nov. 28, 1860.

"The Question of Compromise," *New Harmony Advertiser*, Jan. 12, 1861.

"The Legal Condition of the Insurgent States," *Evening Post*, Oct. 21, 1863.

"The Pardoning Power. Historical Precedents," *N. Y. Tribune*, Dec. 12, 1863.

"Domestic Tranquility or Civil War," *Indianapolis Journal*, Sept. 13, 1864.

"Negro Suffrage and Representative Population," *N. Y. Tribune*, June 24, 1865.

"The Constitutional Guaranty of a Republican Form of Government," *Evening Post*, Nov. 25, 1865.

"Shall There Be Guarantees for the Future or Shall Restoration Be Unconditional?" *N. Y. Tribune*, May 19, 1866.

"Spiritualism as a Phase of the Religious Sentiment of the Day," *Report of Addresses at a Meeting* [of the Free Religious Association] . . . *May 30, 1867* (Boston, 1867), 16–28.

"Address," *Semi-Centennial Anniversary of Odd-Fellowship, at Indianapolis, Indiana, April 26, 1869* (Indianapolis, 1869), 11–29.

"Address . . . at Terre Haute . . . on the Twenty-fourth Anniversary of Modern Spiritualism," *Religio-Philosophical Journal*, Apr. 20, 1872.

7. PERIODICALS EDITED

The New Harmony Gazette (wk.), Oct. 18, 1826–May 2, 1827; Mar. 19–June 11, 1828; July 23–Oct. 22, 1828.

The New Harmony and Nashoba Gazette, or the Free Enquirer (wk.), Oct. 29, 1828–Feb. 25, 1829.

The Free Enquirer (wk.), Apr. 11, 1829–Nov. 10, 1831. Owen was nominally co-editor and co-proprietor of these periodicals from July 23, 1828 to Oct. 20, 1832.

The New York Daily Sentinel. Owen was managing editor from Feb. 15, 1830 until the spring of 1831.

The Crisis (London, wk.), Nov. 3, 1832–Apr. 20, 1833.

8. PRINTED LETTERS AND OTHER MANUSCRIPTS

"A New Harmony Letter of 1851," *Indiana Magazine of History*, XXVII, 50–53 (Mar. 1931). Owen to Sarah T. Bolton, July 6, 1851.

"Robert Dale Owen and Indiana's Common School Fund," Harlow Lindley, ed., *Indiana Magazine of History*, xxv, 52–60 (Mar. 1929).

"Some Correspondence of Robert Dale Owen," Louis M. Sears, ed., *Mississippi Valley Historical Review*, x, 306–324 (Dec. 1923). Extracts from the Trist Papers.

9. HANDBILLS

A Candidate's Defence against a Base Accusation [July 1836]. (ISL)

A Few Explanations from a Candidate [July 1837]. (ISL)

The Last Calumny [July 1843]. (ISL)

To My Constituents [Aug. 1836]. (ISL)

To the Citizens of Posey County, Apr. 10, 1837. (ISL)

To the Voters of Posey County. Handbills I, II, III [May, June, 1836]. (ISL)

10. MISCELLANEOUS

"Spiritualism," *Johnson's New Universal Cyclopaedia* (N.Y., 1878), IV, Part 1, 435–437. Signed article, written in 1872.

APPENDIX II

BIBLIOGRAPHY

To KEEP this Bibliography within reasonable bounds and to make it, at the same time, useful for other scholars, certain arbitrary limits have been set. Almost all secondary works, general accounts as well as monographs, have been left out on the grounds that they are probably familiar to students of American history. Certain types of primary materials — notably handbills and broadsides, gazetteers and registers, travel accounts, the collected writings of statesmen, and various compilations of sources — have been excluded. These omissions, partly remedied by complete citations in the footnotes, have been made in order to describe fully the manuscripts, documents, newspapers, and periodicals consulted.

PRIMARY

I. MANUSCRIPTS

A. PAPERS OF OWEN'S CONTEMPORARIES

Allen, William (LC)
Andrew, John A. (MHS)
Bentham, Jeremy (BM)
Bolton, Francis D. (LWI)
Brownson, Orestes A., Transcripts (NDUL)
Buchanan, James (HSP)
Bryant, William C. (NYPL)
Burns, Alexander, Jr. (LWI)
Chase, Salmon P. (HSP, LC)
Cooke, Jay (HSP)
Draper, Lyman (WHS)
Dreer, Ferdinand J. (HSP)
Duyckinck, Evert A. (NYPL)
Embree, Elisha (ISL)
English, William H. (CUL, IHS)
Everett, Edward (MHS)
Force, Peter (LC)
Fretageot, Marie D. (Private)
Garrison, William L. (BPL)
Greeley, Horace (NYPL)
Holt, Joseph (LC)
Howells, William D. (HCL)

Johnson, Andrew (LC)
Kennedy, John P., Diary (PI)
Lane, Joseph, Transcripts (OHS)
Macdonald, Archibald J. (YUL)
Macdonald, Donald, Diary (Private)
Maclure, William (LWI)
Morton, Samuel G. (PLC)
Noble, Noah (ISL)
Owen, Jane D., Scrapbook (ROMM)
Owen, Richard (Private)
Owen, Robert (HHM)
Owen, Robert Dale (LWI, Private). For a description of the Owen family papers, see Appendix I.
Place, Francis (BM)
Smith, Caleb B. (LC)
Southard, Mathew R. (ISL)
Stanton, Edwin M. (LC)
Sumner, Charles (HCL)
Taylor, Fauntleroy & Co. (LWI)
Van Buren, Martin (LC)

B. AUTOGRAPH COLLECTIONS

Chamberlain (BPL)
Dreer (HSP)
Ford (NYPL)
Gratz (HSP)
Harvard University

Indiana State Library
New York Historical Society
Purdue University
Smith, Valette (ISL)
Washburn (MHS)

C. MISCELLANEOUS

American Freedmen's Inquiry Commission, Miscellaneous Papers. (HCL)

"Correspondence Explanatory of the Details of a Plan of Buildings for a Smithsonian Institution." (LWI)

Indiana University, "Excerpts from the Minutes of the Board of Trustees." (Furnished the author by the Hon. W. L. Bryan).

"Journal of the Free Land Association of New Harmony." (LWI)

"Minutes of the Convention Forming the Constitution of the New Harmony Community of Equality [Jan. 25–Feb. 6, 1826]." (Private)

New Harmony Thespian Society, "Minutes." (LWI)

New Harmony Workingmen's Institute, "Minutes." (LWI)

"Preamble and Constitution of the Woman's Suffrage [Rights from 1851–1869] Association of Indiana, with Names of Charter Members; Minutes of Annual Meetings etc." (IHS)

2. PUBLIC DOCUMENTS

A large number of documents, printed and unprinted, national, state, and foreign, has been consulted in tracing Owen's public life.

A. NATIONAL

Federal documents have been drawn upon for Owen's activity in Congress, for his connection with the Smithsonian Institution, for his mission to Naples, and for his role during the Civil War and Reconstruction.

The chief printed ones include the *Congressional Globe*, the journals of the Senate and the House, together with the journal of the executive proceedings of the former, the statutes at large, and various Congressional reports. The census shed some light on the growth of spiritualism.

Important compilations of national documents were: William M. Malloy, ed., *Treaties, Conventions, International Acts, Protocols and Agreements between the United States of America and Other Powers, 1776–1937* (4 v., Wash., 1910–1937); William J. Rhees, ed., *The Smithsonian Institution: Documents Relative to Its Origin and History, 1835–1899* (2 v., Wash., 1901), and *The Smithsonian Institution: Journal of the Board of Regents etc.* (Wash., 1879); James D. Richardson, *A Compilation of the Messages and Papers of the Presidents, 1789–1897* (10 v., Wash., 1896–1897); *War of the Rebellion: a Compilation of the Official Records of the Union and Confederate Armies* (70 v., Wash., 1880–1901).

Government reports by Owen are included in the list of his writings in Appendix I. An important special source is Benjamin B. Kendrick, *The Journal of the Joint Committee of Fifteen on Reconstruction* (Columbia University, *Studies*, LXII, N. Y., 1914). The following reports of the Board of Regents of the Smithsonian Institution proved to be very helpful.

1846: 29 Cong., 2 Sess., *Reports*, no. 211.
1847: 30 Cong., 1 Sess., *Senate Misc. Reports*, no. 23.
1848: 30 Cong., 2 Sess., *House Misc. Reports*, no. 48.
1849: 31 Cong., 1 Sess., *Senate Misc. Reports*, no. 120.
1850: Spl. Sess., Mar. 1851, *Senate Misc. Reports*, no. 1.
1851: 32 Cong., 1 Sess., *Senate Misc. Reports*, no. 108.
1852: 32 Cong., 2 Sess., *Senate Misc. Reports*, no. 53.
1853: 33 Cong., 1 Sess., *Senate Misc. Reports*, no. 73.
1854: 33 Cong., 2 Sess., *Senate Misc. Reports*, no. 24.
1855: 34 Cong., 1 Sess., *House Misc. Reports*, no. 113.

The most important unprinted national documents used were the instructions to and despatches from the legation at Naples, 1853 to 1858, formerly at the Department of State, now in the National Archives.

B. STATE

State documents have provided much of the material pertaining to Owen's part in the Indiana legislature and in the convention that framed the constitution of 1851. They have also revealed his services as a Trustee of Indiana University and as the agent to purchase arms for the Hoosier soldiers during the Civil War. Local archives disclosed some of his business dealings.

The chief printed documents include the journals of the General Assembly, the journal and debates of the Constitutional Convention of 1850, the general and local laws, the revised statutes, especially those of 1852, and the documentary journals of the various legislative sessions.

Extremely valuable were the following unprinted documents: the archives of the Adjutant General of Indiana (ISL); the official correspondence and telegrams of Gov. O. P. Morton, 1861–1866 (ISL); the "Deed Book," "Order Book," and "Will Record," in the Posey County Courthouse, Mt. Vernon, Indiana.

C. FOREIGN

The most important collection of foreign documents bearing upon this biography was Matias Romero, ed., *Correspondencia de la Legacion Mexicana en Washington durante la Intervencion Extranjera, 1860–1868* (10 t., Mexico City, 1870–1879). That compilation was indispensable for Owen's connection with the scheme for a Congressional guarantee of a loan to the Juarez government.

3. NEWSPAPERS AND PERIODICALS

Newspapers, periodicals, and publications that partake of the character of both have contributed much to this biography. They have shown how Owen was regarded in his day by friend and by foe; they have often constituted the basis for special studies made by the author on movements in which Owen participated. Only those files used intensively are listed.

A. NATIONAL

Nationally important newspapers and periodicals have depicted Owen's career in politics and have indicated the contemporary notice taken of the New Harmony experiment, the rise of labor, the founding of the Smithsonian Institution, and the progress of spiritualism.

(*1*) *New York*

For the reception given the Owens in 1825 and the comments on their coöperative colony: *American* (1825, LC); *Enquirer* (1826–1827, LC); *Mercantile Advertiser* (1825, LC); *National Advocate* (1825, LC); *N. Y. National Advocate* (1825–1826, LC).

Papers hostile to the Working Men's Party: *Advertiser* (1829–1832, LC); *American* (1829–1832, LC); *Commercial Advertiser* (1829–1832, NYHS); *Courier and Enquirer* (1829–1832, NYPL); *Enquirer* (1829, LC); *Evening Post* (1829–1831, NYHS); *Journal of Commerce* (1829–1831, NYPL); *Morning Herald* (1829–1830, NYHS).

To estimate Owen's national prominence while in Congress: *Courier and Enquirer* (1843–1847, LC); *Evening Post* (1843–1848, LC); *Express* (1843–1847, LC); *Globe* (1845–1848, LC); *Herald* (1843–1853, LC); *Journal of Commerce* (1843–1848, LC); *Morning News* (1843–1846, LC); *Plebeian* (1843–1845, NYSL); *Sun* (1845–1848, LC, NYPL, broken files); *Tribune* (1843–1853, LC); *True Sun* (1844–1846, LC).

For Owen's contribution to the problems of the Civil War and Reconstruction: *Evening Post* (1860–1866, LC); *Herald* (1860–1867, LC); *Times* (1862–1866, LC); *Tribune* (1861–1866, LC); *World* (1862–1867, LC).

(*2*) *Washington*

Except for the *Washington City Chronicle* (later the *American Spectator,* 1828–1831, LC), which engaged in a controversy with *The Free Enquirer,* the newspapers of the national capital were useful only for politics and the establishment of the Smithsonian Institution. The following, all in the Library of Congress, were consulted: *American* (1847); *Chronicle* (1865–1866); *Constitution* (1844–1845); *Globe* (1843–1845); *Madisonian* (1843–1845); *National Intelligencer* (1843–1853, 1865–1866); *National Whig* (1847–1848); *Republic* (1853); *Saturday Evening News* (1846–1850); *Spectator* (1843–1844); *Union* (1845–1853).

(*3*) *Philadelphia*

Valuable for the fullest Eastern accounts of the New Harmony experiment: *Democratic Press* (1825–1827, LC); *National Gazette* (1825–1829, LC); *Poulson's American Advertiser* (1825, LC).

During his political career Owen was frequently criticized by the *North American* (1843–1853, LC).

For the Civil War period and the Katie King affair: *Inquirer* (1861–1862, 1874–1875, LC); *Press* (1860–1864, 1874–1875, LC).

(4) Others

Cincinnati papers carried brief notices of the New Harmony community, especially the *Emporium* (1825–1826, LC) and the *Liberty Hall and Gazette* (1825–1827, LC). Similar notices were found in the *American Journal of Science and Arts* (New Haven, 1824–1829, HCL) and *Niles' Register* (Baltimore, 1824–1829, HCL).

For Owen's prominence in national affairs: Baltimore *American* (1843–1847, HCL, LC) and *Sun* (1843–1847, LC); Charleston *Mercury* (1843–1847, LC); Chicago *Tribune* (1866, LC); Cincinnati *Commercial* (1862–1866, LC) and *Gazette* (1860–1862, HCL); Louisville *Journal* (1840–1843, ISL); Richmond *Enquirer* (1843–1847, LC). See also among the periodicals: *Nation* (N. Y., 1865–1866, LC); *Niles' Register* (Baltimore, 1843–1847, LC); and the *United States Magazine and Democratic Review* (N. Y., 1837–1853, LC).

On the nation-wide interest in plank roads: *American Railroad Journal* (Phila. & N. Y., 1847–1851, LC); *De Bow's Commercial Review* (New Orleans, 1849–1851, LC); Hunt's *Merchants' Magazine* (N. Y., 1849–1853, LC); *Plough, Loom, and Anvil* (Phila., 1848–1852, LC); and the *Western Journal* (St. Louis, 1848–1852, LC).

B. INDIANA

To appreciate Owen's preoccupation with politics during his middle years one must examine intensively the Indiana newspapers. Only there can be found his speeches in the state legislature, his course during the numerous presidential and Congressional canvasses, and his public letters on national and local topics.

(1) New Harmony

For the social experiment and its aftermath: *New Harmony Gazette* (1825–1829) and *Disseminator* (1828–1831, 1834–1836, and a broken file for 1837–1841).

For Owen's political progress and later developments in New Harmony: *Advertiser* (1858–1861); *Indiana Statesman* (1842–1846); *Register* (1867–1877); and *Western Atlas* (1846–1847).

All of these are to be found in the Library of the Workingmen's Institute, New Harmony.

(2) Indianapolis

From 1836 to 1853 and from 1860 to 1877 every issue of at least two Indianapolis papers, one of each party, has been examined. These journals were invaluable both for tracing Owen's career in politics and for judging how he was regarded after he had ceased to play a vital role in Hoosier affairs.

The Democratic newspapers include: *Indiana Democrat* (1836–1841, IPL, ISL, LC); *Indiana Democrat* (1845–1846, ISL); *Indiana State*

Guard (1860–1861, IPL); *Indiana State Sentinel* (title varies, 1841–1853, 1860–1865, 1868–1877, IPL, ISL); *Indiana Statesman* (1850–1852, IPL, ISL); *Indianapolis Herald* (1865–1868, IPL).

The Whig and Republican newspapers include: *Indiana Journal* (title varies, 1836–1853, 1860–1877, IPL, ISL); *Spirit of '76* (1840, ISL).

Other journals consulted were the *Indiana Farmer* (1838–1839, IPL); *Family Visitor* (1848–1850, IPL, ISL); *Locomotive* (1849–1853, ISL); *News* (1869–1877, ISL).

(3) Others

For sampling public opinion and studying political campaigns in Owen's Congressional district the most valuable Whig papers were the Corydon *Investigator* (1835–1839, LC); Evansville *Journal* (1843–1853, WL, broken file); and Leavenworth *Arena* (1838–1841, ISL). The most important Democratic sheets were the Evansville *South-Western Sentinel* (Mar. 1840, LC) and the Princeton *Democratic Clarion* (1846–1853, ISL, PPL).

Newspapers of other Indiana towns were searched for data on the proceedings of the state legislature and Constitutional Convention and for the various presidential and Senatorial contests. On the Democratic side: Aurora *Dearborn County Democrat* (1838–1840, ISL); Covington *People's Friend* (1847–1850, ISL); Lafayette *Courier* (1847–1850, ISL); Lawrenceburg *Democratic Register* (1851–1852, ISL) and *Independent Press* (1850–1851, ISL); Logansport *Democratic Pharos* (1851–1853, ISL) and *Herald* (1837–1840, ISL); Madison *Courier* (1845, 1849–1853, ISL); New Albany *Democrat* (1847–1849, ISL) and *Ledger* (1849–1853, 1860–1866, ISL); Terre Haute *Wabash Enquirer* (1838–1841, ISL); Vincennes *Western Sun* (1840–1842, ISL). On the Whig side: Bloomington *Post* (1835–1841, ISL); Brookville *Indiana American* (1847–1853, ISL); Delphi *Journal* (1850–1852, ISL); Lafayette *Journal* (1850–1851, ISL); Lawrenceburg *Political Beacon* (1837–1840, ISL); Logansport *Journal* (1849–1852, ISL) and *Telegraph* (1836–1840, ISL, broken file); Madison *Banner* (1851–1853, ISL) and *Tribune* (1851–1852, ISL); New Albany *Tribune* (1852–1853, ISL); Richmond *Palladium* (1848–1853, ISL); South Bend *St. Joseph Valley Register* (1850–1851, ISL, broken file).

Except for a few brief notices in the Evansville *Gazette* (1824–1825, LC), Lawrenceburg *Indiana Palladium* (1824–1829, ISL), and the Vincennes *Western Sun* (1824–1829, ISL), Hoosier editors paid scant attention to the community experiment at New Harmony.

C. LABOR

On the New Harmony experiment: *New Harmony Gazette* (1825–1829, LWI) and the *Co-operative Magazine* (London, 1826–1830, BM, HCL, ISL).

For the rise of labor in New York City: *Evening Journal* (1829–1830, NYHS); *Free Enquirer* (1829–1835, LWI); *Sentinel* (1830–1832, WHS);

Working Man's Advocate (1829–1830, LWI), all of New York City, and the Philadelphia *Mechanics' Free Press* (1828–1831, HSP).

For Owen's connection with the British workers: London *Crisis* (1832–1834, LC, NYPL).

For Owen's relation to American labor after 1831: *Harbinger* (1845–1849, HCL); *Phalanx* (1843–1845, HCL); *Working Man's Gazette* (1844–1845, LC); and *Young America* (1845–1846, NYPL), all of New York City.

D. FREETHOUGHT

In addition to the *New Harmony Gazette* and *Free Enquirer*, American freethought from 1825 to 1833 can best be studied in the *Correspondent* (N.Y., 1827–1829, HCL); *Delaware Free Press* (Wilmington, 1830, 1832–1833, AAS, WHS transcripts); and the *Telescope* (N. Y., 1826–1828, LC).

What freethinkers said of Owen after 1833 may be discovered in the *Beacon* (N. Y., 1836–1846, LC); *Boston Investigator* (1835–1853, 1858–1862, 1867–1876, BPL, LC, NYPL); and the *Index* (Toledo & N. Y., 1870–1877, LC).

Owen's place among British secularists was revealed in the *Crisis*; *Gauntlet* (1833, BM); *National Reformer* (1860, LC); *New Moral World* (1834–1846, LWI); *Prompter* (1830–1831, BM); *Reasoner* (1846–1861, LC); *Robert Owen's Journal* (1850–1852, ISL); *Robert Owen's Millennial Gazette* (1856–1858, LC, LWI); and *Robert Owen's Rational Quarterly Review* (1853, BM, HCL), all of London.

E. ANTISLAVERY

For Owen's changing views on slavery and the different ways in which he was regarded by abolitionists see: *Free Soil Banner* (*Indianapolis*, 1848, IPL); *Free Territory Sentinel* (1848–1849, ISL) and *Indiana True Democrat* (1850–1852, ISL), both of Centreville; *Liberator* (Boston, 1846–1848, 1862–1865, LC); *National Anti-Slavery Standard* (N. Y., 1846–1847, 1860–1866, LC); *National Era* (Washington, 1847–1853, LC).

F. SPIRITUALIST

A definitive history of American spiritualism must be based upon a wider examination of spiritualist periodicals than any writer has yet made. The most valuable ones for this biography were the *Banner of Light* (Boston, 1857–1877, HCL) and the *Religio-Philosophical Journal* (Chicago, 1865–1866, 1868–1877, NL).

Other American journals consulted were: *American Spiritual Magazine* (Memphis, 1875–1877, LC); *American Spiritualist* (Cleveland & N. Y., 1871–1872, WHS); *Brittan's Journal* (N. Y., 1873–1874, LC); *Herald of Progress* (N. Y., 1860–1864, HCL, LC, broken file); *Present Age* (N. Y. & Chicago, 1871–1872, LC); *Spiritual Age* (Boston, 1858–1860, HCL); *Spiritual Scientist* (Boston, 1874–1877, BPL); *Spiritual Telegraph* (N. Y., 1852–1859, AAS); *Western Star* (Boston, 1872, LC).

British periodicals drawn upon were: *British Spiritual Telegraph* (Keighley, 1857–1859, BM, LC); and *Human Nature* (1867–1876, HCL); *Medium and Daybreak* (1870–1877, YUL); *Spiritual Magazine* (1860–1877, LC, NYPL); *Spiritualist Newspaper* (1869–1877, HCL), all of London.

4. BOOKS AND PAMPHLETS

No attempt is made to list all the books and pamphlets consulted for this biography. The footnotes indicate the main primary sources for the various chapters. The purpose of this section of the Bibliography is to evaluate briefly, by topics, the more valuable of these works, always excluding Owen's writings detailed in Appendix I.

For the English background the *Life of Robert Owen Written by Himself* (2 v., London, 1857–1858), while not altogether accurate, was very useful. See also George J. Holyoake's *History of Co-Operation in England* (2 v., London, 1875–1877) and *Sixty Years of an Agitator's Life* (2 v., London, 1892).

In sketching the New Harmony community the author found Paul Brown's *Twelve Months in New Harmony* (Cincinnati, 1827) more credible than have earlier writers. The most helpful contemporary accounts and letters were: Victor C. Duclos, "Diary and Recollections" and "The Letters of William Pelham Written in 1825 and 1826," both printed in *Indiana as Seen by Early Travelers* (Harlow Lindley, ed., Indianapolis, 1916); George Flower, *History of the English Settlements in Edwards County* (*Chicago Historical Society's Collections*, I, Chicago, 1882); Joel Hiatt, ed., "The Diary of William Owen, from November 10, 1824 to April 20, 1825," Indiana Historical Society, *Publications*, IV (Indianapolis, 1906), 7–134; Thomas Pears, Jr., ed., "New Harmony, an Adventure in Happiness. The Papers of Thomas and Sarah Pears," Indiana Historical Society, *Publications*, XI (Indianapolis, 1933), 7–96. The Pears and Pelham correspondence, together with the Macdonald diary, the Maclure-Fretageot letters, and the Owen manuscripts, constitute an indispensable body of material that was not available when the supposedly definitive history of the community was written by Lockwood (*post*).

To round out the picture of Owen the reformer that emerges from his own writings during the New York years, the following have been drawn upon: Abner Cunningham, *An Address Submitted to the Consideration of R. D. Owen, Kneeland, Houston, and Others of the Infidel Party* (N. Y., 1833); Frances Wright D'Arusmont, *Biography, Notes, and Personal Letters* (N. Y., 1844); Ezra S. Ely, *The Duty of Christian Freemen to Elect Christian Rulers* (Phila., 1828); L. S. Everett, *An Exposure of the Principles of the "Free Enquirers"* (Boston, 1831); William Gibbons, *An Exposition of Modern Scepticism, in a Letter Addressed to the Editors of the Free Enquirer* (3rd edn., Wilmington, 1830); Amos Gilbert, *Memoir of Frances Wright* (Cincinnati, 1855) and "Sketch of the Life of Thomas Skidmore," *Free Enquirer*, Mar. 30, Apr. 6, 13, 1834; [George Houston?] *Robert Dale Owen Unmasked by His Own Pen* (N. Y., 1830, BA); Charles Knowlton, *The Fruits of Philosophy; or the Private Companion of Young Married People* (2d edn., Boston, 1833, HCL); Thomas Skidmore, *Moral Physiology Exposed and Refuted* (N. Y.,

1831, NYSL) and *The Rights of Man to Property!* (N. Y., 1829); Frances Wright, *Course of Popular Lectures* (N. Y., 1829) and *A Few Days in Athens* (N. Y., 1831). See also the printed proceedings of workingmen's meetings and the anti-labor broadsides cited in the footnotes.

Helpful for understanding Owen's Indiana years were: Rosamond Dale Owen, *My Perilous Life in Palestine* (N. Y., 1929) and "Robert Dale Owen and Mary Jane Robinson," *History of Woman Suffrage* (Elizabeth C. Stanton, Susan B. Anthony, & Matilda J. Gage, eds., N. Y., 1881), I, 293-306; Walter R. D. Owen, *A Glimpse of the Early History of New Harmony* (Evansville, 1898); O. H. Smith, *Early Indiana Trials and Sketches* (Cincinnati, 1858); William W. Woollen, *Biographical and Historical Sketches of Early Indiana* (Indianapolis, 1883); and the novels of Edward Eggleston. Useful for specific events were: *Proceedings at the Presentation to the Hon. Robert Dale Owen of a Silver Pitcher, on Behalf of the Women of Indiana* (New Albany, 1851); *The Town of New Harmony and the Rev. Benjamin Halsted; Being a Report of the Proceedings of a Meeting . . . Held . . . 13th April 1842* (Evansville, 1842).

For Owen's career in national politics manuscripts, documents, and newspapers were the most important sources. Special mention, however, should be made of the *Memoirs of John Quincy Adams, Comprising Portions of His Diary from 1795-1848* (C. F. Adams, ed., 12 v., Phila., 1874-1877); F. B. Carpenter, *Six Months at the White House with Abraham Lincoln* (N. Y., 1867); and the *Diary of James K. Polk during His Presidency, 1845-1849* (M. M. Quaife, ed., 4 v., Chicago, 1910). Useful contemporary pamphlets dealing with the Smithsonian Institution were: David H. Arnot, *Animadversions on the Proceedings of the Regents of the Smithsonian Institution* (N. Y., 1847); *Report of the Hon. James Meacham . . . on the Distribution of the Smithsonian Fund* (Wash., 1854); *Report of the Special Committee of the Board of Regents . . . on the Distribution of the Income of the Smithsonian Fund* (Wash., 1854). Indispensable for Owen's connection with the proposed Mexican loan in 1865-1866 were: Herman Sturm, *The Republic of Mexico and Its American Creditors* (Indianapolis, 1869); Lew Wallace, *An Autobiography* (2 v., N. Y., 1905).

For Owen's interest in spiritualism and relation to post-war literature, reform, and religion see: Orestes A. Brownson, "Owen on Spiritualism," *Catholic World*, XIV, 803-812 (Mar. 1872); Henry T. Child, *Narratives of the Spirits of . . . John and Katie King* (Phila., 1874); William Crookes, *Researches in the Phenomena of Spiritualism* (London, 1874); John B. Ellis, *Free Love and Its Votaries; or, American Socialism Unmasked* (N. Y., 1870); [William Fishbough], "Spiritualism," *New American Cyclopaedia* (George Ripley & C. A. Dana, eds., N. Y., 1862), XV, 1-4; Emma Hardinge, *Modern American Spiritualism* (N. Y., 1870); three works by D. D. Home, *Incidents in My Life* (N. Y., 1863), *Incidents in My Life. Second Series* (N. Y., 1874), *Lights and Shadows of Spiritualism* (N. Y., 1877); F. J. Lippitt, "Was It Katie King?" *Galaxy*,

XVIII, 754–766 (Dec. 1874); John H. Noyes, *Dixon and His Copyists* ([Wallingford], 1871) and *History of American Socialisms* (Phila., 1870); Henry S. Olcott, *People from the Other World* (Hartford, 1875); Epes Sargent, *Planchette; or, the Despair of Science* (Boston, 1869), *The Proof Palpable of Immortality* (Boston, 1875), "Spiritualism," *American Cyclopaedia* (George Ripley & C. A. Dana, eds., N. Y., 1876), XV, 275–278; Elizabeth C. Stanton, Susan B. Anthony, & Matilda J. Gage, eds., *History of Woman Suffrage* (6 v., N. Y., 1881–1922); Sarah E. L. Taylor, ed., *Fox-Taylor Automatic Writing, 1869–1892. Unabridged Record* (Minneapolis, [1932]); A. Leah [Fox] Underhill, *The Missing Link in Modern Spiritualism* (N. Y., 1885); *The Year-Book of Spiritualism for 1871* (Hudson Tuttle & J. M. Peebles, eds., Boston, 1871); Alfred R. Wallace, *My Life* (2 v., London, 1905) and *On Miracles and Modern Spiritualism* (London, 1875). See also the annual proceedings of the Free Religious Association.

SECONDARY

A large number of books and articles, familiar to historians, have been consulted in the preparation of this biography. Most of these secondary works, either ignoring Owen or mentioning him but briefly, were useful only in providing the background against which Owen performed. Some contain misleading and erroneous statements concerning his thought and activity.

The three best sketches of Owen's life — George B. Lockwood, *The New Harmony Movement* (N. Y., 1905), ch. 25, Norman E. Himes in the *Encyclopaedia of the Social Sciences* (N. Y., 1933), XI, 517–518, and Broadus Mitchell in the *Dictionary of American Biography* (N. Y., 1934), XIV, 118–120 — stress unduly his youthful radicalism and minimize his preoccupation with politics during his middle years and with spiritualism during his later ones. This tendency to regard Owen as a social reformer arises also from the fact that those books which discuss him most fully treat such matters as the New Harmony experiment and the rise of labor in New York, matters that came early in Owen's life.[1]

In addition to the three sketches just cited, there are a few articles of varying merit dealing solely with Owen: Arthur H. Estabrook, "The Family History of Robert Owen," *Indiana Magazine of History*, XIX, 63–101 (Mar. 1923), replete with errors; Nora C. Fretageot, "The Robert Dale Owen Home in New Harmony," *Indiana History Bulletin*, I, extra no. (June 1924), 15–26, based partly on documents, partly on tradition; Norman E. Himes, "Robert Dale Owen, the Pioneer of American Neo-Malthusianism," *American Journal of Sociology*, XXXV, 529–547 (Jan. 1930), important and stimulating but from which the present writer, on the basis of more exhaustive research, dissents on several points; Louis

---

[1] While this biography was in galley proof, there appeared *The Incorrigible Idealist: Robert Dale Owen in America* by Elinor Pancoast and Anne E. Lincoln. Within the limits set for themselves, the authors have made a worth-while contribution, but with many of their interpretations the present writer cannot agree.

M. Sears, "Robert Dale Owen as a Mystic," *Indiana Magazine of History*, XXIV, 15–25 (Mar. 1928) and "Robert Dale Owen's Mission to Naples," *Indiana History Bulletin*, VI, extra no. 2 (May 1929), 43–51, adequate commentaries on certain source materials.

For some of the events and movements in which Owen played a part there are virtually no secondary works of value. Such is the case with American freethought after 1825, the early years of the Smithsonian Institution, the attempt to nominate Joseph Lane for the presidency in 1852, the Mexican loan episode of 1865–1866, and, most important of all, the history of American spiritualism. J. M. Robertson, *A History of Freethought in the Nineteenth Century* (2 v., N. Y., 1930), is inadequate for the United States; and G. Adolf Koch, *Republican Religion (American Religion Series*, VII, N. Y., 1933), does not cover the years after 1825. The unsatisfactory character, for this study, of George B. Goode's *The Smithsonian Institution, 1846–1896: The History of the First Half-Century* (Wash., 1897), is exceeded only by that of Webster P. True's *The Smithsonian Institution (Smithsonian Scientific Series*, I, N. Y., 1929). On spiritualism Frank Podmore, *Modern Spiritualism. A History and a Criticism* (2 v., London, 1902), and George Lawton, *The Drama of Life after Death (American Religion Series*, VI, N. Y., 1932), are the best; but the former has nothing on American spiritualism after 1860, while the latter is essentially an account of the contemporary movement. For all of these matters, neglected by social historians, the author has made special studies of his own.

For other events and movements in which Owen was concerned secondary works could be drawn upon. The most useful follow.

For Robert Owen and his work: G. D. H. Cole, *Robert Owen* (Boston, 1925); Frank Podmore, *Robert Owen, a Biography* (2 v., London, 1906).

For the New Harmony experiment: George B. Lockwood, *The New Harmony Movement* (N. Y., 1905), is still the fullest general account, although the present writer differs from many of Lockwood's conclusions. A ground-breaking work when undertaken, the book should now be supplemented by the many new sources, mentioned above, made available since Lockwood wrote. The chapters on Robert Dale Owen and education should be used with caution. Later accounts, such as Caroline D. Snedeker's *Town of the Fearless* (Garden City, 1931), have been superficial, borrowing heavily from Lockwood and repeating his errors. H. B. Weiss & G. M. Ziegler, *Thomas Say, Early American Naturalist* (Springfield, Ill., 1931), is an exception to that generalization, but it has little that is new on the community experiment. There is no biography of Maclure; but George P. Merrill, *The First One Hundred Years of American Geology* (New Haven, 1924) is helpful. Studies of Joseph Neef and David Dale Owen are in progress.

For Frances Wright and Nashoba: A. J. G. Perkins & Theresa Wolfson, *Frances Wright, Free Enquirer* (N. Y., 1939); William R. Waterman, *Frances Wright* (Columbia University, *Studies*, CXV, N. Y., 1924).

For the beginnings of American birth control: Norman E. Himes, *Medical History of Contraception* (Baltimore, 1936).

For the rise of the workingmen in New York: John R. Commons and others, *History of Labour in the United States* (4 v., N. Y., 1918–1935).

For the Indiana years: Jacob P. Dunn, *Greater Indianapolis* (2 v., Chicago, 1910) and *Indiana and Indianans* (5 v., Chicago, 1919); Logan Esarey, *A History of Indiana* (2 v., Indianapolis, 1915–1918) and "Internal Improvements in Early Indiana," Indiana Historical Society, *Publications*, V (Indianapolis, 1912), 47–158; Nora C. Fretageot, *Historic New Harmony, a Guide* (3d edn., n. p., 1934); Henry C. Hubbart, *The Older Middle West, 1840–1880* (N. Y., 1936); Charles Kettleborough, "Indiana on the Eve of the Civil War," Indiana Historical Society, *Publications*, VI (Indianapolis, n. d.), 137–169; Charles B. Murphy, "The Political Career of Jesse D. Bright," Indiana Historical Society, *Publications*, X (Indianapolis, 1931), 99–145; Ralph L. Rusk, *The Literature of the Middle Western Frontier* (2 v., N. Y., 1926); James A. Woodburn, "Party Politics in Indiana during the Civil War," American Historical Association, *Report for 1902*, 223–251.

For the plank road craze: Joseph A. Durrenberger, *Turnpikes. A Study of the Toll Road Movement in the Middle Atlantic States and Maryland* (Valdosta, Ga., 1931), is more valuable than the title suggests.

For national politics, 1839–1867: The standard works and monographs on banking, the tariff, expansion, the Mexican War, the Civil War, and Reconstruction have been consulted; very few have much to say about Owen.

For a more detailed account, with fuller documentation, of all phases of Owen's career, see the author's manuscript dissertation in the Harvard College Library.

INDEX

INDEX

seeks Owen's aid, 214; attacks Owen, 215; replied to by Owen, 216; on election of 1847, 239–240

Evans, Robert M., 166, 173, 175

Evansville, Indiana, interest in New Harmony experiment, 31; Owen buys land at, 139, 163; terminus of Central Canal, 142–143, 166; lawyers hostile to Owen, 166; and plank roads, 264; churches and Barnes will, 386

Evansville Journal, prints Stinson-Lane circular, 167 n. 12; on election of 1847, 239; criticizes Owen family appointments, 241. *See also* Chandler, John J.; Chandler, William H.

Evening Journal, becomes a labor paper, 89–90; advertises Hall of Science, 90; prints essays on guardianship, 94; conservatives gain control of, 90, 94; repudiates Owen, 95; heads faction of workingmen, 96–97; joins National Republicans, 97, 98

Evening Post, 181, 332; prints Owen's letter to Stanton, 353; praises, 353; on progress of spiritualism, 395; obituary of Owen, 415. *See also* Bryant, William C.

Everett, Linus S., 77; articles in *Trumpet,* 74; attacks *Moral Physiology,* 81

Every Woman's Book, 78; Owen's views on, 61, 77, 78; prospectus of printed at New Harmony, 60. *See also* Carlile, Richard

Evil, question of, Owen on, 8, 58

Evolution, doctrine of, criticized by Owen, 388

Expansion, territorial, 176–179; not an issue in election of 1843, 178; young Democrats urge, 181; Owen sees no danger in, 185–186, 190; Owen on in 1866, 375. *See also* Oregon boundary dispute; Texas, annexation of

Factory Act of 1819, 10

Factory system, 3, 7, 10; Owen's family and, 3–4

Fauntleroy, Jane Dale Owen (Mrs. Robert H. Fauntleroy), 6, 113, 126;

teaches in London, 112–113; settles in New Harmony, 119, 125; Owen's fondness for, 128; marries Robert H. Fauntleroy, 129; breaks down village snobbery, 130; lectures at New Harmony Institute, 130; acts in "William Tell," 133; visits Europe, 301, 308

Fauntleroy, Robert H., 129, 234, 254

Faux, William, 21

Feiba-Peveli community, 34, 54

Fellenberg, Philip E. von, 11–13, 100

Felton, Cornelius C., 339

Female education, Owen on, 76

Feminism. *See* Female education; Married women, property rights of; Woman; Woman suffrage; Woman's rights movement

Ferdinand II, 308, 313; Owen's audiences with, 309, 310, 320; wishes Owen's rank raised, 312, 314; in Owen's autobiography, 316; detested in United States, 308, 309; quashes Sartorio case, 310

Ferris, Benjamin, 74

Fessenden, William P., 369, 370, 371

Few Days in Athens, 49, 68

Flower, Richard, 19, 20

Footfalls on the Boundary of Another World, begun, 327; manuscript read, 327, 328; described, 329–331, 334; reception, 332–334, 337, 338; English edition, 336; allusion to in Congress, 363; place in American spiritualism, 334–335; on Owen's grave, 414

Fourierism, 26, 227; Owen avoids, 46, 213, 292

Fourteenth Amendment, 367–371; Owen's draft, 368 n. 18; Owen's draft criticized, 370–371; action by Committee, 369–370; in Owen's autobiography, 371–372, 399

Fox, Catherine, 323, 338, 402

Fox, Margaret, 402

Franklin, Benjamin, 79

Fredericksoord, 22

"Free banking," 270, 285

Free Enquirer, begun, 63; described, 66–68; editors, 66–67; circulation, 68; becomes leading freethought journal, 67–68; articles of reprinted,